MW00344783

*The 100 Greatest Baseball Games
of the 20th Century Ranked*

To Tim,

With all my best wishes

Joe Dittmar

ALSO BY JOSEPH J. DITTMAR

*Baseball Records Registry: The Best and Worst
Single-Day Performances and the Stories Behind Them*
(McFarland, 1997)

*Baseball's Benchmark Boxscores:
Summaries of the Record-Setting Games*
(McFarland, 1990)

# The 100 Greatest Baseball Games of the 20th Century Ranked

*by*
JOSEPH J. DITTMAR

McFarland & Company, Inc., Publishers
*Jefferson, North Carolina, and London*

*Front cover, clockwise from upper left:* Fans at Yankee Stadium; an aerial shot of Crosley Field; the Mets celebrating at Shea Stadium; a fan's view of the Polo Grounds. (All photographs courtesy of the Baseball Hall of Fame Library)

**Library of Congress Cataloguing-in-Publication Data**

Dittmar, Joseph J.
    The 100 greatest baseball games of the 20th century ranked / by Joseph J. Dittmar.
        p.    cm.
    Includes bibliographical references and index.
    ISBN 0-7864-0915-0 (softcover : 50# alkaline paper) ∞
    1. Baseball — United States — History — 20th century.
    2. Baseball — Records — United States.   I. Title: One hundred greatest baseball games of the twentieth century ranked.   II. Title.
GV863.A1D58   2000
796.357'0973'0904 — dc21                  00-32870

British Library cataloguing data are available

©2000 Joseph J. Dittmar. All rights reserved

*No part of this book may be reproduced or transmitted in any form or by any means, electronic or mechanical, including photocopying or recording, or by any information storage and retrieval system, without permission in writing from the publisher.*

Manufactured in the United States of America

*McFarland & Company, Inc., Publishers*
  *Box 611, Jefferson, North Carolina 28640*
    *www.mcfarlandpub.com*

To my children, the pride of my life:
Clint, Laura, and Gwen

# Acknowledgments

With heartfelt thanks the author would like to acknowledge the integral role played by a group of generous contributors in forging this anthology. In particular the following provided immeasurable input:

The entire Retrosheet organization, especially their indomitable leader Dave Smith, supplied most of the boxscores contained herein. In addition, their play-by-play accounts afforded grist for much of the narrative. Retrosheet also supplied data on dozens of other games that were considered but missed the cutoff for the top 100.

Gary Gillette and The Baseball Workshop supplied data for games played from 1984 through 1996. Total Sports was the data source for games played from 1997 through 1999.

Friend and respected colleague Lyle Spatz furnished not only personal remembrances but also a host of editing suggestions. His grasp of baseball's evolving ambiance, as well as his remarkable knowledge of the New York clubs, is reflected in this work

Jim "Snuffy" Smith, esteemed baseball historian, suggested scores of games for inclusion and offered an eagle eye in editing.

The entire staff at the National Baseball Hall of Fame and Museum who smiled while making endless trips to their photographic files and provided the images contained within.

Finally, many thanks for the suggestions from friends, baseball historians, and co-workers who avidly follow the game, namely Bill Deane, Bob Herzog, Tom Ruane, Bob Shaefer, Dave Vincent, Jim Weigand, and Jeff Zimmerman. It is with regret that all of your favorites could not be included.

# Table of Contents

# Introduction

What constitutes a *great* baseball game? Is it a high scoring contest or a pitchers' duel? a thrilling World Series game? a playoff game? a suspenseful regular season or record setting game? For some fans a great game may have been branded by youth, before life's other distractions took hold — when impression and opinion were unfettered by historical perspective. Can we evoke the greatest games by mathematically calculating the chances of an identical or similar event's occurring? Is a perfect game a greater event than overcoming a 12-run deficit to win? (The former occurred 14 times this century while the latter happened but twice.) How can one measure emotion or compare similar events that occurred in World Series games against regular season contests? Some games are staged in a context that invites greatness, such as the seventh game of a World Series, the final game of a pennant race, or an expected record streak. Others are deemed great only in retrospect.

Regardless of who compiles a list of greatest games, personal preference is certain to be heavily weighted. October 1, 1950, was an exhilarating day for Philadelphia fans, but one that broke the hearts of their Brooklyn counterparts and may be resurrected only through deep hypnosis. How then can one make a sensible determination of the greatest games? To achieve some semblance of objectivity, criteria must be established for the selection process. This collection considered two major categories: Drama/Excitement and Game Importance. 

In the Drama/Excitement arena, the author measured individual pitching efforts, pitching duels, individual batting performances, combatant offenses, comebacks, lead changes, extra innings, team rivalries, records set, and games won in the final at-bat. Game Importance surfaced in pennant races, playoffs, and the World Series, with greater consideration given to games that ended a season or series. The more ingredients a game possessed, the higher it was rated. Particularly challenging was the comparison of games from the first several decades with those of the concluding years. Because live radio or TV broadcasts were unavailable, newspaper accounts provided the main source for assessing relative merits.

It was decided early in the formation of this anthology that to be included

1

a game must have been competitive as well as exciting. Omitted are games such as the Red Sox annihilation of the Browns, 29–4. Bostonians may consider it one of the greatest games of the century, but it certainly didn't keep fans in St. Louis on the edge of their seats. Also excluded are games notable only as famous firsts, such as the premier night game or radio broadcast; personal milestone games such as players reaching 3,000 hits or 300 wins; and hitting and pitching streaks. Those categories alone could generate another 100 games of the century. In sum, each contest herein, while possibly woven into the fabric of a short series, stands on its own single-game merits.

While examples of all types of games were considered for inclusion, to profess examination of the more than 100,000 games played in the 20th century would be glorious delusion. Published sources as well as individual remembrances were researched, although it is almost certain that some of the reader's choosing were omitted. However, among the most satisfying facets of the National Pastime is its capacity to invite such comparisons and arguments year after year, generation after generation, usually without the satisfaction of persuasion. Most fans cling steadfastly to individual criteria of excellence, and the following collection reflects similar personal standards.

What better way to conclude a century of major league baseball games than to suggest a mere 100 that stand as the greatest? It is, at best, a risky venture. Nevertheless, not only has the author extracted what he considers the greatest games, but he also has the audacity to rank them. This is intended to arouse and stimulate discussion. Follow now as we revisit and relive baseball at its best.

# Boxscore Legend

| | |
|---|---|
| 1B | First base |
| 2B | Doubles in offensive section; second base in umpire section |
| 3B | Triples in offensive section; third base in umpire section |
| AB | Official at-bats |
| AT | Attendance |
| BB | Bases on balls allowed by pitchers |
| BK | Balk |
| CI | Catcher's interference or any defensive interference allowing a batter to reach base |
| CS | Runner caught stealing |
| DP | Double plays |
| ER | Errors in the boxscore summary; earned runs allowed by pitchers |
| H | Hits: made by batters, allowed by pitchers |
| HP | Hit by pitch (batter's name in parentheses); home plate in umpire section |
| HR | Home runs |
| I | Runs batted in |
| IP | Innings pitched: .1 = one-third of an inning; .2 = two-thirds of an inning |
| L | Losing pitcher |
| LF | Left field in umpire section |
| OB | Left on base |
| PB | Passed ball |
| PK | Runners picked off base |
| R | Runs: scored by batters, allowed by pitchers |
| RF | Right field in umpire section |
| SB | Stolen base |
| SF | Sacrifice fly |
| SH | Sacrifice hit |
| SO | Strikeouts by pitchers |
| TI | Time of game |
| UM | Umpire |
| W | Winning pitcher |
| WP | Wild pitch |

# THE GREATEST GAMES

## *The Miracle at Coogan's Bluff* 1

BROOKLYN (NL) at NEW YORK (NL)
Wednesday, October 3, 1951, Polo Grounds
Giants 5, Dodgers 4

The century's greatest game promised to be the emotional crescendo of a two-month escalation in tension between two clubs, their players, and their fans. On the afternoon of August 11, the Brooklyn Dodgers held a runaway 13½ game lead over their National League cross-town rivals, the New York Giants. But then the Giants caught fire, winning 16 straight and 37 of their last 44 contests, including their final seven. The Dodgers barely hung on, winning a 14-inning cliffhanger over the Phillies in their final regularly scheduled game just to tie the upstarts. What resulted was only the third major league playoff in the 20th century, and the first to extend three games. Meanwhile, about 800 yards away, just across the Harlem River, were the New York Yankees, waiting to meet the victors in the World Series.

The first game of the playoff went to the Giants, 3–1, but Brooklyn countered in the second game behind rookie Clem Labine, 10–0. Each club's magic number had been reduced to one with a single game remaining.

October 3 was a gray day under Coogan's Bluff, damp and shrouded in mist. In the estimation of announcer Gordon McLendon, nearly half of the 34,320 who made their way into the park were of Brooklyn persuasion. *The New York Times* reported that a larger crowd was discouraged by the threat of rain.

Sal "The Barber" Maglie, the gritty 34-year-old veteran, was the pitching choice of New York manager Leo Durocher. It was an obvious selection as Maglie, the Giants' ace with a 23–6 record, had beaten the Dodgers in five of six confrontations this season, and would be working with three days rest. On the other hand his Brooklyn counterpart was workhorse Don Newcombe, who, at 20–9, was pitching in his fourth game in eight days. "Newk" was 5–2 against the Giants this year, with one of those losses coming against Maglie.

5

Thomson gets a hug from Giants president Horace Stoneham (National Baseball Hall of Fame Library, Cooperstown, New York).

    The Barber was uncharacteristically wild in the opening frame, walking Pee Wee Reese and Duke Snider before Jackie Robinson singled home Reese. A Bobby Thomson base-running blunder in the second aborted a potentially big inning for the home team, who could do little else with Newcombe. After six innings the boys from Coogan's Bluff had no runs and just three hits. Combined with Labine's hitless pitching over the final five frames a day earlier, the New

York offense appeared spent. Announcer McLendon described the home team's situation as "darker than the inside of an inkwell."

The Giants finally tallied and tied it in the seventh on a double by Monte Irvin, Whitey Lockman's sacrifice bunt, and Thomson's sacrifice fly. New York hopes were soon dashed, however, when the Dodgers exploded for three runs in the top of the eighth, aided by two poor fielding plays by third baseman Thomson. Newcombe struck out the side in the bottom of the eighth, leaving the Giants dangling and gasping for breath as they approached what was likely their final inning of the season.

With New York trailing 4–1 to start the bottom of the ninth, McLendon gazed across the Harlem River. Declaring Yankee Stadium, already bedecked in World Series bunting, "as far away as the Taj Mahal," the announcer held out little hope for the Giant faithful. The public address announcer could be heard directing sportswriters to pick up their World Series passes in the Dodgers' clubhouse. But the Giants weren't finished as they dug in against a tiring Newcombe. Alvin Dark led off with a single to right, and Don Mueller followed with another. Monte Irvin popped out, but Whitey Lockman doubled to left, scoring Dark and making it 4–2. Mueller injured his ankle sliding into third and, as he was carried from the field, Newcombe left under his own power. From the Dodgers' bullpen, wearing number 13, strode veteran starter/reliever Ralph Branca to guide the Dodgers to the Taj Mahal.

Waiting at the plate was Thomson, who through his blundering baserunning

| *Brooklyn* | AB | R | H | I |
|---|---|---|---|---|
| Furillo C, rf | 5 | 0 | 0 | 0 |
| Reese P, ss | 4 | 2 | 1 | 0 |
| Snider D, cf | 3 | 1 | 2 | 0 |
| Robinson J, 2b | 2 | 1 | 1 | 1 |
| Pafko A, lf | 4 | 0 | 1 | 1 |
| Hodges G, 1b | 4 | 0 | 0 | 0 |
| Cox B, 3b | 4 | 0 | 2 | 1 |
| Walker R, c | 4 | 0 | 1 | 0 |
| Newcombe D, p | 4 | 0 | 0 | 0 |
| Branca R, p | 0 | 0 | 0 | 0 |
| | 34 | 4 | 8 | 3 |

| *New York* | AB | R | H | I |
|---|---|---|---|---|
| Stanky E, 2b | 4 | 0 | 0 | 0 |
| Dark A, ss | 4 | 1 | 1 | 0 |
| Mueller D, rf | 4 | 0 | 1 | 0 |
| Hartung C, pr | 0 | 1 | 0 | 0 |
| Irvin M, lf | 4 | 1 | 1 | 0 |
| Lockman W, 1b | 3 | 1 | 2 | 1 |
| Thomson B, 3b | 4 | 1 | 3 | 4 |
| Mays W, cf | 3 | 0 | 0 | 0 |
| Westrum W, c | 0 | 0 | 0 | 0 |
| Rigney B, ph | 1 | 0 | 0 | 0 |
| Noble R, c | 0 | 0 | 0 | 0 |
| Maglie S, p | 2 | 0 | 0 | 0 |
| Thompson H, ph | 1 | 0 | 0 | 0 |
| Jansen L, p | 0 | 0 | 0 | 0 |
| | 30 | 5 | 8 | 5 |

| *Brooklyn* | IP | H | R | ER | BB | SO |
|---|---|---|---|---|---|---|
| Newcombe | 8.1 | 7 | 4 | 4 | 2 | 2 |
| Branca (L) | 0.0 | 1 | 1 | 1 | 0 | 0 |
| | 8.1 | 8 | 5 | 5 | 2 | 2 |

| *New York* | IP | H | R | ER | BB | SO |
|---|---|---|---|---|---|---|
| Maglie | 8.0 | 8 | 4 | 4 | 4 | 6 |
| Jansen (W) | 1.0 | 0 | 0 | 0 | 0 | 0 |
| | 9.0 | 8 | 4 | 4 | 4 | 6 |

| Brooklyn | 100 | 000 | 030 — 4 |
|---|---|---|---|
| New York | 000 | 000 | 104 — 5 |

OB: Brooklyn 7, New York 3; DP: Brooklyn 2; 2B: Thomson, Irvin, Lockman; HR: Thomson (32); CS: Snider; SH: Lockman; WP: Maglie; TI: 2:28; AT: 34,320; UM: HP Jorda, 1B Conlan, 2B Stewart, 3B Goetz

and poor fielding had contributed greatly to the Giant deficit. But Bobby was not to be taken lightly. He already had 31 home runs this season and had connected off Branca in Game One of the playoff. McLendon, prophetic, described the "Royal Scot" as "dangerous as a Great Dane behind a meat counter."

McLendon struggled to be heard above the crowd, now full-throated in its partisan yowls and exhortations. The first pitch to Thomson was a strike on the inside corner. Branca's next offering never crossed the plate. Bobby smashed it on a low line into the left-field bleachers several rows over the 17-foot wall at the "315 FT" sign. Giants announcer Russ Hodges could hardly contain himself. As he screamed into the microphone five times, "The Giants win the pennant," hysterical fans and teammates ran onto the field to congratulate Thomson, who was mobbed at home plate. The club's 157th game became a reflection of the entire season, and the miracle that the Giants planted nearly eight weeks earlier had borne the sweetest fruit.

# 2 Shangri-La in Schenley Park

NEW YORK (AL) at PITTSBURGH (NL)
Thursday, October 13, 1960, Forbes Field
Pirates 10, Yankees 9

A scriptwriter hardly could have dreamed of a more storied ending to the baseball season — a favored perennial winner and a post-season stranger meeting for one last chance to call themselves world champions. The New York Yankees, winners of 10 American League pennants during the last 13 years, and the Pittsburgh Pirates, who last saw a pennant fly atop Forbes Field in 1927, each won their league's flag in convincing fashion. Matched now in a climactic World Series, no fewer than 75 records were set and another 27 tied, most of an offensive nature. The records, however, were forgotten amid the emotional upheaval of the seventh game.

The first six games witnessed an awesome display of power by the Bronx Bombers. They embarrassed the Pirates in Games Two, Three and Six by a combined score of 38 to 3. In far less spectacular fashion Pittsburgh won their three contests by a combined total of only 14 to 8. More pyrotechnics were now waiting as the grand finale showcased a stunning parade of heroes, one after another in bewildering abundance.

The curtain closer unfolded in Pittsburgh on a sunny, hazy, 70-degree day. Pirate manager Danny Murtaugh sent his ace, Vernon Law, to the mound. A 20-game winner during the regular season, Law had already won Games One and Four. New York skipper Casey Stengel countered with Bob Turley, winner of Game Two.

It didn't take long for the adrenalin to begin flowing in the Steel City. Screams of delight shook the ballpark in the opening frame when Bob Skinner walked and Rocky Nelson sent a towering fly to right that just cleared the 30-foot screen about 350 feet from the plate. In the second frame Turley gave way to 22-year-old Bill Stafford as the Bucs tallied another pair making it 4–0.

Law held the New Yorkers in check until Bill Skowron homered leading off the fifth. In the sixth the workhorse, having put in nearly 300 innings of work during the year, showed signs of fatigue. Despite the appearance of Pittsburgh's remarkable reliever, Elroy Face, the Bombers erupted for four more runs vaulting them into a 5–4 lead. The newest hero was Yogi Berra, whose three-run circuit blast cast a pall over the crowd.

In the top of the eighth New York touched Face for another pair of runs, making it 7–4. Yankee left-hander Bobby Shantz was pitching brilliantly in relief, and only six outs remained. But announcer Chuck Thompson reminded listeners that when trailing after the sixth inning, the Pirates that season had come back to win 29 times. For New Yorkers it would become a haunting statistic.

The first batter in the home half of the eighth, Gino Cimoli, singled to right. That got the crowd buzzing with anticipation. Next followed the most decisive play of the Series. Billy Virdon hit a sharp grounder toward Tony Kubek at shortstop, a tailor-made double play ball. But destiny intervened. The ball took a bad hop and struck Kubek in the throat, knocking him backward where he sat stunned. Instead of two outs and no Pirate baserunners, the Bucs had runners at first and second. Dick Groat seized the opportunity and singled home Cimoli. A luckless Shantz was relieved by Jim Coates. Skinner sacrificed his mates to second and third, but Nelson flied out to right, too shallow to score the sixth run. Next up was Roberto Clemente, who dribbled a roller to the right of the mound. First baseman Skowron fielded the ball, but Coates was late covering first. Clemente was safe, and the Pirates narrowed the gap to 7–6. Hal Smith, who had replaced Burgess in the top of the frame, then stepped to the plate. The one-time Yankee farmhand selected a 2–2 pitch and unloaded a majestic blast over the ivy-covered brick wall in left center and into Schenley Park, more than 400 feet from home plate. The delirious throng rendered the announcers inaudible, and the ancient steel rafters vibrated like tuning forks. When he finally could be heard, announcer Thompson described Forbes Field "as an outdoor insane asylum" and labeled Smith's first World Series home run "one of the all-time great moments in baseball history." His partner, Jack Quinlin, called the blast "one of the most dramatic home runs of all time." The Pirates had regained the lead at 9–7 with but an inning to play. Little did they know there was much more to follow.

Murtaugh entrusted the miraculous Pittsburgh lead to Bob Friend, an 18-game winner who had been pummeled in the Series. Friend took the mound having allowed seven earned runs in six innings pitched and an 0–2 record, but the Yankees showed no pity by chasing him with two quick singles. On came lefty Harvey Haddix to retire Roger Maris, but Mickey Mantle singled home the Bombers' eighth run. Then with Yankees at the corners, Berra grounded sharply to first. A double play would have ended the Series, and Nelson went for it, although in unorthodox fashion. Rocky stepped on first to retire Berra and was about to throw to second. Mantle, recognizing he had little chance of making second base and no longer in a forceout position, dove back into first, barely eluding Nelson's tag. Meanwhile, another New York run scored to tie the game. That set the stage for one last hero.

With the crowd relatively quiet, Bill Mazeroski led off the bottom of the ninth against Ralph Terry. The second pitch was a high fastball that was launched into the memories of baseball fans forever. As the ball sailed over the familiar "406 FT" sign, Mazeroski danced around the bases waving his helmet with glee, and Pittsburgh won their first World Championship in 35 years.

| New York | AB | R | H | I |
|---|---|---|---|---|
| Richardson B, 2b | 5 | 2 | 2 | 0 |
| Kubek T, ss | 3 | 1 | 0 | 0 |
| DeMaestri J, ss | 0 | 0 | 0 | 0 |
| Long D, ph | 1 | 0 | 1 | 0 |
| McDougald G, pr-3b | 0 | 1 | 0 | 0 |
| Maris R, rf | 5 | 0 | 0 | 0 |
| Mantle M, cf | 5 | 1 | 3 | 2 |
| Berra Y, lf | 4 | 2 | 1 | 4 |
| Skowron B, 1b | 5 | 2 | 2 | 1 |
| Blanchard J, c | 4 | 0 | 1 | 1 |
| Boyer C, 3b-ss | 4 | 0 | 1 | 1 |
| Turley B, p | 0 | 0 | 0 | 0 |
| Stafford B, p | 0 | 0 | 0 | 0 |
| Lopez H, ph | 1 | 0 | 1 | 0 |
| Shantz B, p | 3 | 0 | 1 | 0 |
| Coates J, p | 0 | 0 | 0 | 0 |
| Terry R, p | 0 | 0 | 0 | 0 |
| | 40 | 9 | 13 | 9 |

| Pittsburgh | AB | R | H | I |
|---|---|---|---|---|
| Virdon B, cf | 4 | 1 | 2 | 2 |
| Groat D, ss | 4 | 1 | 1 | 1 |
| Skinner B, lf | 2 | 1 | 0 | 0 |
| Nelson R, 1b | 3 | 1 | 1 | 2 |
| Clemente R, rf | 4 | 1 | 1 | 1 |
| Burgess S, c | 3 | 0 | 2 | 0 |
| Christopher J, pr | 0 | 0 | 0 | 0 |
| Smith H, c | 1 | 1 | 1 | 3 |
| Hoak D, 3b | 3 | 1 | 0 | 0 |
| Mazeroski , 2b | 4 | 2 | 2 | 1 |
| Law V, p | 2 | 0 | 0 | 0 |
| Face R, p | 0 | 0 | 0 | 0 |
| Cimoli G, ph | 1 | 1 | 1 | 0 |
| Friend B, p | 0 | 0 | 0 | 0 |
| Haddix H, p | 0 | 0 | 0 | 0 |
| | 31 | 10 | 11 | 10 |

| New York | IP | H | R | ER | BB | SO |
|---|---|---|---|---|---|---|
| Turley | 1.0 | 2 | 3 | 2 | 1 | 0 |
| Stafford | 1.0 | 2 | 1 | 2 | 1 | 0 |
| Shantz | 5.0 | 4 | 3 | 3 | 1 | 0 |
| Coates | 0.2 | 2 | 2 | 2 | 0 | 0 |
| Terry (L) | 0.1 | 1 | 1 | 1 | 0 | 0 |
| | 8.0 | 11 | 10 | 10 | 3 | 0 |

| Pittsburgh | IP | H | R | ER | BB | SO |
|---|---|---|---|---|---|---|
| Law | 5.0 | 4 | 3 | 3 | 1 | 0 |
| Face | 3.0 | 6 | 4 | 4 | 1 | 0 |
| Friend | 0.0 | 2 | 2 | 2 | 0 | 0 |
| Haddix (W) | 1.0 | 1 | 0 | 0 | 0 | 0 |
| | 9.0 | 13 | 9 | 9 | 2 | 0 |

| New York | 000 | 014 | 022 – 9 |
|---|---|---|---|
| Pittsburgh | 220 | 000 | 051 – 10 |

OB: New York 6, Pittsburgh 1; ER: Maris; DP: New York 3; 2B: Boyer; HR: Nelson, Skowron, Berra, Smith, Mazeroski; SH: Skinner; TI: 2:36; AT: 36,683; UM: HP Jackowski, 1B Chylak, 2B Boggess, 3B Stevens, LF Stan Landes, RF Honochick

# The Longest Game Ever Played 3

BROOKLYN (NL) at BOSTON (NL)
Saturday, May 1, 1920, Braves Field
Robins 1, Braves 1

In Boston on May Day, 1920, clouds and light rain overshadowed the city. But the 4,500 avid fans that ventured to Braves Field were richly rewarded by witnessing a 26-inning game, the longest contest in major league history.

The drizzle stopped by game time, but during the following three hours and fifty minutes records galore fell. In a show of endurance inconceivable by today's standards, Brooklyn Robins' Leon Cadore and Boston's Joe Oeschger both went the distance in what amounted to nearly a tripleheader.

Amazingly both pitchers strengthened as the contest dragged on. Cadore didn't allow a hit after a 20th-inning single. And Oeschger, who permitted just three runners to reach third base during the entire game, pitched what amounts to a no-hitter over the final third of the game. Brooklyn scored its only run in the fifth on a walk, fielder's choice, and single. Boston tallied in the sixth on a triple and a single.

Despite the contest's duration, outstanding defensive plays and the suspense of several game-ending situations kept the crowd on the edge of their seats. The Braves loaded the bases in the ninth with only one away, but a Robins double play ended the threat. In the 15th, Boston blew another golden opportunity after their first two batters reached safely, but Cadore induced two ground-outs and a fly ball to close the door. Several runners were thrown out at the plate including Brooklyn's Ed Konetchy in the 17th. Then, with the bases loaded and only one out, Konetchy was cut down on a thrilling 1–2–3–2 double play. Boston's Boeckel was also thrown out at the plate in the sixth.

With darkness falling and no lights, the game was called after 26 innings with the score tied at 1–1. Among the records set this day were those of Braves teammates Charlie Pick and Tony Boeckel, who each collected 11 official at-bats. Boston first baseman Walter Holke amassed 42 putouts while Oeschger tossed 21 consecutive scoreless frames. Brooklyn's Cadore established new benchmarks when he faced 96 batters and had 12 assists. Team marks were set by the Braves with 119 fielding chances and the Robins' outfield with 24 chances. The two clubs also combined for 72 assists.

As was the custom of the time, this game was replayed in its entirety later in the season. On June 25, as part of a doubleheader, Boston prevailed 4–2 — in nine innings. Although replayed, this contest stands as official.

| Brooklyn | AB | R | H | I |
|---|---|---|---|---|
| Olson I, 2b | 10 | 0 | 1 | 1 |
| Neis B, rf | 10 | 0 | 1 | 0 |
| Johnston J, 3b | 10 | 0 | 2 | 0 |
| Wheat Z, lf | 9 | 0 | 2 | 0 |
| Myers H, cf | 2 | 0 | 1 | 0 |
| Hood W, pr-cf | 6 | 0 | 1 | 0 |
| Konetchy E, 1b | 9 | 0 | 1 | 0 |
| Ward C, ss | 10 | 0 | 0 | 0 |
| Krueger E, c | 2 | 1 | 0 | 0 |
| Elliott R, c | 7 | 0 | 0 | 0 |
| Cadore L, p | 10 | 0 | 0 | 0 |
|  | 85 | 1 | 9 | 1 |

| Boston | AB | R | H | I |
|---|---|---|---|---|
| Powell R, cf | 7 | 0 | 1 | 0 |
| Pick C, 2b | 11 | 0 | 0 | 0 |
| Mann L, lf | 10 | 0 | 2 | 0 |
| Cruise W, rf | 9 | 1 | 1 | 0 |
| Holke W, 1b | 10 | 0 | 2 | 0 |
| Boeckel T, 3b | 11 | 0 | 3 | 1 |
| Maranville R, ss | 10 | 0 | 3 | 0 |
| O'Neil M, c | 2 | 0 | 0 | 0 |
| Christenbury L, ph | 1 | 0 | 1 | 0 |
| Gowdy H, c | 6 | 0 | 1 | 0 |
| Oeschger J, p | 9 | 0 | 1 | 0 |
|  | 86 | 1 | 15 | 1 |

| Brooklyn | IP | H | R | ER | BB | SO |
|---|---|---|---|---|---|---|
| Cadore | 26.0 | 15 | 1 | 1 | 5 | 7 |

| Boston | IP | H | R | ER | BB | SO |
|---|---|---|---|---|---|---|
| Oeschger | 26.0 | 9 | 1 | 1 | 4 | 7 |

| Brooklyn | 000 | 010 | 000 | 000 | 000 | 000 | 000 | 000 | 00 — 1 |
|---|---|---|---|---|---|---|---|---|---|
| Boston | 000 | 001 | 000 | 000 | 000 | 000 | 000 | 000 | 00 — 1 |

OB: Brooklyn 11, Boston 17; ER: Olson, Ward, Pick 2; DP: Brooklyn 1, Boston 1; 2B: Maranville, Oeschger; 3B: Cruise; SB: Myers, Hood; CS: Myers, Boeckel; PK: Neis, Hood, Mann; SH: Hood; Powell, Cruise, Holke, O'Neil, Oeschger; WP: Oeschger; TI: 3:50; AT: 4,500; UM: McCormick, Hart

# 4 Haddix Is Perfect for Twelve Innings

### PITTSBURGH (NL) at MILWAUKEE (NL)
### Tuesday, May 26, 1959, County Stadium
### Braves 1, Pirates 0

Since the birth of the National League in 1876, no pitcher had ever started and carried a perfect game beyond the ninth inning, at least until this night when veteran Harvey "The Kitten" Haddix took the mound. The 155-pound, 33-year-old southpaw was facing the first-place Braves, who led the league in hitting a year earlier and now had seven regulars batting over .300. In addition, Milwaukee stacked their lineup with seven right-handed batters.

Prior to the contest, Harvey's warm-up pitches were as sluggish as the rest of his body. He was fighting a cold but told manager Danny Murtaugh he would go as far as he could. His effort turned out to be a masterpiece, one that many claim as the best pitching performance in baseball history.

In the clubhouse, Haddix comtemplates the night's events (National Baseball Hall of Fame Library, Cooperstown, New York).

The night was cold and damp, but the Kitten was brilliant. His battery-mate, Smoky Burgess, later said Haddix had pinpoint control of all four of his pitches — fastball, curve, slider, and change up. So amazing was his control that the Pittsburgh Press reported he stayed ahead of every batter until the 12th inning when Andy Pafko worked a 2–0 count before bouncing back to the mound.

There were few threats to his perfection. In the third, Johnny Logan's liner was snared with a short leap by shortstop Dick Schofield. Centerfielder Bill Virdon made a fine catch on a short liner in the 11th, and third baseman Don Hoak made a great stop of a bounder in the 12th. Everything else was routine. Even

| Pittsburgh | AB | R | H | I |
|---|---|---|---|---|
| Schofield D, ss | 6 | 0 | 3 | 0 |
| Virdon B, cf | 6 | 0 | 1 | 0 |
| Burgess S, c | 5 | 0 | 0 | 0 |
| Nelson R, 1b | 5 | 0 | 2 | 0 |
| Skinner B, lf | 5 | 0 | 1 | 0 |
| Mazeroski B, 2b | 5 | 0 | 1 | 0 |
| Hoak D, 3b | 5 | 0 | 2 | 0 |
| Mejias R, rf | 3 | 0 | 1 | 0 |
| Stuart D, ph | 1 | 0 | 0 | 0 |
| Christopher J, rf | 1 | 0 | 0 | 0 |
| Haddix H, p | 5 | 0 | 1 | 0 |
| | 47 | 0 | 12 | 0 |

| Milwaukee | AB | R | H | I |
|---|---|---|---|---|
| O'Brien J, 2b | 3 | 0 | 0 | 0 |
| Rice D, ph | 1 | 0 | 0 | 0 |
| Mantilla F-2b | 1 | 1 | 0 | 0 |
| Mathews E, 3b | 4 | 0 | 0 | 0 |
| Aaron H, rf | 4 | 0 | 0 | 0 |
| Adcock J, 1b | 5 | 0 | 1 | 1 |
| Covington W, lf | 4 | 0 | 0 | 0 |
| Crandall D, c | 4 | 0 | 0 | 0 |
| Pafko A, cf | 4 | 0 | 0 | 0 |
| Logan J, ss | 4 | 0 | 0 | 0 |
| Burdette L, p | 4 | 0 | 0 | 0 |
| | 38 | 1 | 1 | 1 |

| Pittsburgh | IP | H | R | ER | BB | SO |
|---|---|---|---|---|---|---|
| Haddix (L) | 12.2 | 1 | 1 | 0 | 1 | 8 |

| Milwaukee | IP | H | R | ER | BB | SO |
|---|---|---|---|---|---|---|
| Burdette (W) | 13.0 | 12 | 0 | 0 | 0 | 2 |

| Pittsburgh | 000 | 000 | 000 | 000 | 0 — 0 |
|---|---|---|---|---|---|
| Milwaukee | 000 | 000 | 000 | 000 | 1 — 1 |

OB: Pittsburgh 8, Milwaukee 1; ER: Hoak; DP: Milwaukee 3; 2B: Adcock; SH: Mathews; TI: 2:54; AT: 19,194; UM: Smith, Dascoli, Secory, Dixon

the rain, which began falling lightly in the seventh, couldn't put a damper on his performance. Beginning in the ninth the partisan crowd, recognizing Harvey's achievement, gave him a standing ovation after each inning.

While Haddix was getting all the attention, Lew Burdette was tossing a gem unnoticed. During 13 innings he allowed more than one hit in only two frames and never walked a batter. Pittsburgh collected three hits in the third, but some shabby baserunning helped Burdette escape. In the ninth two Pirates singled, but both were left stranded. Burdette faced no other threats.

Flawlessness finally ended for Haddix in the 13th when Felix Mantilla sent a routine grounder to Hoak. The third baseman fielded it cleanly but short-hopped his throw to first. Rocky Nelson failed to dig it out, and the Braves had their first baserunner. The official scorer ruled it an error, so Haddix still had a no-hitter. Eddie Mathews then sacrificed Mantilla to second. Hank Aaron, the league's leading hitter, was walked intentionally to get to the slow-footed Joe Adcock, who hadn't gotten a ball out of the infield all night. On a 1–0 count, Adcock smashed a low liner toward right-center that just cleared the fence, but with the field shrouded in mist, mass confusion reigned. Mantilla scored, but Aaron, not realizing the ball left the park and thinking the game was over, ran past second then across the pitcher's mound toward the dugout. Adcock, running with his head down, passed Aaron and rounded third. Under instructions from an equally confused coaching staff, both runners returned to the basepaths in an attempt to get it right.

Frank Dascoli, chief of the umpire crew, ruled that Adcock was out for having passed Aaron, but because Aaron retraced his steps and crossed the plate, his run counted. Several newspapers reported the final score as 2–0, but several others printed the final tally as 1–0. It wasn't until the following day that National League president Warren Giles ruled that because Adcock passed

Aaron at second base, his hit was to be scored a double. That made Aaron's run superfluous and the official score 1–0.

In later years information surfaced that made Haddix's masterpiece even more astonishing. Bob Buhl, who sat in the Milwaukee bullpen that night, divulged that the Braves used binoculars to steal the signs of catcher Burgess all night and relayed them to the hitters through a series of towel waving movements. Adcock, however, claimed he did not partake in the practice.

# *Fisk Extends the Series to Seven Games* 5

CINCINNATI (NL) at BOSTON (AL)
Tuesday, October 21, 1975, Fenway Park
Red Sox 7, Reds 6

This World Series had it all — good pitching, terrific fielding plays, explosive offense and plenty of drama. Veteran writers proclaimed it one of the more exciting Series in memory. After five games Cincinnati's Big Red Machine held the edge over the Boston Red Sox three games to two, and their manager, Sparky Anderson, had every intention of ending the Fall Classic this night. Captain Hook, as he was affectionately known, was not bashful about replacing pitchers on the mound and promised to use seven in this game if necessary to take home the championship. Underdog Boston, meanwhile, took advantage of a three-day rain delay to start their Game One pitcher Luis Tiant.

It was a clear crisp night in Boston, with the wind favoring the hitters. Radio announcer Curt Gowdy told the listening audience that "with the wind blowing out, this is a hold-your-breath ballpark." Throughout the first five innings, he repeated the potential influence of Mother Nature on batted balls.

The Red Sox needed this game to stay alive, and in the opening frame they drew first blood. After two outs Carl Yastrzemski and Carlton Fisk singled. Rookie Fred Lynn then smashed a towering drive into right–center field that cleared the Boston bullpen and landed ten rows deep in the bleachers.

Tiant held the 3–0 lead until the fifth. With two on and one out, Ken Griffey tripled to deep left-center driving home Cincinnati's first two runs. Johnny Bench then singled to tie the game.

In the Cincinnati seventh, with two on and two out, George Foster doubled home a pair, giving the Reds their first lead at 5–3. Crowd noise was non-existent,

| Cincinnati | AB | R | H | I |
|---|---|---|---|---|
| Rose P, 3b | 5 | 1 | 2 | 0 |
| Griffey K, rf | 5 | 2 | 2 | 2 |
| Morgan J, 2b | 6 | 1 | 1 | 0 |
| Bench J, c | 6 | 0 | 1 | 1 |
| Perez T, 1b | 6 | 0 | 2 | 0 |
| Foster G, lf | 6 | 0 | 2 | 2 |
| Concepcion D, ss | 6 | 0 | 1 | 0 |
| Geronimo C, cf | 6 | 1 | 2 | 1 |
| Nolan G, p | 0 | 0 | 0 | 0 |
| Chaney D, ph | 1 | 0 | 0 | 0 |
| Norman F, p | 0 | 0 | 0 | 0 |
| Billingham J, p | 0 | 0 | 0 | 0 |
| Armbrister E, ph | 0 | 1 | 0 | 0 |
| Carroll C, p | 0 | 0 | 0 | 0 |
| Crowley T, ph | 1 | 0 | 1 | 0 |
| Borbon P, p | 1 | 0 | 0 | 0 |
| Eastwick R, p | 0 | 0 | 0 | 0 |
| McEnaney W, p | 0 | 0 | 0 | 0 |
| Driessen D, ph | 1 | 0 | 0 | 0 |
| Darcy P, p | 0 | 0 | 0 | 0 |
| | 50 | 6 | 14 | 6 |

| Boston | AB | R | H | I |
|---|---|---|---|---|
| Cooper C, 1b | 5 | 0 | 0 | 0 |
| Drago D, p | 0 | 0 | 0 | 0 |
| Miller R, ph | 1 | 0 | 0 | 0 |
| Wise R, p | 0 | 0 | 0 | 0 |
| Doyle D, 2b | 5 | 0 | 1 | 0 |
| Yastrzemski C, lf-1b | 6 | 1 | 3 | 0 |
| Fisk C, c | 4 | 2 | 2 | 1 |
| Lynn F, cf | 4 | 2 | 2 | 3 |
| Petrocelli R, 3b | 4 | 1 | 0 | 0 |
| Evans D, rf | 5 | 0 | 1 | 0 |
| Burleson R, ss | 3 | 0 | 0 | 0 |
| Tiant L, p | 2 | 0 | 0 | 0 |
| Moret R, p | 0 | 0 | 0 | 0 |
| Carbo B, ph-lf | 2 | 1 | 1 | 3 |
| | 41 | 7 | 10 | 7 |

| Cincinnati | IP | H | R | ER | BB | SO |
|---|---|---|---|---|---|---|
| Nolan | 2.0 | 3 | 3 | 3 | 0 | 2 |
| Norman | 0.2 | 1 | 0 | 0 | 2 | 0 |
| Billingham | 1.1 | 1 | 0 | 0 | 1 | 1 |
| Carroll | 1.0 | 1 | 0 | 0 | 0 | 0 |
| Borbon | 2.0 | 1 | 2 | 2 | 2 | 1 |
| Eastwick | 1.0 | 2 | 1 | 1 | 1 | 2 |
| McEnaney | 1.0 | 0 | 0 | 0 | 1 | 0 |
| Darcy P (L) | 2.0 | 1 | 1 | 1 | 0 | 1 |
| | 11.0 | 10 | 7 | 7 | 7 | 7 |

| Boston | IP | H | R | ER | BB | SO |
|---|---|---|---|---|---|---|
| Tiant | 7.0 | 11 | 6 | 6 | 2 | 5 |
| Moret | 1.0 | 0 | 0 | 0 | 0 | 0 |
| Drago | 3.0 | 1 | 0 | 0 | 0 | 1 |
| Wise (W) | 1.0 | 2 | 0 | 0 | 0 | 1 |
| | 12.0 | 13 | 6 | 6 | 2 | 7 |

Cincinnati   000   030   210   000 — 6
Boston       300   000   030   001 — 7

OB: Cincinnati 11, Boston 9; ER: Burleson; DP: Cincinnati 1, Boston 1; 2B: Doyle, Evans, Foster; 3B: Griffey; HR: Lynn, Geronimo, Carbo, Fisk; SB: Concepcion; SH: Tiant; HP: by Drago (Rose); TI: 4:01; AT: 35,205; UM: HP Davidson, 1B Frantz, 2B Colosi, 3B Barnett, LF Stello, RF Maloney

especially after Cesar Geronimo led off the visitor's eighth with a home run. The round-tripper spelled the end for Tiant, who left to a standing ovation, but trailing 6–3.

Meanwhile, Captain Hook's fifth pitcher, Pedro Borbon, was coasting along as the announcers quipped that the only empty seats in the park were in the Cincinnati bullpen. Borbon had walked one and retired the other six batters he faced without a ball leaving the infield. Sox fans braced themselves for another long, unhappy winter.

But in the bottom of the eighth, after Lynn opened with a single and Rico Petrocelli walked, the crowd came to life. Rawly Eastwick replaced Borbon, struck out Dwight Evans, and retired Rick Burleson on a liner to left. Pinch-hitting for Roger Moret, Bernie Carbo then strode to the plate. Carbo had been a first round draft pick of Cincinnati in 1965 (ahead of Johnny Bench) and relished the chance to impress his old mates. After fouling off a 3–2 pitch, Carbo launched Eastwick's next offering 400 feet, into the center field seats, knotting the contest at six. It was Bernie's second pinch home run of the Series, and the theatrics ignited the crowd.

Boston could not have had a better opportunity to win it in the ninth. With bases loaded and no outs, Lynn lifted a shallow fly to left. Foster hovered near the foul line, where the stands encroached within a few feet of fair territory, and made the catch. Contrary to the screams of Boston third base coach Don Zimmer, Denny Doyle tagged up and dashed for the plate. Foster's throw was nearly perfect. Bench reached slightly up the first base line for the peg then tagged out Doyle for a double play. That broke the back of the Sox rally, and Petrocelli ended the suspense by grounding out.

In the 11th another spectacular defensive play saved the game, this time for Boston. With Griffey at first and one out, Joe Morgan lifted a fly ball deep to right field. Evans raced back, leaped above the wall and pulled down a certain home run. He then fired back to the infield where Griffey was easily doubled off first.

Cincinnati again threatened in the 12th frame against Rick Wise, who became the last of a dozen pitchers to enter the game. With one out the Reds collected a pair of singles, but Wise retired the next two batters.

Pat Darcy, who had taken the mound for Cincinnati in the 10th, had retired six straight Red Sox. But leading off the home 12th was Fisk. On a 1–0 pitch the catcher lofted a towering drive deep to left as more than 35,000 pairs of eyes strained to see if it would stay fair. Amid a deafening roar Fisk waved the ball fair as it slammed high off the foul pole and gave Boston one of the most dramatic victories in World Series history.

# *Koufax Was Perfect;*
# *Hendley Almost* 6

## CHICAGO (NL) at LOS ANGELES (NL)
### Thursday, September 9, 1965, Dodger Stadium
### Dodgers 1, Cubs 0

For five years Sandy Koufax had been one of the most dominating pitchers ever to stalk the baseball diamond. This would be the fourth of five consecutive seasons leading the league in ERA; the third of five leading in strikeouts;

| Chicago | AB | R | H | I |
|---|---|---|---|---|
| Young D, cf | 3 | 0 | 0 | 0 |
| Beckert G, 2b | 3 | 0 | 0 | 0 |
| Williams B, rf | 3 | 0 | 0 | 0 |
| Santo R, 3b | 3 | 0 | 0 | 0 |
| Banks E, 1b | 3 | 0 | 0 | 0 |
| Browne B, lf | 3 | 0 | 0 | 0 |
| Krug C, c | 3 | 0 | 0 | 0 |
| Kessinger D, ss | 2 | 0 | 0 | 0 |
| Amalfitano J, ph | 1 | 0 | 0 | 0 |
| Hendley B, p | 2 | 0 | 0 | 0 |
| Kuenn H, ph | 1 | 0 | 0 | 0 |
| | 27 | 0 | 0 | 0 |

| Los Angeles | AB | R | H | I |
|---|---|---|---|---|
| Wills M, ss | 3 | 0 | 0 | 0 |
| Gilliam J, 3b | 3 | 0 | 0 | 0 |
| Kennedy J, 3b | 0 | 0 | 0 | 0 |
| Davis W, cf | 3 | 0 | 0 | 0 |
| Johnson L, lf | 2 | 1 | 1 | 0 |
| Fairly R, rf | 2 | 0 | 0 | 0 |
| Lefebvre J, 2b | 3 | 0 | 0 | 0 |
| Tracewski D, 2b | 0 | 0 | 0 | 0 |
| Parker W, 1b | 3 | 0 | 0 | 0 |
| Torborg J, c | 3 | 0 | 0 | 0 |
| Koufax S, p | 2 | 0 | 0 | 0 |
| | 24 | 1 | 1 | 0 |

| Chicago | IP | H | R | ER | BB | SO |
|---|---|---|---|---|---|---|
| Hendley (L) | 8 | 1 | 1 | 0 | 1 | 3 |

| Los Angeles | IP | H | R | ER | BB | SO |
|---|---|---|---|---|---|---|
| Koufax (W) | 9 | 0 | 0 | 0 | 0 | 14 |

| Chicago | 000 | 000 | 000 — 0 |
|---|---|---|---|
| Los Angeles | 000 | 010 | 00x — 1 |

OB: Chicago 0, Los Angeles 1; ER: Krug; 2B: Johnson; SB: Johnson; SH: Fairly; TI: 1:43; AT: 29, 139; UM: Vargo, Pelekoudas, Jackowski, Pryor

and the sixth in a row in holding opponents to the lowest batting average. And the unassuming Dodger had already tossed three no-hitters. Baseball fans were, in fact, shocked when he lost.

His mound opponent was, like Koufax, a 6'2" left-hander, but that's where the similarity ended. Chicago's Bob Hendley, in his fifth major league campaign, possessed an unimpressive 37–42 lifetime record, an ERA approaching 4.00, and an opponents' on-base percentage that customarily exceeded .300. This day, however, Hendley pitched the game of his life, allowing just one hit, and the lone run to score did so without the benefit of that hit.

Each hurler retired the first 12 batters to face him. Then in the Dodger half of the fifth, Lou Johnson led off with a walk. After Ron Fairly bunted him to second, Johnson tried to steal third. Cubs' rookie backstop, Chris Krug, unleashed a wild throw attempting to catch the thief, and Lou waltzed home. Thus the Dodgers scored the game's only run without a hit and without getting a ball out of the infield.

The only other offense, and the only hit of the game, was provided again by Johnson in the seventh. With two outs the former Cub blooped a double just beyond the reach of first baseman Ernie Banks but was left stranded when Fairly grounded out.

The Cubs came close to ruining perfection several times. In the opening frame Glenn Beckert smashed a hard drive down the left field line that was foul by inches. Byron Browne hit a line drive in the second inning that center fielder Willie Davis caught belt high, and first baseman Wes Parker had to dig a throw by Maury Wills out of the dirt in the sixth. The first three pitches in the seventh to Billy Williams were balls before Koufax tossed two strikes, and Williams flied lazily to left.

With one run behind him Koufax turned on the heat and retired eight of the last 12 Cubs on strikes. With the hometown fans roaring with each strike, Sandy fanned the final six batters, the last five swinging. The final two batters were pinch-hitters. His 14 strikeouts marked the 18th time that season he reached double figures and ran his total to 332, just 16 shy of Bob Feller's record. (Koufax went on to eclipse the mark, finishing with 382.) Feeding the Cubs a diet of 113 fastballs and curves, the great lefty had tossed no-hitters in four successive seasons, making him the first to reach that plateau.

# Twins Capture Championship in Extra-Inning Finale 7

ATLANTA (NL) at MINNESOTA (AL)
Sunday, October 27, 1991, Metrodome
Twins 1, Braves 0

Commissioner Fay Vincent's claim that this was "probably the greatest World Series ever" was more than mere propaganda. The Cinderella opponents each finished last in their division the previous season. Five games, including the seventh, were decided by one run; four saw ties unknotted in the home half of the final inning; and three games, including the final, took extra innings to decide. In addition, this was only the second seventh-game in history to span extra innings as well as only the second Game Seven in which only one run was scored.

Despite several first place divisional finishes, the Braves were appearing in their first World Series since moving to Atlanta a quarter-century earlier. The Twins, meanwhile, had been crowned world champions four years earlier, in 1987.

Two right-handers squared off for this seventh game. John Smoltz, in his fourth season, was a rising star for Atlanta. His boyhood idol, veteran Jack Morris, opposed him. Morris was a workhorse; a tough, wily veteran who made 34-plus starts in nine of the past 10 seasons, all with Detroit. As a free agent, Morris joined the Twins for the 1991 campaign.

Smoltz and Morris handcuffed the batters for seven innings, allowing only two runners to reach third. In the third inning Dan Gladden doubled and advanced

| Atlanta | AB | R | H | I |
|---------|----|----|----|----|
| Smith L, dh | 4 | 0 | 2 | 0 |
| Pendleton T, 3b | 5 | 0 | 1 | 0 |
| Gant R, cf | 4 | 0 | 0 | 0 |
| Justice D, rf | 3 | 0 | 1 | 0 |
| Bream S, 1b | 4 | 0 | 0 | 0 |
| Hunter B, lf | 4 | 0 | 1 | 0 |
| Olson G, c | 4 | 0 | 0 | 0 |
| Lemke M, 2b | 4 | 0 | 1 | 0 |
| Belliard R, ss | 2 | 0 | 1 | 0 |
| Blauser J, ph-ss | 1 | 0 | 0 | 0 |
|  | 35 | 0 | 7 | 0 |

| Minnesota | AB | R | H | I |
|-----------|----|----|----|----|
| Gladden D, lf | 5 | 1 | 3 | 0 |
| Knoblauch C, 2b | 4 | 0 | 1 | 0 |
| Puckett K, cf | 2 | 0 | 0 | 0 |
| Hrbek K, 1b | 3 | 0 | 0 | 0 |
| Davis C, dh | 4 | 0 | 1 | 0 |
| Brown J, ph | 0 | 0 | 0 | 0 |
| Larkin G, ph | 1 | 0 | 1 | 1 |
| Harper B, c | 4 | 0 | 2 | 0 |
| Mack S, rf | 4 | 0 | 1 | 0 |
| Pagliarulo M, 3b | 3 | 0 | 0 | 0 |
| Gagne G, ss | 2 | 0 | 0 | 0 |
| Bush R, ph | 1 | 0 | 1 | 0 |
| Newman A, pr-ss | 0 | 0 | 0 | 0 |
| Sorrento P, ph | 1 | 0 | 0 | 0 |
| Leius S, ss | 0 | 0 | 0 | 0 |
|  | 34 | 1 | 10 | 1 |

| Atlanta | IP | H | R | ER | BB | SO |
|---------|----|----|----|----|----|----|
| Smoltz | 7.1 | 6 | 0 | 0 | 1 | 4 |
| Stanton | 0.2 | 2 | 0 | 0 | 1 | 0 |
| Peña (L) | 1.1 | 2 | 1 | 1 | 3 | 1 |
|  | 9.1 | 10 | 1 | 1 | 5 | 5 |

| Minnesota | IP | H | R | ER | BB | SO |
|-----------|----|----|----|----|----|----|
| Morris (W) | 10.0 | 7 | 0 | 0 | 2 | 8 |

```
Atlanta     000  000  000  0 — 0
Minnesota   000  000  000  1 — 1
```

OB: Atlanta 8, Minnesota 12; DP: Atlanta 3, Minnesota 1; 2B: Gladden 2, Hunter, Pendleton; SH: Belliard, Knoblauch; HP: by Smoltz (Hrbek); WP: Morris; TI: 3:23; AT: 55,118; UM: HP Denkinger, 1B Wendelstedt, 2B Coble, 3B Tata, LF Reed, RF Montague

to third on a fly ball, but Smoltz fanned Kirby Puckett to end the inning. The Braves put runners at the corners in the fifth, but Morris got Terry Pendleton on a pop-up and sat down Ron Gant on strikes.

Both teams threatened in the eighth. Lonnie Smith led off the visitors' half with a single to right. As he broke to steal second, Pendleton smashed a ball deep to left-center that caromed off the wall. Smith lost sight of the ball and hesitated around second base. By the time he recovered, he could get only as far as third, with Pendleton pulling into second with a double. Though Smith might have scored on the play had he relied on his third-base coach, his lapse still left the Braves in good position to break into the scoring column. Next, Ron Gant was out on a slow roller to first and the runners could not advance. Twins' manager Tom Kelly then decided to walk David Justice intentionally, loading the bases. The strategy worked to perfection as Sid Bream grounded into a 3–2–3 double play.

A similar fate befell Minnesota in the home half of the eighth. A pair of singles surrounding a pop-up put Twins at the corners with one away. Mike Stanton replaced Smoltz and intentionally walked Puckett to load the bases. Kent Hrbek then sent a soft line drive toward second. Atlanta second baseman Mark Lemke caught it easily and stepped on the bag to double-up Chuck Knoblauch, who had foolishly left at the crack of the bat.

Minnesota threatened again in the ninth. Two singles, the second a bunt, put Twins at first and second with no outs. Stanton injured himself fielding the bunt and was replaced by Alejandro Peña, who immediately induced Shane Mack to ground into a 4–6–3 double play. With a runner on third, Mike Pagliarulo was intentionally passed, but pinch-hitter Paul Sorrento fanned to send the game into extra innings.

While the Twins were threatening to end the game in the ninth, a conference was held in their dugout. Manager Kelly wanted to relieve Morris if the game went into extra innings, but Jack insisted on staying in. Pitching coach Dick Such cast the tie-breaking vote, and Morris returned to the mound, retiring the Braves in order in the tenth.

Gladden opened the home tenth with a broken-bat double into left-center. After Knoblauch sacrificed him to third, the strategizing in both dugouts accelerated. Peña intentionally walked both Puckett and Hrbek to load the bases. As Gene Larkin stepped up to pinch-hit for Jarvis Brown, the Atlanta outfielders moved in close enough to catch a short fly and throw out Gladden at the plate. Meanwhile, the home crowd of 55,000 was on its feet, waving its white homer-hankies.

The switch-hitting Larkin, batting for only the fourth time in the Series, responded with a fly ball to left-center, over the outfielders' heads. Gladden jumped on home plate, and a wild celebration in the Metrodome began.

# Joss and Walsh Struggle for the Pennant 8

## CHICAGO (AL) at CLEVELAND (AL)
### Friday, October 2, 1908, League Park
### Naps 1, White Sox 0

The 1908 American League pennant race was among the most exciting of the century. On the morning of October 2, three clubs, each with five games remaining, had a chance to fly the championship flag. Here's how they stacked up:

|          | W  | L  | GB  | Games Remaining: Schedule |
|----------|----|----|-----|---------------------------|
| Detroit  | 87 | 61 | —   | 5: 2 Home vs. St. Louis; 3 Away vs. Chicago |
| Cleveland| 87 | 62 | 0.5 | 5: 2 Home vs. Chicago; 3 Away vs. St. Louis |
| Chicago  | 85 | 62 | 1.5 | 5: 2 Away vs. Cleveland; 3 Home vs. Detroit |

In Cleveland that afternoon were pitted two of the best pitchers in the league — Adrian "Addie" Joss of the hometown Naps (named after their player-manager

| Chicago | AB | R | H | I |
|---|---|---|---|---|
| Hahn E, rf | 3 | 0 | 0 | 0 |
| Jones F, cf | 3 | 0 | 0 | 0 |
| Isbell F, 1b | 3 | 0 | 0 | 0 |
| Dougherty P, lf | 3 | 0 | 0 | 0 |
| Davis G, 2b | 3 | 0 | 0 | 0 |
| Parent F, ss | 3 | 0 | 0 | 0 |
| Schreckengost O, c | 2 | 0 | 0 | 0 |
| Shaw A, c | 0 | 0 | 0 | 0 |
| | 0 | | | |
| White D, ph | 1 | 0 | 0 | 0 |
| Tannehill L, 3b | 2 | 0 | 0 | 0 |
| Donahue J, ph | 1 | 0 | 0 | 0 |
| Walsh E, p | 2 | 0 | 0 | 0 |
| Anderson J, ph | 1 | 0 | 0 | 0 |
| | 27 | 0 | 0 | 0 |

| Cleveland | AB | R | H | I |
|---|---|---|---|---|
| Good W, rf | 4 | 0 | 0 | 0 |
| Bradley B, 3b | 4 | 0 | 0 | 0 |
| Hinchman B, lf | 3 | 0 | 0 | 0 |
| Lajoie N, 2b | 3 | 0 | 1 | 0 |
| Stovall G, 1b | 3 | 0 | 0 | 0 |
| Clarke N, c | 3 | 0 | 0 | 0 |
| Birmingham J, cf | 3 | 1 | 2 | 0 |
| Perring G, | 2 | 0 | 1 | |
| Joss A, p | 3 | 0 | 0 | 0 |
| | 28 | 1 | 4 | 0 |

| Chicago | IP | H | R | ER | BB | SO |
|---|---|---|---|---|---|---|
| Walsh (L) | 8.0 | 4 | 1 | 0 | 1 | 15 |

| Cleveland | IP | H | R | ER | BB | SO |
|---|---|---|---|---|---|---|
| Joss (W) | 9.0 | 0 | 0 | 0 | 0 | 3 |

| | | | |
|---|---|---|---|
| Chicago | 000 | 000 | 000 — 0 |
| Cleveland | 001 | 000 | 00x — 1 |

OB: Chicago 0, Cleveland 4; ER: Isbell; SB: Lajoie, Birmingham 2, Perring; WP: Walsh; PB: Schreckengost; TI: 1:40; AT: 10,598; UM: Connolly, O'Loughlin

Nap Lajoie) and spitballer Big Ed Walsh of the Chicago White Sox. Walsh was compiling one of the most spectacular pitching seasons of the century. Before it was over, the right-hander would amass a 40–15 log with 11 shutouts, 464 innings pitched, 269 strikeouts, 7 saves, 42 complete games, and a 1.42 ERA. Joss, a fan favorite in the Cleveland area, would finish at 24–11 with 9 shutouts, a league leading 1.16 ERA, and only 30 walks in 325 innings.

Both clubs were hoping the Tigers would stumble in St. Louis, and neither could afford to lose another game. Thus the two future Hall of Famers locked horns in what everyone expected to be a pitcher's duel. With the hopes of three teams at stake, completing the game was deemed a top priority: officials advanced the time of the first pitch to 2:30 P.M. lessening the chance that an extra-inning contest might be postponed by encroaching darkness. By the start of the action, more than 10,000 excited fans had crammed into League Park, exceeding by 1,000 its seating capacity. The skies were clear and the temperature was in the 50s.

A pitcher's duel is exactly what the fans got. The first batter didn't reach base until Cleveland's Joe Birmingham led off the third with a single. As Joe took his lead off first, Walsh fired to first sacker Frank Isbell. Birmingham took off for second and would have been out easily had not Isbell's throw hit the runner and bounded into the outfield. Joe went all the way to third on the play. With no outs, Walsh bore down and got the next two batters on a ground-out and a strikeout. He was almost out of the inning when he got two strikes on Wilbur Good. But the next delivery, a wild pitch, got past catcher Ossie Schreckengost, and Isbell scored an unearned run. On the very next pitch, Good struck out. Ironically, neither Isbell nor Schreckengost was a regular. Isbell was filling in for a slumping Jiggs Donahue, and Schreckengost was replacing an injured Billy Sullivan.

The Naps had a few more scoring opportunities, but Walsh was equal to the task. In the fourth Lajoie singled with two outs and stole second but was left stranded. In the eighth the first two Naps singled and advanced on a passed ball, but Walsh struck out the next two batters and a third grounded out. Big Ed struck out 15, including the great Lajoie twice, but it wasn't enough.

Joss pitched the game of his life, a perfect one, by retiring all 27 batters to face him. Twenty-two Sox failed to get the ball out of the infield as Joss made efficient use of his 74 pitches. He also had some help from his defense. In the second frame first baseman George Stovall made a fine play on a high toss from shortstop George Perring. Lajoie made at least five great plays scooping grounders around second base, and Joss himself made a great play on a slow roller toward third in the fifth inning. In the ninth, Chicago manager Fielder Jones showed his desperation when he sent three pinch-hitters to the plate, but to no avail. The final out was punctuated by another fine play by Stovall, who scooped third baseman Bill Bradley's throw out of the dirt.

Despite the heroics of the two clubs, neither was able to overtake Detroit. The Tigers, however, were forced to win their final game of the season to earn the pennant.

# *The Double No-Hitter* 9

CINCINNATI (NL) at CHICAGO (NL)
Wednesday, May 2, 1917, Weeghman Park
Reds 1, Cubs 0

More than 200 no-hitters have been pitched in major league baseball, but only once have two no-hitters been tossed in the same game. On a frigid, early spring day at Weeghman Park (now known as Wrigley Field) two of the National League's best, Cincinnati's Fred Toney and Chicago's Jim "Hippo" Vaughn, matched up for one of the most celebrated games in baseball history. For the only time in the century neither pitcher allowed a hit from innings one through nine.

Each hurler walked just two batters, but none of the baserunners got as far as second. Vaughn, a 6'4" left-hander, overpowered the Cincinnati nine, striking out 10 and allowing only one ball to leave the infield. In addition to his two free passes, another batter reached first by way of an error. But thanks to

| Cincinnati | AB | R | H | I |
|---|---|---|---|---|
| Groh H, 3b | 1 | 0 | 0 | 0 |
| Getz G, 3b | 1 | 0 | 0 | 0 |
| Kopf L, ss | 4 | 1 | 1 | 0 |
| Neale G, cf | 4 | 0 | 0 | 0 |
| Chase H, 1b | 4 | 0 | 0 | 0 |
| Thorpe J, rf | 4 | 0 | 1 | 1 |
| Shean D, 2b | 3 | 0 | 0 | 0 |
| Cueto M, lf | 3 | 0 | 0 | 0 |
| Huhn E, c | 3 | 0 | 0 | 0 |
| Toney F, p | 3 | 0 | 0 | 0 |
| | 30 | 1 | 2 | 1 |

| Chicago | AB | R | H | I |
|---|---|---|---|---|
| Zeider R, ss | 4 | 0 | 0 | 0 |
| Wolter H, rf | 4 | 0 | 0 | 0 |
| Doyle L, 2b | 4 | 0 | 0 | 0 |
| Merkle F, 1b | 4 | 0 | 0 | 0 |
| Williams C, cf | 2 | 0 | 0 | 0 |
| Mann L, lf | 3 | 0 | 0 | 0 |
| Wilson A, c | 3 | 0 | 0 | 0 |
| Deal C, 3b | 3 | 0 | 0 | 0 |
| Vaughn H, p | 3 | 0 | 0 | 0 |
| | 30 | 0 | 0 | 0 |

| Cincinnati | IP | H | R | ER | BB | SO |
|---|---|---|---|---|---|---|
| Toney (W) | 10.0 | 0 | 0 | 0 | 2 | 3 |

| Chicago | IP | H | R | ER | BB | SO |
|---|---|---|---|---|---|---|
| Vaughn (L) | 10.0 | 2 | 1 | 0 | 2 | 10 |

| Cincinnati | 000 | 000 | 000 | 1 — 1 |
|---|---|---|---|---|
| Chicago | 000 | 000 | 000 | 0 — 0 |

OB: Cincinnati 1, Chicago 2; ER: Zeider, Williams; DP: Chicago 2; SB: Chase; CS: Neale; TI: 1:45; AT: 2,500; UM: Orth, Rigler

one caught-stealing and two double plays, no Reds were left on base through nine innings.

With one out in the visitor's tenth Larry Kopf, who had hit into two double plays and hadn't gotten a ball out of the infield, lined a sharp single to right off of Vaughn. *The Chicago Tribune* reported: "Fred Merkle made a desperate lunge to his right with one hand stretched out and perhaps came within a foot of the ball, but it was out of reach and the terrible suspense was broken." Greasy Neale flied out to center for the second out. Hal Chase, another batter who hadn't gotten the ball out of the infield, then smashed a low liner straight at Cy Williams in center for what some say should have been the third out. It was not an easy play, however, and Cy couldn't hold onto the ball. The official scorer gave him an error, but Cubs manager Fred Mitchell claimed the ball hit the ground a few feet in front of Williams. Chase stopped at first while Kopf dashed to third.

Next up was former Olympian Jim Thorpe. Chase stole second before Thorpe beat a ball into the muddy turf down the third base line. Newspaper accounts vary on the details of what happened next, but apparently Vaughn chased the ball while his battery mate, Art Wilson, waited at the plate. Some accounts claimed that Wilson also went after the ball. Vaughn got to the ball, realized he had no chance to throw out the fleet-footed Thorpe, and tried to toss it to Wilson to cut down Kopf trying to score. But Wilson was either returning to home plate or expecting Vaughn to throw to first. Whatever the circumstances, the throw bounced off Wilson, enabling Kopf to score the first run of the game. Chase too, tried to score, but Wilson quickly retrieved the ball and tagged him out. Thorpe, given credit for an infield single, was the only Red left on base the entire game.

The home team still had a chance to win this incredible contest. Larry Doyle led off the bottom of the tenth, and Toney struck him out. Merkle then thrilled the fans by sending a deep drive to left that forced Manuel Cueto against the wall to make the catch. Williams also brought the crowd to its feet when he smashed a long drive to right that was foul by only a foot. But Toney regained his composure and fanned Cy to end the game.

The fabled contest drew much praise but none more significant than that from Reds' manager Christy Mathewson. For many years the premier pitcher of the National League, Mathewson called this game the finest exhibition of pitching he ever witnessed.

# *Coombs and Harris Battle for 24 Innings* 10

PHILADELPHIA (AL) at BOSTON (AL)
Saturday, September 1, 1906, Huntington Avenue Grounds
Athletics 4, Red Sox 1

Under ideal weather conditions and in front of an overflow crowd, the Boston Red Sox entertained the Philadelphia Athletics in the longest game played to that date. Lasting 24 innings, the game was laced with numerous scoring opportunities squelched by dazzling pitching and spectacular fielding. To make it even more remarkable, both starters went the distance.

Fans continued to pour into the park even after all the seats were filled. As was custom of the era, excess patrons were permitted to stand in the periphery of the outfield, separated from the action by only a rope. Special ground rules were invoked in such cases, and this day was no exception. Any ball being lost among the standing spectators was predetermined to be a triple. Six such hits were scattered throughout the game, and one eventually became instrumental in its outcome.

Two young right-handed pitchers faced one another. Philadelphia's Jack Coombs, with a 5–7 record, was only a few months removed from Colby College in Maine. Boston's Joe Harris lost his first 14 games of the campaign and now possessed a 2–17 log. For this one day, however, both pitched like they were invincible. Coombs fanned 18 batters, a mark that was not exceeded in a single game for 56 years. Colby Jack faced 89 batters and Harris 87, establishing American League records that withstood the test of the century. In effect each hurler pitched through the opposing lineup nearly ten times.

The Athletics opened the scoring in the third inning. With one out, Coombs

| Philadelphia | AB | R | H | I |
|---|---|---|---|---|
| Hartzel T, lf | 10 | 1 | 2 | 0 |
| Lord B, cf | 9 | 0 | 1 | 0 |
| Davis H, 1b | 4 | 0 | 0 | 0 |
| Schreckengost ph,1b | 6 | 1 | 2 | 1 |
| Seybold S, rf | 10 | 1 | 1 | 1 |
| Murphy D, 2b | 9 | 0 | 2 | 1 |
| Cross M, ss | 9 | 0 | 1 | 0 |
| Knight J, 3b | 7 | 0 | 5 | 0 |
| Powers M, c | 9 | 0 | 1 | 0 |
| Coombs J, p | 9 | 1 | 1 | 0 |
| | 82 | 4 | 16 | 3 |

| Boston | AB | R | H | I |
|---|---|---|---|---|
| Hayden J, rf | 9 | 0 | 2 | 0 |
| Parent F, ss | 10 | 1 | 4 | 0 |
| Stahl C, cf | 7 | 0 | 2 | 1 |
| Ferris H, 2b | 9 | 0 | 1 | 0 |
| Hoey J, lf | 10 | 0 | 2 | 0 |
| Grimshaw M, 1b | 8 | 0 | 2 | 0 |
| Morgan R, 3b | 7 | 0 | 0 | 0 |
| Carrigan B, c | 5 | 0 | 1 | 0 |
| Freeman B, ph | 1 | 0 | 0 | 0 |
| Criger L, c | 4 | 0 | 0 | 0 |
| Harris J, p | 9 | 0 | 1 | 0 |
| | 79 | 1 | 15 | 1 |

| Philadelphia | IP | H | R | ER | BB | SO |
|---|---|---|---|---|---|---|
| Coombs (W) | 24.0 | 15 | 1 | 1 | 6 | 18 |

| Boston | IP | H | R | ER | BB | SO |
|---|---|---|---|---|---|---|
| Harris (L) | 24.0 | 16 | 4 | 3 | 2 | 14 |

```
Philadelphia   001  000  000  000  000  000  000  003 — 4
Boston         000  001  000  000  000  000  000  000 — 1
```

OB: Philadelphia 11, Boston 16; ER: Murphy, Cross, Carrigan; DP: Philadelphia 1, Boston 1; 2B: Ferris, Parent; 3B: Parent, Schreckengost, Murphy, Knight 2, Seybold; SB: Hartzel, Lord, Cross, Knight, Combs 2, Stahl; CS: Murphy, Knight 2, Hayden, Hoey, Grimshaw, Morgan 2; SH: Lord, Knight, Ferris, Morgan 2; HP: by Coombs (Stahl), by Harris (Murphy); TI: 4:47; AT: 18,084; UM: Hurst

singled and stole second. He moved to third on an infield out and scored when Harris was late covering on a ground ball to first.

Boston tied it in the sixth as Freddy Parent tripled into the crowd standing in right field and came home on Chick Stahl's single.

For the next 17 innings no other runner crossed the plate despite ample opportunities.

• In the eighth each team got a runner to second with two outs, but Bris Lord grounded out for Philadelphia, and Parent struck out for Boston.

• Philadelphia's Monte Cross opened the 10th by drawing a base on balls and was sacrificed to second by Jack Knight. But Joe Harris fanned Mike Powers and got Coombs on a pop-up to first.

• With two outs in the 11th the Athletics' Ossie Schreckengost pinch-hit for Harry Davis and tripled into the crowd, but Harris retired Socks Seybold on a bouncer back to the box.

• Philadelphia repeated their two-out threat in the 12th when Jack Knight also tripled. Harris again was equal to the task, retiring Powers on a fly ball to right.

• Boston, too, threatened in the 12th. Stahl singled and was sacrificed by Hobe Ferris. After Coombs struck out Jack Hoey, manager Connie Mack ordered Moose Grimshaw walked. The strategy paid off when Coombs then fanned Red Morgan.

• Opportunity knocked again for the Red Sox in the 14th as Parent led off with a double. But Coombs went to work by fanning Stahl and Ferris, and then induced Hoey to ground out.

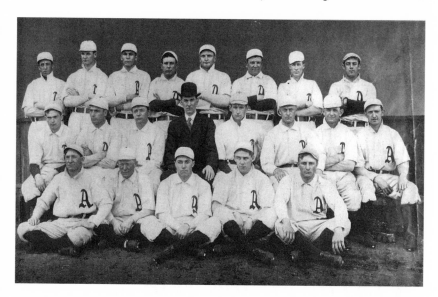

Coombs was still in college when the 1906 team photo was snapped (National Baseball Hall of Fame Library, Cooperstown, New York).

• Both clubs put runners in scoring position in the 15th. For Philadelphia, with one out, Knight tripled in his second consecutive plate appearance. But Powers flied out to shallow center, and Coombs grounded out. Grimshaw led off for Boston in the bottom half of the inning and was safe on Monte Cross' throwing error. After Morgan sacrificed, manager Mack ordered pinch-hitter Buck Freeman intentionally walked. Freeman became incensed at the strategy, and after three straight wide ones, jumped across the plate to swing at the fourth offering. For his impetuousness, Buck was declared out, quashing hopes of a rally and drawing the ire of the Boston press. Coombs then took control by striking out Harris. That marked the third inning in which the youngster had slammed the door on a Boston threat with a strikeout.

• Coombs again shined in the 18th. With one out Jack Hayden walked, and Parent singled, sending Hayden to third. Connie Mack then displayed extraordinary confidence in his rookie hurler by ordering Stahl walked, loading the bases. With the infield drawn in to double-play depth, Coombs again responded by fanning both Ferris and Hoey.

• The 19th inning again tested Coombs. Grimshaw led off and was safe on an error. Morgan sacrificed, but Lou Criger flied out to center and Harris struck out. For the fifth time Coombs had extinguished the threat with a strikeout.

• In the 20th, after two were out, Knight singled for Philadelphia and stole second. Powers, however, fanned.

After the 20th inning, neither team had a batter reach second base until the fateful 24th. In that frame Coombs struck out, and Topsy Hartzel singled and stole second. Lord also struck out, and with two strikes on Schreckengost, the inning once more appeared fruitless for Philadelphia. But the famine was broken when he singled home Hartzel, and both Socks Seybold and Danny Murphy followed with triples. In the bottom of the frame, with darkness quickly closing in, Coombs sealed the Philadelphia victory.

The marathon provided several heroes other than Coombs and Harris. The Boston infield handled 56 chances without an error and made several spectacular plays. Philadelphia backstop Mike Powers was a tower of strength behind the plate, establishing two records. To century's end, no backstop caught more innings in a game without an error or accepted more chances (25) in a major league game. He also threw out five runners attempting to steal, including two in the seventh inning.

# 11 *The Pirates Win a Muddy Championship*

WASHINGTON (AL) at PITTSBURGH (NL)
Thursday, October 15, 1925, Forbes Field
Pirates 9, Senators 7

It was one of those games that under normal circumstances may not have been played, but this was the deciding game of the World Series. Already the finale had been delayed one day because of rain. So the cold temperatures, wet grounds, and a slow, misty drizzle couldn't dissuade nearly 43,000 exuberant fans from packing Pittsburgh's Forbes Field. Sixteen years had passed since the Pirates had entered baseball's last dance, and nothing could dissuade their supporters. By the time it was all told, they saw an unfolding parade of heroes slipping and sloshing through mud and sawdust to wear the crown once again.

Vic Aldridge, winner of Games Two and Five, toed the rubber for the Pirates, while the venerable Walter Johnson took the hill for Washington. For the 37-year-old right-hander, winner of Games One and Four, this would be his last World Series appearance.

The outcome looked promising for Washington in the opening frame as Pittsburgh, it seemed, tried to give away the game. Aldridge was both hittable and wild, and his teammates put on a display unbefitting championship play. By the time the opening half-inning ended, the Senators scored four runs on

| Washington | AB | R | H | I |
|---|---|---|---|---|
| Rice S, cf | 5 | 2 | 2 | 0 |
| Harris B, 2b | 5 | 0 | 0 | 0 |
| Goslin G, lf | 4 | 2 | 1 | 0 |
| Harris J, rf | 3 | 1 | 1 | 2 |
| Judge J, 1b | 3 | 1 | 1 | 1 |
| Bluege O, 3b | 4 | 0 | 1 | 1 |
| Peckinpaugh R, ss | 3 | 1 | 1 | 1 |
| Ruel M, c | 4 | 0 | 0 | 0 |
| Johnson W, p | 4 | 0 | 0 | 0 |
|  | 35 | 7 | 7 | 5 |

| Pittsburgh | AB | R | H | I |
|---|---|---|---|---|
| Moore E, 2b | 4 | 3 | 1 | 1 |
| Carey M, cf | 5 | 3 | 4 | 2 |
| Cuyler K, rf | 4 | 0 | 2 | 3 |
| Barnhart C, lf | 5 | 0 | 1 | 1 |
| Oldham R, p | 0 | 0 | 0 | 0 |
| Traynor P, 3b | 4 | 0 | 1 | 1 |
| Wright G, ss | 4 | 0 | 1 | 0 |
| McInnis S, 1b | 4 | 0 | 2 | 0 |
| Smith E, c | 4 | 0 | 1 | 0 |
| Yde E, pr | 0 | 1 | 0 | 0 |
| Gooch J, c | 0 | 0 | 0 | 0 |
| Aldridge V, p | 0 | 0 | 0 | 0 |
| Morrison J, p | 1 | 1 | 1 | 0 |
| Grantham G, ph | 1 | 0 | 0 | 0 |
| Kremer R, p | 1 | 0 | 0 | 0 |
| Bigbee C, ph-lf | 1 | 1 | 1 | 1 |
|  | 38 | 9 | 15 | 9 |

| Washington | IP | H | R | ER | BB | SO |
|---|---|---|---|---|---|---|
| Johnson (L) | 8.0 | 15 | 9 | 5 | 1 | 3 |

| Pittsburgh | IP | H | R | ER | BB | SO |
|---|---|---|---|---|---|---|
| Aldridge | 0.1 | 2 | 4 | 4 | 3 | 0 |
| Morrison | 3.2 | 4 | 2 | 2 | 0 | 2 |
| Kremer (W) | 4.0 | 1 | 1 | 1 | 0 | 1 |
| Oldham (S) | 1.0 | 0 | 0 | 0 | 0 | 2 |
|  | 9.0 | 7 | 7 | 7 | 3 | 5 |

```
Washington    400   200   010 — 7
Pittsburgh    003   010   23x — 9
```

OB: Washington 5, Pittsburgh 7; ER: Moore, Cuyler, Peckinpaugh 2; CI: Smith; DP: Washington 1; 2B: Carey 3, Moore, Harris, Cuyler 2, Smith, Bigbee; 3B: Traynor; HR: Peckinpaugh; SB: Carey; SH: Cuyler; WP: Aldridge 2; TI: 2:31; AT: 42,856; UM: HP McCormick, 1B Moriarty, 2B Rigler, 3B Owens.

just two hits and left the bases loaded. Added ingredients included three walks, two wild pitches, a catcher's interference, and an error.

Things settled down until the home half of the third when, amid the drizzle and hurrying darkness, the Pirates reached Johnson. Sopping wet and spattered with mud, the Buccaneers stroked three singles and a double to close to within one run at 4–3.

Despite the howling crowd, Washington wasted no time in retaliation. Two singles and a double added another pair of runs to the Senators' lead in the top of the fourth.

Pittsburgh kept it close as they pushed across one run in the bottom of the fifth. With the field shrouded in mist, the first two batters, Max Carey and Kiki Cuyler, each doubled making it 6–4. But Johnson closed the door and retired the next three batters with no further damage.

In the seventh the Pirates drew even for the first time by scoring two unearned runs. It all started when Washington shortstop Roger Peckinpaugh dropped Eddie Moore's pop-up for his seventh error of the Series. Then Carey used his fourth hit of the game to double home Moore and make it 6–5. Pie Traynor next lined a ball into the fog of right–center field, and in their pursuit the Washington outfielders disappeared into the darkness. The expectant crowd was on its feet cheering as Carey scored and Traynor splashed through the mud, rounding third. From right fielder Joe Harris to second baseman Bucky Harris and on to catcher Muddy Ruel, the wet ball made its way home to await Traynor. Pittsburgh tied it at six, but their lead run easily was tagged out.

Atoning for his misdeeds, Peckinpaugh smashed a solo homer over the left field screen in the eighth. Sensing a championship within their grasp, Roger was mobbed and congratulated by his teammates upon returning to the dugout.

Johnson solidified the Senators' expectations by retiring the first two Pirates in the bottom of the eighth. The old warhorse was only four outs away from repeating his heroics of a year earlier, when he won Game Seven for a Washington championship. But Pittsburgh would have none of it. A pair of doubles deadlocked the score once again as the enthusiasm of the soaked crowd could not be dampened. Johnson then walked Moore but induced Carey to send a grounder to short. This should have ended the inning with the game tied, but Peckinpaugh made a high throw toward second allowing all the runners safe harbor. When Cuyler doubled home another pair, pandemonium erupted. The Pirates again had come back, only this time it was to take a 9–7 lead.

Reliever Red Oldham, a left-hander seeing his first action of the Series, was brought in to nail down the title for Pittsburgh. Oldham faced just three batters, fanning the first and last. With the last strike, and ignoring the mud, the crowd swarmed onto the field in mass celebration that lasted into the Allegheny night.

# 12 *Larsen Was Perfect*

BROOKLYN (NL) at NEW YORK (AL)
Monday, October 8, 1956, Yankee Stadium
Yankees 2, Dodgers 0

The Fall Classic of 1956 marked the sixth time in 10 years that the New York Yankees and Brooklyn Dodgers met in the World Series. Brooklyn, fresh on the heels of their first World Championship, opened the Series at home and won both games. But New York bounced back with wins in Games Three and Four, setting the stage for the pivotal fifth game scheduled in Yankee Stadium.

Brooklyn sent their 39-year-old veteran Sal Maglie to the mound. In the twilight of his career, Maglie found new life when traded to the Dodgers earlier in

| Brooklyn | AB | R | H | I |
|---|---|---|---|---|
| Gilliam J, 2b | 3 | 0 | 0 | 0 |
| Reese P, ss | 3 | 0 | 0 | 0 |
| Snider D, cf | 3 | 0 | 0 | 0 |
| Robinson J, 3b | 3 | 0 | 0 | 0 |
| Hodges G, 1b | 3 | 0 | 0 | 0 |
| Amoros S, lf | 3 | 0 | 0 | 0 |
| Furillo C, rf | 3 | 0 | 0 | 0 |
| Campanella R, c | 3 | 0 | 0 | 0 |
| Maglie S, p | 2 | 0 | 0 | 0 |
| Mitchell D, ph | 1 | 0 | 0 | 0 |
| | 27 | 0 | 0 | 0 |

| New York | AB | R | H | I |
|---|---|---|---|---|
| Bauer H, rf | 4 | 0 | 1 | 1 |
| Collins J, 1b | 4 | 0 | 1 | 0 |
| Mantle M, cf | 3 | 1 | 1 | 1 |
| Berra Y, c | 3 | 0 | 0 | 0 |
| Slaughter E, lf | 2 | 0 | 0 | 0 |
| Martin B, 2b | 3 | 0 | 1 | 0 |
| McDougald G, ss | 2 | 0 | 0 | 0 |
| Carey A, 3b | 3 | 1 | 1 | 0 |
| Larsen D, p | 2 | 0 | 0 | 0 |
| | 26 | 2 | 5 | 2 |

| Brooklyn | IP | H | R | ER | BB | SO |
|---|---|---|---|---|---|---|
| Maglie (L) | 8.0 | 5 | 2 | 2 | 2 | 5 |

| New York | IP | H | R | ER | BB | SO |
|---|---|---|---|---|---|---|
| Larsen (W) | 9.0 | 0 | 0 | 0 | 0 | 7 |

```
Brooklyn    000  000  000 — 0
New York    000  101  00x — 2
```

OB: Brooklyn 0, New York 3; DP: Brooklyn 2; HR: Mantle; SH: Larsen; TI: 2:06; AT: 64,519; UM: HP Pinelli, 1B Soar, 2B Boggess, 3B Napp, LF Gorman, RF Runge

the season. He finished with a 13–5 regular season mark, including a no-hitter, and had beaten Whitey Ford in the Series opener. Slated to start for New York was 27-year-old Don Larsen. During the regular campaign Larsen started 20 games, completed six, and relieved in another 18. With his unorthodox no-wind-up delivery he started Game Two of the Series but was wild and banished to the showers during the second inning. Now, three days later, the story would be much different.

Larsen's first inning of work was inauspicious. Fifteen pitches included a full count to Pee Wee Reese and a line drive to right by Duke Snider. In retrospect, Reese's appearance marked the only three-ball count of the day for Larsen.

Leading off the second, Brooklyn's Jackie Robinson sent a vicious, head-high line drive to the left of third baseman Andy Carey. The ball glanced off his glove but fortuitously bounded to Gil McDougald at shortstop. McDougald alertly fielded it and threw to first, nipping Robinson by a half step.

Larsen needed only seven pitches to retire the Dodgers in the third. In the top of the fourth, Duke Snider smashed a drive into the lower right field seats as umpire Ed Runge gave it a long hard look before calling it foul. During the action, radio announcer Mel Allen commented that, given the sellout crowd, the dark canvas backdrop normally in center field, which contrasted with the white ball and thereby aided hitters, had been removed.

The home half of the fourth provided the game's first baserunner and all the runs Larsen would need when Mickey Mantle stroked one just inside the foul pole, not far from where Snider's clout landed a half inning earlier. Yogi Berra then lined a ball into center where Snider made a diving shoestring catch.

In the top of the fifth with one out, Gil Hodges hit a deep fly to left-center on which Mantle made a spectacular one-handed running catch. The next batter, Sandy Amoros, sent another long fly ball into the seats in right field. The announcers paused while waiting for Runge to call it foul. Later in the clubhouse, right fielder Hank Bauer claimed the ball was foul by no more than three inches. Runge said it was more like six inches foul.

The Yankees added a second run in the sixth when Carey led off with a single, was sacrificed to second by Larsen, and scored on Hank Bauer's single.

In the top of the seventh the crowd began to buzz with anticipation as Larsen retired Brooklyn on seven pitches. His assortment of fastballs, sliders, and slow curves had the Dodgers stymied. The eighth saw the visitors hit the ball hard but to no avail, while Maglie in the bottom of the inning kept his club alive by striking out the side.

The Dodgers' last chance opened with Carl Furillo fouling off four balls before flying out to right. Roy Campanella then grounded out to second, setting the stage for what announcer Vin Scully called the "most dramatic plate appearance in baseball history."

Sal Maglie was the scheduled batter, but pinch-hitter Dale Mitchell strode to the plate. The first pitch was a ball outside. Two strikes followed, one called and one swinging. Mitchell next sent a foul into the left field stands. Then, on Larsen's 97th pitch, home plate umpire Babe Pinelli called strike three! Pandemonium erupted. Berra ran to meet Larsen and jumped into his arms as teammates encircled the pair. Yogi called it the best-pitched game he ever caught, despite having worked two no-hitters by Allie Reynolds. Pinelli, who called balls and strikes for 31 years, described Larsen's effort as the "greatest pinpoint control I've ever seen." A most unlikely character had tossed not only the first no-hitter in World Series history but also baseball's first perfect game in 34 years.

# 13 *Marlins Ride Their Payroll to the Title*

CLEVELAND (AL) at FLORIDA (NL)
Sunday, October 26, 1997, Pro Player Stadium
Marlins 3, Indians 2

For baseball traditionalists, 1997 was a bitter pill to swallow. Free agency had previously afforded clubs willing to pay high ransom an opportunity for post-season action. Now the baseball establishment inaugurated inter-league play, and the dreaded wild-card concept created havoc. Culminating affairs, a second place club in the National League and a team with the fourth best record in the American League each reached the World Series.

| Cleveland | AB | R | H | I |
|---|---|---|---|---|
| Vizquel O, ss | 5 | 0 | 1 | 0 |
| Fernandez T, 2b | 5 | 0 | 2 | 2 |
| Ramirez M, rf | 3 | 0 | 0 | 0 |
| Justice D, lf | 5 | 0 | 0 | 0 |
| Williams M, 3b | 2 | 0 | 0 | 0 |
| Alomar Jr. S, c | 5 | 0 | 1 | 0 |
| Thome J, 1b | 4 | 1 | 1 | 0 |
| Grissom M, cf | 4 | 1 | 1 | 0 |
| Wright J, p | 2 | 0 | 0 | 0 |
| Assenmacher P, p | 0 | 0 | 0 | 0 |
| Jackson M, p | 0 | 0 | 0 | 0 |
| Anderson B, p | 0 | 0 | 0 | 0 |
| Giles B, ph | 1 | 0 | 0 | 0 |
| Mesa J, p | 0 | 0 | 0 | 0 |
| Nagy C, p | 0 | 0 | 0 | 0 |
| | 36 | 2 | 6 | 2 |

| Florida | AB | R | H | I |
|---|---|---|---|---|
| White D, cf | 6 | 0 | 0 | 0 |
| Renteria E, ss | 5 | 0 | 3 | 1 |
| Sheffield G, rf | 4 | 0 | 1 | 0 |
| Daulton D, 1b | 3 | 0 | 0 | 0 |
| Conine J, ph-1b | 1 | 0 | 0 | 0 |
| Nen R, p | 0 | 0 | 0 | 0 |
| Cangelosi J, ph | 1 | 0 | 0 | 0 |
| Powell J, p | 0 | 0 | 0 | 0 |
| Alou M, lf | 5 | 1 | 1 | 0 |
| Bonilla B, 3b | 5 | 1 | 2 | 1 |
| Johnson C, c | 4 | 0 | 1 | 0 |
| Zaun G, pr-c | 1 | 0 | 0 | 0 |
| Counsell C, 2b | 3 | 1 | 0 | 1 |
| Leiter A, p | 0 | 0 | 0 | 0 |
| Cook D, p | 0 | 0 | 0 | 0 |
| Floyd C, ph | 0 | 0 | 0 | 0 |
| Abbott K, ph | 1 | 0 | 0 | 0 |
| Alfonseca A, p | 0 | 0 | 0 | 0 |
| Heredia F, p | 0 | 0 | 0 | 0 |
| Eisenreich J, 1b | 1 | 0 | 0 | 0 |
| | 40 | 3 | 8 | 3 |

| Cleveland | IP | H | R | ER | BB | SO |
|---|---|---|---|---|---|---|
| Wright | 6.1 | 2 | 1 | 1 | 5 | 7 |
| Assenmacher | 0.2 | 0 | 0 | 0 | 0 | 1 |
| Jackson | 0.2 | 0 | 0 | 0 | 0 | 1 |
| Anderson | 0.1 | 0 | 0 | 0 | 0 | 0 |
| Mesa | 1.2 | 4 | 1 | 1 | 0 | 2 |
| Nagy (L) | 1.0 | 2 | 1 | 0 | 1 | 0 |
| | 10.2 | 8 | 3 | 2 | 6 | 11 |

| Florida | IP | H | R | ER | BB | SO |
|---|---|---|---|---|---|---|
| Leiter | 6.0 | 4 | 2 | 2 | 4 | 7 |
| Cook | 1.0 | 0 | 0 | 0 | 0 | 2 |
| Alfonseca | 1.1 | 0 | 0 | 0 | 1 | 1 |
| Heredia | 0.0 | 1 | 0 | 0 | 0 | 0 |
| Nen | 1.2 | 1 | 0 | 0 | 0 | 3 |
| Powell (W) | 1.0 | 0 | 0 | 0 | 1 | 0 |
| | 11.0 | 6 | 2 | 2 | 6 | 13 |

```
Cleveland  002  000  000  00 — 2
Florida    000  000  101  01 — 3
```

OB: Cleveland 8, Florida 12; ER: Ramirez, Fernandez; DP: Cleveland, Florida; 2B: Renteria; HR: Bonilla; SB: Vizquel 2; SH: Wright; SF: Counsell; TI: 4:10; AT: 67,204; UM: HP Montague, 1B Ford, 2B West, 3B Kosc, LF Marsh, RF Kaiser.

The biggest free-agent spender during the prior winter was the Florida Marlins, and their investment bore fruit. In just their fifth year in the league, the Marlins rode the backs of their new players to produce the franchise's first winning season and to battle their way into the World Series. Their opponent, the Cleveland Indians, by contrast, was an original member of the American League. But the Tribe hadn't tasted a World Championship for nearly a half-century, and the club showed up with a retooled roster, as well.

The two teams took turns winning over the first six games. When the curtain rose for the deciding game in front of an exuberant Florida crowd, everyone was on their feet for the opening pitch from left-hander Al Leiter. Toeing the rubber for the visitors was rookie right-hander Jaret Wright, thrown into a pressure cooker at only 21 years of age. On an 80-degree night both starters pitched well for six innings before a parade of ten relievers marched to the mound.

The Indians opened the scoring in the top of the third when a clutch two-out single by Tony Fernandez drove home a pair. It made a temporary hero out of the four-time Gold Glove winner but would be forgotten by game's end.

With two outs in the fifth inning Cleveland pushed another runner to third base, but Leiter thrilled the crowd by fanning David Justice to end the frame.

The Marlins squandered a golden opportunity in the sixth when Manny Ramirez misplayed a line drive by Darren Daulton into a three-base error. Wright extinguished the threat by getting Moises Alou to fly out.

Florida finally got on the board in the seventh. Bobby Bonilla, in the throes of a 4 for 26 Series, connected with Wright's first offering, driving it over the wall in right-center. It was only the Marlins second hit but made it 2–1.

A walk, force-out, and single put Indians at the corners in the ninth, and Marlins closer Rob Nen was summoned to the mound. Nen was having a horrendous World Series. In only three innings he had allowed seven hits and four runs but now got Marquis Grissom to ground to shortstop Edgar Renteria. The 21 year old threw home and caught Sandy Alomar trying to score. It was a crucial play that kept the Marlins within one run. Nen then slammed the door closed as pinch-hitter Brian Giles flied out.

The bottom of the ninth was the last chance for Florida, and Cleveland sent in their ace reliever, Jose Mesa, to nail down the championship. The stadium rocked when Moises Alou led off with a single. Mesa struck out Bonilla, but Charles Johnson singled Alou to third. Craig Counsell then lined a ball to right field deep enough for Alou to tag and score, tying the game and sending it into extra innings. At this point announcer Vin Scully lauded the play of both clubs and expressed his hope that the championship would not be determined by a gaffe.

Florida had an opportunity to win it in the bottom of the tenth when, with one out, Renteria and Gary Sheffield singled. But Mesa struck out pinch-hitter John Cangelosi, and Charles Nagy came on to retire Alou.

Bonilla led off the bottom of the eleventh with a single, but Greg Zaun popped out. Then an unfortunate play tarnished a drama-filled classic when Counsell hit a spinning grounder between first and second. Fernandez got to the ball in plenty of time hoping to start a double play. It's unclear whether he took his eye off the ball or was distracted by Bonilla passing by, but the ball scooted beneath his glove for an error. Bonilla went to third with the championship run, and Jim Eisenreich was intentionally walked to fill the bases.

Fernandez temporarily atoned for his miscue by fielding Devon White's grounder and throwing home to nip Bonilla for out number two. But the high wire act and the 1997 season ended when the next batter, Renteria, singled over second, and Counsell skipped across the plate. Scully's fear materialized, and the club that led the majors in one-run games added the most important one to their trophy case.

# *Phillies Comeback Wins NLCS in Extra Innings* 14

PHILADELPHIA (NL) at HOUSTON (NL)
Sunday, October 12, 1980, The Astrodome
Phillies 8, Astros 7

Many baseball observers consider the 1980 five-game National League Championship Series the most exciting of the century. In only one of the five encounters was the eventual winner leading after five innings, and in that struggle they later fell behind and were forced to fashion a late-inning comeback. In addition, four victories were decided in extra innings, including the final game. Throughout the Series, fans in both Houston and Philadelphia were treated to heart-pounding drama, lead changes, scintillating plays, and unexpected outcomes. And just when it seemed the combatants had stretched baseball drama to the absolute limit in Game Four, they topped themselves in the finale.

The deciding game was not a pitcher's duel, although it looked that way for six innings. Several great defensive plays limited the scoring, but there were ample baserunners throughout. From the very first pitch, the boisterous Astrodome crowd cheered each Nolan Ryan delivery. Owner of four no-hitters, the future Hall of Fame right-hander was trying to bring Houston its first National League Championship. Ryan was opposed by 22-year-old Marty Bystrom, an undefeated rookie with a 5–0 mark during the month of September.

In the first inning, the Astros combined a single, a steal, and a two-out double by Jose Cruz to open the scoring. They would have added another but for a dazzling defensive play by second baseman Manny Trillo.

The Phillies countered with their own two-out rally in the top of the second when Bob Boone sent a 99-mile-per-hour fastball back through the middle. That scored two of the visitors and gave Philadelphia a 2–1 lead.

In the home half, after a walk to Luis Pujols, Craig Reynolds doubled into the right-field corner. Pujols, running on an injured ankle, was waved home as Bake McBride stopped the ball before it reached the wall. Bake fired to the cutoff man, Manny Trillo, who made a near perfect relay to catcher Bob Boone. Boone made a backhanded, one-handed catch of the relay and applied a sweep tag on Pujols, barely nipping him. It was a scintillating play that saved a run and temporarily quieted the crowd. Reynolds was then stranded on third as Ryan grounded out.

In the third, with Terry Puhl on first, Joe Morgan brought the crowd to its feet as he drove a pitch to deep center field, where Garry Maddox finally caught up with it about 390 feet from home plate.

| Philadelphia | AB | R | H | I |
|---|---|---|---|---|
| Rose P, 1b | 3 | 0 | 1 | 1 |
| McBride B, rf | 3 | 0 | 0 | 0 |
| Moreland K, ph | 1 | 0 | 0 | 1 |
| Aviles R, pr | 0 | 1 | 0 | 0 |
| McGraw T, p | 0 | 0 | 0 | 0 |
| Vukovich G, ph | 1 | 0 | 0 | 0 |
| Ruthven D, p | 0 | 0 | 0 | 0 |
| Schmidt M, 3b | 5 | 0 | 0 | 0 |
| Luzinski G, lf | 3 | 0 | 1 | 0 |
| Smith L, pr | 0 | 0 | 0 | 0 |
| Christenson L, p | 0 | 0 | 0 | 0 |
| Reed R, p | 0 | 0 | 0 | 0 |
| Unser D, ph-rf | 2 | 2 | 2 | 1 |
| Trillo M, 2b | 5 | 1 | 3 | 2 |
| Maddox G, cf | 4 | 1 | 1 | 1 |
| Bowa L, ss | 5 | 1 | 2 | 0 |
| Boone B, c | 3 | 1 | 2 | 2 |
| Bystrom M, p | 2 | 0 | 0 | 0 |
| Brusstar W, p | 0 | 0 | 0 | 0 |
| Gross G, lf | 2 | 1 | 1 | 0 |
| | 39 | 8 | 13 | 8 |

| Houston | AB | R | H | I |
|---|---|---|---|---|
| Puhl T, cf | 6 | 3 | 4 | 0 |
| Cabell E, 3b | 5 | 0 | 1 | 0 |
| Morgan J, 2b | 5 | 0 | 1 | 1 |
| Cruz J, lf | 3 | 1 | 2 | 2 |
| Walling D, rf | 5 | 2 | 1 | 1 |
| LaCorte F, p | 0 | 0 | 0 | 0 |
| Howe A, 1b | 4 | 0 | 2 | 1 |
| Bergman D, pr-1b | 1 | 0 | 0 | 0 |
| Pujols L, c | 1 | 0 | 0 | 0 |
| Ashby A, ph-c | 3 | 0 | 1 | 1 |
| Reynolds C, ss | 5 | 1 | 2 | 0 |
| Ryan N, p | 3 | 0 | 0 | 0 |
| Sambito J, p | 0 | 0 | 0 | 0 |
| Forsch K, p | 0 | 0 | 0 | 0 |
| Woods G, ph-rf | 1 | 0 | 0 | 0 |
| Heep D, ph | 1 | 0 | 0 | 0 |
| | 43 | 7 | 14 | 6 |

| Philadelphia | IP | H | R | ER | BB | SO |
|---|---|---|---|---|---|---|
| Bystrom | 5.1 | 7 | 2 | 1 | 2 | 1 |
| Brusstar | 0.2 | 0 | 0 | 0 | 0 | 0 |
| Christenson | 0.2 | 2 | 3 | 3 | 1 | 0 |
| Reed | 0.1 | 1 | 0 | 0 | 0 | 0 |
| McGraw | 1.0 | 4 | 2 | 2 | 0 | 2 |
| Ruthven (W) | 2.0 | 0 | 0 | 0 | 0 | 0 |
| | 10.0 | 14 | 7 | 6 | 3 | 3 |

| Houston | IP | H | R | ER | BB | SO |
|---|---|---|---|---|---|---|
| Ryan | 7.0 | 8 | 6 | 6 | 2 | 8 |
| Sambito | 0.1 | 0 | 0 | 0 | 0 | 0 |
| Forsch | 0.2 | 2 | 1 | 1 | 0 | 1 |
| LaCorte (L) | 2.0 | 3 | 1 | 1 | 1 | 1 |
| | 10.0 | 13 | 8 | 8 | 3 | 10 |

```
Philadelphia   020   000   050   1 — 8
Houston        100   001   320   0 — 7
```

OB: Philadelphia 5, Houston 10; ER: Trillo, Luzinski; DP: Houston 2; 2B: Cruz, Reynolds, Trillo, Unser, Maddox; 3B: Howe; SB: Puhl; CS: Rose; SH: Cabell, Boone; WP: Christenson; TI: 3:38; AT: 44,802; UM: HP Vargo, 1B Crawford, 2B Engel, 3B Tata, LF Froeming, RF Harvey

Bystrom was the beneficiary of another dramatic play in the fifth. With two outs and Enos Cabell on second, Cruz smashed a grounder toward right. Trillo's throw pulled Pete Rose off first base, and Cabell raced for home. But Rose alertly recovered and threw to Boone to cut down Cabell. It was the second potential Astros' run to die at the plate.

Houston drove Bystrom to the showers in the sixth as they tied the score. Greg Luzinski got his glove on Denny Walling's fly ball to left field but couldn't hold on to it. Art Howe's ground-out moved Walling to second before pinch-hitter Alan Ashby singled home the tying run, making it 2–2. The momentum clearly had swung in the Astros' direction.

Throughout the 1980 campaign, Houston preferred to score their runs without benefit of the home run, socking only 75. In the seventh, they assembled a typical rally. Two singles, a walk, sacrifice, wild pitch, and a triple scored three runs and sent the fans into a frenzy. Houston had overtaken Philadelphia and led 5–2, evoking a comment from CBS announcer Jerry Coleman that the Astros had practically sewn it up. Microphone mate Jack Buck echoed Coleman in proclaiming Houston's first pennant.

Meanwhile, Ryan had worked his way into a pitching groove, striking out six Phillies from the third through the seventh frames. Philadelphia did manage several hits and walks, but potential rallies were killed when Pete Rose was caught stealing and the Houston defense pulled off two twin-killings. During this stretch, Coleman and Buck reminded the listening audience how effective Ryan was when staked to a late-inning lead. Outside the announcer's booth, the fans could be heard boiling over with confidence.

But as they had done a day earlier, the Phillies astonished the announcers as well as the Astrodome crowd in the eighth. On just six pitches, Philadelphia loaded the bases on three singles. Rose then walked, forcing in a run. Pinch-hitter Keith Moreland grounded into a fielders' choice, but another run scored, making it 5–4. With the fans on their feet, screaming and waving their orange hats with every delivery, Mike Schmidt fanned for out number two. Pinch-hitter Del Unser continued the drama with a single to right, knocking in the tying run. Houston's three-run lead had evaporated, and Philadelphia had runners at first and second. Manny Trillo then doubled both runners home, pushing the Phils ahead, 7–5. But it was still far from over.

In the home eighth, Houston struck back. Reliever Tug McGraw, appearing in his fifth consecutive game and seventh in ten days, put runners at the corners with one out. Again the crowd was on its feet as Cabell struck out, but both Joe Morgan and Cruz singled to tie the game once more. At this point, a veteran Philadelphia columnist reported he could actually feel the Astrodome shaking.

The Phillies again threatened to take the lead in the ninth. But with runners at the corners and two down, pinch-hitter George Vukovich worked the count full before grounding out. Dick Ruthven, normally a starter, took the mound for Philadelphia and retired the Astros in order in the bottom of the ninth. The fans, now accustomed to nine-inning no-decisions, settled back for their fourth consecutive extra-inning game.

In the top of the tenth, Unser and Maddox each doubled to put another lead run on the board, but nothing was safe in this Series. Despite the crowd's deafening shouts of encouragement to the Astros batters, Ruthven continued his mastery and retired the side in order, sending the Phillies to their first World Series in 30 years.

# 15 Brooklyn Finally Wears the Crown

BROOKLYN (NL) at NEW YORK (AL)
Tuesday, October 4, 1955, Yankee Stadium
Dodgers 2, Yankees 0

October commonly had been a month of frustration for Brooklyn baseball fans. Seven times the Dodgers appeared in the World Series, and seven times they went home disappointed. For this year's opponent, the New York Yankees, the story was quite different. The American League pennant winners were seeking their 17th World Championship and their sixth in seven years. Five of the Yankees' recent triumphs had come at the expense of these Dodgers.

Brooklyn made a shambles of the National League race by winning 22 of their first 24 games and never looking back. They clinched by September 8, but when they lost the first two games of the World Series, it appeared another bleak autumn. No team to date had prevailed after losing the first two contests.

The Bums stormed back, however, winning the next three at home. But after New York won Game Six, it appeared that order had been restored to the baseball world.

Game Seven was held in the Bronx and pitted Brooklyn's 23-year-old Johnny Podres against the veteran Tommy Byrne. Each southpaw had already won one game, but it took more than good pitching to win this championship. Several terrific fielding plays and ample good fortune were instrumental in the outcome. Each club also battled without a star player: Jackie Robinson of the Dodgers and Mickey Mantle of the Yankees had each been lost to injury.

In the second inning Bill Skowron bounced a drive into the right-field seats for a ground-rule double. But there were already two outs, and Podres escaped without damage.

Lady Luck intervened on behalf of the Dodgers in the third frame. With two outs Rizzuto walked, and Billy Martin singled him to second. Gil McDougald next chopped a bouncer toward third that would have made for a difficult fielding play. Fortunately for Brooklyn, as Rizzuto slid into the base, the batted ball hit him for the third out.

With one out in the top of the fourth, Roy Campanella doubled and moved to third on an infield out. Gil Hodges then singled home the game's first run.

Yogi Berra opened the home half of the fourth with a looping fly to left-center that should have been caught. When both Junior Gilliam and Duke Snider misplayed it, the ball fell untouched and was recorded as a double. Podres then went to work and retired the next three hitters.

| Brooklyn | AB | R | H | I |
|---|---|---|---|---|
| Gilliam J, lf-2b | 4 | 0 | 1 | 0 |
| Reese P, ss | 4 | 1 | 1 | 0 |
| Snider D, cf | 3 | 0 | 0 | 0 |
| Campanella R, c | 3 | 1 | 1 | 0 |
| Furillo C, rf | 3 | 0 | 0 | 0 |
| Hodges G, 1b | 2 | 0 | 1 | 2 |
| Hoak D, 3b | 3 | 0 | 1 | 0 |
| Zimmer D, 2b | 2 | 0 | 0 | 0 |
| Shuba G, ph | 1 | 0 | 0 | 0 |
| Amoros S, lf | 0 | 0 | 0 | 0 |
| Podres J, p | 4 | 0 | 0 | 0 |
| | 29 | 2 | 5 | 2 |

| New York | AB | R | H | I |
|---|---|---|---|---|
| Rizzuto P, ss | 3 | 0 | 1 | 0 |
| Martin B, 2b | 3 | 0 | 1 | 0 |
| McDougald G, 3b | 4 | 0 | 3 | 0 |
| Berra Y, c | 4 | 0 | 1 | 0 |
| Bauer H, rf | 4 | 0 | 0 | 0 |
| Skowron B, 1b | 4 | 0 | 1 | 0 |
| Cerv B, cf | 4 | 0 | 0 | 0 |
| Howard E, lf | 4 | 0 | 1 | 0 |
| Byrne T, p | 2 | 0 | 0 | 0 |
| Grim B, p | 0 | 0 | 0 | 0 |
| Mantle M, ph | 1 | 0 | 0 | 0 |
| Turley B, p | 0 | 0 | 0 | 0 |
| | 33 | 0 | 8 | 0 |

| Brooklyn | IP | H | R | ER | BB | SO |
|---|---|---|---|---|---|---|
| Podres (W) | 9.0 | 8 | 0 | 0 | 2 | 4 |

| New York | IP | H | R | ER | BB | SO |
|---|---|---|---|---|---|---|
| Byrne (L) | 5.1 | 3 | 2 | 1 | 3 | 2 |
| Grim | 1.2 | 1 | 0 | 0 | 1 | 1 |
| Turley | 2.0 | 1 | 0 | 0 | 1 | 1 |
| | 9.0 | 5 | 2 | 1 | 5 | 4 |

| Brooklyn | 000 | 101 | 000 — 2 |
|---|---|---|---|
| New York | 000 | 000 | 000 — 0 |

OB: Brooklyn 8, New York 8; ER: Skowron; DP: Brooklyn 1; 2B: Skowron, Campanella, Berra; CS: Gilliam; SH: Snider, Campanella; SF: Hodges; WP: Grim; TI: 2:44; AT: 62,465; UM: HP Honochick, 1B Dascoli, 2B Summers, 3B Ballanfant, LF Flaherty, RF Donatelli

The Dodgers had several opportunities in the sixth to pile on more runs. Pee Wee Reese led off with a single, and Snider was safe when Skowron bungled his sacrifice bunt. Campanella then successfully bunted both runners into scoring position. Byrne intentionally walked Carl Furillo, loading the bases, and was relieved by Bob Grim. A sacrifice fly by Gil Hodges scored the Dodgers' second run. A wild pitch and another walk re-loaded the bases, but George Shuba, pinch-hitting for Don Zimmer, grounded out, ending the threat. Although Shuba failed in his pinch-hitting appearance, it set off a series of critical substitutions. Gilliam moved to second base, and Sandy Amoros came into the game to play left field. The timing was impeccable.

New York made a serious bid to score in the bottom of the sixth as Martin walked and McDougald bunted safely. Next came the game's pivotal play. Berra hit a drive to left that sailed toward the foul line. Amoros raced at top speed, extended his arm and caught the ball just a few feet from the stands. It was a marvelous catch, but he also turned and fired the ball back to the infield, where McDougald was doubled off first. Podres then got Hank Bauer to ground out, preserving Brooklyn's slim lead.

One last scoring opportunity arose for the Yankees in the eighth as two of the first three batters singled. But Podres engaged his finest pitching and retired Berra on a pop-up and Bauer on a strikeout.

In the ninth, Podres retired the Yankees in order, igniting revelry in Flatbush and ending the cries of "Wait till next year."

# 16 Slaughter's Race for the Roses

BOSTON (AL) at ST. LOUIS (NL)
Tuesday, October 15, 1946, Sportsmans Park
Cardinals 4, Red Sox 3

With World War II ended, returning veterans restocked major league rosters. The Boston Red Sox were particularly rejuvenated with the return of Ted Williams, Bobby Doerr, Johnny Pesky, Dom DiMaggio, Hal Wagner, and pitchers Tex Hughson, Joe Dobson, and Mickey Harris. Those nine helped lift the Sox from a seventh place finish in 1945 to the World Series a year later. They not only claimed the American League pennant but did so in decisive fashion. Outdistancing their nearest rival by 12 games, Boston coasted during the last weeks of the campaign. Manager Joe Cronin later felt the letdown was partly responsible for their poor showing in this Series.

The Cardinals, too, bathed in the sun of returning veterans. Their top four pitchers, Howie Pollet, Murray Dickson, Harry Brecheen, and Al Brazle, all wore military uniforms a year earlier. Also serving their country were starting outfielders Harry Walker, Enos Slaughter and Terry Moore. But probably the biggest smile appeared on the faces of Cardinal fans when one of the game's greatest hitters, Stan Musial, returned to the ballyard. Despite this near total facelift, however, St. Louis couldn't shake the Brooklyn Dodgers, and the two teams faced off in the major leagues' first playoff.

The Cardinals made short work of their rivals, dispatching them in two games.

In the drama-filled World Series, the heavily favored Red Sox won Games One, Three, and Five, while the Cardinals prevailed in the even numbered games. Game Seven was played in St. Louis under a brilliant autumn sun, with the thermometer hovering in the 70s.

Boston's 25-game winner, Dave "Boo" Ferriss, squared off against Murray Dickson, the owner of the National League's best winning percentage at .714 (15–6).

The Red Sox scored early. After the game's first two batters singled, DiMaggio brought home Wally Moses with a sacrifice fly. They nearly had more when Williams drove a ball to deep center field. With the outfield shifted far toward right, center fielder Moore made a long run and lunged for a spectacular catch.

Red Schoendienst started the Cardinal first with a single to left. When Williams bobbled the ball, Red streaked for second but was thrown out. Ted's throw saved a run, because two batters later, Musial doubled to left. Slaughter ended the inning by striking out.

| Boston | AB | R | H | I |
|---|---|---|---|---|
| Moses W, rf | 4 | 1 | 1 | 0 |
| Pesky J, ss | 4 | 0 | 1 | 0 |
| DiMaggio D, cf | 3 | 0 | 1 | 3 |
| Culberson L, pr-cf | 0 | 0 | 0 | 0 |
| Williams T, lf | 4 | 0 | 0 | 0 |
| York R, 1b | 4 | 0 | 1 | 0 |
| Campbell P, pr | 0 | 0 | 0 | 0 |
| Doerr B, 2b | 4 | 0 | 2 | 0 |
| Higgins M, 3b | 4 | 0 | 0 | 0 |
| Wagner H, c | 2 | 0 | 0 | 0 |
| Russell R, ph | 1 | 1 | 1 | 0 |
| Partee R, c | 1 | 0 | 0 | 0 |
| Ferriss D, p | 2 | 0 | 0 | 0 |
| Dobson J, p | 0 | 0 | 0 | 0 |
| Metkovich G, ph | 1 | 1 | 1 | 0 |
| Klinger B, p | 0 | 0 | 0 | 0 |
| Johnson E, p | 0 | 0 | 0 | 0 |
| McBride T, ph | 1 | 0 | 0 | 0 |
| | 35 | 3 | 8 | 3 |

| St. Louis | AB | R | H | I |
|---|---|---|---|---|
| Schoendienst R, 2b | 4 | 0 | 2 | 1 |
| Moore T, cf | 4 | 0 | 1 | 0 |
| Musial S, 1b | 3 | 0 | 1 | 0 |
| Slaughter E, rf | 3 | 1 | 1 | 0 |
| Kurowski W, 3b | 4 | 1 | 1 | 0 |
| Garagiola J, c | 3 | 0 | 0 | 0 |
| Rice D, c | 1 | 0 | 0 | 0 |
| Walker H, lf | 3 | 1 | 2 | 2 |
| Marion M, ss | 2 | 0 | 0 | 0 |
| Dickson M, p | 3 | 1 | 1 | 1 |
| Brecheen H, p | 1 | 0 | 0 | 0 |
| | 31 | 4 | 9 | 4 |

| Boston | IP | H | R | ER | BB | SO |
|---|---|---|---|---|---|---|
| Ferriss | 4.1 | 7 | 3 | 3 | 1 | 2 |
| Dobson | 2.2 | 0 | 0 | 0 | 2 | 2 |
| Klinger (L) | 0.2 | 2 | 1 | 1 | 1 | 0 |
| Johnson | 0.1 | 0 | 0 | 0 | 0 | 0 |
| | 8.0 | 9 | 4 | 4 | 4 | 4 |

| St. Louis | IP | H | R | ER | BB | SO |
|---|---|---|---|---|---|---|
| Dickson | 7.0 | 5 | 3 | 3 | 1 | 3 |
| Brecheen (W) | 2.0 | 3 | 0 | 0 | 0 | 1 |
| | 9.0 | 8 | 3 | 3 | 1 | 4 |

```
Boston     100  000  020 — 3
St.Louis   010  020  01x — 4
```

OB: Boston 6, St. Louis 8; ER: Kurowski; 2B: Musial, Kurowski, Dickson, Metkovich, DiMaggio, Walker; SH: Marion; TI: 2:17; AT: 36,143; UM: HP Barlick, 1B Berry, 2B Ballanfant, 3B Hubbard

In the second, Boston squandered a golden opportunity. Doerr opened with a single, went to second on a throwing error, and advanced to third on an infield out. After Dickson retired the next two batters without further damage, he walked to the dugout amid a standing ovation. The cheering barely subsided when Whitey Kurowski led off the home half of the second with a double to left-center. Whitey moved to third on a ground-out by Joe Garagiola and tied the game on a sacrifice fly by Walker.

There were no more hits and few plays to cheer until the Cardinals' fifth, when Walker started with a single. Marty Marion sacrificed Walker to second — an intriguing strategy with the pitcher next up. But Dickson was an excellent hitting pitcher and justified his manager's decision by doubling to left, scoring Walker with the go-ahead run. With the impassioned crowd on its feet, Schoendienst then singled home Dickson, making it 3–1. When Moore also singled, the Sox made a pitching change, bringing on Dobson to face Musial, the National League batting champion. The tension-filled at-bat ended with Musial grounding out but moving the runners to second and third. That brought to the plate Slaughter who was intentionally passed, loading the bases. Now the hometown fans were frantic and sensed the kill. But Dobson was equal to the task and got Kurowski on a ground-out, bringing the attack to an end.

Neither club could muster a base hit in the sixth or seventh innings. In the eighth, Cardinal fans were quieted as a single and a double put two Sox in scoring position and sent Dickson to the showers. Out of the St. Louis bullpen strode Brecheen. The southpaw, who had won Games Two and Six, looked as if he would get out of the inning when he struck out Moses and got Pesky on a shallow liner to right. But with two outs, DiMaggio slammed a double off the right-field wall. Both runners scored and the game was again deadlocked. Dom, however, pulled a muscle running to second and had to be replaced by Leon Culberson, a move that shortly led to serious consequences. Brecheen then got Williams on a pop-up to avert any further damage.

The Cardinals retaliated in the bottom of the eighth. With veteran Bob Klinger taking the hill for Boston, Slaughter led off by singling. Klinger routinely retired the next two Redbirds, holding the baserunner at first. Then occurred the pivotal play of the Series. Walker doubled to left-center bringing the screaming crowd to its feet. Amid the uproar, Culberson fielded it cleanly and relayed to Pesky, neither thinking Slaughter would try to score. But in an electrifying dash, he rounded third while Pesky hesitated with his relay to home. By the time Pesky realized Slaughter's daring, it was too late. St. Louis had recaptured the lead.

In the top of the ninth the first two Sox singled, and a forceout put runners at the corners. But Brecheen dashed Boston hopes by inducing a pop-up and an easy ground-out. The first left-hander to win three World Series games was then hoisted to the shoulders of jubilant Cardinals and carried into the clubhouse.

# 17 *The End of a 35-Year Wait*

PHILADELPHIA (NL) at BROOKLYN (NL)
Sunday, October 1, 1950, Ebbets Field
Phillies 4, Dodgers 1

The 1950 season was a roller-coaster ride for the club Philadelphia called the Whiz Kids. From mid–May until mid–July the youngest team in the National League bounced in and out of first place six times. Finally, on July 25, they checked into the penthouse and never left. It was a precarious position, however, with the Dodgers and Giants right on their heels until they caught fire in August.

| *Philadelphia* | AB | R | H | I | | *Brooklyn* | AB | R | H | I |
|---|---|---|---|---|---|---|---|---|---|---|
| Waitkus E, 1b | 5 | 1 | 1 | 0 | | Abrams C, lf | 2 | 0 | 0 | 0 |
| Ashburn R, cf | 5 | 1 | 0 | 0 | | Reese P, ss | 4 | 1 | 3 | 1 |
| Sisler D, lf | 5 | 2 | 4 | 3 | | Snider D, cf | 4 | 0 | 1 | 0 |
| Mayo J, lf | 0 | 0 | 0 | 0 | | Robinson J, 2b | 3 | 0 | 0 | 0 |
| Ennis D, rf | 5 | 0 | 2 | 0 | | Furillo C, rf | 4 | 0 | 0 | 0 |
| Jones W, 3b | 5 | 0 | 1 | 1 | | Hodges G, 1b | 4 | 0 | 0 | 0 |
| Hamner G, ss | 4 | 0 | 0 | 0 | | Campanella R, c | 4 | 0 | 1 | 0 |
| Seminick A, c | 3 | 0 | 1 | 0 | | Cox B, 3b | 3 | 0 | 0 | 0 |
| Caballero P, pr | 0 | 0 | 0 | 0 | | Russell J, ph | 1 | 0 | 0 | 0 |
| Lopata S, c | 0 | 0 | 0 | 0 | | Newcombe D, p | 3 | 0 | 0 | 0 |
| Goliat M, 2b | 4 | 0 | 1 | 0 | | Brown T, ph | 1 | 0 | 0 | 0 |
| Roberts R, p | 2 | 0 | 1 | 0 | | | 33 | 1 | 5 | 1 |
| | 38 | 4 | 11 | 4 | | | | | | |

| *Philadelphia* | IP | H | R | ER | BB | SO | | *Brooklyn* | IP | H | R | ER | BB | SO |
|---|---|---|---|---|---|---|---|---|---|---|---|---|---|---|
| Roberts (W) | 10.0 | 5 | 1 | 1 | 3 | 2 | | Newcombe (L) | 10.0 | 11 | 4 | 4 | 2 | 3 |

Philadelphia   000   001   000   3 — 4
Brooklyn       000   001   000   0 — 1

OB: Philadelphia 7, Brooklyn 5; DP: Philadelphia 1, Brooklyn 1; 2B: Reese; HR: Reese, Sisler;
   CS: Caballero; SH: Roberts; TI: 2:35; AT: 35,073; UM: Goetz, Dascoli, Jorda, Donatelli

By September 19, the Whiz Kids held a nine game lead over the Dodgers but had suffered a number of threatening personnel setbacks. On September 10 left-hander Curt Simmons, at 17–8, ended his season when he was called to active military duty. Several days later right-hander Bubba Church was struck in the face by a line drive and couldn't pitch for a week. And one day after Church went down, Bob Miller injured his pitching arm and was ineffective for the balance of the campaign. In addition, catcher Andy Seminick suffered a badly injured ankle and played the remaining games full of painkillers. All these events took their toll on the Phillies, who watched their lead slowly slip away. During the last two weeks of the season, while the Whiz Kids dropped seven of nine, the resurgent Dodgers won 12 of 15 and reduced the Philadelphia lead to two games. The schedule makers had had either luck or astounding foresight on their side, for entering the final weekend of the season the Phillies and Dodgers were to meet for two games in Brooklyn.

On Saturday, September 30, the Dodgers beat the Whiz Kids handily, 7–3. If Brooklyn could win the last game on Sunday, there would be a three-game playoff to determine the National League pennant.

It was a sunny, mild day in Ebbets Field that attracted the season's best gate, 35,073. Each team sent its best pitcher to the mound — Don Newcombe for Brooklyn and Robin Roberts for Philadelphia. Roberts, who just celebrated his 24th birthday a day earlier, had already logged 294 innings this year. To compensate for his team's pitching shortage he was making his fifth start in a week.

Pitching dominated the first five innings, as only six batters reached base. In the sixth the Phillies finally scored on three singles, all after there were two outs. The Dodgers also scored after two outs but in freakish fashion. Pee Wee Reese lofted a high fly to right. For a moment it appeared it might be caught, but the ball bounced lazily off the screen above the right-field wall and came to rest on the top edge of the wall. Reese, unsure of what happened, sped around the bases. Only when he reached third did he see the umpire giving the home run signal. Veteran observers had never seen anything like it.

There were no other serious threats until the bottom of the ninth. Cal Abrams led off with a walk and Reese singled him to second. Snider then lined Roberts's first pitch to center for a single. Abrams was waved home with the game winner, but center fielder Richie Ashburn came in quickly and made an accurate throw to the plate. Abrams was out by 15 feet and the decision to send the runner has been debated ever since.

With one out and runners on second and third, the Dodgers still had an excellent opportunity to win. The Phillies intentionally passed Jackie Robinson, loading the bases. The capacity crowd was in an uproar, but Roberts was equal to the challenge. He retired Carl Furillo on a pop-up and Gil Hodges on a fly-out to send the game into extra innings.

Roberts led off the tenth with a single, and Eddie Waitkus followed suit. Ashburn tried to sacrifice the runners along, but Newcombe made a good play to get a force at third. That brought Dick Sisler to the plate. Sisler loved to hit in Ebbets Field, having stroked three homers there this year. Dick had also singled in each of his last three plate appearances, but Newcombe got two quick strikes on him. With the count 1–2, Sisler drove the next offering to deep left-center, into the seats 348 feet away, giving the Whiz Kids a commanding 4–1 advantage. All that was needed for the pennant was for Roberts to retire the Dodgers in the home half of the inning. He did, in routine fashion, for his 20th victory. The Brooklyn bubble burst, and Philadelphia began to celebrate its first pennant since 1915.

# 18 *Gibson's Victorious Home Run Hobble*

OAKLAND (AL) at LOS ANGELES (NL)
Saturday, October 15, 1988, Dodger Stadium
Dodgers 5, Athletics 4

Team losing. Insurmountable odds. Time running out. Hero rises from sick bed to hit a home run and win the game. This is the script for fantasies, Saturday afternoon matinees, and the first game of the 1988 World Series.

| Oakland | AB | R | H | I |
|---|---|---|---|---|
| Lansford C, 3b | 4 | 1 | 0 | 0 |
| Henderson D, cf | 5 | 0 | 2 | 0 |
| Canseco J, rf | 4 | 1 | 1 | 4 |
| Parker D, lf | 2 | 0 | 0 | 0 |
| Javier S, pr-lf | 1 | 0 | 1 | 0 |
| McGwire M, 1b | 3 | 0 | 0 | 0 |
| Steinbach T, c | 4 | 0 | 1 | 0 |
| Hassey R, c | 0 | 0 | 0 | 0 |
| Hubbard G, 2b | 4 | 1 | 2 | 0 |
| Weiss W, ss | 4 | 0 | 0 | 0 |
| Stewart D, p | 3 | 1 | 0 | 0 |
| Eckersley D, p | 0 | 0 | 0 | 0 |
| | 34 | 4 | 7 | 4 |

| Los Angeles | AB | R | H | I |
|---|---|---|---|---|
| Sax S, 2b | 3 | 1 | 1 | 0 |
| Stubbs F, 1b | 4 | 0 | 0 | 0 |
| Hatcher M, lf | 3 | 1 | 1 | 2 |
| Marshall M, rf | 4 | 1 | 1 | 0 |
| Shelby J, cf | 4 | 0 | 1 | 0 |
| Scioscia M, c | 4 | 0 | 1 | 1 |
| Hamilton J, 3b | 4 | 0 | 0 | 0 |
| Griffin A, ss | 2 | 0 | 1 | 0 |
| Davis M, ph | 0 | 1 | 0 | 0 |
| Belcher T, p | 0 | 0 | 0 | 0 |
| Heep D, ph | 1 | 0 | 0 | 0 |
| Leary T, p | 0 | 0 | 0 | 0 |
| Woodson T, ph | 1 | 0 | 0 | 0 |
| Holton B, p | 0 | 0 | 0 | 0 |
| Gonzalez J, ph | 1 | 0 | 0 | 0 |
| Peña A, p | 0 | 0 | 0 | 0 |
| Gibson K, ph | 1 | 1 | 1 | 2 |
| | 32 | 5 | 7 | 5 |

| Oakland | IP | H | R | ER | BB | SO |
|---|---|---|---|---|---|---|
| Stewart | 8.0 | 6 | 3 | 3 | 2 | 5 |
| Eckersley (L) | 0.2 | 1 | 2 | 2 | 1 | 1 |
| | 8.2 | 7 | 5 | 5 | 3 | 6 |

| Los Angeles | IP | H | R | ER | BB | SO |
|---|---|---|---|---|---|---|
| Belcher | 2.0 | 3 | 4 | 4 | 4 | 3 |
| Leary | 3.0 | 3 | 0 | 0 | 1 | 3 |
| Holton | 2.0 | 0 | 0 | 0 | 1 | 0 |
| Peña (W) | 2.0 | 1 | 0 | 0 | 0 | 3 |
| | 9.0 | 7 | 4 | 4 | 6 | 9 |

```
Oakland       040  000  000 — 4
Los Angeles   200  001  002 — 5
```

OB: Oakland 10, Los Angeles 5; DP: Oakland 1; 2B: Henderson; HR: Hatcher, Canseco, Gibson; SB: Canseco, Sax, Davis; HP: by Belcher (Canseco), by Stewart (Sax); WP: Stewart; BK: Stewart; TI: 3:04; AT: 55,983; UM: HP Harvey, 1B Merrill, 2B Froemming, 3B Cousins, LF Crawford, RF McCoy

The team losing was the Los Angeles Dodgers, who were trailing the Oakland Athletics, 4–3, and were down to their last out. The odds were steepened by the presence of one of the game's top relievers, Dennis Eckersley. And rising from a trainer's table and hobbling to the plate was the Dodgers' emotional leader, Kirk Gibson. Add to the odds a nail-biting full count before Gibson cracked a long fly over the right field wall to win the game. It was indeed a fantasy finish.

More than three hours earlier, the Dodgers' Tim Belcher tossed the first pitch of the game. He was opposed by Oakland's 21-game winner, Dave Stewart.

Belcher was wild in the opening frame — giving up a single, a walk, and hitting a batter — but escaped without allowing a run.

Stewart also opened by hitting a batter, Steve Sax, and one out later Mickey Hatcher gave the Dodgers a two-run lead on a home run to left-center.

Belcher's wildness continued into the second inning as he gave up a single, then issued two free passes. The first of those walks went to Stewart, who hadn't batted all year. It was also the first walk given to a World Series pitcher in seven years. With the bases loaded, third-year slugger Jose Canseco left little doubt where his rising rocket to center field was going. The grand slam vaulted Oakland into a 4–2 lead.

From the second until the ninth, only one runner reached third base. That was in the Dodger sixth when three singles narrowed the gap to 4–3.

Protecting a one-run lead entering the bottom of the ninth, the Athletics called upon their ace reliever. Eckersley easily retired the first two batters before walking pinch-hitter Mike Davis. That set the stage for Gibson.

Out of the dugout he limped, pained by a sprained ligament in his right knee and a severely pulled hamstring in his left leg. He was in obvious pain as he fouled off several pitches en route to working the count full. One strike away from defeat, Gibson suddenly electrified the crowd by lining the next pitch over the right field wall, bringing his team an unlikely 5–4 victory. As television cameras captured the drama for posterity, Gibson limped into a fist-in-the-air home run trot before 55,000 delirious fans.

# 19 Cleveland Wins with Nine in the Ninth

WASHINGTON (AL) at CLEVELAND (AL)
Thursday, May 23, 1901, League Park
Blues 14, Senators 13

With the American League as we know it barely one month old, perhaps the most remarkable comeback in major league history transpired. In the bottom of the ninth, with two outs and nobody on base, the Cleveland Blues (later Indians) exploded from an eight-run deficit (13–5) to overtake the Washington Senators in spectacular fashion.

As the batboys began packing equipment, a handful of fans remained only to scoff at the home club. Bill Hoffer, Blues pitcher, absorbed considerable insult when he was the first to bat and satisfied his tormentors by striking out. Ollie Pickering then grounded out. What happened next, between 5:18 P.M. and 5:28 P.M., strains the limits of belief.

    • Jack McCarthy singled, agitating the spectators at the seemingly useless delay.

    • Bill Bradley also singled, detaining the loyal attendees from their dinners.

    • Candy LaChance swung and missed twice, leaving the Senators one strike from victory. But LaChance singled home McCarthy, making it 13–6.

| Washington | AB | R | H | I |
|---|---|---|---|---|
| Farrell J, cf | 6 | 1 | 0 | 3 |
| Dungan S, rf | 6 | 0 | 1 | 2 |
| Quinn J, 2b | 5 | 1 | 2 | 2 |
| Foster P, lf | 5 | 1 | 3 | 0 |
| Everett B, 1b | 3 | 1 | 0 | 0 |
| Grady M, c | 4 | 2 | 2 | 2 |
| Clingman B, ss | 4 | 2 | 2 | 0 |
| Coughlin B, 3b | 3 | 3 | 2 | 0 |
| Patten C, p | 4 | 2 | 2 | 1 |
| Lee W, p | 0 | 0 | 0 | 0 |
|  | 40 | 13 | 14 | 10 |

| Cleveland | AB | R | H | I |
|---|---|---|---|---|
| Pickering O, rf | 6 | 1 | 1 | 1 |
| McCarthy J, lf | 5 | 2 | 2 | 0 |
| Bradley B, 3b | 5 | 2 | 4 | 1 |
| LaChance C, 1b | 5 | 1 | 3 | 2 |
| Wood B, c | 4 | 1 | 1 | 0 |
| Scheibeck F, ss | 5 | 2 | 4 | 4 |
| Genins F, cf | 4 | 1 | 1 | 1 |
| Eagan T, 2b | 4 | 2 | 1 | 0 |
| Hoffer B, p | 4 | 1 | 1 | 1 |
| Beck E, ph | 1 | 1 | 1 | 2 |
|  | 43 | 14 | 19 | 12 |

| Washington | IP | H | R | ER | BB | SO |
|---|---|---|---|---|---|---|
| Patten | 8.2 | 16 | 11 | 7 | 3 | 3 |
| Lee (L) | 0.0 | 3 | 3 | 3 | 0 | 0 |
|  | 8.2 | 19 | 14 | 10 | 3 | 3 |

| Cleveland | IP | H | R | ER | BB | SO |
|---|---|---|---|---|---|---|
| Hoffer (W) | 9 | 14 | 13 | 6 | 3 | 0 |

| Washington | 050 | 130 | 202 — 13 |
|---|---|---|---|
| Cleveland | 000 | 040 | 019 — 14 |

OB: Washington 7, Cleveland 7; ER: Foster, Grady, Bradley 2, Wood, Scheibeck; DP: Washington 1; 2B: Coughlin, Scheibeck, Beck; 3B: Dungan; SB: Grady, Clingman; SH: Everett, Clingman, Coughlin, Patten; HP: By Patten (Wood); PB: Grady; TI: 2:00; AT: 1,620; UM: Joe Cantillon

- Bob Wood was hit by a pitch, and still Washington needed only one more out.
- Frank Scheibeck doubled, clearing the bases (13–9) and altering the interests of the remaining fans.
- Frank Genins singled home Scheibeck (13–10); the crowd now swarmed around the infield to urge their heroes on. Time was called to push the horde back.
- With the count 2–1 to Truck Eagan, Watty Lee relieved Washington starter Casey Patten.
- Lee completed the walk to Eagan.
- Erve Beck, pinch-hitting for Hoffer, lifted a ball deep to left. The Senators' Pop Foster, with his back to the wall, had the ball glance off his glove for a double, driving in Cleveland's 11th and 12th runs. Now the crowd was hysterical.
- When Pickering got his first hit of the day to tie the game, pandemonium erupted. The remaining fans ran onto the field, tossing hats, umbrellas, canes, and cushions into the air. For several minutes there was serious danger of forfeit.
- Pickering took second on a passed ball before McCarthy singled. Foster fumbled the ball in left field, affording Pickering a chance to cross the plate with the winning run.

The frantic crowd flooded the field, hoisted the players to their shoulders, and carried them to the dressing room. One strike from defeat, the Blues had written one of the greatest comeback stories in sports history.

# 20 *Lavagetto Breaks Up Bevens's No-Hitter*

NEW YORK (AL) at BROOKLYN (NL)
Friday, October 3, 1947, Ebbets Field
Dodgers 3, Yankees 2

Before the 1947 season began the Yankees hired Dodger coach Chuck Dressen away from Brooklyn. The incident stimulated such public animosity between the two clubs that Commissioner Happy Chandler was forced to intervene. Among the accusations were several that smacked of gambling. In the end Chandler suspended Dressen for 30 days and Brooklyn manager Leo Durocher for the balance of the season for "consorting" with gamblers. Each team was fined $2,000. Fittingly the two were to meet seven months later for a drama-filled, seven-game World Series.

With the Yankees leading two games to one, the two clubs met for Game Four in Brooklyn's Ebbets Field. The thriller provided a storybook finish with tragic overtones.

New York started Bill Bevens, a mediocre 7–13 right-hander who was a few weeks shy of his 31st birthday. Bevens experienced a lot of bad luck throughout the regular season, in part the residue of his 77 walks in only 165 innings pitched. Rookie Harry Taylor, who had a promising season aborted because of an elbow injury in August, got the call for the Dodgers.

The Yankees wasted no time feasting on Taylor. The first two batters, Snuffy Stirnweiss and Tommy Henrich, both singled, and Yogi Berra reached first on an error. Another walk, to Joe DiMaggio, forced in a New York run and sent Taylor to an early shower. Hal Gregg assumed the pitching duties for Brooklyn and extinguished the rally. In the home half of the first, the Dodgers worked Bevens for two walks but both runners were left stranded.

In the third, DiMaggio walked. George McQuinn then tapped a ball near the plate, and Brooklyn catcher Bruce Edwards threw wildly to first. DiMaggio, on a sign from third base coach Chuck Dressen, tried to score on the errant throw but was cut down easily at the plate. The play provided the second-guessers with ample grist during the following few days. In the same frame the Dodgers' Eddie Stanky led off with a walk and advanced to second on a Bevens wild pitch. But Johnny Lindell helped the Yanks escape damage with a tumbling catch of Jackie Robinson's foul fly.

New York added an insurance run in the fourth when Billy Johnson tripled, and Lindell doubled him home.

The Dodgers finally took advantage of Bevens's wildness in the fifth. Leading

**Lavagetto shattered Bevens's bid for glory (National Baseball Hall of Fame Library, Cooperstown, New York).**

off, both Spider Jorgensen and Hal Gregg walked. Although Brooklyn had yet to hit safely, they now had six free passes from the big right-hander. Stanky sacrificed both runners into scoring position. Pee Wee Reese then sent a ground ball to shortstop Phil Rizzuto, who threw to third to nip a scampering Gregg. Jorgenson scored on the play, making it 2–1.

| New York | AB | R | H | I |
|---|---|---|---|---|
| Stirnweiss S, 2b | 4 | 1 | 2 | 0 |
| Henrich T, rf | 5 | 0 | 1 | 0 |
| Berra Y, c | 4 | 0 | 0 | 0 |
| DiMaggio J, cf | 2 | 0 | 0 | 1 |
| McQuinn G, 1b | 4 | 0 | 1 | 0 |
| Johnson B, 3b | 4 | 1 | 1 | 0 |
| Lindell J, lf | 3 | 0 | 2 | 1 |
| Rizzuto P, ss | 4 | 0 | 1 | 0 |
| Bevens B, p | 3 | 0 | 0 | 0 |
| | 33 | 2 | 8 | 2 |

| Brooklyn | AB | R | H | I |
|---|---|---|---|---|
| Stanky E, 2b | 1 | 0 | 0 | 0 |
| Lavagetto C, ph | 1 | 0 | 1 | 2 |
| Reese P, ss | 4 | 0 | 0 | 1 |
| Robinson J, 1b | 4 | 0 | 0 | 0 |
| Walker D, rf | 2 | 0 | 0 | 0 |
| Hermanski G, lf | 4 | 0 | 0 | 0 |
| Edwards B, c | 4 | 0 | 0 | 0 |
| Furillo C, cf | 3 | 0 | 0 | 0 |
| Gionfriddo A, pr | 0 | 1 | 0 | 0 |
| Jorgensen S, 3b | 2 | 1 | 0 | 0 |
| Taylor H, p | 0 | 0 | 0 | 0 |
| Gregg H, p | 1 | 0 | 0 | 0 |
| Vaughan A, ph | 0 | 0 | 0 | 0 |
| Behrman H, p | 0 | 0 | 0 | 0 |
| Casey H, p | 0 | 0 | 0 | 0 |
| Reiser P, ph | 0 | 0 | 0 | 0 |
| Miksis E, pr | 0 | 1 | 0 | 0 |
| | 26 | 3 | 1 | 3 |

| New York | IP | H | R | ER | BB | SO |
|---|---|---|---|---|---|---|
| Bevens (L) | 8.2 | 1 | 3 | 3 | 10 | 5 |

| Brooklyn | IP | H | R | ER | BB | SO |
|---|---|---|---|---|---|---|
| Taylor | 0.0 | 2 | 1 | 0 | 1 | 0 |
| Gregg | 7.0 | 4 | 1 | 1 | 3 | 5 |
| Behrman | 1.1 | 2 | 0 | 0 | 0 | 0 |
| Casey (W) | 0.2 | 0 | 0 | 0 | 0 | 0 |
| | 9.0 | 8 | 2 | 1 | 4 | 5 |

```
New York    100   100   000 — 2
Brooklyn    000   010   002 — 3
```

OB: New York 9, Brooklyn 8; ER: Reese, Edwards, Berra, Jorgensen; DP: Brooklyn 3; 2B: Lindell, Lavagetto; 3B: Johnson; SB: Rizzuto, Reese, Gionfriddo; SH: Stanky, Bevens; WP: Bevens; TI: 2:20; AT: 33,443; UM: HP Goetz, 1B McGowen, 2B Pinelli, 3B Rommel, LF Boyer, RF Magerkurth

To start the eighth, Hank Behrman replaced Gregg on the mound for Brooklyn. Behrman withstood an error by Jorgensen to get out of the eighth frame but ran into serious trouble in the ninth. Lindell singled, but was forced at second when Rizzuto hit into a fielder's choice. Bevens sacrificed but all were safe on a late throw to second. When Stirnweiss singled to center, the Yankees had the bases loaded and a golden opportunity to put the game out of reach.

Brooklyn called in their ace reliever, Hugh Casey, to face the dangerous Henrich. On Casey's first pitch, Henrich grounded sharply back to the mound starting a snappy 1–2–3 double play and pulling the Dodgers out of potential disaster. They still had no hits but were only one run down.

Bevens's high wire act finally caught up with him in the strategy-filled, fatal ninth. After Bruce Edwards flied out, Carl Furillo collected the Dodgers' ninth walk. When Jorgensen fouled out, Bevens was one out away from the first World Series no-hitter. Al Gionfriddo, running for Furillo while Pete Reiser batted for Casey, stole second. This changed the Yankees thinking about pitching to Reiser. Although the talented outfielder was injured and couldn't run well, New York decided to walk him. It was the tenth walk awarded Brooklyn and put the winning run on base. Eddie Miksis was immediately commissioned to run for Reiser.

The cat-and-mouse game reached another level when, for only the second time this season, Eddie Stanky was lifted for a pinch-hitter. Cookie Lavagetto was an aging veteran who had seen limited action during the season but was always a dangerous hitter. Cookie swung and missed, leaving Bevens only two strikes away from fame and victory. But fate had its day as Lavagetto drilled the next offering off the right field wall, and it bounced around long enough for Gionfriddo to score the tying run and Miksis to tally the game winner. Bevens's near fame had turned into an unforgetable loss.

## The Longest Post-Season Game 21

NEW YORK (NL) at HOUSTON (NL)
Wednesday, October 15, 1986, The Astrodome
Mets 7, Astros 6

Intense, emotional, mentally straining — this is how players described the longest post-season game of the century. With the Mets leading Houston in the National League Championship Series three games to two, the clubs engaged in a drama-filled 16-inning struggle. New York tied it in the ninth after being shut out for eight innings, and both teams scored in the 14th and 16th before a Houston rally fell just short. The thriller culminated a 64-inning, six-game series that resulted in a combined victory margin of only 10 runs.

The Astros jumped on Mets' starter Bob Ojeda for three runs in the opening frame, and then their starter, Bob Knepper, went to work. Through the first eight innings the left-hander allowed just two singles and a walk. Entering the ninth, he was coasting behind a 3–0 lead.

Pinch-hitter Lenny Dykstra represented the first real scoring threat for New York as he led off the ninth with a triple. A single, ground-out, and a double scored two and sent Knepper to the showers. Relief ace Dave Smith then entered the game but was wild. He walked the next two batters, loading the bases, before Ray Knight sent the tying run home on a sacrifice fly. Another intentional walk re-loaded the sacks, but Smith struck out pinch-hitter Danny Heep on a 3–2 count. Houston went down in order in the home half, sending the battle into extra innings.

The Mets turned over the pitching duties to Roger McDowell, who preserved the tie with five nearly perfect innings of relief.

| New York | AB | R | H | I |
|---|---|---|---|---|
| Wilson M, cf-lf | 7 | 1 | 1 | 1 |
| Mitchell K, lf | 4 | 0 | 0 | 0 |
| Elster K, ss | 3 | 0 | 0 | 0 |
| Hernandez K, 1b | 7 | 1 | 1 | 1 |
| Carter G, c | 5 | 0 | 2 | 0 |
| Strawberry D, rf | 5 | 2 | 1 | 0 |
| Knight R, 3b | 6 | 1 | 1 | 2 |
| Teufel T, 2b | 3 | 0 | 1 | 0 |
| Backman W, ph-2b | 2 | 1 | 1 | 1 |
| Santana R, ss | 3 | 0 | 1 | 0 |
| Heep D, ph | 1 | 0 | 0 | 0 |
| McDowell R, p | 1 | 0 | 0 | 0 |
| Johnson H, ph | 1 | 0 | 0 | 0 |
| Orosco J, p | 0 | 0 | 0 | 0 |
| Ojeda B, p | 1 | 0 | 0 | 0 |
| Mazzilli L, ph | 1 | 0 | 0 | 0 |
| Aguilera R, p | 0 | 0 | 0 | 0 |
| Dykstra L, ph-cf | 4 | 1 | 2 | 1 |
| | 54 | 7 | 11 | 6 |

| Houston | AB | R | H | I |
|---|---|---|---|---|
| Doran B, 2b | 7 | 1 | 2 | 0 |
| Hatcher B, cf | 7 | 2 | 3 | 2 |
| Garner P, 3b | 3 | 1 | 1 | 1 |
| Walling D, ph-3b | 4 | 0 | 0 | 0 |
| Davis G, 1b | 7 | 1 | 3 | 2 |
| Bass K, rf | 6 | 0 | 1 | 0 |
| Cruz J, lf | 6 | 0 | 1 | 1 |
| Ashby A, c | 6 | 0 | 0 | 0 |
| Thon D, ss | 3 | 0 | 0 | 0 |
| Reynolds C, ph-ss | 3 | 0 | 0 | 0 |
| Knepper B, p | 2 | 0 | 0 | 0 |
| Smith D, p | 0 | 0 | 0 | 0 |
| Puhl T, ph | 1 | 0 | 0 | 0 |
| Andersen L, p | 0 | 0 | 0 | 0 |
| Pankovitz J, ph | 1 | 0 | 0 | 0 |
| Lopez A, p | 0 | 0 | 0 | 0 |
| Calhoun J, p | 0 | 0 | 0 | 0 |
| Lopes D, ph | 0 | 1 | 0 | 0 |
| | 56 | 6 | 11 | 6 |

| New York | IP | H | R | ER | BB | SO |
|---|---|---|---|---|---|---|
| Ojeda | 5.0 | 5 | 3 | 3 | 2 | 1 |
| Aguilera | 3.0 | 1 | 0 | 0 | 0 | 1 |
| McDowell | 5.0 | 1 | 0 | 0 | 0 | 2 |
| Orosco (W) | 3.0 | 4 | 3 | 3 | 1 | 5 |
| | 16.0 | 11 | 6 | 6 | 3 | 9 |

| Houston | IP | H | R | ER | BB | SO |
|---|---|---|---|---|---|---|
| Knepper | 8.1 | 5 | 3 | 3 | 1 | 6 |
| Smith | 1.2 | 0 | 0 | 0 | 3 | 2 |
| Andersen | 3.0 | 0 | 0 | 0 | 1 | 1 |
| Lopez (L) | 2.0 | 5 | 3 | 3 | 2 | 2 |
| Calhoun | 1.0 | 1 | 1 | 1 | 1 | 0 |
| | 16.0 | 11 | 7 | 7 | 8 | 11 |

| New York | 000 | 000 | 003 | 000 | 010 | 3 — 7 |
|---|---|---|---|---|---|---|
| Houston | 300 | 000 | 000 | 000 | 010 | 2 — 6 |

OB: New York 9, Houston 5; ER: Bass; DP: Houston 2; 2B: Garner, Davis, Hernandez, Straw-
berry; 3B: Dykstra; HR: Hatcher; CS: Bass 2; SH: Orosco; SF: Knight; WP: Calhoun 2;
TI: 4:42; AT: 45,718; UM: HP Brocklander, 1B Harvey, 2B Weyer, 3B Pulli, LF Rennert,
RF West

In the 14th the Mets forged a lead on a single, walk, and another single by
Wally Backman. Only two outs from defeat, Billy Hatcher saved the Astros with
a home run that bounced off the foul screen in left.

On to the 16th the two clubs played before the Mets struck again. A pop
fly double by Darryl Strawberry and a single by Knight gave New York another
lead. There followed a walk, two wild pitches by Jeff Calhoun, and a single by
Dykstra all of which pushed the visitors out in front by a 7–4 margin. But the
Astros weren't through yet. A walk and three singles brought Houston to within
one run of tying, and with two on and two outs, the Astrodome trembled with
anticipation. Kevin Bass then worked the count full before Jesse Orosco fanned
him, and the crowd's groans reverberated through the dome. New York had won
its first pennant in 13 years.

# Red Sox Prevail in World Series Game Number Eight 22

NEW YORK (NL) at BOSTON (AL)
Wednesday, October 16, 1912, Fenway Park
Red Sox 3, Giants 2

The 1912 World Series between the New York Giants and Boston Red Sox was scheduled for seven games, but Game Two ended in a 6–6 tie, called after 11 innings on account of darkness. Rather than continue play the following day, the game was replayed in its entirety, resulting in an eight-game Series.

The final contest was a thriller, but one not without controversial undertones. On a cold sunny day a crowd of only 17,034, nearly half that of a day earlier, turned out for the deciding contest in Fenway Park, which had opened that April. The Royal Rooters, the Sox most loyal and vociferous group of fans, boycotted because their favorite seats had not been held for them on Tuesday. They also influenced substantial numbers of sympathizers by fueling rumors that management had engaged Sox pitcher Buck O'Brien to lay down in Game Six to increase the length of the Series and further pad the purse. Nonetheless, the game went on and matched New York great Christy Mathewson against Boston's 22-year-old Hugh Bedient.

The first scoring threat resulted from some shoddy Boston fielding in the top of the second. But with runners at second and third and two outs, Bedient retired Mathewson on an easy fly ball to left.

The Giants did break into the scoring column in the third. After Josh Devore walked and moved to third on two ground-ball outs, Red Murray doubled him home.

In the fourth, New York squandered a golden opportunity. Buck Herzog led off with a double to left and was sacrificed to third. But Bedient again choked off the rally by getting Art Fletcher on a pop-up and Mathewson on a fly-out to right.

The defensive play of the game was made with New York batting in the fifth. Larry Doyle drove a deep fly to right that had enough lift to clear the short wall, but Harry Hooper raced back and leaped to pull it down for an out. In the same frame Boston's Heinie Wagner sent Murray to the fence in left for a long out.

Boston blew their first serious scoring opportunity in the sixth. With two outs, Steve Yerkes stood at third and Duffy Lewis at first. Whether a double steal

| New York | AB | R | H | I |
|---|---|---|---|---|
| Devore J, rf | 3 | 1 | 1 | 0 |
| Doyle L, 2b | 5 | 0 | 0 | 0 |
| Snodgrass F, cf | 4 | 0 | 1 | 0 |
| Murray R, lf | 5 | 1 | 2 | 1 |
| Merkle F, 1b | 5 | 0 | 1 | 1 |
| Herzog B, 3b | 5 | 0 | 2 | 0 |
| Meyers C, c | 3 | 0 | 0 | 0 |
| Fletcher A, ss | 3 | 0 | 1 | 0 |
| McCormick M, ph | 1 | 0 | 0 | 0 |
| Shafer T, ss | 0 | 0 | 0 | 0 |
| Mathewson C, p | 4 | 0 | 1 | 0 |
| | 38 | 2 | 9 | 2 |

| Boston | AB | R | H | I |
|---|---|---|---|---|
| Hooper H, rf | 5 | 0 | 0 | 0 |
| Yerkes S, 2b | 4 | 1 | 1 | 0 |
| Speaker T, cf | 4 | 0 | 2 | 1 |
| Lewis D, lf | 4 | 0 | 0 | 0 |
| Gardner L, 3b | 3 | 0 | 1 | 1 |
| Stahl J, 1b | 4 | 1 | 2 | 0 |
| Wagner H, ss | 3 | 0 | 1 | 0 |
| Cady H, c | 4 | 0 | 0 | 0 |
| Bedient H, p | 2 | 0 | 0 | 0 |
| Henriksen O, ph | 1 | 0 | 1 | 1 |
| Wood J, p | 0 | 0 | 0 | 0 |
| Engle C, ph | 1 | 1 | 0 | 0 |
| | 35 | 3 | 8 | 3 |

| New York | IP | H | R | ER | BB | SO |
|---|---|---|---|---|---|---|
| Mathewson (L) | 9.2 | 8 | 3 | 1 | 5 | 4 |

| Boston | IP | H | R | ER | BB | SO |
|---|---|---|---|---|---|---|
| Bedient | 7.0 | 6 | 1 | 1 | 3 | 2 |
| Wood (W) | 3.0 | 3 | 1 | 1 | 1 | 2 |
| | 10.0 | 9 | 2 | 2 | 4 | 4 |

```
New York   001  000  000  1 — 2
Boston     000  000  100  2 — 3
```

OB: New York 11, Boston 9; ER: Wagner, Doyle, Gardner 2, Speaker, Snodgrass; 2B: Murray 2, Herzog, Gardner, Henriksen, Stahl; SB: Devore; CS: Snodgrass, Meyers, Devore; SH: Meyers; SF: Gardner; TI: 2:37; AT: 17,034; UM: HP O'Loughlin, 1B Rigler, 2B Klem, 3B Evans

was signaled is not known, but Lewis took off for second. Giants catcher Chief Myers faked a throw to second and threw to Mathewson instead. The pitcher wheeled and tossed to third, catching Yerkes off the base for the third out.

The home team finally dented the plate in the seventh. With two outs and runners at first and second, Olaf Henriksen pinch hit for Bedient and doubled down the third base line to knot it at one. Another hit at this point would have scored two more and broken the spirit of New York, but Mathewson got Hooper on a fly ball to center.

Smokey Joe Wood, winner of 34 games during the regular season and two more in this Series, replaced Bedient and had no trouble with the Giants in the eighth and ninth. Meanwhile, Boston's Jake Stahl doubled with one out in the bottom of the ninth, but Mathewson retired the next two Sox on routine fly balls, sending the game into extra innings.

Despair cast a shadow over Fenway in the top of the tenth as the Giants pushed across the lead run on Murray's double and Fred Merkle's RBI single. The Red Sox were down to their final three outs.

Clyde Engle led off the home tenth with a routine fly ball to left-center. Fred Snodgrass and Murray both had plenty of time to make the catch, and Snodgrass called off his teammate. But the ball no sooner hit his glove than it bounced out for a crucial error. Next, Hooper drove a ball to deep left-center. Snodgrass temporarily atoned for his miscue with a great running catch, but Engle tagged and went to second. Mathewson then walked Yerkes on five pitches. Tris Speaker, a .383 hitter during the regular season, was up next, and Mathewson got him to pop-up in foul territory near the first base bag. Mathewson, catcher Meyers, and first baseman Merkle each may have caught it, but confusion reigned, and what should have been the Series-ending out became just a foul ball. Reporters claimed it would have been an easy catch for Merkle, but the second crucial misplay of the inning gave Speaker new life. He took full advantage of it and singled to right driving home Engle with the tying run. On a throw to the plate, Yerkes went to third and Speaker to second. Hoping for an inning-ending double play, Lewis was walked intentionally, loading the bases. With the Boston crowd imploring Larry Gardner, he drove a long fly to right that scored Yerkes with the championship run.

# *Robinson Leads Dodgers into a Playoff* 23

BROOKLYN (NL) at PHILADELPHIA (NL)
Sunday, September 30, 1951, Shibe Park
Dodgers 9, Phillies 8

In one of the most dramatic pennant races of the century, the New York Giants surged from 13½ games behind on August 11 to tie the Brooklyn Dodgers on the last Friday of the season. By Sunday, with just one game remaining on the schedule, the two were still deadlocked. Both contenders were on the road, the Giants in Boston and the Dodgers in Philadelphia, making this a story of two games rather than one.

Many of the Brooklyn faithful followed their club into the Quaker City to see the final showdown. Those who weren't late were dealt a blow to the solar plexus as Philadelphia crashed into the scoring column, putting four runs across in the second inning. While Brooklyn's Preacher Roe was being sent to the showers, the score was flashed in Boston, where the optimistic Giants were leading the Braves.

The Dodgers got one back in the top of the third, but the Phillies increased their lead to 6–1 in the home half. This further fueled the Giant pennant hopes, as they couldn't help but keep an eye on the Philadelphia score.

Brooklyn fought back, scoring one in the fourth and three in the fifth to reduce the lead to 6–5. During the three-run rally, Jackie Robinson atoned for some earlier disappointments by tripling home a run. He had ended a first-inning rally by hitting into a double play, struck out in the fourth, and blamed himself for failing to snare Richie Ashburn's RBI infield-single in the second.

| Brooklyn | AB | R | H | I |
|---|---|---|---|---|
| Furillo C, rf | 7 | 1 | 2 | 1 |
| Reese P, ss | 6 | 0 | 3 | 1 |
| Snider D, cf | 7 | 1 | 3 | 1 |
| Robinson J, 2b | 6 | 2 | 2 | 2 |
| Campanella R, c | 7 | 1 | 2 | 0 |
| Pafko A, lf | 7 | 0 | 1 | 1 |
| Hodges G, 1b | 5 | 1 | 2 | 0 |
| Cox B, 3b | 6 | 1 | 1 | 0 |
| Roe P, p | 0 | 0 | 0 | 0 |
| Branca R, p | 0 | 1 | 0 | 0 |
| Russell J, ph | 1 | 0 | 0 | 0 |
| King C, p | 0 | 0 | 0 | 0 |
| Labine C, p | 0 | 0 | 0 | 0 |
| Belardi W, ph | 1 | 0 | 0 | 0 |
| Erskine C, p | 0 | 0 | 0 | 0 |
| Walker R, ph | 1 | 0 | 1 | 2 |
| Thompson D, pr | 0 | 1 | 0 | 0 |
| Newcombe D, p | 2 | 0 | 0 | 0 |
| Podbielan B, p | 0 | 0 | 0 | 0 |
|  | 56 | 9 | 17 | 8 |

| Philadelphia | AB | R | H | I |
|---|---|---|---|---|
| Pellagrini E, 2b | 6 | 1 | 2 | 3 |
| Ashburn R, cf | 8 | 0 | 4 | 1 |
| Jones W, 3b | 4 | 0 | 1 | 0 |
| Ennis D, lf | 8 | 0 | 1 | 0 |
| Brown T, 1b | 2 | 1 | 1 | 1 |
| Waitkus E, 1b | 6 | 0 | 0 | 0 |
| Clark M, rf | 1 | 0 | 0 | 0 |
| Nicholson B, ph-rf | 6 | 2 | 2 | 0 |
| Hamner G, ss | 5 | 3 | 2 | 1 |
| Seminick A, c | 2 | 1 | 0 | 0 |
| Church B, p | 2 | 0 | 1 | 2 |
| Drews K, p | 2 | 0 | 1 | 0 |
| Roberts R, p | 1 | 0 | 0 | 0 |
|  | 53 | 8 | 15 | 8 |

| Brooklyn | IP | H | R | ER | BB | SO |
|---|---|---|---|---|---|---|
| Roe | 1.2 | 5 | 4 | 4 | 1 | 1 |
| Branca | 1.1 | 2 | 2 | 2 | 2 | 1 |
| King | 1.0 | 3 | 2 | 2 | 0 | 0 |
| Labine | 1.0 | 1 | 0 | 0 | 1 | 2 |
| Erskine | 2.0 | 2 | 0 | 0 | 0 | 0 |
| Newcombe | 5.2 | 1 | 0 | 0 | 6 | 3 |
| Podbielan (W) | 1.1 | 1 | 0 | 0 | 0 | 0 |
|  | 14.0 | 15 | 8 | 8 | 10 | 7 |

| Philadelphia | IP | H | R | ER | BB | SO |
|---|---|---|---|---|---|---|
| Church | 4.1 | 6 | 5 | 5 | 3 | 3 |
| Drews | 3.0 | 5 | 3 | 3 | 0 | 2 |
| Roberts (L) | 6.2 | 6 | 1 | 1 | 0 | 1 |
|  | 14.0 | 17 | 9 | 9 | 3 | 6 |

```
Brooklyn       001  130  030  000  01 — 9
Philadelphia   042  020  000  000  00 — 8
```

OB: Brooklyn 9, Philadelphia 18; ER: Jones, Robinson; DP: Philadelphia 3; 2B: Jones, Hamner, Pellagrini, Snider, Walker, Campanella; 3B: Reese, Campanella, Robinson, Hamner; HR: Brown, Robinson; SH: Jones 2, Robinson, Pellagrini; HP: by King (Jones), by Newcombe (Pellagrini); WP: Branca; TI: 4:30; AT: 31,755; UM: HP Jorda, 1B Gore, 2B Warneke, 3B Goetz

In the bottom of the fifth, Brooklyn hopes suffered another blow as the Phillies added two, making it 8–5. Meanwhile the scoreboard showed the Giants leading the Braves, 3–1, with zeroes extending closer and closer to the ninth in Boston.

It was while Philadelphia was batting in the sixth that the final score at Boston was posted — New York 3, Boston 2. A roar accompanied the posting, and Robinson looked over his shoulder at the scoreboard. All the Dodgers now knew they had to win this game. As for the Giants, they had won 37 of their last 44 games to clinch at least a tie for the pennant.

Two innings later, the Dodgers rallied. Two singles, a double, and another single enabled three Brooklyn runs to tie the game.

As the battle extended into the ninth, each team had 20-game winners on the mound: Don Newcombe for Brooklyn and Robin Roberts for Philadelphia. Duke Snider reached second base in the ninth inning with only one out before

Roberts retired Roy Campanella and Andy Pafko to send the game into extra innings.

In the 10th the Phillies put the winning run on second with two down, but Newcombe fanned Del Ennis to keep Brooklyn hopes alive.

The Dodgers also got a runner to second base with two outs in the 11th, but Roberts got Robinson on a pop-up for the third out. In the bottom half, with a runner aboard and two outs, Andy Seminick drilled a liner down the left field line that was targeted for two bases and possibly the winning run. But Pafko made a sensational catch to save the day for Brooklyn.

The tattered honor of Flatbush hung by a thread in the 12th as the Phillies loaded the bases with only one out. Here Newcombe again fanned Ennis. But when Eddie Waitkus smacked a line drive to the right of the second base bag, it appeared to most that the game was over. Riding the train from Boston to New York, the Giants players could only listen to the announcers describe a remarkable diving catch by Robinson. Jackie fell hard and writhed in pain, but surrounded by relieved teammates, groggily walked toward the dugout to a non-partisan standing ovation.

Philadelphia threatened again in the 13th. With two down, a tiring Newcombe walked both Seminick and Roberts. Reliever Bud Podbielan came in to record the third out.

Roberts retired the first two batters in the 14th when Robinson stepped to the plate. On a 1–1 count, Jackie drove a towering fly into the left field upper deck, bringing Dodgers' president Walter O'Malley, general manager Buzzie Bavasi, and their wives out of their seats in near hysteria. For the first time in the game, the Dodgers led.

But the drama hadn't ended. Ashburn led off in the home half with a sharp single to left and was sacrificed to second. Ennis worked the count full before popping out to first. Waitkus, who nearly ended it earlier, now lifted an easy fly ball to left. As Pafko clutched it, several hundred Dodger fans swarmed onto the field and mobbed their heroes, who would soon begin a dramatic playoff series with the Giants. Upon reaching the train station in Brooklyn, Robinson was greeted with placards that read "Jackie Robinson for Borough President."

# 24 Ruth Tosses a 14-Inning Masterpiece

BROOKLYN (NL) at BOSTON (AL)
Monday, October 9, 1916, Braves Field
Red Sox 2, Robins 1

Modern baseball fans, on reading accounts of Game Two of the 1916 World Series, may be scandalized by the goings-on at Braves Field that October afternoon. There were the expected events, of course: great outfield catches, right-hander versus left-hander strategic moves, hair-raising plays at the plate, defensive decoys. But, in addition, the game had to be halted at one point because fans were making too much noise, a shortstop purposely caused a baserunner to trip and crash to the ground on his way to third, a batter was removed in mid-count because he failed to bunt successfully, and betting odds were openly discussed and changed throughout the contest. Regardless, *New York Times* columnist Hugh Fullerton called it the greatest World Series game ever played.

In 1916, to take advantage of greater seating capacity, the American League Boston Red Sox played their home World Series games in the National League Park just a short distance away. Braves Field had the largest outfield in the major leagues, the closest fence being more than 400 feet away from home plate.

Gray skies greeted the 44,000 spectators for Game Two. On the mound for the visiting Brooklyn Robins was left-hander Sherry Smith, whom reporters denounced as a second-rate hurler. Pitching for the home club was the American League's best pitcher — 21-year-old Babe Ruth. The young southpaw had fashioned a 23–12 record with a league-leading 1.75 ERA. Smith proved the scribes wrong, for despite one scoring opportunity after another, a pitcher's duel ensued.

Brooklyn scored first. With two outs in the top of the first, Hy Myers sent a long line drive to spacious right-center field that scooted between the outfielders and rolled to the distant fence for an inside-the-park home run. The Robins had another scoring opportunity in the third when Smith lined a ball down the right field line, but outfielder Harry Hooper made a swift recovery and threw him out as the Robin tried for a triple.

Boston finally got into the scoring column in the third when Everett Scott led off with a triple, bringing to life the home crowd. They erupted when Ruth's ground-out allowed Scott to score.

In the fifth, with two outs, Boston's Pinch Thomas was rudely interrupted in his bid for a triple. About halfway between second and third, Brooklyn shortstop Ivy Olsen tripped him, nearly precipitating a battle royal. Umpire Bill

| Brooklyn | AB | R | H | I |
|---|---|---|---|---|
| Johnston J, rf | 5 | 0 | 1 | 0 |
| Daubert J, 1b | 5 | 0 | 0 | 0 |
| Myers H, cf | 6 | 1 | 1 | 1 |
| Wheat Z, lf | 5 | 0 | 0 | 0 |
| Cutshaw G, 2b | 5 | 0 | 0 | 0 |
| Mowrey M, 3b | 5 | 0 | 1 | 0 |
| Olsen I, ss | 2 | 0 | 1 | 0 |
| Miller O, c | 5 | 0 | 1 | 0 |
| Smith S, p | 5 | 0 | 1 | 0 |
| | 43 | 1 | 6 | 1 |

| Boston | AB | R | H | I |
|---|---|---|---|---|
| Hooper H, rf | 6 | 0 | 1 | 0 |
| Janvrin H, 2b | 6 | 0 | 1 | 0 |
| Walker T, cf | 3 | 0 | 0 | 0 |
| Walsh J, ph-cf | 3 | 0 | 0 | 0 |
| Hoblitzel D, 1b | 2 | 0 | 0 | 0 |
| McNally M, pr | 0 | 1 | 0 | 0 |
| Lewis D, lf | 3 | 0 | 1 | 0 |
| Gardner L, 3b | 5 | 0 | 0 | 0 |
| Gainer D, ph | 1 | 0 | 1 | 1 |
| Scott E, ss | 4 | 1 | 2 | 0 |
| Thomas P, c | 4 | 0 | 1 | 0 |
| Ruth B, p | 5 | 0 | 0 | 1 |
| | 42 | 2 | 7 | 2 |

| Brooklyn | IP | H | R | ER | BB | SO |
|---|---|---|---|---|---|---|
| Smith (L) | 13.1 | 7 | 2 | 2 | 6 | 2 |

| Boston | IP | H | R | ER | BB | SO |
|---|---|---|---|---|---|---|
| Ruth (W) | 14.0 | 6 | 1 | 1 | 3 | 4 |

| Brooklyn | 100 | 000 | 000 | 000 | 00 — 1 |
|---|---|---|---|---|---|
| Boston | 001 | 000 | 000 | 000 | 01 — 2 |

OB: Brooklyn 5, Boston 9; ER: Cutshaw, Mowrey, Gardner; DP: Brooklyn 2, Boston 1; 2B: Smith, Janvrin; 3B: Scott, Thomas; HR: Myers; CS: Johnston 2; SH: Lewis 2, Olsen 2, Thomas; TI: 2:29; AT: 47,373; UM: HP Dinneen, All Bases Quigley, RF Connolly, LF O'Day

Dinneen quickly separated the combatants and awarded Thomas third base. This further incited the crowd, who continued to howl at every opportunity. It all went for naught, however, when Smith next fanned Ruth on three swings.

The Red Sox were robbed of a scoring opportunity again in the sixth when Hooper sent a sinking line drive into center only to see Hy Myers make the defensive play of the day with a running, tumbling, shoe-top catch.

With runners at the corners and only one out in the eighth, Brooklyn looked as if they finally might take the lead, but Smith grounded to a drawn-in infield, starting an involved rundown. Ruth eventually tagged out Mike Mowrey at home. The Babe then retired the next batter to preserve the 1–1 tie and further energize the now frenzied fans.

Myers once again saved the game for Brooklyn in the bottom of the ninth. It was a sudden-death situation as the Red Sox put runners at the corners with no outs. Dick Hoblitzel next lined sharply to center, but Myers caught it and fired home. The runner on third tagged and tried to score the game winner, but the throw was perfect. Smith continued his mastery, sending the game into extra innings.

The Royal Rooters, that vociferous group of Sox fans whose members attended all the games and even composed their own band, delighted in agitating the opposition with derisive songs. They were now fueled by the fact that while Smith was apparently tiring, Ruth grew stronger with each passing inning. By the time Brooklyn batted in the eleventh, manager Wilbert Robinson could stand the mayhem no longer. Calling time, he approached chief umpire Dinneen and had the Royal Rooter band stopped, a move that incited more cheering, flag waving, and verbal abuse.

Meanwhile, Ruth iced the Robins' bats, allowing not a hit after the eighth inning. Now in the home half of the 14th, Boston finally reached a tiring Smith. A leadoff walk and sacrifice put the winning run in scoring position. Pinch-hitter Del Gainer then cracked a single into a left field so dark that many could not follow the flight of the ball. Brooklyn left fielder Zack Wheat desperately tried to hurry a throw home, but it was off line, and the Royal Rooters struck up their band once again.

# 25 Buckner's Unfortunate Error

BOSTON (AL) at NEW YORK (NL)
Saturday, October 25, 1986, Shea Stadium
Mets 6, Red Sox 5

Baseball history is littered with crucial defensive misplays and mistakes in judgment. Some, like Ruth's caught-stealing to end the 1926 World Series, have brought an abrupt conclusion to a team's season, leaving no chance for redemption. Others, not quite as grave, have gained in perceived importance with the passing of time. The Merkle Boner, an innocent action that was often overlooked in its time, has since been elevated to the level of damnable offense for having cost the Giants the pennant in 1908. But few consider that the Giants had several weeks remaining in their season to offset the gaffe. Game Six of the 1986 Fall Classic provided the annals with another such lapse that, while serious, perhaps unfairly stigmatized a player with the onus of a lost season.

Looking for their first championship in 68 campaigns, the Boston Red Sox were now on the verge, leading the New York Mets three series games to two. A victory this night would ignite Beantown and liberate the frustrated souls of players who had previously guided the Sox to three seventh-game World Series losses and 11 second-place American League finishes.

The storybook game began as a duel between the teams' best pitchers — Boston's Roger Clemens and New York's Bob Ojeda — but ended as a battle of bullpens and memorable late rallies.

Boston hopes initially were aroused when the Sox scored a run in each of first two frames. Dwight Evans doubled home a run in the first, and Marty Barrett singled home another in the second. Behind the 24-4 Clemens, who allowed no hits through the first four innings, it appeared the 68-year drought might end.

In the fifth the Mets finally dented the hitting and the scoring columns.

Stanley walks off the field as the Mets celebrate (National Baseball Hall of Fame Library, Cooperstown, New York).

Darryl Strawberry led off with a single, stole second and scored on Ray Knight's single. Another single, an error and a double play allowed Knight to tally an unearned run, making it 2–2.

The Red Sox regained the lead in the seventh thanks in part to a throwing error by Knight. They nearly added a fourth run, but Mookie Wilson threw out Jim Rice at the plate.

With a 3–2 lead, Boston nearly broke it open in the eighth as they loaded the bases with two outs. But Jesse Orosco extinguished the fire by retiring Bill Buckner on a fly ball to center. During the futile rally Clemens was lifted for a pinch-hitter. The ace right-hander had developed a blister on the middle finger of his pitching hand and felt it had compromised his effectiveness. It was about this time that a Boston clubhouse man asked to borrow the Mets' champagne because the visitors had left theirs home. Twenty cases were sent to the Sox' dressing room.

Needing just six outs for their long awaited championship, ace reliever Calvin Schiraldi assumed the Boston pitching duties. The right-hander, thanks to two misplayed bunts, quickly got into trouble by allowing the Mets to load the bases with only one out. With the frantic crowd roaring, Gary Carter hit a sacrifice fly to tie the game at three, but Schiraldi escaped any further damage.

The Mets blew a golden opportunity to win it in the bottom of the ninth. A walk and an error put their first two men aboard, but Schiraldi disposed of pinch-hitter Howard Johnson, Lee Mazzilli, and Lenny Dykstra to send it into extra innings.

| Boston | AB | R | H | I |
|---|---|---|---|---|
| Boggs W, 3b | 5 | 2 | 3 | 0 |
| Barrett M, 2b | 4 | 1 | 3 | 2 |
| Buckner B, 1b | 5 | 0 | 0 | 0 |
| Rice J, lf | 5 | 0 | 0 | 0 |
| Evans D, rf | 4 | 0 | 1 | 2 |
| Gedman R, c | 5 | 0 | 1 | 0 |
| Henderson D, cf | 5 | 1 | 2 | 1 |
| Owen S, ss | 4 | 1 | 3 | 0 |
| Clemens R, p | 3 | 0 | 0 | 0 |
| Greenwell M, ph | 1 | 0 | 0 | 0 |
| Schiraldi C, p | 1 | 0 | 0 | 0 |
| Stanley B, p | 0 | 0 | 0 | 0 |
|  | 42 | 5 | 13 | 5 |

| New York | AB | R | H | I |
|---|---|---|---|---|
| Dykstra L, cf | 4 | 0 | 0 | 0 |
| Backman W, 2b | 4 | 0 | 1 | 0 |
| Hernandez K, 1b | 4 | 0 | 1 | 0 |
| Carter G, c | 4 | 1 | 1 | 1 |
| Strawberry D, rf | 2 | 1 | 0 | 0 |
| Aguilera R, p | 0 | 0 | 0 | 0 |
| Mitchell K, ph | 1 | 1 | 1 | 0 |
| Knight R, 3b | 4 | 2 | 2 | 2 |
| Wilson M, lf | 5 | 0 | 1 | 0 |
| Santana R, ss | 1 | 0 | 0 | 0 |
| Heep D, ph | 1 | 0 | 0 | 0 |
| Elster K, ss | 1 | 0 | 0 | 0 |
| Johnson H, ph-ss | 1 | 0 | 0 | 0 |
| Ojeda B, p | 2 | 0 | 0 | 0 |
| McDowell R, p | 0 | 0 | 0 | 0 |
| Orosco J, p | 0 | 0 | 0 | 0 |
| Mazzilli L, ph-rf | 2 | 1 | 1 | 0 |
|  | 36 | 6 | 8 | 3 |

| Boston | IP | H | R | ER | BB | SO |
|---|---|---|---|---|---|---|
| Clemens | 7.0 | 4 | 2 | 1 | 2 | 8 |
| Schiraldi (L) | 2.2 | 4 | 4 | 3 | 2 | 1 |
| Stanley | 0.0 | 0 | 0 | 0 | 0 | 0 |
|  | 9.2 | 8 | 6 | 4 | 4 | 9 |

| New York | IP | H | R | ER | BB | SO |
|---|---|---|---|---|---|---|
| Ojeda | 6.0 | 8 | 2 | 2 | 2 | 3 |
| McDowell | 1.2 | 2 | 1 | 0 | 3 | 1 |
| Orosco | 0.1 | 0 | 0 | 0 | 0 | 0 |
| Aguilera (W) | 2.0 | 3 | 2 | 2 | 0 | 3 |
|  | 10.0 | 13 | 5 | 4 | 5 | 7 |

| Boston | 110 | 000 | 100 | 2 — 5 |
|---|---|---|---|---|
| New York | 000 | 020 | 010 | 3 — 6 |

OB: Boston 14, New York 8; ER: Evans, Knight, Elster, Gedman, Buckner; DP: Boston 1, New York 1; 2B: Evans, Boggs; HR: Henderson; SB: Strawberry 2; SH: Owen, Dykstra, Backman; SF: Carter; HP: by Aguilera (Buckner); WP: Stanley; TI: 4:02; AT: 55,078; UM: HP Ford, 1B Kibler, 2B Evans, 3B Wendelstedt, LF Brinkman, RF Montague

When Dave Henderson led off the Boston 10th with a home run, it looked as if the Sox finally had their championship. And when Barrett followed Wade Boggs's double with an RBI single, a celebration seemed certain.

In the bottom of the tenth Schiraldi retired the first two batters, and the message board in left briefly flashed: "Congratulations, Red Sox." With a 2–1 count on Carter, Boston was only two strikes away from World Series' rings. But Carter singled, as did rookie pinch-hitter Kevin Mitchell. Schiraldi then got two strikes on Knight, needing just one more to end it, but the veteran third baseman atoned for his earlier error by singling and making it 5–4. With runners at the corners, Bob Stanley replaced Schiraldi. Wilson fouled off several pitches before Stanley uncorked a wild pitch that enabled Mitchell to score the tying run and moved Knight to second. After fouling off several more offerings, Wilson grounded a ball toward first, tight to the line. The behobbled Buckner managed to square himself in front of the slow grounder, but the ball slipped under his glove and trickled into right field. Knight raced home as the Mets erupted from their dugout. A miraculous comeback had transpired, and Boston's haunted past had risen spectre-like once again.

# *Wrigley Winds Were Blowing Straight Out* 26

PHILADELPHIA (NL) at CHICAGO (NL)
Thursday, May 17, 1979, Wrigley Field
Phillies 23, Cubs 22

Mother Nature was as responsible for making this one of the greatest games of the century as were the players. With a strong wind blowing out from home plate toward the ivy-covered walls, players and announcers alike predicted plenty of scoring before this game even began.

Each starting pitcher retired but one batter, although Philadelphia left-hander Randy Lerch contributed to the mayhem with a home run before throwing his first pitch. Routine fly balls were blown away from fielders and beyond the outfield walls with such regularity that fans witnessed 23 hits and 21 runs before the home team batted in the third inning. Phillies announcer Richie Ashburn pleaded to "get the married men off the field" as managers began looking for volunteers to take the mound. Retired as a player for 17 years, Ashburn longed to "go down there and grab a bat."

Through four and one-half innings, the elements seemed to favor the visitors, with the Phillies grabbing a 21–9 lead. In the top of the fifth, Nino Espinosa, a hurler who mercifully would not pitch this day, came off the bench to pinch run and eventually was forced himself to bat.

But Cubs manager Herman Franks knew that his club had plenty of outs before succumbing. In the middle of the fifth, the momentum shifted as Chicago rallied for seven runs, making it 21–16. The fireworks included two home runs, one a grand slam by Bill Buckner. The Cubs added three more in the sixth, making it 21–19.

Though the Phils added an insurance run in the top of the seventh, the momentum was still clearly on the side of the home team. Chicago had mauled the best of the visitors' relievers, and the Philadelphia audience felt as if they were at the mercy of Cub bats. Sure enough, Chicago scored three more runs in the bottom of the eighth to complete their miraculous comeback. With the score tied at 22 and Chicago ace reliever Bruce Sutter in the game, the odds now favored the home team.

Philadelphia failed to score in the top of the ninth and called on Rawley Eastwick to carry them into extra innings. The erratic reliever carried an ERA of 8.00, but he set down the Cubs in order for the first time in the game.

Sutter routinely retired the first two Phillies in the top of the 10th. Then Mike Schmidt, who had homered nearly four hours earlier, picked a high fastball

| Philadelphia | AB | R | H | I |
|---|---|---|---|---|
| McBride B, rf | 8 | 2 | 3 | 1 |
| Bowa L, ss | 8 | 4 | 5 | 1 |
| Rose P, 1b | 7 | 4 | 3 | 4 |
| Schmidt M, 3b | 4 | 3 | 2 | 4 |
| Unser D, lf | 7 | 1 | 1 | 2 |
| Maddox G, cf | 4 | 3 | 4 | 4 |
| Gross G, pr-cf | 2 | 1 | 1 | 1 |
| Boone B, c | 4 | 2 | 3 | 5 |
| Meoli R, 2b | 5 | 0 | 1 | 0 |
| Lerch R, p | 1 | 1 | 1 | 1 |
| Bird D, p | 1 | 1 | 0 | 0 |
| Luzinski G, ph | 0 | 0 | 0 | 0 |
| Espinosa N, pr-ph | 1 | 1 | 0 | 0 |
| McGraw T, p | 0 | 0 | 0 | 0 |
| Reed R, p | 0 | 0 | 0 | 0 |
| McCarver T, ph | 1 | 0 | 0 | 0 |
| Eastwick R, p | 0 | 0 | 0 | 0 |
| | 53 | 23 | 24 | 23 |

| Chicago | AB | R | H | I |
|---|---|---|---|---|
| DeJesus I, ss | 6 | 4 | 3 | 1 |
| Vail M, rf | 5 | 2 | 3 | 1 |
| Burris R, p | 0 | 0 | 0 | 0 |
| Thompson S, ph-rf | 2 | 1 | 1 | 0 |
| Buckner B, 1b | 7 | 2 | 4 | 7 |
| Kingman D, lf | 6 | 4 | 3 | 6 |
| Ontiveros S, 3b | 7 | 2 | 1 | 1 |
| Martin J, cf | 6 | 2 | 3 | 3 |
| Sutter B, p | 0 | 0 | 0 | 0 |
| Foote B, c | 6 | 1 | 3 | 1 |
| Sizemore T, 2b | 4 | 2 | 2 | 1 |
| Caudill B, p | 0 | 0 | 0 | 0 |
| Murcer B, ph-rf | 2 | 0 | 1 | 0 |
| Lamp D, p | 0 | 0 | 0 | 0 |
| Moore D, p | 1 | 0 | 1 | 1 |
| Hernandez W, p | 1 | 0 | 0 | 0 |
| Dillard S, ph-2b | 1 | 2 | 1 | 0 |
| Biittner L, ph | 1 | 0 | 0 | 0 |
| Kelleher M, 2b | 1 | 0 | 0 | 0 |
| | 56 | 22 | 26 | 22 |

| Philadelphia | IP | H | R | ER | BB | SO |
|---|---|---|---|---|---|---|
| Lerch | 0.1 | 5 | 5 | 5 | 0 | 0 |
| Bird | 3.2 | 8 | 4 | 4 | 0 | 2 |
| McGraw | 0.2 | 4 | 7 | 4 | 3 | 1 |
| Reed | 3.1 | 9 | 6 | 6 | 0 | 0 |
| Eastwick (W) | 2.0 | 0 | 0 | 0 | 0 | 1 |
| | 10.0 | 26 | 22 | 19 | 3 | 4 |

| Chicago | IP | H | R | ER | BB | SO |
|---|---|---|---|---|---|---|
| Lamp | 0.1 | 6 | 6 | 6 | 0 | 0 |
| Moore | 2.0 | 6 | 7 | 7 | 2 | 1 |
| Hernandez | 2.2 | 7 | 8 | 6 | 7 | 1 |
| Caudill | 1.1 | 2 | 1 | 1 | 2 | 3 |
| Burris | 1.2 | 1 | 0 | 0 | 0 | 0 |
| Sutter (L) | 2.0 | 2 | 1 | 1 | 1 | 1 |
| | 10.0 | 24 | 23 | 21 | 12 | 6 |

Philadelphia   708   240   100   1 — 23
Chicago        600   373   030   0 — 22

OB: Philadelphia 15, Chicago 7; ER: Kingman, DeJesus, Schmidt 2; DP: Philadelphia 2; 2B: Bowa 2, Martin, Maddox 2, Rose 2, Foote, DeJesus, Boone; 3B: Moore, Gross; HR: Schmidt 2, Boone, Lerch, Maddox, Buckner, Martin, Kingman 3, Ontiveros; SB: Bowa, Meoli; SF: Unser, Gross; HP: by Hernandez (Boone); TI: 4:03; AT: 14,952; UM: HP Cavenaugh, Pomponi, Maher, Riccio

and drove it far beyond the left field ivy, giving his club a 23–22 edge. Eastwick again retired three consecutive batters in the bottom of the 10th to elicit a sigh of relief from Philadelphians. Meanwhile, Chicago players and fans alike sat stunned as one of the greatest offensive shows of the century ended with barely a whimper.

# Detroit's Greatest Opening Day *27*

MILWAUKEE (AL) at DETROIT (AL)
Thursday, April 25, 1901, Bennett Park
Tigers 14, Brewers 13

The newly declared major league, the American League, marked its second day in business with one of its greatest games when the club from Detroit emerged victorious from a ninth-inning, 13–4 deficit.

For both the visitors from Milwaukee and the Tigers, this marked the first league game. The scene was Bennett Park, located at Michigan and Trumbull Avenues, where later Navin Field, Briggs Stadium, and Tiger Stadium would stand. Capacity in the wooden structure was approximately 8,000, but for this inaugural match the humanity that engulfed the park numbered more than 10,000. The overflow, mostly in the outfield, eventually affected the game's outcome as it was agreed that balls hit into the masses would be ground-rule doubles.

The Brewers jumped out to a 7–0 lead after three innings, thanks in part to five Tiger errors. After six innings it was 7–3, and Milwaukee manager Hugh Duffy decided to remove starter Pink Hawley and give another pitcher, Pete Dowling, some work. Duffy's crew tacked on three more runs in both the seventh and eighth, giving them a very comfortable 13–3 edge. Detroit added a fourth run in the bottom of the eighth.

The visitors went down in order in the top of the ninth, setting the stage for Detroit's miraculous deliverance. Here's how it happened:

• Doc Casey led off with a ground-rule double into the crowd standing in left field.

• Jimmy Barrett beat out a slow roller toward third base while Casey moved to third.

• Kid Gleason singled to center, knocking in Casey and making it 13–5.

• When Ducky Holmes doubled home Barrett, the crowd enthusiasm intensified, unnerving Dowling.

• Pop Dillon also drove a ball into the crowd for a ground-rule double, sending home Gleason and Holmes, and making it 13–8.

• Kid Elberfeld notched the Tigers' third consecutive double, this one into the crowd in right-center. Dillon scored and Detroit trailed by only four runs. At this point player-manager Duffy walked in from his center field position and ordered Dowling from the mound in favor of Bert Husting.

| Milwaukee | AB | R | H | I |
|---|---|---|---|---|
| Waldron I, rf | 5 | 1 | 0 | 0 |
| Gilbert B, 2b | 6 | 1 | 3 | 0 |
| Hallman B, lf | 5 | 1 | 0 | 0 |
| Anderson J, 1b | 4 | 1 | 2 | 0 |
| Conroy W, ss | 5 | 4 | 4 | 3 |
| Duffy H, cf | 4 | 2 | 1 | 1 |
| Burke J, 3b | 5 | 2 | 3 | 4 |
| Leahy T, c | 4 | 1 | 1 | 1 |
| Hawley P, p | 3 | 0 | 1 | 2 |
| Dowling P, p | 1 | 0 | 1 | 0 |
| Husting B, p | 0 | 0 | 0 | 0 |
|  | 42 | 13 | 16 | 11 |

| Detroit | AB | R | H | I |
|---|---|---|---|---|
| Casey D, 3b | 6 | 3 | 2 | 0 |
| Barrett J, cf | 5 | 1 | 1 | 0 |
| Gleason K, 2b | 6 | 2 | 3 | 2 |
| Holmes D, rf | 6 | 2 | 2 | 2 |
| Dillon P, 1b | 6 | 3 | 4 | 5 |
| Elberfeld K, ss | 4 | 1 | 2 | 2 |
| Nance D, lf | 5 | 0 | 1 | 1 |
| Buelow F, c | 4 | 1 | 1 | 0 |
| Miller R, p | 0 | 0 | 0 | 0 |
| Frisk E, p | 5 | 1 | 3 | 1 |
|  | 47 | 14 | 19 | 13 |

| Milwaukee | IP | H | R | ER | BB | SO |
|---|---|---|---|---|---|---|
| Hawley | 6.0 | 5 | 3 | 2 | 1 | 0 |
| Dowling | 2.0 | 10 | 7 | 7 | 1 | 3 |
| Husting (L) | 0.2 | 4 | 4 | 0 | 1 | 1 |
|  | 8.2 | 19 | 14 | 9 | 3 | 4 |

| Detroit | IP | H | R | ER | BB | SO |
|---|---|---|---|---|---|---|
| Miller | 2.1 | 6 | 7 | 4 | 1 | 0 |
| Frisk (W) | 6.2 | 10 | 6 | 6 | 3 | 2 |
|  | 9.0 | 16 | 13 | 10 | 4 | 2 |

```
Milwaukee    025  000     330 — 13
Detroit      000  210   01 (10) — 14
```

OB: Milwaukee 8, Detroit 10; ER: Hallman, Conroy, Burke 2, Gleason, Holmes, Dillon, Nance, Elberfeld 3; 2B: Conroy, Duffy, Burke, Casey, Gleason, Dillon 4, Elberfeld 2; SB: Casey, Gleason; SH: Hallman, Leahy; WP: Dowling, Husting, Frisk; PB: Leahy; TI: 2:35; AT: 10,023; UM: Sheridan, Mannassau

• Doc Nance grounded out for the first Tiger out of the frame, but the game had to be temporarily halted. The frenzied crowd had encroached on the out-fielders, making play impossible. To avoid the possibility of forfeit, Detroit players ran from their bench and pushed the throng back toward the outfield walls.

• Fritz Buelow, the eighth Detroit batter this inning, walked; the home-town crowd began throwing hats and coats into the air.

• Emil Frisk fueled the frenzy by singling to left and driving home Elber-feld. It was then 13–10.

• Casey made his second plate appearance of the inning and beat out a bunt, loading the sacks.

• Barrett temporarily silenced the multitude by striking out for the second out. The Tigers still trailed by three runs.

• Gleason hit a sharp grounder to third that should have ended the con-test, but Jimmy Burke fumbled it, allowing Buelow to score Detroit's 11th run.

• Holmes beat out a slow roller to third that made it 13–12.

• Dillon delivered the coup de grâce by again doubling into the crowd. Casey scored the tying run and Gleason was right behind him with the win-ning tally.

With Dillon's double, the delirious multitude surged onto the field, hoisted Pop to their shoulders and paraded in triumph around the grounds.

# Tigers Overcome a 12-Run Deficit 28

CHICAGO (AL) at DETROIT (AL)
Sunday, June 18, 1911, Bennett Park
Tigers 16, White Sox 15

Baseball record keepers, fans, and players had never witnessed anything like it. Trailing by 12 runs after four and one-half innings, the Detroit Tigers clawed their way back to emerge victorious.

In the early rounds, the game belonged entirely to the Chicago White Sox and their veteran hurler Doc White. The Sox routed Tiger starter Ed Summers in the very first inning with seven runs on five hits and three walks. The Tigers reacted with a token run in the second, but Chicago piled on three more in each of the fourth and fifth frames. White was coasting with a 13–1 lead, but things soon began to unravel.

Detroit chipped away with four runs in their half of the fifth and three in the sixth, making it 13–8. Batting for himself in the seventh, White started another Chicago rally that produced two additional runs. They were the last runs scored by the visitors, who then held a 15–8 advantage. At this point, Chicago manager Hugh Duffy replaced White with Fred Olmstead.

Olmstead temporarily halted the Tiger comeback with a shutout seventh inning. He was not so fortunate in the eighth, however. Two walks and five singles pushed five more runs across for Detroit, narrowing the gap to 15–13 with only two outs. Future Hall of Famer Ed Walsh, whom the Detroit *Free Press* referred to as "the imperial guard of Duffy's army," was summoned to extinguish the rally. Walsh did just that by fanning pinch-hitter Biff Schaller to end the inning and preserve Chicago's fragile two-run lead.

Walsh still looked overpowering in the bottom of the ninth when he struck out the first Tiger batter. But Davey Jones singled and Donie Bush doubled him to third. That brought to the plate Ty Cobb, who already had four hits. On a 2–1 pitch, the speedy Cobb chopped a high bouncer toward third baseman Harry Lord. Lord's hurried throw and Cobb arrived at first almost simultaneously, both in the dirt. Ty started to slide about 10 feet before the bag, kicking up a dust storm and actually colliding with the first baseman. The ball was lost in the confusion, and as it rolled into foul territory, Cobb raced to second while both runners scored. The game was now tied, and Cobb, hatless, pants torn, and covered in dirt, danced around the keystone sack taunting Walsh and the White Sox.

Cobb's derision continued as Wahoo Sam Crawford stepped into the batters box. With a 2–1 count, Crawford blistered Walsh's next offering over the head of the center fielder, enabling Cobb to score the game winner uncontested. Most of the hometown fans had left early in disgust, but the loyal few who

| Chicago | AB | R | H | I |
|---|---|---|---|---|
| McIntyre M, rf | 5 | 4 | 4 | 2 |
| Lord H, 3b | 6 | 2 | 4 | 3 |
| Callahan N, lf | 5 | 1 | 1 | 2 |
| Bodie P, cf | 4 | 1 | 1 | 1 |
| Zeider R, ss | 5 | 2 | 0 | 0 |
| Collins S, 1b | 4 | 0 | 0 | 0 |
| Tannehill L, 2b | 4 | 1 | 2 | 0 |
| Payne F, c | 5 | 2 | 2 | 2 |
| White D, p | 3 | 2 | 2 | 1 |
| Olmstead F, p | 1 | 0 | 0 | 0 |
| Walsh E, p | 0 | 0 | 0 | 0 |
| | 42 | 15 | 16 | 11 |

| Detroit | AB | R | H | I |
|---|---|---|---|---|
| Drake D, lf | 4 | 1 | 0 | 0 |
| Jones D, ph-lf | 1 | 1 | 1 | 0 |
| Bush D, ss | 5 | 3 | 1 | 2 |
| Cobb T, cf | 6 | 3 | 5 | 5 |
| Crawford S, rf | 5 | 2 | 3 | 3 |
| Delahanty J, 1b | 4 | 0 | 1 | 3 |
| Moriarty G, 3b | 5 | 1 | 1 | 1 |
| O'Leary C, 2b | 5 | 1 | 3 | 0 |
| Stanage O, c | 3 | 1 | 1 | 0 |
| Casey J, c | 1 | 1 | 1 | 0 |
| Schaller B, ph | 1 | 0 | 0 | 0 |
| Schmidt B, c | 0 | 0 | 0 | 0 |
| Summers E, p | 0 | 0 | 0 | 0 |
| Works R, p | 1 | 0 | 1 | 1 |
| Mullin G, ph | 1 | 0 | 1 | 0 |
| Covington B, p | 1 | 1 | 1 | 0 |
| Mitchell C, p | 1 | 1 | 1 | 0 |
| Lathers C, ph | 1 | 0 | 0 | 0 |
| | 45 | 16 | 21 | 15 |

| Chicago | IP | H | R | ER | BB | SO |
|---|---|---|---|---|---|---|
| White | 6.0 | 12 | 8 | 8 | 1 | 2 |
| Olmstead | 1.2 | 5 | 5 | 5 | 2 | 0 |
| Walsh (L) | 0.2 | 4 | 3 | 3 | 0 | 2 |
| | 8.1 | 21 | 16 | 16 | 3 | 4 |

| Detroit | IP | H | R | ER | BB | SO |
|---|---|---|---|---|---|---|
| Summers | 0.1 | 4 | 7 | 4 | 2 | 0 |
| Works | 4.2 | 5 | 6 | 4 | 2 | 2 |
| Covington | 2.0 | 5 | 2 | 2 | 0 | 3 |
| Mitchell (W) | 2.0 | 2 | 0 | 0 | 0 | 2 |
| | 9.0 | 16 | 15 | 10 | 6 | 7 |

| Chicago | 700 | 330 | 200 — 15 |
|---|---|---|---|
| Detroit | 010 | 043 | 053 — 16 |

OB: Chicago 8, Detroit 8; ER: Lord, Payne, Bush, Cobb, Stanage 2; DP: Chicago 1; 2B: Bush, Crawford; 3B: Cobb, Crawford, Lord, Payne; SB: Lord, Callahan, Zeider 2; CS: Bodie; SH: Callahan, Collins; HP: by Olmstead (Delahanty); WP: Works, White; TI: 2:24; AT: 10,111; UM: Perrine, Dinneen

remained then madly poured onto the field and carried their heroes, Cobb and Crawford, to the clubhouse. Surmounting a 12-run deficit to victory would be seen just once more during the balance of the century.

# 29 *Athletics Overcome a 12-Run Deficit*

CLEVELAND (AL) at PHILADELPHIA (AL)
Monday, June 15, 1925, Shibe Park
Athletics 17, Indians 15

Of the more than 150,000 games played this century, the greatest deficit from which any team ever rebounded to win was 12. It happened twice, once in 1911 and again in June 1925.

The Philadelphia Athletics hosted the Cleveland Indians in Shibe Park, and the hurlers on both clubs were in a very generous mood. After a fruitless first, the Indians pounded five Philadelphia pitchers and scored in each of the next six innings. Twice Cleveland held 12-run advantages, and by the time the Athletics stepped to the plate in the eighth they trailed by a score of 15–3.

Philadelphia then pulled victory from the deepest hole in major league history.

- Chuck Galloway innocently led off with a base on balls.
- Manager Mack could see no reason to bother with a pinch-hitter for Tom Glass, the fifth A's hurler. Tom batted for himself and flied out to right.
- Max Bishop, sometimes called "Camera Eye" because of his affinity for walks, coaxed one of his specialties.
- Jimmy Dykes then ripped a line drive triple toward the scoreboard in right-center, driving both runners home. The score was then 15–6, causing little concern.
- Bill Lamar, on a 16-game hit streak, singled to center, knocking home Dykes. It was then 15–7.
- Cleveland player-manager Tris Speaker ordered By Speece to the hill. Al Simmons greeted him with a single that bounced strangely over the head of first baseman Ray Knode. *The Cleveland Plain Dealer* reported that the ball would have been an out if the Shibe Park turf had not been in such deplorable condition.
- Frank Welch, who earlier replaced an injured Bing Miller, also singled to right, scoring Lamar and making it 15–8.
- Connie Mack must have felt the game was still out of reach, because he then allowed Charlie Berry to bat — Charlie had his first major league at-bat only a few innings earlier. But the youngster continued the onslaught with an RBI single, however, pulling the A's to within six, at 15–9.
- Speaker had seen enough of Speece and relieved him with Carl Yowell. But Yowell then walked Jim Poole, loading the sacks.
- For the second time in the inning, Galloway batted. This time he lashed a single to left, driving home two mates. With the score then 15–11, Speaker had enough of his marginal pitchers and brought on his ace, George Uhle. This was a time-tested, dependable right-hander whom *The Cleveland Plain Dealer* dubbed "the flower of Mr. Speaker's casting corps."
- Tom Glass, the next scheduled hitter, had made the only out in the inning when it didn't much matter. Now Mack knew he had enough momentum to catch the Tribe, so he dispatched Sammy Hale to pinch-hit. Uhle induced Hale to hit a sharp grounder to short, but the ball took a bad hop over Joe Sewell's head for another single and another run, the A's 12th.
- In a bizarre strategic move, Hale sprinted toward second on an attempted steal. The ball and Hale arrived simultaneously, but when the sphere hit the runner, he was declared safe.

| Cleveland | AB | R | H | I |
|---|---|---|---|---|
| Jamieson C, lf | 6 | 2 | 5 | 3 |
| McNulty P, rf | 1 | 0 | 0 | 0 |
| Lee C, rf | 4 | 1 | 2 | 3 |
| Speaker T, cf | 6 | 1 | 2 | 2 |
| Sewell J, ss | 6 | 1 | 4 | 2 |
| Myatt G, c | 6 | 3 | 2 | 1 |
| Spurgeon F, 2b | 6 | 2 | 2 | 0 |
| Lutzke R, 3b | 4 | 2 | 2 | 0 |
| Knode R, 1b | 5 | 3 | 4 | 2 |
| Sewell L, ph | 1 | 0 | 0 | 0 |
| Miller J, p | 5 | 0 | 1 | 0 |
| Speece B, p | 0 | 0 | 0 | 0 |
| Yowell C, p | 0 | 0 | 0 | 0 |
| Uhle G, p | 0 | 0 | 0 | 0 |
|  | 50 | 15 | 24 | 13 |

| Philadelphia | AB | R | H | I |
|---|---|---|---|---|
| Bishop M, 2b | 4 | 1 | 2 | 2 |
| Dykes J, 3b | 6 | 2 | 2 | 2 |
| French W, pr | 0 | 1 | 0 | 0 |
| Lamar B, lf | 5 | 3 | 4 | 2 |
| Simmons A, cf | 6 | 2 | 3 | 3 |
| Miller B, rf | 2 | 0 | 0 | 0 |
| Welch F, rf | 3 | 1 | 1 | 2 |
| Perkins C, c | 2 | 0 | 0 | 0 |
| Berry C, c | 2 | 1 | 2 | 1 |
| Cochrane M, c | 0 | 0 | 0 | 0 |
| Poole J, 1b | 4 | 3 | 2 | 0 |
| Galloway C, ss | 3 | 2 | 2 | 3 |
| Rommel E, p | 0 | 0 | 0 | 0 |
| Baumgartner S, p | 0 | 0 | 0 | 0 |
| Foxx J, ph | 1 | 0 | 0 | 0 |
| Heimach F, p | 0 | 0 | 0 | 0 |
| Stokes A, p | 0 | 0 | 0 | 0 |
| Glass T, p | 1 | 0 | 0 | 0 |
| Hale S, ph-3b | 1 | 1 | 1 | 1 |
| Walberg R, p | 0 | 0 | 0 | 0 |
|  | 40 | 17 | 19 | 17 |

| Cleveland | IP | H | R | ER | BB | SO |
|---|---|---|---|---|---|---|
| Miller | 7.1 | 12 | 8 | 8 | 6 | 1 |
| Speece | 0.0 | 3 | 3 | 3 | 0 | 0 |
| Yowell | 0.0 | 1 | 2 | 2 | 1 | 0 |
| Uhle (L) | 0.2 | 3 | 4 | 4 | 1 | 0 |
|  | 8.0 | 19 | 17 | 17 | 8 | 1 |

| Philadelphia | IP | H | R | ER | BB | SO |
|---|---|---|---|---|---|---|
| Rommel | 1.1 | 3 | 4 | 4 | 1 | 0 |
| Baumgartner | 0.2 | 2 | 0 | 0 | 0 | 1 |
| Heimach | 1.1 | 6 | 4 | 4 | 0 | 1 |
| Stokes | 1.2 | 5 | 4 | 4 | 1 | 3 |
| Glass (W) | 3.0 | 7 | 3 | 2 | 0 | 1 |
| Walberg | 1.0 | 1 | 0 | 0 | 0 | 2 |
|  | 9.0 | 24 | 15 | 14 | 2 | 8 |

```
Cleveland      042  242  1    0   0 — 15
Philadelphia   011  001  1  (13)  x — 17
```

OB: Cleveland 11, Philadelphia 9; ER: Berry, Galloway; DP: Cleveland 2; 2B: Jamieson, Lee, Speaker, Dykes, Lamar, Poole; 3B: Lee, Dykes, Poole; HR: J. Sewell, Myatt, Simmons; SB: Jamieson, Myatt, Spurgeon, Lutzke, Hale; SF: Lee, Glass; HP: by J.Miller (Welch); WP: Rommel, Stokes; TI: 3:00; AT: 8,000; UM: Owens, Dinneen, Rowland

   • Next, Bishop singled to center driving home Galloway and Hale. The A's then trailed by only one run, 15–14.
   • Dykes sent a roller to short that might have been an inning-ending double play. But Dykes beat the throw to first after Bishop was forced at second. With two outs, Walt French entered the fray as a pinch runner for Dykes.
   • Bill Lamar, the next batter, was having his finest season (he would finish at .356) and had four hits thus far in the game. What happened next would be hotly debated in most baseball circles. With the tying run (French) on first, two outs, and clean-up hitter Al Simmons on deck, Lamar was intentionally walked, sending the tying run into scoring position. To make the strategy even more debatable, Simmons stepped to the plate carrying a .385 batting average. In Cleveland's defense, Lamar batted left-handed, Simmons right-handed, and Uhle threw right-handed.
   • Simmons didn't allow the fans or the press much time to debate the wisdom of the strategy, driving Uhle's third pitch high and far. It went so high that

it became only the second ball ever to land on the roof atop the upper deck in left. As Simmons rounded the bases, pandemonium erupted. Fans sailed straw hats and indiscriminate debris onto the field. Neighborhood rooftops that served as inexpensive bleachers had their construction severely tested as fans stomped feet and jumped for joy. The A's players hooted, howled, slapped each other's backs, and tossed their bats about. Even the venerable Connie Mack, normally stoic, tossed his scorecard into the air and shook hands with most of the team members while his son Earle, the nominal captain, turned cartwheels in front of the bench.

• After everyone settled down, Welch flied out to right for the final out of the inning.

The Athletics had been ruthlessly efficient. The nine players who got hits and the four players who walked all scored. No one was left on base in the inning. Rube Walberg then dismissed the Indians in the ninth to give the A's a share of the all-time comeback record. For A's hurler Tom Glass this was a very special game — his first major league victory and the last big-league game in which he ever pitched.

# *Dodgers Finally Win a Playoff* 30

MILWAUKEE (NL) at LOS ANGELES (NL)
Tuesday, September 29, 1959, Memorial Coliseum
Dodgers 6, Braves 5

While in Brooklyn, the Dodgers were involved in the National League's first two playoffs, bowing to both the Cardinals in 1946 and the Giants in 1951. Now, in just their second year on the West Coast, they were again tied for first after 154 games. It was an unexpected finish for Los Angeles, after holding first place in late April, they disappeared beneath the front-running Giants for most of the season. It wasn't until September 20, after sweeping San Francisco in a three game series, that they once again breathed first-place air. The remaining week of the regular season provided a thrilling conclusion as the Milwaukee Braves, pennant winners the last two seasons, finished with an identical record.

On a cold, drizzling night in Milwaukee, the Dodgers took Game One in

| Milwaukee | AB | R | H | I |
|---|---|---|---|---|
| Bruton B, cf | 6 | 0 | 0 | 0 |
| Mathews E, 3b | 4 | 2 | 2 | 1 |
| Aaron H, rf | 4 | 1 | 2 | 0 |
| Torre F, 1b | 3 | 0 | 1 | 2 |
| Maye L, lf | 2 | 0 | 0 | 0 |
| Pafko A, ph-lf | 1 | 0 | 0 | 0 |
| Slaughter E, ph | 1 | 0 | 0 | 0 |
| DeMerit J, lf | 0 | 0 | 0 | 0 |
| Spangler A, ph-lf | 0 | 0 | 0 | 0 |
| Logan J, ss | 3 | 1 | 2 | 0 |
| Schoendienst R, 2b | 1 | 0 | 0 | 0 |
| Vernon M, ph | 1 | 0 | 0 | 0 |
| Cottier C, 2b | 0 | 0 | 0 | 0 |
| Adcock J, ph | 1 | 0 | 0 | 0 |
| Avila B, 2b | 0 | 0 | 0 | 0 |
| Crandall D, c | 6 | 1 | 1 | 0 |
| Mantilla F, 2b-ss | 5 | 0 | 1 | 1 |
| Burdette L, p | 4 | 0 | 1 | 0 |
| McMahon D, p | 0 | 0 | 0 | 0 |
| Spahn W, p | 0 | 0 | 0 | 0 |
| Jay J, p | 1 | 0 | 0 | 0 |
| Rush B, p | 1 | 0 | 0 | 0 |
| | 44 | 5 | 10 | 4 |

| Los Angeles | AB | R | H | I |
|---|---|---|---|---|
| Gilliam J, 3b | 5 | 0 | 1 | 0 |
| Neal C, 2b | 6 | 2 | 2 | 1 |
| Moon W, rf-lf | 6 | 1 | 3 | 1 |
| Snider D, cf | 4 | 0 | 1 | 0 |
| Lillis B, pr | 0 | 1 | 0 | 0 |
| Williams S, p | 2 | 0 | 0 | 0 |
| Hodges G, 1b | 5 | 2 | 2 | 0 |
| Larker N, lf | 4 | 0 | 2 | 2 |
| Pignatano J, pr-c | 1 | 0 | 1 | 0 |
| Roseboro J, c | 3 | 0 | 0 | 0 |
| Furillo C, ph-rf | 2 | 0 | 2 | 1 |
| Wills M, ss | 5 | 0 | 1 | 0 |
| Drysdale D, p | 1 | 0 | 0 | 0 |
| Podres J, p | 1 | 0 | 0 | 0 |
| Churn C, p | 0 | 0 | 0 | 0 |
| Demeter D, ph | 1 | 0 | 0 | 0 |
| Koufax S, p | 0 | 0 | 0 | 0 |
| Labine C, p | 0 | 0 | 0 | 0 |
| Essegian C, ph | 0 | 0 | 0 | 0 |
| Fairly R, ph-cf | 2 | 0 | 0 | 0 |
| | 48 | 6 | 15 | 5 |

| Milwaukee | IP | H | R | ER | BB | SO |
|---|---|---|---|---|---|---|
| Burdette | 8.0 | 10 | 5 | 5 | 0 | 4 |
| McMahon | 0.0 | 1 | 0 | 0 | 0 | 0 |
| Spahn | 0.1 | 1 | 0 | 0 | 0 | 0 |
| Jay | 2.1 | 1 | 0 | 0 | 1 | 1 |
| Rush (L) | 1.0 | 2 | 1 | 0 | 1 | 0 |
| | 11.2 | 15 | 6 | 5 | 2 | 5 |

| Los Angeles | IP | H | R | ER | BB | SO |
|---|---|---|---|---|---|---|
| Drysdale | 4.1 | 6 | 4 | 3 | 2 | 3 |
| Podres | 2.1 | 3 | 0 | 0 | 1 | 1 |
| Churn | 1.1 | 1 | 1 | 1 | 0 | 0 |
| Koufax | 0.2 | 0 | 0 | 0 | 3 | 1 |
| Labine | 0.1 | 0 | 0 | 0 | 0 | 1 |
| Williams (W) | 3.0 | 0 | 0 | 0 | 3 | 3 |
| | 12.0 | 10 | 5 | 4 | 9 | 9 |

| Milwaukee | 210 | 010 | 010 | 000 — 5 |
|---|---|---|---|---|
| Los Angeles | 100 | 100 | 003 | 001 — 6 |

OB: Milwaukee 13, Los Angeles 11; ER: Snider, Neal, Mantilla 2; DP: Milwaukee 1, Los Angeles 1; 2B: Aaron; 3B: Neal, Crandall; HR: Neal, Mathews; CS: Moon; SF: Mantilla, Furillo; HP: by Jay (Pignatano); WP: Podres; PB: Pignatano; TI: 4:06; AT: 36,528; UM: HP Barlick, 1B Boggess, 2B Donatelli, 3B Conlan, LF Jackowski, RF Gorman

the best-of-three playoff. Game Two moved to warm Los Angeles and the Dodgers' new home, Memorial Coliseum, a structure never intended for baseball. Its distinguishing feature was a 42-foot-high screen in left field that was just 251 feet down the line. The scheduled starters for Game Two were Milwaukee's Lew Burdette, at 21–15, and the Dodgers' Don Drysdale, who carried a 17–13 mark.

Neither club wasted any time breaking into the scoring column. With one out in the first, Eddie Mathews singled, Hank Aaron doubled, and Frank Torre drove both home with a single. The Dodgers got one back in their half when Charley Neal tripled and Wally Moon singled him home.

Two singles and an error enabled the Braves to extend their lead to 3–1 in the second, and Burdette kept it that way until the fourth, when Neal lofted a high fly over the friendly screen.

In the fifth, Eddie Mathews clouted his 46th home run of the season down the right-field line. The third baseman's shot gave him the home run crown and the Braves a 4–2 advantage.

Milwaukee again threatened in the seventh. Mathews and Aaron singled, but Wally Moon's throw from right field caught Mathews trying for third. A wild pitch moved Aaron to third, and Torre walked before pinch-hitter Enos Slaughter popped out.

When Del Crandall tripled in the eighth and was driven home by Felix Mantilla's sacrifice fly, the Braves' lead extended to a comfortable 5–2. Burdette seemed to be strengthening as the Dodgers went down in order in the home half.

Once again the Braves threatened in the ninth when a young and wild Sandy Koufax walked the bases loaded after recording two outs. Clem Labine was summoned, and he temporarily relieved the tension by fanning pinch-hitter Mickey Vernon. But with a three-run lead and three outs to go, Vernon's strikeout didn't seem important at the time.

Burdette's apparent control of the game slipped sharply when the first three Dodgers singled in the ninth. With the bases loaded and the suspense nearly unbearable, Milwaukee's ace reliever, Don McMahon, was called to preserve the win. But the drama continued as Norm Larker singled home two runs, making it 5–4. Grizzled veteran Carl Furillo then hit a sacrifice fly to tie the game at five. When Maury Wills next singled, Los Angeles had runners at first and second with only one out and a chance to pull off a miraculous win. At this point, Joey Jay took the hill for Milwaukee and retired the next two Dodgers, sending the game into extra innings. Hollywood couldn't have written a better script.

Neither team got a hit in the 10th, but in the 11th both clubs loaded the bases. The Braves failed to score as pinch-hitter Joe Adcock grounded into a force-out. The Dodgers met the same fate when Neal also grounded out.

In the 12th Milwaukee went down in order, and it looked like the same fate awaited Los Angeles after the first two batters were retired. But Gil Hodges walked, and Joe Pignatano singled him to second. Furillo then drilled a sharp grounder through the box on which Mantilla made a brilliant stop. His desperate throw to first bounced past Torre, however, enabling Hodges to cross the plate, and sending the Dodgers on their way to the World Series.

Los Angeles had escaped multiple Milwaukee threats and fought tenaciously to get back in the game. Four times the Braves stranded a runner at third, twice with the bases loaded; and the Dodgers never led in the game until their final at-bat. So scintillating was the roller-coaster ride, that both manager Walter Alston and veteran first baseman Gil Hodges called this game their greatest pennant thrill.

# 31 *Phillies Overcome an 11-Run Deficit*

PHILADELPHIA (NL) at CHICAGO (NL)
Saturday, April 17, 1976, Wrigley Field
Phillies 18, Cubs 16

Shortly after this game began, Philadelphia fans turned off their televisions in disgust. After only two innings, the Cubs led 7–1, and then it got worse: The third inning provided Chicago with five additional tallies, making it 12–1. But nearly four hours after it began, Mike Schmidt and company fashioned a miracle, coming back to win in the tenth, 18–16, and tying the National League record for the greatest deficit surmounted for victory. In the process, Schmidt joined an elite group of sluggers by belting four home runs and becoming the first National Leaguer of the century to connect for four consecutive round-trippers in a game.

Garry Maddox gave the Phillies an early 1–0 lead on a solo home run, but the Cubs came back with a vengeance. Both Steve Swisher and Rick Monday took advantage of Wrigley Field's 20-mile-per-hour wind by homering in a seven-run retort. Chicago heaped on an additional five runs in the third, thanks to four hits, a walk, and two hit-batsmen. After just three innings it was 12–1, and three Philadelphia hurlers had already seen their ERAs explode.

The Phillies scrounged out a meager run in the fourth, but Chicago balanced the scales with one of their own on Monday's second circuit blast.

In the fifth, Schmidt got into the act, smashing a two-run homer off Rick Reuschel that narrowed the cub lead to 13–4, and this time the Cubs did not retaliate.

Philadelphia chipped away with three more runs in the seventh. A single, triple, sacrifice, and Schmidt's second homer to left did the damage. The slugger's solo blast with two outs made it 13–7.

Mike Garman took the mound for Chicago in the eighth but never got out of the inning, as the Phillies pounded him for four hits, a walk, and five runs, including Schmidt's third consecutive home run. It was the third baseman's longest clout of the day, landing high in the center-field bleachers and testing the memory of old-timers, who couldn't recall the last player to reach that frontier. The Cubs had squandered their early 11-run leads and now held a slim 13–12 margin.

The ninth brought still more pain for the Cub faithful. After Bob Boone tied it with a leadoff homer, a single, triple, and squeeze bunt gave Philadelphia a 15–13 advantage. Chicago hadn't scored since the fourth inning, and

| Philadelphia | AB | R | H | I |
|---|---|---|---|---|
| Cash D, 2b | 6 | 1 | 2 | 2 |
| Bowa L, ss | 6 | 3 | 3 | 1 |
| Johnstone J, rf | 5 | 2 | 4 | 2 |
| Luzinski G, lf | 5 | 0 | 1 | 1 |
| Brown O, lf | 0 | 0 | 0 | 0 |
| Allen D, 1b | 5 | 2 | 1 | 2 |
| Schmidt M, 3b | 6 | 4 | 5 | 8 |
| Maddox G, cf | 5 | 2 | 2 | 1 |
| McGraw T, p | 0 | 0 | 0 | 0 |
| McCarver T, ph | 1 | 1 | 1 | 0 |
| Underwood T, p | 0 | 0 | 0 | 0 |
| Lonborg J, p | 0 | 0 | 0 | 0 |
| Boone B, c | 6 | 1 | 3 | 1 |
| Carlton S, p | 1 | 0 | 0 | 0 |
| Schueler R, p | 0 | 0 | 0 | 0 |
| Garber G, p | 0 | 0 | 0 | 0 |
| Hutton T, ph | 0 | 0 | 0 | 0 |
| Reed R, p | 0 | 0 | 0 | 0 |
| Martin J, ph | 1 | 0 | 0 | 0 |
| Twitchell W, p | 0 | 0 | 0 | 0 |
| Tolan B, ph-cf | 3 | 2 | 2 | 0 |
|  | 50 | 18 | 24 | 18 |

| Chicago | AB | R | H | I |
|---|---|---|---|---|
| Monday R, cf | 6 | 3 | 4 | 4 |
| Cardenal J, lf | 5 | 1 | 1 | 0 |
| Summers C, lf | 0 | 0 | 0 | 0 |
| Mitterwald G, ph | 1 | 0 | 0 | 0 |
| Wallis J, lf | 1 | 0 | 0 | 0 |
| Madlock B, 3b | 7 | 2 | 3 | 3 |
| Morales J, rf | 5 | 2 | 1 | 0 |
| Thornton A, 1b | 4 | 3 | 1 | 1 |
| Trillo M, 2b | 5 | 0 | 2 | 3 |
| Swisher S, c | 6 | 1 | 3 | 4 |
| Rosello D, ss | 4 | 1 | 2 | 1 |
| Kelleher M, ss | 2 | 0 | 1 | 0 |
| Reuschel R, p | 1 | 2 | 0 | 0 |
| Garman M, p | 0 | 0 | 0 | 0 |
| Knowles D, p | 0 | 0 | 0 | 0 |
| Reuschel P, p | 0 | 0 | 0 | 0 |
| Schultz B, p | 0 | 0 | 0 | 0 |
| Adams M, ph | 1 | 1 | 1 | 0 |
|  | 48 | 16 | 19 | 16 |

| Philadelphia | IP | H | R | ER | BB | SO |
|---|---|---|---|---|---|---|
| Carlton | 1.2 | 7 | 7 | 7 | 2 | 1 |
| Schueler | 0.2 | 3 | 3 | 3 | 0 | 0 |
| Garber | 0.2 | 2 | 2 | 2 | 1 | 1 |
| Reed | 2.0 | 1 | 1 | 1 | 1 | 1 |
| Twitchell | 2.0 | 0 | 0 | 0 | 1 | 1 |
| McGraw (W) | 2.0 | 4 | 2 | 2 | 1 | 2 |
| Underwood | 0.2 | 2 | 1 | 1 | 0 | 1 |
| Lonborg (S) | 0.1 | 0 | 0 | 0 | 0 | 0 |
|  | 10.0 | 19 | 16 | 16 | 6 | 7 |

| Chicago | IP | H | R | ER | BB | SO |
|---|---|---|---|---|---|---|
| R. Reuschel | 7.0 | 14 | 7 | 7 | 1 | 4 |
| Garman | 0.2 | 4 | 5 | 5 | 1 | 1 |
| Knowles (L) | 1.1 | 3 | 4 | 4 | 0 | 0 |
| P. Reuschel | 0.0 | 3 | 2 | 2 | 1 | 0 |
| Schultz | 1.0 | 0 | 0 | 0 | 0 | 0 |
|  | 10.0 | 24 | 18 | 18 | 3 | 5 |

| Philadelphia | 010 | 120 | 353 | 3 — 18 |
|---|---|---|---|---|
| Chicago | 075 | 100 | 002 | 1 — 16 |

OB: Philadelphia 8, Chicago 12; DP: Philadelphia 1, Chicago 1; 2B: Cardenal, Madlock 2, Thornton, Boone, Adams; 3B: Johnstone, Bowa; HR: Maddox, Swisher, Boone, Monday 2, Schmidt 4; SH: R. Reuschel, Johnstone; SF: Luzinski, Cash; HP: by Schueler (R. Reuschel), by Garber (Thornton), by Twitchell (Monday); BK: Schultz; TI: 3:42; AT: 28,287; UM: Olsen, Davidson, Rennert, Vargo

their once towering lead was completely wiped out. Now they were in jeopardy of losing.

In the bottom of the ninth, the Phillies' sixth hurler of the game, Tug McGraw, got the first batter on a fly-out to right. He needed just two outs to salt away this colossal comeback. But the Cubs finally responded with a single, a double, and a two-run single by Steve Swisher that sent the struggle into extra innings.

When the Phillies leadoff batter walked to start the 10th, the Cubs brought in Paul Reuschel (Rick's brother) to face Schmidt. Paul had no more success than his brother, however, as Schmidt lined a high fastball into the center-field bleachers for his fourth consecutive home run, giving the Phillies a 17–15 lead.

Later, a single, double, and sacrifice fly added run number 18 to the Phillies' scorecard.

It took two more Philadelphia pitchers to retire the Cubs in the bottom of the 10th, but not before another Chicago run scored on a pair of doubles. When the tying run came to the plate, the Phillies brought on starter Jim Lonborg. In his only relief appearance of the season, Lonborg threw one pitch and got a ground ball to third, ending one of baseball history's wildest contests.

# 32 Washington's Wait Ends at Last

NEW YORK (NL) at WASHINGTON (AL)
Friday, October 10, 1924, Griffith Stadium
Senators 4, Giants 3

The World Series of 1924 introduced a pair of strangers. Harboring years of frustration, the Washington Senators were making their first appearance in the Fall Classic, while in the opposing dugout sat a perennial entry, the favored New York Giants.

Led by the masterful John McGraw, the Giants were a baseball machine. This would be their fourth consecutive appearance against an American League champion, having beaten the Yankees in two of the three previous Series.

There was little to choose between the two teams as they alternated victories during the first six games. Washington's famed 18-year veteran Walter Johnson had not pitched particularly well, losing Games One and Five, but teammate Tom Zachary was sterling in winning games Two and Six.

Now the championship boiled down to a single contest. And what a game it was — drama-filled situations, strategic moves, and great pitching were all involved.

Animated Senator fans, longing to raise a championship flag, packed Griffith Stadium. Among them were President Calvin Coolidge and the First Lady, who were seen standing and cheering throughout the thrill-packed contest.

Managerial strategizing began even before the first pitch, as Washington skipper Bucky Harris sent right-hander Curley Ogden to the mound. It was Ogden's first appearance in the Series and was designed to deplete McGraw's reserve strength. Encouraging more lefties in the Giant lineup, Harris planned

Field captains for the 1924 World Series: Frankie Frisch of the Giants (left) and Bucky Harris of the Senators (National Baseball Hall of Fame Library, Cooperstown, New York).

to switch immediately to left-handed George Mogridge. The ruse failed, however, as McGraw kept his lineup intact even after Mogridge entered the game.

Neither club scored until the fourth, when Harris hit Washington's first ball past the infield and clear over the left-field wall. That 1–0 advantage lasted until the sixth, when New York combined a walk, two singles, two Washington errors, and a sacrifice fly to push across three runs. It was during this frame that McGraw and Harris played another cat-and-mouse substitution game with right-handers versus left-handers.

| New York | AB | R | H | I |
|---|---|---|---|---|
| Lindstrom F, 3b | 5 | 0 | 1 | 0 |
| Frisch F, 2b | 5 | 0 | 2 | 0 |
| Youngs R, rf-lf-rf | 2 | 1 | 0 | 0 |
| Kelly G, cf-1b | 6 | 1 | 1 | 0 |
| Terry B, 1b | 2 | 0 | 0 | 0 |
| Meusel I, ph-lf-rf-lf | 3 | 0 | 1 | 1 |
| Wilson H, lf-cf | 5 | 1 | 1 | 0 |
| Jackson T, ss | 6 | 0 | 0 | 0 |
| Gowdy H, c | 6 | 0 | 1 | 0 |
| Barnes V, p | 4 | 0 | 0 | 0 |
| Nehf A, p | 0 | 0 | 0 | 0 |
| McQuillan H, p | 0 | 0 | 0 | 0 |
| Groh H, ph | 1 | 0 | 1 | 0 |
| Southworth B, pr | 0 | 0 | 0 | 0 |
| Bentley J, p | 0 | 0 | 0 | 0 |
| | 45 | 3 | 8 | 1 |

| Washington | AB | R | H | I |
|---|---|---|---|---|
| McNeely E, cf | 6 | 0 | 1 | 1 |
| Harris B, 2b | 5 | 1 | 3 | 3 |
| Rice S, rf | 5 | 0 | 0 | 0 |
| Goslin G, lf | 5 | 0 | 2 | 0 |
| Judge J, 1b | 4 | 0 | 1 | 0 |
| Bluege O, ss | 5 | 0 | 0 | 0 |
| Taylor T, 3b | 2 | 0 | 0 | 0 |
| Leibold N, ph | 1 | 1 | 1 | 0 |
| Miller R, 3b | 2 | 0 | 0 | 0 |
| Ruel M, c | 5 | 2 | 2 | 0 |
| Ogden C, p | 0 | 0 | 0 | 0 |
| Mogridge G, p | 1 | 0 | 0 | 0 |
| Marberry F, p | 1 | 0 | 0 | 0 |
| Tate B, ph | 0 | 0 | 0 | 0 |
| Shirley M, pr | 0 | 0 | 0 | 0 |
| Johnson W, p | 2 | 0 | 0 | 0 |
| | 44 | 4 | 10 | 4 |

| New York | IP | H | R | ER | BB | SO |
|---|---|---|---|---|---|---|
| Barnes | 7.2 | 6 | 3 | 3 | 1 | 6 |
| Nehf | 0.2 | 1 | 0 | 0 | 0 | 0 |
| McQuillan | 1.2 | 0 | 0 | 0 | 0 | 1 |
| Bentley (L) | 1.1 | 3 | 1 | 0 | 1 | 0 |
| | 11.1 | 10 | 4 | 3 | 2 | 7 |

| Washington | IP | H | R | ER | BB | SO |
|---|---|---|---|---|---|---|
| Ogden | 0.1 | 0 | 0 | 0 | 1 | 1 |
| Mogridge | 4.2 | 4 | 2 | 1 | 1 | 3 |
| Marberry | 3.0 | 1 | 1 | 0 | 1 | 3 |
| Johnson (W) | 4.0 | 3 | 0 | 0 | 3 | 5 |
| | 12.0 | 8 | 3 | 1 | 6 | 12 |

```
New York     000  003  000  000 — 3
Washington   000  100  020  001 — 4
```

OB: New York 14, Washington 8; ER: Taylor, Judge, Bluege 2, Jackson 2, Gowdy; DP: New York 2, Washington 1; 2B: Lindstrom, Leibold, Goslin, Ruel; 3B: Frisch; HR: Harris; SB: Youngs; SH: Lindstrom; SF: Meusel; TI: 3:00; AT: 31,667; UM: HP Dinneen, 1B Quigley, 2B Connolly, 3B Klem

Facing extinction the Senators opened the eighth with only three hits off Giants starter Virgil Barnes. Ossie Bluege popped out to catcher Hank Gowdy, but then a double, single, and walk loaded the sacks. Barnes got the second out on a short line drive to left on which no one could score. With the crowd, including the Coolidges, standing and screaming, Harris grounded a ball toward third. It looked like an easy inning-ending play for third baseman Fred Lindstrom, but the ball suddenly high-hopped over his head and into left field. Two runners scored, tying the game as pandemonium reigned. Washington then had the go-ahead run at second with one of their best hitters, Sam Rice, due to bat. But McGraw called on lefty Art Nehf, who retired Rice on an innocent grounder to first.

The crowd stood and cheered once again in the ninth as Johnson took the mound. But after one out, Frankie Frisch drove a triple to deep center. Facing his third loss of the Series, Johnson intentionally walked Ross Youngs but fanned George Kelly on three pitches. The threat ended when the dangerous Irish Meusel grounded out to third.

In the bottom of the ninth, the Senators could smell the championship after they placed runners at the corners with only one out. While the frenzied crowd roared, McGraw made another strategic pitching change, bringing on right-hander Hugh McQuillan to face righty Ralph Miller. It was a stroke of genius as Miller banged into an inning-ending double play, sending the contest into extra innings.

Each team managed to put runners at first and second with two outs in the eleventh, but neither could score.

Johnson had little trouble retiring the Giants in the twelfth before fate again intervened on behalf of the Senators. After Miller grounded out in the home half, Muddy Ruel hit a high pop up behind home plate. Gowdy staggered beneath it, weaving back and forth before finally stumbling on his discarded mask and dropping the ball. Given another chance Ruel doubled to left as the crowd roared. Johnson grounded to short, but 20-year-old Travis Jackson bobbled it for an error while Ruel held second. Fate then worked overtime as Earl McNeely sent a vicious grounder straight at third baseman Lindstrom. As Fred crouched, the sun streamed through the rear of the grandstand and blinded him. He threw out his hands, but the ball shot over his head and rolled into left field. Ruel, who had been moving on contact, was nearly home by the time Meusel picked up the ball. There was no throw. McNeely got no farther than six feet away from first when the delirious crowd flooded onto the field. By the thousands they surrounded their heroes as thrown hats and cushions littered the field, and torn programs and newspapers fluttered like snow from the upper deck. It took concentrated effort by the police to extricate the players, and long into the Washington night celebrations were heard.

# *Athletics' Explosion Shocks the Cubs* 33

CHICAGO (NL) at PHILADELPHIA (AL)
Saturday, October 12, 1929, Shibe Park
Athletics 10, Cubs 8

After a 15-year absence, Connie Mack returned to the World Series arena, bringing with him what some consider his greatest collection of talent and one that outdistanced the second-place New York Yankees by 18 games. It would be the first of three consecutive post-season appearances for the Athletics, while their opponents, the Chicago Cubs, were returning after an 11-year hiatus.

Philadelphia invaded Chicago in convincing style by winning the first two games. Back in the Quaker City, the Cubs won Game Three and held a commanding

| Chicago | AB | R | H | I |
|---|---|---|---|---|
| McMillan N, 3b | 4 | 0 | 0 | 0 |
| English W, ss | 4 | 0 | 0 | 0 |
| Hornsby R, 2b | 5 | 2 | 2 | 0 |
| Wilson H, cf | 3 | 1 | 2 | 0 |
| Cuyler K, rf | 4 | 2 | 3 | 2 |
| Stephenson R, lf | 4 | 1 | 1 | 1 |
| Grimm C, 1b | 4 | 2 | 2 | 2 |
| Taylor Z, c | 3 | 0 | 0 | 1 |
| Root C, p | 3 | 0 | 0 | 0 |
| Nehf A, p | 0 | 0 | 0 | 0 |
| Blake S, p | 0 | 0 | 0 | 0 |
| Malone P, p | 0 | 0 | 0 | 0 |
| Hartnett G, ph | 1 | 0 | 0 | 0 |
| Carlson H, p | 0 | 0 | 0 | 0 |
|  | 35 | 8 | 10 | 6 |

| Philadelphia | AB | R | H | I |
|---|---|---|---|---|
| Bishop M, 2b | 5 | 1 | 2 | 1 |
| Haas M, cf | 4 | 1 | 1 | 3 |
| Cochrane M, c | 4 | 1 | 2 | 0 |
| Simmons A, lf | 5 | 2 | 2 | 1 |
| Foxx J, 1b | 4 | 2 | 2 | 1 |
| Miller B, rf | 3 | 1 | 2 | 0 |
| Dykes J, 3b | 4 | 1 | 3 | 3 |
| Boley J, ss | 3 | 1 | 1 | 1 |
| Quinn J, p | 2 | 0 | 0 | 0 |
| Walberg R, p | 0 | 0 | 0 | 0 |
| Rommel E, p | 0 | 0 | 0 | 0 |
| Burns G, ph | 2 | 0 | 0 | 0 |
| Grove L, p | 0 | 0 | 0 | 0 |
|  | 36 | 10 | 15 | 10 |

| Chicago | IP | H | R | ER | BB | SO |
|---|---|---|---|---|---|---|
| Root | 6.1 | 9 | 6 | 6 | 0 | 3 |
| Nehf | 0.0 | 1 | 2 | 2 | 1 | 0 |
| Blake (L) | 0.0 | 2 | 2 | 2 | 0 | 0 |
| Malone | 0.2 | 1 | 0 | 0 | 0 | 2 |
| Carlson | 1.0 | 2 | 0 | 0 | 0 | 1 |
|  | 8.0 | 15 | 10 | 10 | 1 | 6 |

| Philadelphia | IP | H | R | ER | BB | SO |
|---|---|---|---|---|---|---|
| Quinn | 5.0 | 7 | 6 | 5 | 2 | 2 |
| Walberg | 1.0 | 1 | 1 | 0 | 0 | 2 |
| Rommel (W) | 1.0 | 2 | 1 | 1 | 1 | 0 |
| Grove (S) | 2.0 | 0 | 0 | 0 | 0 | 4 |
|  | 9.0 | 10 | 8 | 6 | 3 | 8 |

```
Chicago        000   205   100    — 8
Philadelphia   000   000   (10)  0x — 10
```

OB: Chicago 4, Philadelphia 6; ER: Cuyler, Miller, Wilson, Walberg; DP: Philadelphia 1; 2B: Cochrane, Dykes; 3B: Hornsby; HR: Grimm, Simmons, Haas; CS: Miller; SH: Boley, Haas; SF: Taylor; HP: by Malone (Miller); TI: 2:12; AT: 29,921; UM: HP Van Graflan, 1B Klem, 2B Dinneen, 3B Moran

lead in Game Four. After six and one-half innings the score stood Chicago 8, Philadelphia 0. Cub starter Charlie Root, 19–6 during the regular campaign and tough-luck loser of Game One, had held the Athletics to just three hits and hadn't allowed a runner to reach third base. Nine more outs and the Cubs would tie the Series at two games each.

Despite the warmth and sunshine, a powerful storm was brewing in the Athletics' dugout. Al Simmons led off the home half of the seventh with a titanic home run that landed on the roof of the left-field upper deck. At least, the fans thought, they had averted a shutout. Four straight singles followed, tallying a pair of runs and igniting the home crowd. Pinch-hitter George Burns made the first out when he popped out to short, but Max Bishop resumed the single parade, driving home Philadelphia's fourth run. That was all Chicago manager Joe McCarthy could bear, so he beckoned left-hander Art Nehf from the bullpen.

Mule Haas greeted Nehf by crushing a long fly to center field. Hack Wilson raced back and caught up with it, but then lost it in a glaring sun. The elusive sphere fell by his feet and bounded away while both runners as well as Haas circled the bases. It was then 8–7, and still the fury raged.

When Mickey Cochrane walked, McCarthy unceremoniously yanked Nehf and installed right-hander Sheriff Blake. It didn't seem to matter who served them up to the Athletics though, as Simmons, up for the second time, singled to left. Foxx tied it with his second single to right, and the tumultuous crowd erupted once again.

McCarthy was now beside himself and frantically waved to the Chicago bullpen for more help in the person of staff ace Pat Malone. Pat's first effort was to hit Bing Miller in the ribs, loading the bases. Jimmy Dykes, who earlier singled in the frame, then doubled into the left-field corner, sending home the ninth and tenth runs. Malone struck out the next two Athletics as the exhausted crowd fell back into its seats.

The shellshocked Cubs still had six outs, but Mack called on the league's strikeout and earned-run leader, Lefty Grove, to protect the Philadelphia lead. Grove fanned four of the six batters he faced, punctuating the debacle.

Two days later the Cubs gamely carried a 2–0 lead into the bottom of the ninth of Game Five. But using Game Four as their model, the Athletics rallied for three runs and the Series trophy.

# The Johnson-Wood Showdown 34

WASHINGTON (AL) at BOSTON (AL)
Friday, September 6, 1912, Fenway Park
Red Sox 1, Senators 0

By the morning of September 6, 1912, the Boston Red Sox had pulled away from the rest of the American League and were well on their way to the World Series. Behind the success that saw the Sox lead mushroom to 14½ games over both Washington and Philadelphia was the fabled Smokey Joe Wood. The dominating right-hander was amassing one of the finest seasons in pitching annals and would finish with a 34–5 regular-season mark and three World Series victories.

With the Washington Senators in town, Walter Johnson was scheduled to take his turn on the mound this day. Wood was not due to pitch until Saturday, but other circumstances turned this into more than just another regular season game. Johnson earlier in the season had established the American League consecutive win streak record at 16, but Wood was working with an active 13-game streak of his own. Washington management publicly challenged Boston and

| Washington | AB | R | H | I |
|---|---|---|---|---|
| Milan C, cf | 3 | 0 | 1 | 0 |
| Foster E, 3b | 3 | 0 | 1 | 0 |
| Moeller D, rf | 4 | 0 | 0 | 0 |
| Gandil C, 1b | 4 | 0 | 0 | 0 |
| LaPorte F, 2b | 4 | 0 | 2 | 0 |
| Moran R, lf | 3 | 0 | 0 | 0 |
| McBride G, ss | 4 | 0 | 1 | 0 |
| Ainsmith E, c | 2 | 0 | 0 | 0 |
| Johnson W, p | 3 | 0 | 1 | 0 |
| | 30 | 0 | 6 | 0 |

| Boston | AB | R | H | I |
|---|---|---|---|---|
| Hooper H, rf | 4 | 0 | 0 | 0 |
| Yerkes S, 2b | 4 | 0 | 1 | 0 |
| Speaker T, cf | 2 | 1 | 1 | 0 |
| Lewis D, lf | 2 | 0 | 1 | 1 |
| Gardner L, 3b | 3 | 0 | 1 | 0 |
| Engle C, 1b | 3 | 0 | 1 | 0 |
| Wagner H, ss | 3 | 0 | 0 | 0 |
| Cady H, c | 3 | 0 | 0 | 0 |
| Wood J, p | 3 | 0 | 0 | 0 |
| | 27 | 1 | 5 | 1 |

| Washington | IP | H | R | ER | BB | SO |
|---|---|---|---|---|---|---|
| Johnson (L) | 8.0 | 5 | 1 | 1 | 1 | 5 |

| Boston | IP | H | R | ER | BB | SO |
|---|---|---|---|---|---|---|
| Wood (W) | 9.0 | 6 | 0 | 0 | 3 | 9 |

| | | | |
|---|---|---|---|
| Washington | 000 | 000 | 000 — 0 |
| Boston | 000 | 001 | 00x — 1 |

OB: Washington 8, Boston 4; DP: Boston 1; 2B: McBride, LaPorte, Speaker, Lewis; SB: Foster; CS: Speaker; SH: Ainsmith, Lewis, Moran; TI: 1:50; AT: 30,000; UM: Connolly, Hart

Wood to face Johnson to afford the "Big Train" an opportunity to protect his record. Newspapers publicized the challenge and treated the hurlers like prize-fighters, listing their height, weight, biceps measurement, arm span, and so forth.

Droves of fans piled into the still-new Fenway Park, which had opened its doors for the first time just five months earlier. Thousands more than could be seated found their way along the outfield fences while others occupied dangerous territory along the foul lines. So many patrons jammed the area in front of the grandstand that the players were forced to abandon their dugouts and sit on benches along the lines. No one in the crowd was disappointed with the game, but several spectators were injured by foul balls.

Washington had many more scoring opportunities than the home team. They got a runner as far as second base in the fifth, sixth, eighth, and ninth, but Wood always rose to the challenge: Only once did they advance a runner to third. In the third inning a leadoff double and a sacrifice put a runner just 90 feet from home. Johnson then hit back to the box, and Wood came home with his throw, getting the runner on a dazzling play at the plate. Wood walked the next two batters, loading the bases, but struck out Danny Moeller to erase the peril.

In only two innings were the Red Sox able to get runners as far as second base against Johnson. In the second frame, with one out, they stroked back-to-back singles, but second baseman Frank LaPorte made a great running catch in short right field to save a run, and Johnson got the last batter to fly out. Finally, with two outs in the sixth, Boston scored the first and only run of the game on back-to-back doubles by Tris Speaker and Duffy Lewis. Both blows rolled into the fans lining the outfield perimeter.

With a 1–0 lead, the huge crowd remained captivated. The climax came in the ninth when, with the tying run at second and one out, Wood fanned the last two Senators.

# Ventura's Grand-Slam Single in the Fifteenth 35

ATLANTA (NL) at NEW YORK (NL)
Sunday, October 17, 1999, Shea Stadium
Mets 4, Braves 3

It was no surprise that this fifth game of the National League Championship Series was a cliffhanger. After all, three of the first four games were decided by a single run and the other by a mere two runs. The surprise is that it was played at all. Beginning shortly after the first pitch was thrown, a slow but steady rain began and continued for the duration of this five-hour, 46-minute marathon. From late afternoon until far into the night, through 15 drama-packed innings, 45 players struggled with poor footing and wet equipment in what became the longest (in hours) post-season game of the century.

The Atlanta Braves, bidding for their fifth World Series appearance of the decade, had taken a commanding three games to none lead in the NLCS. Struggling to preserve their dignity, the Mets took Game Four.

Game Five also started well for New York. With Atlanta's Greg Maddux on the mound, Ricky Henderson led off with a single before John Olerud smacked a home run over the right-field wall.

The Mets threatened again in the second when Darryl Hamilton reached third with one out, but Maddux choked off the rally.

In the fourth, Atlanta combined doubles by Bret Boone and Chipper Jones to get on the board, then Brian Jordan tied it at 2–2 with a single.

No other runners reached third until the sixth inning, when the Braves loaded the bases with only one down. In a pivotal play, Maddux next missed an attempted squeeze bunt. With the runner on third moving with the pitch, he was tagged out at the plate for an inning-ending double play.

Thanks to two errors by first baseman Ryan Klesko, New York also loaded the sacks in the sixth with one out. Another goose egg went up on the board, however, as Rey Ordoñez grounded into a short-to-first double play.

Atlanta once again loaded the bases in the seventh, but Andruw Jones flied out to left, ending the threat.

For the next seven innings, a parade of relief pitchers dominated as third base showed not a single footprint. Having seen three pinch-runners and eight pinch-hitters enter the game, and with the Mets on their ninth hurler, both benches were nearly depleted. In the bullpen, TV cameras showed Rick Reed, starter from the day before, warming up. This was a desperate time for the Mets.

| Atlanta | AB | R | H | I |
|---|---|---|---|---|
| Williams G, lf | 7 | 0 | 1 | 0 |
| Boone B, 2b | 3 | 1 | 1 | 0 |
| Nixon O, pr | 0 | 0 | 0 | 0 |
| Lockhart K, 2b | 4 | 0 | 2 | 1 |
| Jones C, 3b | 6 | 1 | 3 | 1 |
| Jordan B, rf | 7 | 0 | 2 | 1 |
| Klesko R, 1b | 2 | 0 | 0 | 0 |
| Hunter B, ph-1b | 3 | 0 | 0 | 0 |
| Jones A, cf | 5 | 0 | 0 | 0 |
| Perez E, c | 4 | 0 | 2 | 0 |
| Battle H, pr | 0 | 0 | 0 | 0 |
| Myers G, c | 1 | 0 | 0 | 0 |
| Weiss W, ss | 6 | 1 | 2 | 0 |
| Maddux G, p | 3 | 0 | 0 | 0 |
| Hernandez, ph | 1 | 0 | 0 | 0 |
| Mulholland T, p | 0 | 0 | 0 | 0 |
| Guillen O, ph | 1 | 0 | 0 | 0 |
| Remlinger M, p | 0 | 0 | 0 | 0 |
| Springer R, p | 0 | 0 | 0 | 0 |
| Fabregas J, ph | 1 | 0 | 0 | 0 |
| Rocker J, p | 0 | 0 | 0 | 0 |
| McGlinchy K, p | 1 | 0 | 0 | 0 |
| | 55 | 3 | 13 | 3 |

| New York | AB | R | H | I |
|---|---|---|---|---|
| Henderson R, lf | 5 | 1 | 1 | 0 |
| Rogers K, p | 0 | 0 | 0 | 0 |
| Bonilla B, ph | 1 | 0 | 0 | 0 |
| Dotel O, p | 0 | 0 | 0 | 0 |
| Franco M, ph | 0 | 0 | 0 | 0 |
| Cedeno R, pr | 0 | 1 | 0 | 0 |
| Alfonzo E, 2b | 6 | 0 | 1 | 0 |
| Olerud J, 1b | 6 | 1 | 2 | 2 |
| Piazza M, c | 6 | 0 | 1 | 0 |
| Pratt T, c | 0 | 0 | 0 | 1 |
| Ventura R, 3b | 7 | 0 | 2 | 1 |
| Mora M, rf-cf-rf | 6 | 0 | 1 | 0 |
| Hamilton D, cf | 3 | 0 | 2 | 0 |
| Agbayani B, ph-rf-lf | 1 | 0 | 0 | 0 |
| Ordoñez R, ss | 6 | 0 | 0 | 0 |
| Yoshii M, p | 1 | 0 | 0 | 0 |
| Hershiser O, p | 1 | 0 | 0 | 0 |
| Wendell T, p | 0 | 0 | 0 | 0 |
| Cook D, p | 0 | 0 | 0 | 0 |
| Mahomes P, p | 1 | 0 | 0 | 0 |
| Franco J, p | 0 | 0 | 0 | 0 |
| Benitez A, p | 0 | 0 | 0 | 0 |
| Dunston S, ph-cf | 3 | 1 | 1 | 0 |
| | 53 | 4 | 11 | 4 |

| Atlanta | IP | H | R | ER | BB | SO |
|---|---|---|---|---|---|---|
| Maddux | 7.0 | 7 | 2 | 2 | 0 | 5 |
| Mulholland | 2 0 | 1 | 0 | 0 | 0 | 2 |
| Remlinger | 2.0 | 1 | 0 | 0 | 0 | 2 |
| Springer | 1.0 | 0 | 0 | 0 | 1 | 1 |
| Rocker | 1.1 | 0 | 0 | 0 | 0 | 2 |
| McGlinchy | 1.0 | 2 | 2 | 2 | 4 | 1 |
| | 14.1 | 11 | 4 | 4 | 5 | 13 |

| New York | IP | H | R | ER | BB | SO |
|---|---|---|---|---|---|---|
| Yoshii | 3.0 | 4 | 2 | 2 | 1 | 3 |
| Hershiser | 3.1 | 1 | 0 | 0 | 3 | 5 |
| Wendell | 0.1 | 0 | 0 | 0 | 1 | 1 |
| Cook | 0.0 | 0 | 0 | 0 | 0 | 0 |
| Mahomes | 1.0 | 1 | 0 | 0 | 2 | 1 |
| Franco J | 1.1 | 1 | 0 | 0 | 0 | 2 |
| Benitez | 1.0 | 1 | 0 | 0 | 0 | 1 |
| Rogers | 2.0 | 1 | 0 | 0 | 1 | 1 |
| Dotel | 3.0 | 4 | 1 | 1 | 2 | 5 |
| | 15.0 | 13 | 3 | 3 | 10 | 19 |

```
Atlanta    000  200  000  000  001 — 3
New York   200  000  000  000  002 — 4
```

OB: Atlanta 19, New York 12; ER: Klesko 2, Olerud; DP: Atlanta 2, New York 2; 2B: Perez, Boone, C. Jones 2, Williams, Weiss, Hamilton; 3B: Lockhart; HR: Olerud; SB: Nixon, Battle, Weiss, Agbayani, Dunston; CS: Klesko; SH: A. Jones, Alfonzo; HP: by Hershiser (Boone); TI: 5:46; AT: 55,723; UM: HP Layne, 1B Crawford, 2B Montague, 3B Kellogg

In the 15th inning, both offenses suddenly emerged. Atlanta's Walt Weiss singled and stole second between a pair of outs. With the rain falling even harder, Keith Lockhart tripled to right-center, and the Braves took a daunting 3–2 lead. They would soon regret, however, the 19 runners left on base and the 3-for-18 batting with runners in scoring position.

After fouling off six pitches, Shawon Dunston led off the home half of the 15th with a single to center against 22-year-old rookie Kevin McGlinchy. The youngster then walked pinch-hitter Matt Franco. A sacrifice moved the runners to second and third before McGlinchy walked Olerud intentionally to load the bases. Todd Pratt, who had entered the game in the 14th for an injured Mike Piazza, walked on five pitches to force in the tying run.

With the remaining fans soaked but roaring, Robin Ventura stepped to the plate. The hobbling third baseman was 1-for-18 in the Series but now drove a 1–1 pitch over the right-field wall for an apparent grand slam home run. Such pandemonium erupted that Ventura's teammates rushed onto the field and surrounded him in elation. The three baserunners crossed the plate, but Robin never reached second base, causing much confusion about the final score. At first it flashed on television screens as 7–3, but several minutes later the announcers correctly explained that Ventura could not be credited with a home run because he did not circle the bases. He had touched only first and thus was credited with a single and one RBI, making the final score 4–3. What really mattered to Ventura and the Mets, however, was that they had survived a 482-pitch marathon to play at least one more game.

# *The Most Runs in a Game* 36

## PHILADELPHIA (NL) at CHICAGO (NL)
### Friday, August 25, 1922, Wrigley Field
### Cubs 26, Phillies 23

The decade of the 1920s witnessed baseball's transition from a dead-ball, pitcher-dominated game into the live-ball, offensive era. The bunt-and-sacrifice, one-run-at-a-time tactics gave way to the long-ball, multiple-run strategy. By 1922 the least productive teams were averaging nearly the same number of runs as the most productive teams four years earlier. Never were the effects of the new lively ball more evident than on August 25, 1922, in Chicago, when the Cubs prevailed over the Philadelphia Phillies by a remarkable 26–23 score. Through the end of the century, 49 runs remained the most ever scored in a game.

The normally favorable winds of Wrigley Field were apparently not a factor, as local newspapers made little mention of Mother Nature. Of the three home runs, however, all struck by right-handed batters, two sailed over the right-field facade and one into the center-field bleachers. But it wasn't home runs that turned this into a massacre for the pitchers; it was hits — 51 to be exact — and the 49 runs they gave rise to.

Newspapers from both Philadelphia and Chicago were replete with lists of 20th-century benchmarks that were established or tied. Among them were:

| Philadelphia | AB | R | H | I |
|---|---|---|---|---|
| Wrightstone R, 3b | 7 | 3 | 4 | 4 |
| Parkinson F, 2b | 4 | 1 | 2 | 2 |
| Williams C, cf | 3 | 1 | 0 | 0 |
| Lebourveau B, cf | 4 | 2 | 3 | 2 |
| Walker C, rf | 6 | 2 | 4 | 1 |
| Mokan J, lf | 4 | 2 | 3 | 2 |
| Fletcher A, ss | 3 | 1 | 0 | 0 |
| Smith J, ss | 4 | 2 | 1 | 2 |
| Leslie R, 1b | 1 | 1 | 0 | 1 |
| Lee C, 1b | 4 | 4 | 3 | 0 |
| Henline B, c | 2 | 1 | 2 | 0 |
| Withrow F, c | 4 | 1 | 2 | 3 |
| Ring J, p | 2 | 0 | 1 | 1 |
| Weinert L, p | 4 | 2 | 1 | 1 |
| Rapp G, ph | 0 | 0 | 0 | 0 |
|  | 52 | 23 | 26 | 19 |

| Chicago | AB | R | H | I |
|---|---|---|---|---|
| Heathcote C, cf | 5 | 5 | 5 | 4 |
| Hollocher C, ss | 5 | 2 | 3 | 6 |
| Kelleher J, ss | 1 | 0 | 0 | 0 |
| Terry Z, 2b | 5 | 2 | 2 | 2 |
| Friberg B, 2b | 1 | 0 | 1 | 0 |
| Grimes R, 1b | 4 | 2 | 2 | 2 |
| Callaghan M, rf | 7 | 3 | 2 | 1 |
| Miller H, lf | 5 | 3 | 4 | 6 |
| Krug M, 3b | 5 | 4 | 4 | 1 |
| O'Farrell B, c | 3 | 3 | 2 | 2 |
| Hartnett G, c6 | 0 | 0 | 0 | 0 |
| Kaufmann T, p | 2 | 0 | 0 | 0 |
| Barber T, ph | 1 | 2 | 0 | 0 |
| Stueland G, p | 1 | 0 | 0 | 0 |
| Maisel G, ph | 1 | 0 | 0 | 0 |
| Eubanks U, p | 0 | 0 | 0 | 0 |
| Morris E, p | 0 | 0 | 0 | 0 |
| Osborne T, p | 0 | 0 | 0 | 0 |
|  | 46 | 26 | 25 | 24 |

| Philadelphia | IP | H | R | ER | BB | SO |
|---|---|---|---|---|---|---|
| Ring (L) | 3.1 | 12 | 16 | 6 | 5 | 2 |
| Weinert | 4.2 | 13 | 10 | 5 | 5 | 2 |
|  | 8.0 | 25 | 26 | 11 | 10 | 4 |

| Chicago | IP | H | R | ER | BB | SO |
|---|---|---|---|---|---|---|
| Kaufmann (W) | 4.0 | 9 | 6 | 3 | 3 | 0 |
| Stueland | 3.0 | 7 | 3 | 3 | 2 | 2 |
| Eubanks | 0.2 | 3 | 8 | 4 | 3 | 0 |
| Morris | 0.1 | 4 | 4 | 4 | 1 | 1 |
| Osborne | 1.0 | 3 | 2 | 2 | 2 | 3 |
|  | 9.0 | 26 | 23 | 16 | 11 | 6 |

| Philadelphia | 0 | 3 | 2 | 1 | 3 | 0 | 0 | 8 | 6 — 23 |
|---|---|---|---|---|---|---|---|---|---|
| Chicago | 1 | (10) | 0 | (14) | 0 | 1 | 0 | 0 | x — 26 |

OB: Philadelphia 16, Chicago 9; ER: Wrightstone, Williams, Walker, Lee, Heathcote, Hollocher, Callaghan, Krug, Hartnett; DP: Philadelphia 3; 2B: Parkinson, Walker, Mokan, Terry, Withrow, Heathcote 2, Hollocher, Friberg, Grimes, Krug 2; 3B: Wrightstone, Walker; HR: Miller 2, O'Farrell; SB: Weinert, Hollocher; CS: Williams; SH: Parkinson, Walker, O'Farrell; SF: Leslie, Hollocher; HP: By Weinert (Grimes); WP: Stueland; TI: 3:01 ; AT: 7,100; UM: Hart, Rigler

- Most plate appearances by one team in a nine-inning game (66)
- Most plate appearances by both teams in a nine-inning game (125)
- Most hits by both teams in a nine-inning game (51)
- Most runs by one team in a game (26 [later surpassed])
- Most runs by both teams in a game (49)
- Most at-bats in one inning by one player (3)
- Most team hits in one inning (11 [later surpassed])
- Most runs by one team in one inning (14 [later surpassed])
- Most times reached base safely in a nine-inning game by one player (7)
- Most plate appearances in a nine-inning game by one player (8)
- Most teammates to score one or more runs (13)
- Most players, both clubs, to score one or more runs (22)

In addition the two pitching staffs issued a combined 21 walks, and the fielders gave the offenses plenty of extra outs by committing nine errors.

An innocent 1–0 Cubs lead after one inning exploded into a 25–6 rout after four. But the Phillies had not yet conceded defeat. After seven frames the Cubs held a seemingly insurmountable lead of 26–9, and with only two innings remaining, the outcome appeared settled. Chicago manager, Bill Killefer, decided to afford several of his rookies some mound work. No team, after all, had ever overcome such a deficit, especially with only two innings remaining. The Phillies, however, were about to stage one of the most gallant comeback attempts in baseball history.

The first rookie victim was 19-year-old Poss Eubanks, who was bludgeoned for eight runs while retiring just two batters. It was the last time Eubanks ever graced a major league diamond. Big Ed Morris was the next novice to face the Philadelphia contingent. Ed doused the rally, halting the score at 26–17 with one inning remaining.

Philadelphia bats re-ignited in the final frame. Before Morris could retire a single batter, the visitors crossed the plate four more times, making it 26–21. Chicago's next hopeful savior was rookie Tiny Osborne. The Phillies nudged across two more runs, working the score to 26–23 with two outs and bases loaded. Osborne then faced Bevo Lebourveau who had singled in each of his three plate appearances. Lebourveau now represented the lead run for Philadelphia. This time, however, with the crowd on its feet, Bevo fanned to end the game.

# The 18-Inning Double Shutout 37

WASHINGTON (AL) at DETROIT (AL)
Friday, July 16, 1909, Bennett Park
Nationals 0, Tigers 0

When Washington invaded Detroit in mid–July of 1909, there wasn't much at stake. The Tigers were at the summit of the American League standings while the Nationals were solidly entrenched in the basement. Washington's anemic offense averaged just 2.5 runs per game during the season, so it was no surprise they failed to cross the plate during what amounted to a doubleheader. More surprising was that the best offensive club in the league, the Tigers, was also held scoreless.

In a remarkable display of stamina and talent, Detroit pitcher Oron Edgar Summers, "Kickapoo Ed," went the distance. Washington starter Dolly Gray outpitched Summers during the first eight frames, but an injury forced his replacement in the ninth. At 6:45 P.M., after 18 innings, home plate umpire John Kerin called the game because of darkness, much to the chagrin of both players and spectators. Everyone but the arbiter felt there was plenty of daylight remaining.

For Washington, there were few scoring opportunities.

• They had two hits in the same inning only once — the first. Then, with one down, Clyde Milan bunted safely and Jack Lelivelt singled, but Summers retired Bob Unglaub on a long fly and struck out Jiggs Donahue.

• In the third, Dolly Gray led off with a two-bagger but was doubled off second on a liner to short.

• In the ninth, George Browne opened with a walk, and Milan again bunted safely. After Lelivelt flied out, Unglaub stroked a blooper into right. First baseman Claude Rossman lunged and caught it, then tagged first to double off Milan.

• Speed Kelly was safe on an error to lead off the 13th, and George McBride followed with a single to center. Here Summers got lucky after his next pitch got away from battery mate Oscar Stanage. Kelly thought he could advance, but Stanage recovered in time to catch him in a rundown between second and third. Gabby Street then grounded out, and Bob Groom fanned.

Summers strengthened over the last five innings, allowing only three baserunners on two errors and a walk. All came with two outs, however.

The Tigers could do nothing with Washington's rookie hurler Dolly Gray, getting just a leadoff single and one walk in eight innings. But thanks in part to six free passes by reliever Groom, they had more extra-inning scoring opportunities than did the Nationals.

• Gray had pitched brilliantly through the first eight frames, but with a 3–1 count to Matty McIntyre leading off the ninth, Gray staggered from the mound in great pain, apparently having torn a muscle in his side. In stepped Groom, who completed the walk. Donie Bush was safe on an error, Wahoo Sam Crawford sacrificed both runners, and, with Ty Cobb up, things looked bleak for Washington. But Cobb bounced to Groom, who caught McIntyre at the plate, and then Rossman fanned.

• Germany Schaefer singled in the 10th and worked his way to third base with two outs, but was left stranded.

• McIntyre walked to start the 11th, but neither Crawford nor Cobb could deliver after Bush had sacrificed.

• There were two outs in the 12th after both George Moriarty and Stanage had walked, but Summers couldn't deliver the victory blow.

• In the 15th Stanage led off with a single to center, and Summers tried to sacrifice bunt. Groom, hurrying a throw to second, tossed the ball into center field. The runner took third, and Summers was safe at first. An intentional pass

| Washington | AB | R | H | I |
|---|---|---|---|---|
| Browne G, lf | 6 | 0 | 1 | 0 |
| Milan C, cf | 7 | 0 | 2 | 0 |
| Lelivelt J, rf | 7 | 0 | 1 | 0 |
| Unglaub B, 2b | 7 | 0 | 0 | 0 |
| Donahue J, 1b | 6 | 0 | 0 | 0 |
| Kelly S, 3b | 6 | 0 | 0 | 0 |
| Collins O, ph | 1 | 0 | 0 | 0 |
| Conroy W, 3b | 0 | 0 | 0 | 0 |
| McBride G, ss | 7 | 0 | 1 | 0 |
| Street G, c | 7 | 0 | 1 | 0 |
| Gray D, p | 3 | 0 | 1 | 0 |
| Groom B, p | 4 | 0 | 0 | 0 |
| | 61 | 0 | 7 | 0 |

| Detroit | AB | R | H | I |
|---|---|---|---|---|
| McIntyre M, lf | 5 | 0 | 1 | 0 |
| Bush D, ss | 5 | 0 | 0 | 0 |
| Crawford S, cf | 7 | 0 | 0 | 0 |
| Cobb T, rf | 7 | 0 | 0 | 0 |
| Rossman C, 1b | 8 | 0 | 1 | 0 |
| Moriarty G, 3b | 7 | 0 | 1 | 0 |
| Schaefer G, 2b | 7 | 0 | 2 | 0 |
| Stanage O, c | 4 | 0 | 1 | 0 |
| Killefer R, pr | 0 | 0 | 0 | 0 |
| Schmidt B, c | 1 | 0 | 0 | 0 |
| Summers E, p | 7 | 0 | 0 | 0 |
| | 58 | 0 | 6 | 0 |

| Washington | IP | H | R | ER | BB | SO |
|---|---|---|---|---|---|---|
| Gray | 8.0 | 1 | 0 | 0 | 1 | 0 |
| Groom | 10.0 | 5 | 0 | 0 | 6 | 8 |
| | 18.0 | 6 | 0 | 0 | 7 | 8 |

| Detroit | IP | H | R | ER | BB | SO |
|---|---|---|---|---|---|---|
| Summers | 18.0 | 7 | 0 | 0 | 2 | 10 |

| | | | | | | |
|---|---|---|---|---|---|---|
| Washington | 000 | 000 | 000 | 000 | 000 | 000 — 0 |
| Detroit | 000 | 000 | 000 | 000 | 000 | 000 — 0 |

OB: Washington 9, Detroit 15; DP: Washington 1, Detroit 2; 2B: Gray; SB: Cobb, Unglaub, Moriarty, McBride; CS: Browne, Lelivelt; SH: Bush 3, Crawford; TI: 3:15; AT: 3,078; UM: Kerin, Sheridan

loaded the bases and created a possible force play at the plate. With no outs and the heart of the Tiger lineup on its way, the outcome looked exceedingly grim for Washington. But the next batter, Bush, popped out to third. Crawford then topped a two-strike pitch toward first base as the potential game winner sprinted home. Groom fielded the grounder and made a desperate toss to his battery mate. It was a very close play at the plate, but Street, thinking the runner had beaten the play, and seeing umpire Kerin give the safe signal, began walking toward the bench, followed by his teammates. The Tiger baserunners also began walking toward the clubhouse. But umpire Kerin remained at the plate, beckoning the players. One of them returned to ask, "What's the matter?" "Runner's out," replied Kerin. Amid much shouting and confusion, both teams stormed back onto the field, surrounded Kerin and demanded an explanation. The umpire explained that he had made a mistake, thinking there were only two baserunners and that a tag play was in order. The runner was really out on the force at home. Almost simultaneously, both teams realized that the inning, and the game, was not yet over. Crawford started back toward first as Washington second baseman Unglaub grabbed the ball from teammate Street's hand. Unglaub chased Crawford as the fans screamed and howled. The other Detroit runners also scrambled back to their bases, each avoiding a tag by a National. Once all the baserunners and fielders were back in position, the balance of the Tigers again surrounded Kerin for a few more minutes of animated dispute. After the commotion was settled, there still were only two outs, the bags still were loaded, and Ty Cobb was the next hitter. Groom struck him out, thereby ending one of the most bizarre half-innings in baseball history.

Summers pitched superbly, issuing two walks (one intentional) and allowing seven hits, only one of which came in the last 12 innings. In essence, he tossed a doubleheader shutout. The Nationals' Dolly Gray and Bob Groom, both rookies, combined to better Summers in one pitching department, for they surrendered only six hits through the 18 innings, despite a combined 7–22 won-lost record at the time.

In 1909, tied games were not suspended but rather replayed in their entirety. Thus on August 22, the two clubs replayed this contest, with Detroit winning, 3–1.

Kickapoo Ed Summers had a fine career (68–45, 2.42 ERA), albeit cut short by arm miseries. In 1912, he retired after just five major league campaigns.

# 38 Koufax Is Brilliant in Game Seven

LOS ANGELES (NL) at MINNESOTA (AL)
Thursday, October 14, 1965, Metropolitan Stadium
Dodgers 2, Twins 0

The big question prior to Game Seven of the 1965 World Series was who would get the starting nod for the Los Angeles Dodgers. As reporters crowded into manager Walter Alston's office, the skipper refused to commit himself. He had two of the best pitchers in baseball available. Don Drysdale had finished the regular season third in major league wins, complete games, and shutouts, and had the fourth lowest on-base percentage allowed in the National League. The right-hander also had three days rest since he had beaten Minnesota in Game Four. But the big side-armer was still just the Dodgers second-best moundsman.

Sitting in the trainer's room, receiving his normal fare of therapy, was number one. Bothered all season by an arthritic pitching elbow, Sandy Koufax was the most dominating hurler of his era. This season the left-hander led not just the National League, but both major leagues in wins, winning percentage, complete games, innings pitched, strikeouts, earned run average, lowest opponents' batting average, and the lowest opponents' on-base percentage. In addition, he tossed his fourth no-hitter — a perfect game — and set a new major league record for most strikeouts in a season with 382. There was little doubt who Alston wanted on the mound for the deciding game, but Koufax was tired

| *Los Angeles* | AB | R | H | I |
|---|---|---|---|---|
| Wills M, ss | 4 | 0 | 0 | 0 |
| Gilliam J, 3b | 5 | 0 | 2 | 0 |
| Kennedy J, 3b | 0 | 0 | 0 | 0 |
| Davis W, cf | 2 | 0 | 0 | 0 |
| Johnson L, lf | 4 | 1 | 1 | 1 |
| Fairly R, rf | 4 | 1 | 1 | 0 |
| Parker W, 1b | 4 | 0 | 2 | 1 |
| Tracewski D, 2b | 4 | 0 | 0 | 0 |
| Roseboro J, c | 2 | 0 | 1 | 0 |
| Koufax S, p | 3 | 0 | 0 | 0 |
| | 32 | 2 | 7 | 2 |

| *Minnesota* | AB | R | H | I |
|---|---|---|---|---|
| Versalles Z, ss | 4 | 0 | 1 | 0 |
| Nossek J, cf | 4 | 0 | 0 | 0 |
| Oliva T, rf | 3 | 0 | 0 | 0 |
| Killebrew H, 3b | 3 | 0 | 1 | 0 |
| Battey E, c | 4 | 0 | 0 | 0 |
| Allison B, lf | 4 | 0 | 0 | 0 |
| Mincher D, 1b | 3 | 0 | 0 | 0 |
| Quilici F, 2b | 3 | 0 | 1 | 0 |
| Kaat J, p | 1 | 0 | 0 | 0 |
| Worthington A, p | 0 | 0 | 0 | 0 |
| Rollins R, ph | 0 | 0 | 0 | 0 |
| Klippstein J, p | 0 | 0 | 0 | 0 |
| Merritt J, p | 0 | 0 | 0 | 0 |
| Valdespino S, ph | 1 | 0 | 0 | 0 |
| Perry J, p | 0 | 0 | 0 | 0 |
| | 30 | 0 | 3 | 0 |

| *Los Angeles* | IP | H | R | ER | BB | SO |
|---|---|---|---|---|---|---|
| Koufax (W) | 9.0 | 3 | 0 | 0 | 3 | 10 |

| *Minnesota* | IP | H | R | ER | BB | SO |
|---|---|---|---|---|---|---|
| Kaat (L) | 3.0 | 5 | 2 | 2 | 1 | 2 |
| Worthington | 2.0 | 0 | 0 | 0 | 1 | 0 |
| Klippstein | 1.2 | 2 | 0 | 0 | 1 | 2 |
| Merritt | 1.1 | 0 | 0 | 0 | 0 | 1 |
| Perry | 1.0 | 0 | 0 | 0 | 1 | 1 |
| | 9.0 | 7 | 2 | 2 | 4 | 6 |

| Los Angeles | 000 | 200 | 000 — 2 |
|---|---|---|---|
| Minnesota | 000 | 000 | 000 — 0 |

OB: Los Angeles 9, Minnesota 6; ER: Oliva; 2B: Roseboro, Fairly, Quilici; 3B: Parker; HR: Johnson; CS: Wills; SH: Davis; HP: by Klippstein (Davis); TI: 2:27; AT: 50,596; UM: HP Hurley, 1B Venzon, 2B Flaherty, 3B Sudol, LF Stewart, RF Vargo

and hurting, having shut out the Twins on only four hits in Game Five. Pitching the seventh game would mean he'd be working on just two days rest.

Alston kept his pitching choice confidential until a few hours before the first pitch, when he named his ace. The manager reasoned that if Koufax ran into trouble, he could always bring in Drysdale. The Dodgers' top reliever, Ron Perranoski, was also left-handed, giving Alston a left-right-left arsenal if necessary.

Amid sunny skies and temperatures in the 50s, Koufax got off to a shaky start, walking two in the opening frame. The Twins, however, were unable to capitalize and did little else for four innings.

Minnesota's Jim Kaat kept the slate clean for the home club until the fourth, when Los Angeles scored the only runs of the game. Lou Johnson led off with a home run down the left field line. It was an ominous sign for Twins' fans who realized that the first team to score in every game this Series had gone on to win. Ron Fairly then doubled and was knocked home on a single by Wes Parker, making it 2–0.

In the fifth The Twins seriously threatened. With one out, Frank Quilici doubled to left-center, and Rich Rollins walked before Zoilo Versalles sent a hard grounder down the third base line. Jim Gilliam, the coach who came out of retirement to play third base this season, made a tremendous backhand stop and raced to third for a force out. It was the turning point of the game, for had Versalles's ball gotten through, at least one run, and possibly two, would have scored. Koufax then retired the next batter on a ground-out.

The Dodgers got a runner to third base in both the sixth and seventh frames but couldn't add to their score. Meanwhile Koufax continued to frustrate the Twins. After their fifth inning threat, Koufax allowed just one baserunner for the rest of the game and finished by fanning the last two batters.

In a post-game interview, Minnesota manager Sam Mele was asked his impressions of Koufax. The skipper just shook his head and said the left-hander was the best he'd ever seen.

# 39 Mays Ends the Spahn-Marichal Duel

MILWAUKEE (NL) at SAN FRANCISCO (NL)
Tuesday, July 2, 1963, Candlestick Park
Giants 1, Braves 0

This was a classic confrontation of great pitching against great hitting. When the San Francisco Giants squared off against the Milwaukee Braves on a chilly summer night in Candlestick Park, no one expected to get home so late. But despite two power-packed offensive lineups, a pair of future Hall of Fame pitchers gained control of a game that stretched long into the night. In an era when the save specialist was beginning to make his presence felt, both starters refused to leave the mound and battled on for 16 grueling innings.

Milwaukee's 42-year-old Warren Spahn was in the midst of his 13th and final 20-win campaign. No stranger to finishing what he started, the left-hander would lead the league in complete games for the seventh consecutive year in 1963. Dominican-born Juan Marichal was at the opposite end of his baseball career. Just 25 years old, the Giants' high-kicking right-hander was about to craft his first of six 20-win seasons.

Each stalwart faced an imposing lineup. This Giants club would finish first in both home runs and slugging, and second in runs scored. The top of their lineup read like an All-Star team. The Braves, meanwhile, would finish third in runs scored and featured the dangerous combination of Eddie Mathews and Henry Aaron. Aaron at the time was hitting .311 and leading the major leagues in home runs and RBI. Mathews would lead the league in on-base percentage.

Juan Marichal (National Baseball Hall of Fame Library, Cooperstown, New York).

But this night belonged to Marichal and Spahn — all four hours and ten minutes of it. There were very few scoring threats, as only three batters went to the plate in 15 of the first 30 half-innings. Before the winning blow was struck in the 16th, just three runners reached third base.

In the home half of the second, after one out, Orlando Cepeda singled and stole second. He advanced to third on a long fly out but was left stranded when Spahn retired Jose Pagan on a pop-up.

| Milwaukee | AB | R | H | I |
|---|---|---|---|---|
| Maye L, lf | 6 | 0 | 0 | 0 |
| Bolling F, 2b | 7 | 0 | 2 | 0 |
| Aaron H, rf | 6 | 0 | 0 | 0 |
| Mathews E, 3b | 2 | 0 | 0 | 0 |
| Menke D, 3b | 5 | 0 | 2 | 0 |
| Larker N, 1b | 5 | 0 | 0 | 0 |
| Jones M, cf | 5 | 0 | 1 | 0 |
| Dillard D, ph-cf | 1 | 0 | 0 | 0 |
| Crandall D, c | 6 | 0 | 2 | 0 |
| McMillan R, ss | 6 | 0 | 0 | 0 |
| Spahn W, p | 6 | 0 | 1 | 0 |
| | 55 | 0 | 8 | 0 |

| San Francisco | AB | R | H | I |
|---|---|---|---|---|
| Kuenn H, 3b | 7 | 0 | 1 | 0 |
| Mays W, cf | 6 | 1 | 1 | 1 |
| McCovey W, lf | 6 | 0 | 1 | 0 |
| Alou F, rf | 6 | 0 | 1 | 0 |
| Cepeda O, 1b | 6 | 0 | 2 | 0 |
| Bailey E, c | 6 | 0 | 1 | 0 |
| Pagan J, ss | 2 | 0 | 0 | 0 |
| Davenport J, ph | 1 | 0 | 0 | 0 |
| Bowman E, ss | 3 | 0 | 2 | 0 |
| Hiller C, 2b | 6 | 0 | 0 | 0 |
| Marichal J, p | 6 | 0 | 0 | 0 |
| | 55 | 1 | 9 | 1 |

| Milwaukee | IP | H | R | ER | BB | SO |
|---|---|---|---|---|---|---|
| Spahn (L) | 15.1 | 9 | 1 | 1 | 1 | 2 |

| San Francisco | IP | H | R | ER | BB | SO |
|---|---|---|---|---|---|---|
| Marichal (W) | 16.0 | 8 | 0 | 0 | 4 | 10 |

| Milwaukee | 000 | 000 | 000 | 000 | 000 | 0 — 0 |
|---|---|---|---|---|---|---|
| San Francisco | 000 | 000 | 000 | 000 | 000 | 1 — 1 |

OB: Milwaukee 11, San Francisco 9; ER: Kuenn, Menke; 2B: Spahn, Kuenn; HR: Mays; SB: Cepeda, Maye, Menke; CS: Crandall; TI: 4:10; AT: 15,921; UM: HP Burkhart, 1B Pelekoudas, 2B Walsh, 3B Conlan

The game-winning run nearly scored in the Braves fourth on a two-out rally. After Norm Larker and Mac Jones walked, Del Crandall singled to right-center. Larker tried to score, but the fabulous arm of Willie Mays cut him down at the plate.

Willie McCovey nearly ended it in the bottom of the ninth, but his towering drive to right left the field foul by inches.

It wasn't until the 14th that another runner reached third. Leading off for San Francisco, Harvey Kuenn doubled before Mays was intentionally walked. With the heart of the Giants lineup approaching, Spahn was in trouble. But the great left-hander got McCovey on a pop-up and Felipe Alou on a fly ball to center. He also induced Cepeda to hit a grounder toward third, but Dennis Menke misplayed it, loading the bases. Again Spahn showed his grit by getting Ed Bailey on a fly-out to strangle the rally.

Neither team reached base in the 15th, and the Braves could muster just a single in the top of the 16th. But in the bottom half, after one out, a hitless Mays picked on Spahn's first pitch and sent it over the left-field fence, ending what most consider one of the best pitching performances of the century.

# Monday Climaxes Dodgers' **40** Sprint to the Pennant

LOS ANGELES (NL) at MONTREAL (NL)
Monday, October 19, 1981, Olympic Stadium
Dodgers 2, Expos 1

With their backs to the wall, the Los Angeles Dodgers played their best in the 1981 post-season. After trailing the Houston Astros two games to none in a best-of-five Western Division playoff, the Dodgers reeled off three straight wins. In the National League Championship Series against Montreal, Los Angeles again found themselves in a precarious position, having lost two of the first three. But they won Game Four to reduce the National League season to a single Sunday game in Montreal. Rain postponed the championship match for a day, but on Monday, amid 41-degree temperatures, Canada's first pennant playoff was decided.

Taking the mound for the Dodgers was their 20-year-old rookie phenomenon, Fernando Valenzuela. The pudgy Mexican left-hander had taken the league by storm, winning his first eight games and then leading the majors in shutouts and strikeouts. He was opposed by journeyman right-hander Ray Burris, who had beaten Valenzuela five days earlier. After rocky starts, each hurler pitched superbly, affording the opposition few opportunities to score.

Both teams threatened in the first, but only the Expos scored. With one out, the Dodgers' Bill Russell slashed a triple down the right-field line, but Burris escaped on two ground-outs. Valenzuela was not as fortunate after Tim Raines led off with a double. Rodney Scott bunted, and Raines slid headfirst into third, beating the throw from Valenzuela. When Andre Dawson grounded into a double play, Raines crossed the plate with the game's first run.

Over the next three frames, each team was limited to a single, but Los Angeles finally scored in the fifth. Two singles, a wild pitch, and Valenzuela's ground-out tied the game at 1–1.

Neither pitcher had any further trouble until the bottom of the seventh when, after two outs, Larry Parrish doubled. Jerry White was walked intentionally to get to the left-handed Warren Cromartie, and the strategy succeeded as Cromartie popped out.

The Dodgers wasted a golden opportunity in the eighth. With one away Davey Lopes singled and stole second. When Russell grounded to short, Lopes became caught in a rundown between second and third, ending any serious trouble.

| Los Angeles | AB | R | H | I |
|---|---|---|---|---|
| Lopes D, 2b | 4 | 0 | 1 | 0 |
| Russell B, ss | 4 | 0 | 2 | 0 |
| Baker D, lf | 4 | 0 | 0 | 0 |
| Garvey S, 1b | 4 | 0 | 0 | 0 |
| Cey R, 3b | 3 | 0 | 0 | 0 |
| Monday R, rf | 4 | 2 | 2 | 1 |
| Guerrero P, cf | 4 | 0 | 1 | 0 |
| Scioscia M, c | 3 | 0 | 0 | 0 |
| Valenzuela F, p | 3 | 0 | 0 | 1 |
| Welch B, p | 0 | 0 | 0 | 0 |
| | 33 | 2 | 6 | 2 |

| Montreal | AB | R | H | I |
|---|---|---|---|---|
| Raines T, lf | 4 | 1 | 1 | 0 |
| Scott R, 2b | 3 | 0 | 0 | 0 |
| Dawson A, cf | 4 | 0 | 0 | 0 |
| Carter G, c | 3 | 0 | 1 | 0 |
| Manuel J, pr | 0 | 0 | 0 | 0 |
| Parrish L, 3b | 3 | 0 | 1 | 0 |
| White J, rf | 3 | 0 | 0 | 0 |
| Cromartie W, 1b | 3 | 0 | 0 | 0 |
| Speier C, ss | 3 | 0 | 0 | 0 |
| Burris R, p | 2 | 0 | 0 | 0 |
| Wallach T, ph | 1 | 0 | 0 | 0 |
| Rogers S, p | 0 | 0 | 0 | 0 |
| | 29 | 1 | 3 | 0 |

| Los Angeles | IP | H | R | ER | BB | SO |
|---|---|---|---|---|---|---|
| Valenzuela (W) | 8.2 | 3 | 1 | 1 | 3 | 6 |
| Welch (S) | 0.1 | 0 | 0 | 0 | 0 | 0 |
| | 9.0 | 3 | 1 | 1 | 3 | 6 |

| Montreal | IP | H | R | ER | BB | SO |
|---|---|---|---|---|---|---|
| Burris | 8.0 | 5 | 1 | 1 | 1 | 1 |
| Rogers (L) | 1.0 | 1 | 1 | 1 | 0 | 1 |
| | 9.0 | 6 | 2 | 2 | 1 | 2 |

| | | | |
|---|---|---|---|
| Los Angeles | 000 | 010 | 001 — 2 |
| Montreal | 100 | 000 | 000 — 1 |

OB: Los Angeles 5, Montreal 5; ER: Speier; DP: Los Angeles 1, Montreal 1; 2B: Raines, Parrish; 3B: Russell; HR: Monday; SB: Lopes; SH: Scott; WP: Burris; TI: 2:41; AT: 36,491; UM: HP Wendelstedt, 1B West, 2B Pryor, 3B Gregg, LF Runge, RF Rennert

Expos' vice president Jim Fanning, who replaced Dick Williams as manager six weeks earlier, decided he had gotten the best out of his starter. After pinchhitting for Burris in the eighth, Fanning called on his staff ace, Steve Rogers, to open the ninth. Rogers had allowed only two runs in his last 36 innings, but now he was pitching in relief for the first time in more than three years. The right-hander routinely retired the first two Dodgers before Rick Monday drilled a 3–1 pitch over the center-field wall, giving Los Angeles their first lead of the game. The dream of bringing Canada its first pennant abruptly started to fade.

In the bottom of the ninth, Valenzuela got two outs before walking both Gary Carter and Parrish on full counts. With switch hitter White the next batter, Dodger manager Tommy Lasorda called to the bullpen for right-hander Bob Welch. Lasorda reasoned that he'd rather have White bat left-handed, his weaker side. Welch threw one pitch, and White bounced out to Lopes for the final out, shattering Canadian dreams.

# The Century's Longest Shutout 41

NEW YORK (NL) at HOUSTON (NL)
Monday, April 15, 1968, Astrodome
Astros 1, Mets 0

More innings have been played in a major-league game — once — but this contest stands alone as the longest shutout in baseball history. The New York Mets and the Houston Astros (née Colt 45s), expansion clubs of 1962, had been perennial bottom dwellers during the first six years of their existence. And in each season except 1966, one of the two had scored the fewest runs in the league, with the other never far off the pace. So it's little wonder that if two clubs ever threatened a scoreless infinity, it would be these.

Starting for New York was Tom Seaver, who walked none and allowed just two hits over ten frames. Don Wilson, named to start by Houston manager Grady Hatton, went nine innings and permitted only five hits and three walks. Following the two starters was a parade of 11 relievers, made up of seven Mets and four Astros. As the innings wore on, pitchers looked more and more like Cy Young, and it became apparent that, short of a negotiated truce, the only way this contest would end was through a mistake.

There were plenty of baserunners: The two teams combined for 22 hits and 12 walks. But when it counted, no one could deliver the clutch hit, as each club squandered multiple scoring opportunities.

- With one out in the second, Houston's Hal King doubled and advanced to third on a wild-pitch. But on a subsequent grounder to second, King was thrown out at the plate.
- New York's Ed Kranepool led off the seventh with a single and was sacrificed to second. After a fly-out and a walk, Al Weis ended the frame by grounding out to first.
- In the ninth the Mets put runners on first and second with two outs, but Seaver tapped back to the pitcher.
- The Mets loaded the bases in the 12th with two outs, but Tommie Agee grounded out.
- Houston also threatened in the 12th, putting two on with only one away. But Rusty Staub fouled out, and King struck out.
- Again in the 13th the Astros had two on with one out before pinch-hitter Ivan Murrell flied out, and Ron Davis popped out.
- Some unusual strategy added extra intrigue in the 16th inning. With a Houston runner on first, no outs, the pitcher at bat, and a sacrifice in order,

| New York | AB | R | H | I |
|---|---|---|---|---|
| Weis A, ss | 9 | 0 | 1 | 0 |
| Boswell K, 2b | 10 | 0 | 1 | 0 |
| Agee T, cf | 10 | 0 | 0 | 0 |
| Swoboda R, rf | 10 | 0 | 0 | 0 |
| Shamsky A, lf | 4 | 0 | 2 | 0 |
| Jones C, pr-lf | 6 | 0 | 1 | 0 |
| Kranepool E, 1b | 8 | 0 | 2 | 0 |
| Buchek J, 3b | 2 | 0 | 0 | 0 |
| Charles E, 3b | 6 | 0 | 1 | 0 |
| Grote J, c | 7 | 0 | 2 | 0 |
| Seaver T, p | 3 | 0 | 1 | 0 |
| Taylor R, p | 0 | 0 | 0 | 0 |
| Linz P, ph | 1 | 0 | 0 | 0 |
| Koonce C, p | 0 | 0 | 0 | 0 |
| Short B, p | 0 | 0 | 0 | 0 |
| Selma D, p | 0 | 0 | 0 | 0 |
| Bosch D, ph | 1 | 0 | 0 | 0 |
| Jackson A, p | 0 | 0 | 0 | 0 |
| Harrelson B, ph | 1 | 0 | 0 | 0 |
| Frisella D, p | 1 | 0 | 0 | 0 |
| Cardwell D, ph | 0 | 0 | 0 | 0 |
| Rohr L, p | 0 | 0 | 0 | 0 |
| | 79 | 0 | 11 | 0 |

| Houston | AB | R | H | I |
|---|---|---|---|---|
| Davis R, cf | 10 | 0 | 1 | 0 |
| Miller N, rf | 8 | 1 | 1 | 0 |
| Wynn J, lf | 8 | 0 | 1 | 0 |
| Staub R, 1b | 9 | 0 | 2 | 0 |
| King H, c | 9 | 0 | 1 | 0 |
| Bateman J, ph | 0 | 0 | 0 | 0 |
| Aspromonte B, 3b | 9 | 0 | 0 | 0 |
| Gotay J, 2b | 9 | 0 | 2 | 0 |
| Torres H, ss | 8 | 0 | 3 | 0 |
| Wilson D, p | 2 | 0 | 0 | 0 |
| Thomas L, ph | 1 | 0 | 0 | 0 |
| Buzhardt J, p | 0 | 0 | 0 | 0 |
| Rader D, ph | 1 | 0 | 0 | 0 |
| Coombs D, p | 0 | 0 | 0 | 0 |
| Murrell I, ph | 1 | 0 | 0 | 0 |
| Ray J, p | 2 | 0 | 0 | 0 |
| Blasingame W, p | 2 | 0 | 0 | 0 |
| | 79 | 1 | 11 | 0 |

| New York | IP | H | R | ER | BB | SO |
|---|---|---|---|---|---|---|
| Seaver | 10.0 | 2 | 0 | 0 | 0 | 3 |
| Taylor | 1.0 | 1 | 0 | 0 | 0 | 1 |
| Koonce | 0.1 | 1 | 0 | 0 | 0 | 0 |
| Short | 1.0 | 1 | 0 | 0 | 2 | 1 |
| Selma | 0.2 | 0 | 0 | 0 | 0 | 0 |
| Jackson | 3.0 | 1 | 0 | 0 | 0 | 4 |
| Frisella | 5.0 | 4 | 0 | 0 | 1 | 4 |
| Rohr (L) | 2.1 | 1 | 1 | 0 | 4 | 2 |
| | 23.1 | 11 | 1 | 0 | 7 | 15 |

| Houston | IP | H | R | ER | BB | SO |
|---|---|---|---|---|---|---|
| Wilson | 9.0 | 5 | 0 | 0 | 3 | 5 |
| Buzhardt | 2.0 | 0 | 0 | 0 | 0 | 1 |
| Coombs | 2.0 | 3 | 0 | 0 | 0 | 2 |
| Ray | 7.0 | 2 | 0 | 0 | 1 | 11 |
| Blasingame (W) | 4.0 | 1 | 0 | 0 | 1 | 1 |
| | 24.0 | 11 | 0 | 0 | 5 | 20 |

| New York | 000 | 000 | 000 | 000 | 000 | 000 | 000 | 000 — 0 |
|---|---|---|---|---|---|---|---|---|
| Houston | 000 | 000 | 000 | 000 | 000 | 000 | 000 | 001 — 1 |

OB: New York 16, Houston 16; ER: Wilson, Weis; DP: New York 1, Houston 1; 2B: King Charles; SB: Jones, Charles; CS: Gotay, Miller; SH: Buchek, Miller, Grote, Kranepool, Cardwell; WP: Seaver, Wilson, Rohr; BK: Rohr; TI: 6:06; AT: 14,219; UM: Sudol, Weyer, Williams, Gorman

Mets' manager Gil Hodges ordered left fielder Ron Swoboda into the infield. The strategy became unnecessary, however, as Astros pitcher Jim Ray tried to bunt three times and struck out.

• Ed Charles opened the New York 17th with a double and was sacrificed to third. Pinch-hitter Bud Harrelson failed to execute a suicide squeeze, fouling off three bunt attempts, and Al Weis ended the threat by grounding out.

• The Mets threatened again in the 19th. Leading off, Cleon Jones singled and was sacrificed to second. After Charles was intentionally passed, the runners pulled a double steal. Jim Ray then retired the next two hitters, Jerry Grote and Danny Frisella, on swinging third strikes.

• With two outs in the Houston 19th Jimmy Wynn and Staub singled, but King, with another chance to be the hero, flied out.

• In the 22nd, New York got Grote to second with two outs, but Weis grounded out.

• The Astros also threatened in their half of the 22nd. With one away Staub walked and moved to second on a ground-out. But after an intentional pass, Julio Gotay fanned.

The marathon of impotence finally ended in the last of the 24th. Norm Miller, unsuccessful in seven official at-bats, led off with a single and was balked to second by Les Rohr. After Wynn was intentionally walked, Staub advanced the runners by grounding out to second. John Bateman pinch-hit for King and was also purposely passed, loading the bases. Next, Bob Aspromonte took two balls, fouled one off and then sent a sharp grounder toward the Mets' shortstop. Weis had played brilliantly all night but wasn't quite the man he'd been six hours earlier. Al didn't bend quickly enough for the grounder, and it zipped through his legs into left field, enabling Miller to trot home with the game-winning tally. It was Houston's first run after 35 consecutive scoreless frames, and the first run Mets' pitching allowed after 38 straight scoreless innings.

On the missed double-play ball, an exhausted Weis could say later only that he just plain blew it. Aspromonte, the equally weary batting hero, later said his bat felt like it weighed eight and a half pounds when he carried it to the plate.

The frustrating night was shared by all the Mets, but especially Swoboda and Tommie Agee. Swoboda went down swinging five times; Agee struck out swinging three times and was called out once. Each went 0-for-10, narrowly avoiding an ignominious entry into the record books.

Displays of tenacity and stamina could be found both on the field and in the stands. Not only did opposing catchers Grote and King catch all 24 innings during the six-hour marathon, but about 5,000 fans were still present at the 1:37 A.M. conclusion. An hour earlier, as they stood before Houston came to bat, the scoreboard flashed, "21st Inning Stretch."

# Teams Combine for 15 Runs in the 12th Inning   42

BROOKLYN (FL) at ST. LOUIS (FL)
Tuesday, June 16, 1914, Federal League Park
Terriers 13, Tiptops 12

The success of the major leagues inspired imitation by entrepreneurs, and in 1914 wealthy businessmen formed the Federal League and declared it a "major

| Brooklyn | AB | R | H | I |
|---|---|---|---|---|
| Anderson G, lf | 7 | 2 | 2 | 0 |
| Cooper C, cf | 6 | 1 | 1 | 1 |
| Griggs A, 1b | 6 | 2 | 2 | 0 |
| Murphy D, rf | 4 | 2 | 2 | 3 |
| Hofman S, 2b | 5 | 2 | 4 | 1 |
| Westerzil T, 3b | 6 | 1 | 2 | 2 |
| Gagnier E, ss | 6 | 1 | 1 | 2 |
| Land G, c | 4 | 0 | 0 | 1 |
| Seaton T, p | 6 | 1 | 3 | 2 |
| Houck D, p | 0 | 0 | 0 | 0 |
| Sommers R, p | 0 | 0 | 0 | 0 |
| | 50 | 12 | 17 | 12 |

| St. Louis | AB | R | H | I |
|---|---|---|---|---|
| Marsans A, 2b | 7 | 1 | 5 | 1 |
| Tobin J, rf | 5 | 2 | 2 | 1 |
| Miller W, lf | 5 | 0 | 3 | 3 |
| Kommers F, cf | 5 | 2 | 1 | 0 |
| Miller H, ph | 1 | 0 | 1 | 1 |
| Drake D, 1b | 6 | 2 | 1 | 0 |
| Boucher A, 3b | 6 | 1 | 2 | 2 |
| Bridwell A, ss | 5 | 2 | 2 | 1 |
| Simon M, c | 5 | 1 | 0 | 1 |
| Davenport D, p | 3 | 0 | 0 | 0 |
| Crandall D, ph | 1 | 0 | 1 | 1 |
| Chapman H, pr | 0 | 1 | 0 | 0 |
| Brown M, p | 1 | 0 | 0 | 0 |
| Hartley G, ph | 1 | 1 | 1 | 1 |
| | 51 | 13 | 19 | 12 |

| Brooklyn | IP | H | R | ER | BB | SO |
|---|---|---|---|---|---|---|
| Seaton (L) | 11.1 | 17 | 13 | 11 | 4 | 9 |
| Houck | 0.0 | 1 | 0 | 0 | 1 | 0 |
| Sommers | 0.0 | 1 | 0 | 0 | 0 | 0 |
| | 11.1 | 19 | 13 | 11 | 5 | 9 |

| St. Louis | IP | H | R | ER | BB | SO |
|---|---|---|---|---|---|---|
| Davenport | 9.0 | 8 | 5 | 5 | 4 | 8 |
| Brown (W) | 3.0 | 9 | 7 | 7 | 0 | 3 |
| | 12.0 | 17 | 12 | 12 | 4 | 11 |

```
Brooklyn    300  000  020  007 — 12
St Louis    300  000  002  008 — 13
```

OB: Brooklyn 9, St. Louis 11; ER: Anderson 2, Westerzil, Drake, Brown; DP: St. Louis 1; 2B: Hofman, Bridwell, Westerzil, Cooper; 3B: Westerzil, Griggs; HR: Murphy, Seaton, Tobin; SB: Drake, Boucher, W. Miller, Land, Cooper; SH: Griggs, Murphy, Tobin; SF: Land; HP: by Seaton (W. Miller); WP: Brown; TI: 2:55; AT: 300; UM: Anderson, Van Sickle

league." Lasting but two seasons, it nevertheless is still considered one of history's major leagues by Major League Baseball. Waving lucrative contracts, the owners were able to lure many American and National Leaguers into their fold. Most of the defectors, however, were past their primes and some of them, playing alongside the ample green recruits filling out most rosters, had a hand in a few bizarre games.

This contest saw the Brooklyn entry, the Tiptops, jump out to a 3–0 lead in the top of the first on a single, walk, and Danny Murphy's wallop over the right-field wall. Their host, the St. Louis Terriers, tied it in the home half on four singles, two steals, and an error.

It wasn't until the eighth that either club again crossed the plate. Brooklyn scored twice on a single, double and Tex Westerzil's triple. St. Louis waited until the ninth to tie it again, relying on a clutch two-out single by Ward Miller to send the game into extra innings.

Thirty-seven-year-old Terrier player-manager Mordecai "Three Finger" Brown then installed himself on the mound to start the 10th. He handled the Tiptops easily until the 12th, when the once-great pitching arm was cruelly tested. After striking out Claude Cooper, Art Griggs tripled, Murphy and Solly Hofman singled, and Westerzil doubled. Eddie Gagnier singled, Grover Land sacrificed, Seaton homered, George Anderson singled, and Cooper doubled, giving the visitors a seven-run advantage. Amazingly, despite the fireworks, Brown did not summon relief. So thrilled and confident were the Tiptops with their 12–5 margin, that Griggs ended the frame by purposely waving at three pitches.

But the Terriers weren't about to roll over and die. Twice before they had come from behind to knot the score, and now Jack Tobin led off the bottom of the 12th with a home run. After Ward Miller grounded out, Fred Kommers, Delos Drake, and Al Boucher each singled. Anderson dropped Al Bridwell's fly, and Mike Simon walked. Grover Hartley pinch-hit for his manager and beat out an infield roller. After Armando Marsans singled, Seaton was finally relieved by Duke Houck with the score 12–11. Houck faced only two hitters: Tobin singled, loading the bases, and Miller walked, forcing in the tying run. Then, with the sacks jammed and just one out, Brooklyn's Rudy Sommers was called upon to quiet the hometown fans, who were celebrating with a throwing frenzy. Bats, hats, coats, and anything that wasn't nailed down was being tossed about. Hugh Miller then batted for Kommers and singled home the game-winning eighth run. All totaled, 15 runners had crossed the plate in this 12th inning, the most runs scored in an extra inning in 20th-century major league baseball.

# *Dodgers Clinch in Final Game of the Season* 43

BROOKLYN (NL) at PHILADELPHIA (NL)
Sunday, October 2, 1949, Shibe Park
Dodgers 9, Phillies 7

It was a joyous day for New York baseball fans, who saw two of their teams gain World Series berths on the final day of the regular season. In the American League the schedule makers were omniscient, having pitted the New York Yankees and the Boston Red Sox, with identical records after 153 games, to meet in a season-ending game. The Yankees won a close game, 5–3, although they led throughout. For the Brooklyn Dodgers the story was different.

Entering the last day of the campaign the Dodgers were playing in Philadelphia while holding a one-game lead over the second place St. Louis Cardinals. St. Louis had squandered a near-certain pennant by losing four in a row and six of their last nine but hung onto one last hope. If they could win and the Dodgers lost, a three-game playoff would ensue. Meanwhile, the Dodgers needed only to win their last game to assure themselves of a trip to the World

| Brooklyn | AB | R | H | I |
|---|---|---|---|---|
| Reese P, ss | 5 | 1 | 1 | 0 |
| Jorgensen S, 3b | 3 | 1 | 1 | 0 |
| Edwards B, ph | 1 | 0 | 0 | 0 |
| Miksis E, 3b | 0 | 0 | 0 | 0 |
| Snider D, cf | 4 | 1 | 1 | 1 |
| Robinson J, 2b | 3 | 1 | 1 | 1 |
| Hermanski G, lf | 3 | 1 | 0 | 0 |
| Olmo L, ph-lf | 2 | 0 | 1 | 1 |
| Furillo C, rf | 6 | 2 | 4 | 1 |
| Hodges G, 1b | 4 | 2 | 2 | 1 |
| Campanella R, c | 3 | 0 | 1 | 2 |
| Newcombe D, p | 2 | 0 | 1 | 2 |
| Barney R, p | 1 | 0 | 0 | 0 |
| Banta J, p | 1 | 0 | 0 | 0 |
| | 38 | 9 | 13 | 9 |

| Philadelphia | AB | R | H | I |
|---|---|---|---|---|
| Ashburn R, cf | 6 | 0 | 2 | 1 |
| Hamner G, ss | 5 | 1 | 1 | 1 |
| Sisler D, 1b | 4 | 0 | 1 | 0 |
| Ennis D, lf | 4 | 2 | 2 | 1 |
| Seminick A, c | 5 | 0 | 0 | 0 |
| Nicholson B, rf | 4 | 1 | 1 | 1 |
| Jones W, 3b | 5 | 1 | 1 | 3 |
| Goliat M, 2b | 5 | 1 | 2 | 0 |
| Meyer R, p | 0 | 0 | 0 | 0 |
| Roberts R, p | 0 | 0 | 0 | 0 |
| Blattner B, ph | 0 | 0 | 0 | 0 |
| Thompson J, p | 0 | 0 | 0 | 0 |
| Hollmig S, ph | 1 | 0 | 1 | 0 |
| Simmons C, p | 0 | 0 | 0 | 0 |
| Konstanty J, p | 0 | 0 | 0 | 0 |
| Blatnik J, ph | 1 | 1 | 1 | 0 |
| Heintzelman K, p | 1 | 0 | 0 | 0 |
| Trinkle K, p | 0 | 0 | 0 | 0 |
| Sanicki E, ph | 1 | 0 | 0 | 0 |
| | 42 | 7 | 12 | 7 |

| Brooklyn | IP | H | R | ER | BB | SO |
|---|---|---|---|---|---|---|
| Newcombe | 3.1 | 6 | 4 | 4 | 2 | 2 |
| Barney | 2.1 | 4 | 3 | 3 | 1 | 1 |
| Banta (W) | 4.1 | 2 | 0 | 0 | 1 | 3 |
| | 10.0 | 12 | 7 | 7 | 4 | 6 |

| Philadelphia | IP | H | R | ER | BB | SO |
|---|---|---|---|---|---|---|
| Meyer | 2.2 | 5 | 5 | 5 | 3 | 0 |
| Roberts | 0.1 | 1 | 0 | 0 | 1 | 0 |
| Thompson | 1.0 | 0 | 0 | 0 | 1 | 0 |
| Simmons | 0.0 | 2 | 2 | 2 | 0 | 0 |
| Konstanty | 2.0 | 1 | 0 | 0 | 1 | 1 |
| Heintzelman (L) | 3.1 | 4 | 2 | 2 | 4 | 0 |
| Trinkle | 0.2 | 0 | 0 | 0 | 0 | 0 |
| | 10.0 | 13 | 9 | 9 | 10 | 1 |

```
Brooklyn        005  020  000  2 — 9
Philadelphia    000  412  000  0 — 7
```

OB: Brooklyn 12, Philadelphia 9; ER: Sisler, Seminick, Furillo; DP: Philadelphia 1; 2B: Hollmig, Campanella, Nicholson; HR: Jones; SB: Jorgensen, Robinson 2; CS: Robinson; SH: Banta, Robinson, Miksis; WP: Meyer; PB: Seminick; TI: 3:17; AT: 36,765; UM: HP Goetz, 1B Reardon, 2B Barlick, 3B Jorda

Series. In a game that saw abundant pitching changes, Brooklyn mounted several leads, but the stubborn Phillies clawed back while the Cardinals won in Chicago.

Philadelphia threatened in the first after Richie Ashburn led off with a single. Two ground ball outs pushed him to third, but Del Ennis flied out.

The Dodgers also got a runner to third with two outs in the third frame, but, unlike the Phils, they made the most of their opportunity. Four singles, two walks, a stolen base, and a wild pitch led to a five-run outburst. Don Newcombe had an important two-run single, and Brooklyn confidence swelled.

In the fourth the Phillies retaliated. A single and a walk preceded a Willie Jones home run. Then another single, double, and a sacrifice fly added a fourth run to the Philadelphia scoresheet, making it 5–4. During this frame, Rex Barney replaced Newcombe on the mound for Brooklyn.

The Dodgers added two more in the fifth. Two singles and a Roy Campanella double pushed over the pair and put the visitors in front, 7–4. Campanella moved to third on catcher Andy Seminick's error but languished there as his next three mates were retired by the Phillies' fifth hurler, Jim Konstanty.

In the bottom of the fifth, Philadelphia chipped away with another run. After Ennis walked, Bill Nicholson doubled him home to make it 7–5.

The Phillies rallied again in the sixth, collecting four singles to tie the game. Before the uprising ended, Jack Banta replaced Barney on the hill for Brooklyn, and the lanky right-hander shined in his relief role over the next four innings.

The first two Dodgers reached base in the seventh and two outs later were stationed at second and third. Pee Wee Reese was passed intentionally, but Ken Heintzelman dispatched pinch-hitter Bruce Edwards on a pop-up.

As the game lengthened, word came out of Chicago that the Cardinals had won. Now the Dodgers faced a three-game playoff unless they could capture this game in Philadelphia.

No other runner reached third until the 10th inning, when Reese singled and was sacrificed to second. Duke Snider drove him home with another single and went to second on a play at the plate. Obviously, many in the huge crowd had made a trip south from Brooklyn, as the park now rattled with elation. Jackie Robinson, the National League batting champion, then was passed intentionally before Luis Olmo singled Snider home, making it 9–7.

In the bottom of the 10th the Phillies faced their last chance to play spoiler. Mike Goliat singled with one out, only the second hit off Banta. That brought the potential tying run to the plate. First it appeared in the person of pinch-hitter Ed Sanicki, a powerful late-season call-up who had only three hits for Philadelphia — but all of them home runs. Sanicki took the count full before fanning. The last obstacle was Ashburn, who quietly flied out to Olmo in left. Brooklyn, who had battled back from second place during the final weeks of the season, had squeaked out an extra-inning victory in their last game to advance to the World Series.

# *The Infamous Third Strike That Got Away* 44

NEW YORK (AL) at BROOKLYN (NL)
Sunday, October 5, 1941, Ebbets Field
Yankees 7, Dodgers 4

Anything can happen in Brooklyn. That was the sentiment shared by the Flatbush faithful after witnessing a history of frustrating events transpire in Ebbets Field. This game reinforced that notion.

| New York | AB | R | H | I |
|---|---|---|---|---|
| Sturm J, 1b | 5 | 0 | 2 | 2 |
| Rolfe R, 3b | 5 | 1 | 2 | 0 |
| Henrich T, rf | 4 | 1 | 0 | 0 |
| DiMaggio J, cf | 4 | 1 | 2 | 0 |
| Keller C, lf | 5 | 1 | 4 | 3 |
| Dickey B, c | 2 | 2 | 0 | 0 |
| Gordon J, 2b | 5 | 1 | 2 | 2 |
| Rizzuto P, ss | 4 | 0 | 0 | 0 |
| Donald A, p | 2 | 0 | 0 | 0 |
| Breuer M, p | 1 | 0 | 0 | 0 |
| Selkirk G, ph | 1 | 0 | 0 | 0 |
| Murphy J, p | 1 | 0 | 0 | 0 |
| | 39 | 7 | 12 | 7 |

| Brooklyn | AB | R | H | I |
|---|---|---|---|---|
| Reese P, ss | 5 | 0 | 0 | 0 |
| Walker D, rf | 5 | 1 | 2 | 0 |
| Reiser P, cf | 5 | 1 | 2 | 2 |
| Camilli D, 1b | 4 | 0 | 2 | 0 |
| Riggs L, 3b | 3 | 0 | 0 | 0 |
| Medwick J, lf | 2 | 0 | 0 | 0 |
| Allen J, p | 0 | 0 | 0 | 0 |
| Casey H, p | 2 | 0 | 1 | 0 |
| Owen M, c | 2 | 1 | 0 | 0 |
| Coscarart P, 2b | 3 | 1 | 0 | 0 |
| Higbe K, p | 1 | 0 | 1 | 0 |
| French L, p | 0 | 0 | 0 | 0 |
| Wasdell J, ph-lf | 3 | 0 | 1 | 2 |
| | 35 | 4 | 9 | 4 |

| New York | IP | H | R | ER | BB | SO |
|---|---|---|---|---|---|---|
| Donald | 4.0 | 6 | 4 | 4 | 3 | 2 |
| Breuer | 3.0 | 3 | 0 | 0 | 1 | 2 |
| Murphy (W) | 2.0 | 0 | 0 | 0 | 0 | 1 |
| | 9.0 | 9 | 4 | 4 | 4 | 5 |

| Brooklyn | IP | H | R | ER | BB | SO |
|---|---|---|---|---|---|---|
| Higbe | 3.2 | 6 | 3 | 3 | 2 | 1 |
| French | 0.1 | 0 | 0 | 0 | 0 | 0 |
| Allen | 0.2 | 1 | 0 | 0 | 1 | 0 |
| Casey (L) | 4.1 | 5 | 4 | 0 | 2 | 1 |
| | 9.0 | 12 | 7 | 3 | 5 | 2 |

```
New York    100  200  004 — 7
Brooklyn    000  220  000 — 4
```

OB: New York 11, Brooklyn 8; ER: Owen; DP: New York 1; 2B: Camilli, Keller 2, Wasdell, Walker, Gordon; HR: Reiser; HP: by Allen (Henrich); TI: 2:54; AT: 33,813; UM: HP Goetz, 1B McGowan, 2B Pinelli, 3B Grieve

Playing in their first World Series in 21 seasons, Leo Durocher led the Dodgers against their favored inter-borough rivals, the New York Yankees. For the Yankees, post-season play was nothing new. Joe McCarthy had led them to four consecutive World Championships, from 1936 through 1939, while dominating the best of the National League 16 games to 3. They also prevailed in two of the first three contests this year.

After Mayor La Guardia tossed out the first ball, Game Four commenced under a blistering midsummer-like sun. A pair of right-handers, the Yankees' Atley Donald and the Dodgers' Kirby Higbe, started the game, but neither hung on past the fourth inning.

New York broke on top in the first on a two-out RBI single by Charlie "King Kong" Keller. In the fourth they increased their margin to 3–0 as first baseman Johnny Sturm slashed a bases-loaded single to center.

The home club retaliated in the bottom half with a pair of their own. After Donald retired the first two batters, a pair of walks and Jimmy Wasdell's long double made it 3–2.

The Yankees squandered a golden opportunity in the fifth. After they loaded the bases with two outs, Hugh Casey came in from the bullpen and retired Joe Gordon on a long fly to left. In the bottom of the frame the Dodgers again went to work on Donald. Dixie Walker led off with a double before batting champion Pete Reiser crashed a pitch over the right-field fence. The blow gave the home club its first lead, at 4–3, and sent the crowd into ecstasy.

Then the relievers took control of the action, allowing neither team to mount a serious rally until the ninth. Casey was particularly effective, retiring 12 of the 14 hitters he faced.

Leading off the ninth for New York, Sturm and Red Rolfe both grounded out. Casey had retired seven Yankees in order. And when Tommy Henrich worked the count full, Brooklyn was one pitch away from tying the Series. Casey's next delivery was a grand, sweeping curve. Henrich swung and missed, setting into motion a chaotic series of events. While home plate umpire Larry Goetz raised his arm signaling the third strike, the ball glanced off the glove of Brooklyn backstop Mickey Owen and rolled toward the Dodger dugout. Policemen stationed in the Dodger dugout, thinking the game had ended, charged onto the field to hold back the euphoric crowd. As Owen fought his way through the police to retrieve the ball, Henrich recognized the situation and raced to first, arriving without a throw. Several Yankee players, who were already in the runway and heading toward the visitors' locker room, returned to the dugout. Strangely, however, no one went to the mound to talk with Casey or give him an opportunity to recover.

The Dodgers still needed only one out to tie the Series, but the home club was shaken. The next batter, Joe DiMaggio, blistered a line drive single to left. A moment later Keller drove an 0–2 pitch high against the right-field screen, narrowly missing a home run. It was, however, deep enough to drive home both Henrich with the tying run and DiMaggio with the lead run. The Dodgers seemed paralyzed, and again no manager, coach, or teammate went to comfort or relieve Casey. The right-hander then walked Bill Dickey before Gordon laced a double to left, sending two more mates home and giving New York an astonishing 7–4 lead.

The bottom of the ninth was without incident, as three Dodgers failed to get the ball out of the infield. The shocked Dodgers left the park trailing three games to one and lost the Series the following day.

# *Hubbell's* 45
# *18-Inning Whitewash*

ST. LOUIS (NL) at NEW YORK (NL)
Sunday, July 2, 1933, Polo Grounds
Giants 1, Cardinals 0

Although the New York Giants offense finished sixth in team batting in 1933, their pitching staff kept them atop the National League. The backbone of

## First Game

| St. Louis | AB | R | H | I |
|---|---|---|---|---|
| Martin P, 3b | 7 | 0 | 0 | 0 |
| Frisch F, 2b | 7 | 0 | 0 | 0 |
| Orsatti E, cf | 7 | 0 | 1 | 0 |
| Collins R, 1b | 7 | 0 | 2 | 0 |
| Medwick J, lf | 7 | 0 | 1 | 0 |
| Allen E, rf | 6 | 0 | 0 | 0 |
| Wilson J, c | 6 | 0 | 2 | 0 |
| Durocher L, ss | 3 | 0 | 0 | 0 |
| Hornsby R, ph | 1 | 0 | 0 | 0 |
| Slade G, ss | 1 | 0 | 0 | 0 |
| Carleton T, p | 4 | 0 | 0 | 0 |
| O'Farrell B, ph | 1 | 0 | 0 | 0 |
| Haines J, p | 0 | 0 | 0 | 0 |
| | 57 | 0 | 6 | 0 |

| New York | AB | R | H | I |
|---|---|---|---|---|
| Critz H, 2b | 9 | 0 | 3 | 1 |
| O'Doul L, lf | 4 | 0 | 1 | 0 |
| James B, pr | 0 | 0 | 0 | 0 |
| Davis K, cf | 2 | 0 | 0 | 0 |
| Terry B, 1b | 6 | 0 | 2 | 0 |
| Ott M, rf | 6 | 0 | 0 | 0 |
| Vergez J, 3b | 5 | 0 | 0 | 0 |
| Moore J, cf-lf | 7 | 1 | 0 | 0 |
| Mancuso G, c | 7 | 0 | 1 | 0 |
| Ryan B, ss | 6 | 0 | 2 | 0 |
| Jackson T, ph | 0 | 0 | 0 | 0 |
| Hubbell C, p | 7 | 0 | 1 | 0 |
| | 59 | 1 | 10 | 1 |

| St. Louis | IP | H | R | ER | BB | SO |
|---|---|---|---|---|---|---|
| Carleton | 16.0 | 8 | 0 | 0 | 7 | 7 |
| Haines (L) | 1.2 | 2 | 1 | 1 | 3 | 1 |
| | 17.2 | 10 | 1 | 1 | 10 | 8 |

| New York | IP | H | R | ER | BB | SO |
|---|---|---|---|---|---|---|
| Hubbell (W) | 18.0 | 6 | 0 | 0 | 0 | 12 |

```
St.Louis    000  000  000  000  000  000 — 0
New York    000  000  000  000  000  001 — 1
```

OB: St. Louis 5, New York 19; DP: New York 1; 2B: Orsatti, Collins; 3B: Terry; SH: Slade, Carleton, Davis, Terry, Mancuso, Hubbell; TI: 4:03; AT: 50,000; UM: Klem, Pfirman, Barr

that staff was future Hall of Famer Carl Hubbell, nicknamed "King Carl" and "The Mealticket." Hubbell was at his finest this day when, in the first game of a doubleheader, he tossed a four-hour, 18-inning shutout.

On the morning of July 2, the Giants occupied first place with the Cardinals only three and one-half games behind. St. Louis had just beaten the league leaders in two of the last three games and was looking forward to this twin bill to further tighten the gap. The Giants, as usual, didn't do much hitting but rode the arms of Hubbell and Roy Parmelee to win both games by 1–0 scores, quite a feat considering the Cardinals led the league in both runs scored and RBI this year.

Hubbell's game was extraordinary. Twelve of his 18 innings were perfect. He allowed only six hits (four were of the infield variety), walked none, and permitted only one runner to reach third. The left-hander retired the first 12 batters, later sat down 19 straight, and disposed of an additional ten consecutively near the end of the game. His mound opponent, Tex Carleton, also pitched a magnificent game. But pitching on only two days' rest, he tired after 16 shutout frames and was relieved by Jesse Haines. The Giants reached Haines in the bottom of the 18th when Jo-Jo Moore led off with a walk and was sacrificed to second. Hubbell's ground-out pushed Moore to third, and Hughie Critz singled home the game-winning run.

King Carl's performance was not an anomaly. He proceeded to win 23 games — including 10 shutouts — compiled a 1.66 ERA, hurled 45.1 consecutive scoreless innings, and walked only 47 in 309 innings. And if that wasn't enough, he beat the Senators twice in the World Series and was named the National League MVP.

## Johnson Outduels Williams in 18 Innings 46

CHICAGO (AL) at WASHINGTON (AL)
Wednesday, May 15, 1918, Griffith Stadium
Nationals 1, White Sox 0

In one of the century's greatest pitching matchups, Washington's Walter Johnson outlasted Chicago's Lefty Williams in 18 innings, 1–0. The Chicago southpaw was superb, tossing a perfect game until there were two outs in the seventh, then allowing only seven singles and one walk through the final 11 frames. Lefty's fastball was rising this day as the Nationals made 35 of their outs either by pop-ups or fly balls, including 15 of the first 21 batters. Johnson, however, was equal to the challenge. Although he gave up 10 safeties, including two doubles, he struck out nine and allowed more than one baserunner in only the first and 14th innings. As a result, each team had precious few scoring opportunities.

Not a soul reached third base until the seventh, when Chicago's Eddie Murphy singled and moved ahead on a sacrifice and a ground-out. But there his run died as Shano Collins also grounded out.

The Nationals had several golden scoring opportunities in the eighth. Ray Morgan was hit by a pitch and moved to second on a single by Eddie Foster. Eddie Ainsmith next sent a scorcher back at Williams, who threw to third to force out Morgan. Johnson popped out, but Burt Shotton walked to load the bases. Williams escaped when Doc Lavan flied out.

Both pitchers then dominated as third base remained pristine until the 18th inning. Then, with one out, Chicago's Swede Risberg doubled. Fortunately for Washington, a great play by Shotton in right field limited Risberg to two bags; after the next batter flied out, a passed ball sent Risberg to third instead of home. Johnson then tried to walk Ray Shalk intentionally to get to Williams, whom he had fanned five times. But Shalk reached out and slapped the ball to second for an easy ground-out, ending the threat.

The pitching classic ended in Washington's half of the 18th. After one out, Ainsmith and Johnson both singled, with Ainsmith moving to third. Williams

| Chicago | AB | R | H | I | | Washington | AB | R | H | I |
|---------|----|----|----|----|---|------------|----|----|----|----|
| Leibold N, lf | 7 | 0 | 1 | 0 | | Shotton B, rf | 7 | 0 | 1 | 0 |
| Murphy E, rf | 6 | 0 | 3 | 0 | | Lavan D, ss | 7 | 0 | 0 | 0 |
| Weaver B, ss | 6 | 0 | 2 | 0 | | Milan C, cf | 7 | 0 | 2 | 0 |
| Gandil C, 1b | 7 | 0 | 0 | 0 | | Shanks H, lf | 6 | 0 | 1 | 0 |
| Collins S, cf | 7 | 0 | 0 | 0 | | Judge J, 1b | 7 | 0 | 1 | 0 |
| Risberg S, 2b | 7 | 0 | 1 | 0 | | Morgan R, 2b | 5 | 0 | 0 | 0 |
| McMullin F, 3b | 7 | 0 | 2 | 0 | | Foster E, 3b | 7 | 0 | 1 | 0 |
| Schalk R, c | 6 | 0 | 1 | 0 | | Ainsmith E, c | 7 | 1 | 1 | 0 |
| Williams L, p | 6 | 0 | 0 | 0 | | Johnson W, p | 7 | 0 | 1 | 0 |
| | 59 | 0 | 10 | 0 | | | 60 | 1 | 8 | 0 |

| Chicago | IP | H | R | ER | BB | SO | Washington | IP | H | R | ER | BB | SO |
|---------|----|----|----|----|----|----|------------|----|----|----|----|----|----|
| Williams (L) | 17.1 | 8 | 1 | 1 | 2 | 3 | Johnson (W) | 18.0 | 10 | 0 | 0 | 1 | 9 |

Chicago      000·  000   000   000   000   000 — 0
Washington   000   000   000   000   000   001 — 1

OB: Chicago 8, Washington 10; DP: Washington 1; 2B: Murphy, Risberg; CS: McMullin;
Weaver; SH: Weaver, Schalk; HP: by Williams (Morgan); WP: Williams; PB: Ainsmith;
TI: 2:47; AT: 1,700; UM: Owens, Hildebrand

went to a 2–0 count on Shotton before unleashing a wild pitch over the head
of Shalk. As it rolled to the grandstand, Ainsmith romped home with the game
winner.

Several other facts about this game are noteworthy. Although errors in 1918
occurred at the lively rate of three per nine-inning game, this contest, essentially
a doubleheader, saw none. There were no substitutions, and the game was completed in under three hours. Clark Griffith, a pitcher for 21 seasons and the manager of the Nationals that day, called it the best extra-inning game he had ever seen.

# 47 Understudy Cabrera Assumes Head Role, Saves Braves

PITTSBURGH (NL) at ATLANTA (NL)
Wednesday, October 14, 1992, Fulton County Stadium
Braves 3, Pirates 2

In a sport that often provides a stage for unlikely heroes, Game Seven
of the 1992 NLCS represented something like a Broadway debut for an
unknown.

| Pittsburgh | AB | R | H | I |
|---|---|---|---|---|
| Cole A, rf | 2 | 1 | 0 | 0 |
| McClendon L, ph-rf | 0 | 0 | 0 | 0 |
| Espy C, pr-rf | 0 | 0 | 0 | 0 |
| Bell J, ss | 4 | 1 | 1 | 0 |
| Van Slyke A, cf | 4 | 0 | 2 | 1 |
| Bonds B, lf | 3 | 0 | 1 | 0 |
| Merced O, 1b | 3 | 0 | 0 | 1 |
| King J, 3b | 4 | 0 | 1 | 0 |
| LaValliere M, c | 4 | 0 | 1 | 0 |
| Lind J, 2b | 4 | 0 | 1 | 0 |
| Drabek D, p | 3 | 0 | 0 | 0 |
| Belinda S, p | 0 | 0 | 0 | 0 |
| | 31 | 2 | 7 | 2 |

| Atlanta | AB | R | H | I |
|---|---|---|---|---|
| Nixon O, cf | 4 | 0 | 1 | 0 |
| Blauser J, ss | 4 | 0 | 0 | 0 |
| Pendleton T, 3b | 4 | 1 | 1 | 0 |
| Justice D, rf | 4 | 1 | 0 | 0 |
| Bream S, 1b | 3 | 1 | 1 | 0 |
| Gant R, lf | 2 | 0 | 0 | 1 |
| Berryhill D, c | 3 | 0 | 1 | 0 |
| Lemke M, 2b | 2 | 0 | 1 | 0 |
| Smith L, ph | 1 | 0 | 0 | 0 |
| Belliard R, 2b | 0 | 0 | 0 | 0 |
| Hunter B, ph | 1 | 0 | 0 | 0 |
| Smoltz J, p | 1 | 0 | 0 | 0 |
| Treadway J, ph | 1 | 0 | 1 | 0 |
| Stanton M, p | 0 | 0 | 0 | 0 |
| Smith P, p | 0 | 0 | 0 | 0 |
| Avery S, p | 0 | 0 | 0 | 0 |
| Sanders D, ph | 1 | 0 | 0 | 0 |
| Reardon J, p | 0 | 0 | 0 | 0 |
| Cabrera F, ph | 1 | 0 | 1 | 2 |
| | 32 | 3 | 7 | 3 |

| Pittsburgh | IP | H | R | ER | BB | SO |
|---|---|---|---|---|---|---|
| Drabek (L) | 8.0 | 6 | 3 | 1 | 2 | 5 |
| Belinda | 0.2 | 1 | 0 | 0 | 1 | 0 |
| | 8.2 | 7 | 3 | 1 | 3 | 5 |

| Atlanta | IP | H | R | ER | BB | SO |
|---|---|---|---|---|---|---|
| Smoltz | 6.0 | 4 | 2 | 2 | 2 | 4 |
| Stanton | 0.2 | 1 | 0 | 0 | 1 | 0 |
| Smith | 0.0 | 0 | 0 | 0 | 1 | 0 |
| Avery | 1.1 | 2 | 0 | 0 | 0 | 0 |
| Reardon (W) | 1.0 | 0 | 0 | 0 | 1 | 1 |
| | 9.0 | 7 | 2 | 2 | 5 | 5 |

| | | | | |
|---|---|---|---|---|
| Pittsburgh | 100 | 001 | 000 — 2 |
| Atlanta | 000 | 000 | 003 — 3 |

OB: Pittsburgh 9, Atlanta 7; ER: Lind; DP: Pittsburgh 1; 2B: Van Slyke, Berryhill, Lind, Bell, Bream, King, Pendleton; SH: Drabek; SF: Merced, Gant; WP: Reardon; TI: 3:22; AT: 51,975; UM: HP McSherry, 1B Marsh, 2B Rippley, 3B Darling, LF Davis, RF Montague

The Pittsburgh Pirates, unsuccessful in the NLCS for the past two years, bounced back this year from a three-games-to-one deficit to earn a seventh game appearance. Their opponent, the Atlanta Braves, had vanquished these same Pirates a year earlier before losing in the World Series.

Pittsburgh broke out in front on Orlando Merced's sacrifice fly in the first and then added another run in the sixth on Andy Van Slyke's RBI single.

In the home half of the sixth, the Braves loaded the bases with no outs. Before frenzied fans who waved foam-rubber tomahawks and chanted, Jeff Blauser lined sharply to a drawn-in third baseman, Jeff King. Mark Lemke, the runner at third, momentarily froze in his tracks, enabling King to double him off the bag. The next batter, Terry Pendleton, further thrilled the roaring crowd by scorching a liner to left. But it went straight to Barry Bonds, and the rally was over.

Pittsburgh loaded the bases with two outs in the seventh, but failed to capitalize as Steve Avery, the fourth Atlanta pitcher, retired Van Slyke on a fly ball to center. They blew another chance to add to their lead in the eighth when Merced tried to score from first on a one-out double by King. Merced was cut down at the plate.

Drabek entered the ninth with a 2–0 lead and a five-hit shutout. It appeared the Pirates had reversed the previous year's outcome.

Pendleton led off the bottom half of the ninth with a double to right. David Justice then grounded to the right of second baseman Jose Lind. One of the best defensive second basemen in the league, Lind didn't have far to move, but the ball glanced off his glove. When Drabek then walked Sid Bream on four pitches to load the bases, Pittsburgh brought in their closer, Stan Belinda. Ron Gant promptly smoked a drive to deep left field, plenty far enough to score Atlanta's first run. The tomahawks were chopping, and Braves fans were chanting as Belinda walked Damon Berryhill, again loading the bases. The next batter, pinch-hitter Brian Hunter, popped out to shortstop. With only one out remaining in their season, the Braves sent to the plate Francisco Cabrera. The rookie was barely eligible, having been called up just one day before the deadline. In addition, he had just one post-season at-bat. But on a 2–1 pitch Cabrera singled to left, driving home Justice with the tying run. Bream, not known for his speed, also tried to score with the winning run and slid home just as the ball arrived slightly off line. The Braves had extended their big-time run, and Cabrera was buried beneath a moving mountain of teammates, fans, and photographers.

# 48 Terry, McCovey, and the Winds of Candlestick

NEW YORK (AL) at SAN FRANCISCO (NL)
Tuesday, October 16, 1962, Candlestick Park
Yankees 1, Giants 0

After the New York Yankees and the San Francisco Giants alternated victories during the first six games of the 1962 World Series, they found themselves playing the decisive game under intimidating conditions. The field had finally dried after the three days of rain prior to Game Six, but the wind was gusting as it could only in Candlestick Park. Veering from its normal left-field-to-right-field course, this air current swirled straight in from center at 25 to 35 miles an hour. It didn't matter from which side of the plate a batter stood, the pitchers had the advantage; and the fielders, especially those in the outer gardens, struggled throughout the game.

For San Francisco, this was their first World Series appearance since arriving on the West Coast five years earlier. In New York, it was business as usual — the

| New York | AB | R | H | I |
|---|---|---|---|---|
| Kubek T, ss | 4 | 0 | 1 | 0 |
| Richardson B, 2b | 2 | 0 | 0 | 0 |
| Tresh T, lf | 4 | 0 | 1 | 0 |
| Mantle M, cf | 3 | 0 | 1 | 0 |
| Maris R, rf | 4 | 0 | 0 | 0 |
| Howard E, c | 4 | 0 | 0 | 0 |
| Skowron B, 1b | 4 | 1 | 1 | 0 |
| Boyer C, 3b | 4 | 0 | 2 | 0 |
| Terry R, p | 3 | 0 | 1 | 0 |
| | 32 | 1 | 7 | 0 |

| San Francisco | AB | R | H | I |
|---|---|---|---|---|
| Alou F, rf | 4 | 0 | 0 | 0 |
| Hiller C, 2b | 4 | 0 | 0 | 0 |
| Mays W, cf | 4 | 0 | 1 | 0 |
| McCovey W, lf | 4 | 0 | 1 | 0 |
| Cepeda O, 1b | 3 | 0 | 0 | 0 |
| Haller T, c | 3 | 0 | 0 | 0 |
| Davenport J, 3b | 3 | 0 | 0 | 0 |
| Pagan J, ss | 2 | 0 | 0 | 0 |
| Bailey E, ph | 1 | 0 | 0 | 0 |
| Bowman E, ss | 0 | 0 | 0 | 0 |
| Sanford J, p | 2 | 0 | 1 | 0 |
| O'Dell B, p | 0 | 0 | 0 | 0 |
| Alou M, ph | 1 | 0 | 1 | 0 |
| | 31 | 0 | 4 | 0 |

| New York | IP | H | R | ER | BB | SO |
|---|---|---|---|---|---|---|
| Terry (W) | 9.0 | 4 | 0 | 0 | 0 | 4 |

| San Francisco | IP | H | R | ER | BB | SO |
|---|---|---|---|---|---|---|
| Sanford (L) | 7.0 | 7 | 1 | 1 | 4 | 3 |
| O'Dell | 2.0 | 0 | 0 | 0 | 0 | 1 |
| | 9.0 | 7 | 1 | 1 | 4 | 4 |

| New York | 000 | 010 | 000 — 1 |
|---|---|---|---|
| San Francisco | 000 | 000 | 000 — 0 |

OB: New York 8, San Francisco 4; ER: Pagan; DP: San Francisco 2; 2B: Mays; 3B: McCovey; TI: 2:29; AT: 43,948; UM: HP Landes, 1B Honochick, 2B Barlick, 3B Berry, LF Burkhart, RF Soar

13th appearance in the last 16 years for the Bronx Bombers. Yankees' pitcher Ralph Terry took the mound with his 0–4 lifetime World Series record, and faced an opponent, Jack Sanford, who had beaten him in Game Two.

Through the first four innings there was only one hit in the game. But in the fifth the first two Yankees singled, and Terry walked with no outs. The Giants' strategists elected to play it conservatively. Instead of pulling the infield in, to cut off a run at the plate, they dropped back into double-play depth, conceding a run for two outs. The strategy worked: Tony Kubek promptly smacked into a 6–4–3 twin killing as a run crossed the plate. Sanford then retired Bobby Richardson to avoid further damage.

With two outs in the sixth, Terry still had a perfect game. Ironically, it was mound adversary Sanford who finally singled. Don Larsen, author of a perfect World Series game in 1956 and now sitting in the Giants bullpen, relaxed.

The first serious San Francisco threat came in the seventh. With one out, Willie Mays sent a low twisting liner to left on which Tom Tresh made a spectacular running catch. Had the drive fallen for a hit, the game would have been tied after the next batter, Willie McCovey, crushed a ball into the teeth of the gale. It sailed over Mickey Mantle's head into deep left-center giving McCovey a triple. The Giants fans were on their feet, but Terry silenced them as he struck out Orlando Cepeda to keep the Giants off the board.

In the eighth, New York threatened to widen the gap. After they filled the bases with no outs, Billy O'Dell replaced Sanford. The lefty turned in a magnificent five-pitch performance by getting a forceout at home and then a groundball double play.

There were no further baserunners until the bottom of the ninth, when the Giants threatened not only to tie the game but to win the Series. Pinch-hitter Matty Alou caught the Yankees flatfooted with a beautiful drag bunt for a single. San Francisco fans were now roaring. But again Terry rose to the occasion by striking out both Felipe Alou and Chuck Hiller. New York was then one out away from the championship, but it was a very tough out — Willie Mays. The great center fielder came through with a double down the right-field line, and only a quick recovery by right fielder Roger Maris kept the ball out of the corner and Alou from scoring. San Francisco then had both the tying and winning runs in scoring position with McCovey at the plate.

The Yankees conferred at the mound and decided to let Terry face the big slugger. McCovey energized the crowd by blistering a drive that curved foul down the right-field line. He swung again, and for an instant it appeared the Giants were world champions. But the liner sank quickly into second baseman Richardson's glove, and the jubilant Yankees smothered Terry on the mound.

# 49 *White Sox Win a 25-Inning Marathon*

MILWAUKEE (AL) at CHICAGO (AL)
Started: Tuesday, May 8, 1984, Comiskey Park
Finished: Wednesday, May 9, 1984, Comiskey Park
White Sox 7, Brewers 6

Complaints about the pastime in the latter part of the century included cries of contests taking too much time. Never was that complaint more justified than on this date. Of the more than 150,000 modern major league games, this epic came closest to lasting forever — a mind-numbing eight hours and six minutes. And in terms of innings, only the Boston-Brooklyn duel of May 1, 1920, ate up more frames in the scorecard, and that game encompassed less than four hours. But this contest included more than just length: It was packed with drama.

The legendary game started on a cold evening in Chicago's Comiskey Park, where the White Sox hosted the Milwaukee Brewers. It began Tuesday night and continued into Wednesday morning, being halted because of a league ruling that no inning could commence after 12:59 A.M. Thus for five hours and 29 minutes, through 17 innings, ten pitchers and 506 pitches, the two clubs struggled, only to leave the field tied at 3–3. Players and patrons then rested, and the battle recommenced Wednesday night prior to a regularly scheduled game.

Those who looked for a timely conclusion were greatly disappointed. Three more scoreless frames were played before Milwaukee appeared to clinch it with three in the top of the 21st. But, remarkably, the home team tied it, sending the contest into serious record territory. There was no more scoring until the bottom of the 25th, when Harold Baines concluded matters with a one-out, solo home run.

By the time the 753rd pitch had been thrown, a plethora of major league records had been established or tied, all of which remain on the books at century's end:

- Longest game in terms of time (eight hours, six minutes)
- Longest night game in terms of innings (25 [tied ML mark])
- Most at-bats, one club, extra-inning game (95 [Chicago])
- Most at-bats, both clubs, extra-inning game (175 [tied ML mark])
- Most plate appearances, extra-inning game (104 [Chicago])
- Most individual at-bats in an extra-inning game (11 [Cooper, R. Law, Fisk, and Cruz tied ML record])
- Most individual plate appearances in an extra-inning game (12 [R. Law, Fisk, and Baines tied the ML mark])
- Most innings caught in a game (25 [Fisk])

American League endurance standards were also set and remain in the record books:

- Longest AL game in terms of innings (25)
- Most plate appearances, both clubs, extra-inning game (198)

Chicago opened the scoring in the sixth, but Milwaukee came right back to tie it an inning later.

In the ninth, the Brewers used a double, two singles and several Chicago miscues to put two go-ahead runs on the board. Milwaukee returned the favor as the bottom of the ninth opened with a two-base dropped fly in right. When the next two batters were retired, it should have ended the game, but another double and a singled tied it at 3–3.

The next 11 innings were scoreless, but the teams were not without opportunity. Milwaukee, who got their leadoff man aboard in six of the first 11 extra innings, had a runner on second with one out in the 13th. Before the next batter singled, the runner was picked off, ruining a possible lead tally.

In the 14th three of the first four White Sox batters singled to load the bases, but Brewer reliever Rick Waits escaped with a strikeout and a foul pop.

Opening the 16th, two Brewers singled, but a forceout and a double play extinguished the flame.

A leadoff double by the Brewers in the 18th was followed by a sacrifice to third. After a strategic intentional walk, the inning ended on a double play. The

| Milwaukee | AB | R | H | I |
|---|---|---|---|---|
| Ready R, 3b | 8 | 1 | 1 | 0 |
| Sundberg J, c | 4 | 0 | 3 | 0 |
| Romero E, pr | 0 | 0 | 0 | 0 |
| Schroeder B, c | 4 | 0 | 2 | 0 |
| Yount R, ss | 10 | 1 | 3 | 1 |
| Cooper C, dh | 11 | 1 | 2 | 0 |
| Simmons T, 1b | 7 | 2 | 1 | 0 |
| Oglivie B, lf | 10 | 1 | 2 | 4 |
| Clark B, cf | 2 | 0 | 1 | 0 |
| Manning R, ph-cf | 6 | 0 | 2 | 0 |
| Moore C, rf | 2 | 0 | 0 | 0 |
| James D, ph-rf | 2 | 0 | 0 | 0 |
| Brouhard M, ph-rf | 4 | 0 | 1 | 0 |
| Gantner J, 2b | 10 | 0 | 2 | 0 |
|  | 80 | 6 | 20 | 5 |

| Chicago | AB | R | H | I |
|---|---|---|---|---|
| Law R, cf | 11 | 1 | 4 | 1 |
| Fisk C, c | 11 | 1 | 3 | 1 |
| Walker G, 1b | 4 | 1 | 2 | 0 |
| Squires M, 1b | 2 | 0 | 0 | 0 |
| Hill M, ph-1b | 4 | 0 | 2 | 0 |
| Dotson R, pr | 0 | 1 | 0 | 0 |
| Reed R, p | 1 | 0 | 0 | 0 |
| Bannister F, p | 1 | 0 | 0 | 0 |
| Seaver T, p | 0 | 0 | 0 | 0 |
| Luzinski G, dh | 2 | 0 | 0 | 0 |
| Stegman D, pr-dh-lf | 8 | 0 | 1 | 0 |
| Baines H, rf | 10 | 1 | 2 | 1 |
| Kittle R, lf | 1 | 0 | 0 | 0 |
| Paciorek T, lf-1b | 9 | 1 | 5 | 3 |
| Law V, 3b | 10 | 0 | 1 | 0 |
| Fletcher S, ss | 3 | 0 | 0 | 0 |
| Hairston J, ph | 1 | 0 | 0 | 0 |
| Dybzinski J, ss | 6 | 0 | 2 | 0 |
| Cruz J, 2b | 11 | 1 | 1 | 1 |
|  | 95 | 7 | 23 | 7 |

| Milwaukee | IP | H | R | ER | BB | SO |
|---|---|---|---|---|---|---|
| Sutton | 7.0 | 4 | 1 | 0 | 3 | 6 |
| Ladd | 1.0 | 0 | 0 | 0 | 1 | 0 |
| Fingers | 2.0 | 2 | 2 | 0 | 0 | 2 |
| Tellmann | 3.1 | 3 | 0 | 0 | 1 | 1 |
| Waits | 3.2 | 3 | 0 | 0 | 0 | 3 |
| Porter (L) | 7.1 | 11 | 4 | 3 | 2 | 5 |
|  | 24.1 | 23 | 7 | 3 | 7 | 17 |

| Chicago | IP | H | R | ER | BB | SO |
|---|---|---|---|---|---|---|
| Fallon | 6.0 | 1 | 1 | 1 | 3 | 4 |
| Barojas | 0.0 | 2 | 0 | 0 | 0 | 0 |
| Burns | 3.0 | 3 | 2 | 2 | 3 | 3 |
| Jones | 4.0 | 4 | 0 | 0 | 1 | 4 |
| Agosto | 7.0 | 5 | 0 | 0 | 2 | 1 |
| Reed | 2.2 | 3 | 3 | 3 | 2 | 3 |
| Bannister | 1.1 | 1 | 0 | 0 | 0 | 1 |
| Seaver (W) | 1.0 | 1 | 0 | 0 | 0 | 0 |
|  | 25.0 | 20 | 6 | 6 | 11 | 16 |

```
Milwaukee   000  000  102  000  000  000  003  000  0 — 6
Chicago     000  001  002  000  000  000  003  000  1 — 7
```

OB: Milwaukee 13, Chicago 24; ER: Ready 2, Fisk, Moore; DP: Milwaukee 1, Chicago 6; 2B: Yount, Cruz, Baines, Hill, Ready, Fisk; HR: Oglivie, Baines; SB: Walker, Yount, Manning; CS: Oglivie, Clark, James, Brouhard; PK: Gantner; SH: Moore, Ready, Schroeder, V. Law, Dybzinski; WP: Burns, Jones; TI: 8:06; AT: 14,754; UM: Evans, Kosc, Hendry, Coble

Sox had their best scoring opportunity in the bottom of the same frame when their first two men reached base. A sacrifice moved both runners along. After a foul-out to third, an intentional pass loaded the bases, but a strikeout sent the marathon into another inning.

Milwaukee finally crossed the plate again in the 21st. With two outs and two on, Ben Oglivie seemingly clinched the game with a right field, upper-deck home run giving the Brewers a daunting 6–3 advantage. But the baseball gods had other plans.

Rudy Law led off the bottom of the inning with a routine grounder, but a wild throw put him on second. A single made it 6–4 before another hit and a walk loaded the bases. Tom Paciorek then drove home the tying runs with his fourth single of the game, knotting it at 6–6.

The odyssey came within an eyelash of ending in the bottom of the 23rd. With Dave Stegman on first and one out, Paciorek notched his fifth single, this one to center. When the ball was momentarily bobbled, third-base coach Jim Leyland motioned for Stegman to continue home with the winning run. But the center fielder quickly recovered, and Leyland tried to stop Stegman. As Stegman stumbled, coach and player made faint contact. The game was then briefly interrupted when Milwaukee manager Rene Lachemann argued with the umpires, who called out Stegman. The decision became critical when the next batter singled, but the Sox were then retired on an inning-ending forceout.

With one out in the Chicago half of the 25th, the longest game in history finally ended when Harold Baines connected for his first home run in a month. It was a 420-foot blast into the center-field bullpen.

# Gionfriddo's Catch Saves the Dodgers 50

### BROOKLYN (NL) at NEW YORK (AL)
### Sunday, October 5, 1947, Yankee Stadium
### Dodgers 8, Yankees 6

Considered by many to be the most dramatic of the century, the 1947 World Series pitted the New York Yankees against their inter-borough rivals the Brooklyn Dodgers. The Yankees prevailed in the first two contests but fell behind early in Game Three. Trailing 6–0 after two innings, the Bronx Bombers nearly overtook the Dodgers before succumbing, 9–8, in a thriller. Game Four saw New York's Bill Bevens carry into the ninth what would have been the first no-hitter in Series history before a pinch-hit double with the bases loaded turned him into the losing pitcher. The Yankees rebounded and took Game Five in another nail-biter, 2–1.

As the Series returned to Yankee Stadium, New York held a three-games-to-two advantage. Weather mindful of a mid-summer's day helped beckon a then–Series record 74,065 fans, most of whom soon would be left emotionally exhausted.

No sooner had the crowd returned to their seats after the National Anthem than Eddie Stanky stroked a single to right. In rapid order, Pee Wee Reese and Jackie Robinson also singled, loading the bases. Yankee starter Allie Reynolds then induced a double play off the bat of Dixie Walker as Stanky dented the plate with the game's first run. The next pitch bounced past catcher Sherman Lollar, and Reese also tallied, making it 2–0.

Two innings later, the Dodgers were back for more. A trio of doubles, by Reese, Robinson and Walker chased Reynolds and gave the visitors a commanding 4–0 advantage.

Brooklyn joy quickly melted as the Yankees rallied in an action-packed home third. When Brooklyn left fielder Gene Hermanski missed a diving catch, Lollar had a leadoff double. One out later he advanced to third on a wild pitch, then scored when third baseman Spider Jorgensen fumbled a hot grounder by Snuffy Stirnweiss. Tommy Henrich singled to center, but Stirnweiss was tagged out at third on a great throw by Carl Furillo. A single by Johnny Lindell sent home Henrich, and Joe DiMaggio nearly knocked over Jorgensen with a savage single to left. That brought on reliever Ralph Branca but didn't stop the Yankees. Billy Johnson greeted him with another single, scoring Lindell, and Bobby Brown singled home DiMaggio. Brown's safety left the crowd breathless as Hermanski just missed another diving catch. By the time Rizzuto lined out, allowing patrons to finally reacquaint themselves with their seats, the Yankees had tied it at four.

In the fourth Stirnweiss made a sparkling play to sap a Dodger rally before the Yankees resumed their assault. Singles by Aaron Robinson, Henrich, and Yogi Berra signaled ecstasy for many thousands as the home club assumed their first advantage of the day at 5–4.

The Dodgers narrowly missed regaining the lead in the fifth when, with one aboard, Walker clouted a ball just foul into the upper right-field stands. But they did deliver on the hopes of their fans in the sixth. Three singles, two doubles, and an error knocked the great Yankee reliever Joe Page from the box and vaulted the Dodgers back into the lead at 8–5.

The home sixth provided a dramatic fielding gem that etched the name of a little known player into the minds of baseball fans forever. With two outs and Yankee runners at first and second, Joe DiMaggio rocketed a towering drive that might have cleared the left-field roof in Ebbets Field. But Yankee Stadium was cavernous. Al Gionfriddo, who had entered the game only minutes earlier as part of a multiple substitution, turned his back and raced toward the fence. The five-foot, six-inch speedster arrived at a low metal gate 415 feet from the plate a split second before DiMaggio's drive. Twisting around at the last moment, Gionfriddo reached over his shoulder as well as the gate and felt the ball hit his glove and stick. A cameraman with impeccable timing caught the action on film in an image that to this day can be recalled by thousands. But for that heroic play, the drive certainly would have cleared the fence for a home run and tied the game.

The tenacious Yankees had the crowd on its feet again in the seventh. Facing left-hander Joe Hatten, New York coaxed two walks and an infield single, loading the bases with two outs. But Hatten disappointed the majority by getting Stirnweiss on a fly-out to center.

In the eighth, Henrich thrilled the home crowd as he backed Walker to the wall in right to make a leaping catch of his home run bid.

It all came down to the bottom of the ninth, and the Yankees would not

| Brooklyn | AB | R | H | I |
|----------|----|----|----|----|
| Stanky E, 2b | 5 | 2 | 2 | 0 |
| Reese P, ss | 4 | 2 | 3 | 2 |
| Robinson J, 1b | 5 | 1 | 2 | 1 |
| Walker D, rf | 5 | 0 | 1 | 1 |
| Hermanski G, lf | 1 | 0 | 0 | 0 |
| Miksis E, ph-lf | 1 | 0 | 0 | 0 |
| Gionfriddo A, lf | 2 | 0 | 0 | 0 |
| Edwards B, c | 4 | 1 | 1 | 0 |
| Furillo C, cf | 4 | 1 | 2 | 0 |
| Jorgensen S, 3b | 2 | 0 | 0 | 0 |
| Lavagetto C, ph-3b | 2 | 0 | 0 | 1 |
| Lombardi V, p | 1 | 0 | 0 | 0 |
| Branca R, p | 1 | 0 | 0 | 0 |
| Bragan B, ph | 1 | 0 | 1 | 1 |
| Bankhead D, pr | 0 | 1 | 0 | 0 |
| Hatten J, p | 1 | 0 | 0 | 0 |
| Casey H, p | 0 | 0 | 0 | 0 |
|  | 39 | 8 | 12 | 6 |

| New York | AB | R | H | I |
|----------|----|----|----|----|
| Stirnweiss S, 2b | 5 | 0 | 0 | 1 |
| Henrich T, rf-lf | 5 | 1 | 2 | 0 |
| Lindell J, lf | 2 | 1 | 2 | 1 |
| Berra Y, rf | 3 | 0 | 2 | 1 |
| DiMaggio J, cf | 5 | 1 | 1 | 0 |
| Johnson B, 3b | 5 | 1 | 2 | 1 |
| Phillips J, 1b | 1 | 0 | 0 | 0 |
| Brown B, ph | 1 | 0 | 1 | 1 |
| McQuinn G, 1b | 1 | 0 | 0 | 0 |
| Rizzuto P, ss | 4 | 0 | 1 | 0 |
| Lollar S, c | 1 | 1 | 1 | 0 |
| Robinson A, c | 4 | 1 | 2 | 0 |
| Reynolds A, p | 0 | 0 | 0 | 0 |
| Drews K, p | 2 | 0 | 0 | 0 |
| Page J, p | 0 | 0 | 0 | 0 |
| Newsom B, p | 0 | 0 | 0 | 0 |
| Clark A, ph | 1 | 0 | 0 | 0 |
| Raschi V, p | 0 | 0 | 0 | 0 |
| Houk R, ph | 1 | 0 | 1 | 0 |
| Wensloff B, p | 0 | 0 | 0 | 0 |
| Frey L, ph | 1 | 0 | 0 | 1 |
|  | 42 | 6 | 15 | 6 |

| Brooklyn | IP | H | R | ER | BB | SO |
|----------|----|----|----|----|----|----|
| Lombardi | 2.2 | 5 | 4 | 4 | 0 | 2 |
| Branca (W) | 2.1 | 6 | 1 | 1 | 0 | 2 |
| Hatten | 3.0 | 3 | 1 | 1 | 4 | 0 |
| Casey (S) | 1.0 | 1 | 0 | 0 | 0 | 0 |
|  | 9.0 | 15 | 6 | 6 | 4 | 4 |

| New York | IP | H | R | ER | BB | SO |
|----------|----|----|----|----|----|----|
| Reynolds | 2.1 | 6 | 4 | 3 | 1 | 0 |
| Drews | 2.0 | 1 | 0 | 0 | 1 | 0 |
| Page (L) | 1.0 | 4 | 4 | 4 | 0 | 1 |
| Newsom | 0.2 | 1 | 0 | 0 | 0 | 0 |
| Raschi | 1.0 | 0 | 0 | 0 | 0 | 1 |
| Wensloff | 2.0 | 0 | 0 | 0 | 0 | 0 |
|  | 9.0 | 12 | 8 | 7 | 2 | 2 |

| Brooklyn | 202 | 004 | 000 — 8 |
|----------|-----|-----|---------|
| New York | 004 | 100 | 001 — 6 |

OB: Brooklyn 6, New York 13; ER: Jorgensen, Robinson, McQuinn; DP: New York 1; 2B: Reese, Robinson, Walker, Lollar, Furillo, Bragan; WP: Lombardi; PB: Lollar; TI: 3:19; AT: 74,065; UM: HP Pinelli, 1B Rommel, 2B Goetz, 3B McGowan, LF Boyer, RF Magerkurth

die quietly. A single and a walk forced Brooklyn reliever Hugh Casey out of the bullpen for the fifth time in six games. Casey got the first out before Aaron Robinson singled to load the bases. That brought the winning run to the plate. Pinch-hitter Lonny Frey then hit into a forceout as the sixth New York tallied. With the tying runs at the corners and the crowd screaming for more, Stirnweiss bounced out weakly to Casey, ending the epic struggle and forcing a seventh game.

# 51 *Pennsylvania Blue Laws Lead to Cleveland Extravaganza*

PHILADELPHIA (AL) at CLEVELAND (AL)
Sunday, July 10, 1932, League Park
Athletics 18, Indians 17

In 1932, professional baseball was not permitted on Sunday in Pennsylvania. So the Athletics, on July 10, 1932, despite being in the midst of a home stand, traveled to Cleveland for a single game. The result was a bizarre — but thrilling and record-setting — 18-inning game in Cleveland's League Park.

At first glance, the box score appears to carry several misprints. Not only does it show one player collecting an inconceivable nine hits, but it also reveals a relief pitcher tossing 17 innings, allowing 29 hits, yet emerging victorious! There is no misprint.

Cleveland shortstop Johnny Burnett did indeed gather nine hits in this game, although no other player in the century stroked more than seven in any one contest. His heroics led the Indians in a 33-hit assault, the most by any major league team during the century. Unfortunately for the Tribe, however, it wasn't enough, because the A's parlayed 25 hits of their own into an 18–17 win. The two-club total of 58 hits also remains the century's benchmark for one game.

When the Athletics traveled to Cleveland this day, manager Connie Mack took with him only two pitchers, 20-year-old Lew Krausse and 34-year-old Eddie Rommel. Doubleheaders on July 7, 8, and 9, had drained the staff, so little-used Krausse was to get the start, and Rommel was the emergency backup.

The A's jumped out to a 2–0 lead in the top of the first, but the Indians countered with three in their half on an Earl Averill home run. Mack let Krausse bat in the top of the second, decided he'd seen enough, and summoned Rommel to pitch in the bottom half. The veteran right-hander, mauled for 20 hits during the next eight innings, was not collared with a loss, however; his teammates were knocking the cover off the ball, too, and making spectacular fielding plays. With no relief available, Rommel labored on until Philadelphia finally scored an unanswered run in the 18th. By then, his 17 innings of relief work established the still-standing American League record, and the 29 hits allowed are the most by any pitcher — starter or reliever — in one game in the 20th-century.

The 10,000 spectators were treated to a seesaw battle that included three ties, six Philadelphia leads, and three Cleveland leads. No margin was safe or

| Philadelphia | AB | R | H | I | | Cleveland | AB | R | H | I |
|---|---|---|---|---|---|---|---|---|---|---|
| Haas M, rf | 9 | 3 | 2 | 0 | | Porter D, rf | 10 | 3 | 3 | 2 |
| Cramer D, cf | 8 | 2 | 2 | 1 | | Burnett J, ss | 11 | 4 | 9 | 2 |
| Dykes J, 3b | 10 | 2 | 3 | 4 | | Averill E, cf | 9 | 3 | 5 | 4 |
| Simmons A, lf | 9 | 4 | 5 | 2 | | Vosmik J, lf | 10 | 2 | 2 | 1 |
| Foxx J, 1b | 9 | 4 | 6 | 8 | | Morgan E, 1b | 11 | 1 | 5 | 4 |
| McNair E, ss | 10 | 0 | 2 | 1 | | Myatt G, c | 7 | 2 | 1 | 0 |
| Heving J, c | 4 | 0 | 0 | 0 | | Cissell B, 2b | 9 | 1 | 4 | 3 |
| Madjeski E, c | 5 | 0 | 0 | 0 | | Kamm W, 3b | 7 | 1 | 2 | 0 |
| Williams D, 2b | 8 | 1 | 2 | 0 | | Brown C, p | 4 | 0 | 2 | 0 |
| Krausse L, p | 1 | 0 | 0 | 0 | | Hudlin W, p | 0 | 0 | 0 | 0 |
| Rommel E, p | 7 | 2 | 3 | 1 | | Ferrell W, p | 5 | 0 | 0 | 0 |
| | 80 | 18 | 25 | 17 | | | 83 | 17 | 33 | 16 |

| Philadelphia | IP | H | R | ER | BB | SO | | Cleveland | IP | H | R | ER | BB | SO |
|---|---|---|---|---|---|---|---|---|---|---|---|---|---|---|
| Krausse | 1.0 | 4 | 3 | 3 | 1 | 0 | | Brown | 6.2 | 13 | 8 | 7 | 1 | 3 |
| Rommel (W) | 17.0 | 29 | 14 | 13 | 9 | 7 | | Hudlin | 0.0 | 0 | 2 | 2 | 2 | 0 |
| | 18.0 | 33 | 17 | 16 | 10 | 7 | | Ferrell (L) | 11.1 | 12 | 8 | 6 | 4 | 7 |
| | | | | | | | | | 18.0 | 25 | 18 | 15 | 7 | 10 |

| | | | | | | | |
|---|---|---|---|---|---|---|---|
| Philadelphia | 201 | 201 | 702 | 000 | 000 | 201 — 18 |
| Cleveland | 300 | 311 | 601 | 000 | 000 | 200 — 17 |

OB: Philadelphia 15, Cleveland 24; DP: Philadelphia 2, Cleveland 2; 2B: Haas, Dykes, Foxx, McNair, Porter, Burnett 2, Vosmik, Morgan 2, Myatt, Cissell, Kamm; 3B: Williams; HR: Foxx 3, Averill; SB: Cissell; SH: Kamm, Ferrell; WP: Rommel 2; TI: 4:05; AT: 10,000; UM: Hildebrand, Owens

situation secure as the Indians overcame a five-run deficit in the seventh, and the Athletics scored 16 of their 18 runs after two were retired.

With two outs and the bases empty in the ninth, the Tribe led 14–13, but a routine grounder was booted, giving the A's life. Al Simmons followed with a walk before Jimmie Foxx slashed a double to left, scoring both runners and giving his team their fourth lead, 15–14.

In the bottom of the ninth, Willie Kamm led off with a double to left, but the next two batters were retired. Burnett, who already had five hits, then singled home the game-tying run. Averill also singled, sending Burnett to third with the winning run. Again, the A's were on the brink of defeat, and the home crowd was about to celebrate when Joe Vosmik sent a low liner toward the right-field line. But right fielder Mule Haas raced to his left, lunged, somersaulted, and arose with the ball, saving the game for Philadelphia.

The Indians had another golden opportunity in the 11th. With one out, a walk and Burnett's double put runners at second and third. Averill was intentionally walked, but Vosmik grounded sharply into a thrilling 4–2–3 double play. The A's had again narrowly escaped defeat.

In the bottom of the 12th, Eddie Morgan opened with a double to center. After a fly-out, Bill Cissell lined a single to left. Thinking third baseman Jimmy Dykes might spear the ball, Morgan hesitated just long enough to be thrown out on a close play at the plate.

After six consecutive scoreless innings, the Athletics finally broke through in the 16th on Foxx's third home run into the left-field bleachers. This two-run shot gave the A's a 17–15 lead and left Indians fans distraught. The home half of the inning was another nail-biter. A lead-off double and Burnett's ninth hit put runners at the corners. Averill then flied out for the first out, but it was deep enough to drive home a run, making it 17–16. Vosmik singled and Morgan singled, tying the game and putting Indians at first and second with only one away. A force-out at second left runners at the corners with two outs. Cissell then sent shrieks through the faithful with a deep fly to right that looked like it would hit the wall. But once again Haas was there to leap high and make a one-handed, game-saving catch.

In the 18th and final frame, the Athletics were again fortunate, and this time it left them victorious. After the first two batters were retired, Foxx singled to left. Eric McNair also singled to left and, when the ball took a high hop over Vosmik's head and rolled to the wall, Foxx was able to score from first with the lead run. The Indians' chance to recover proved anticlimactic as they were retired in order.

Following this marathon, the two teams packed their bags and traveled back to Philadelphia for a Monday doubleheader.

# 52 Cardinals Prevail in a 25 Inning Epic

ST. LOUIS (NL) at NEW YORK (NL)
Wednesday, September 11, 1974, Shea Stadium
Cardinals 4, Mets 3

Fans with the stamina to stay awake until 3:12 a.m. this night in Shea Stadium witnessed the second longest baseball game in history. In a contest that established a host of new benchmarks, the St. Louis Cardinals defeated the New York Mets in a titanic, 25-inning struggle, 4–3. Some of the following records were later tied, but none were exceeded as the century closed.

Major League records:
- The longest night game in major league history (25 innings)
- Most official at-bats by two teams (175)
- Most plate appearances by two teams (202)
- Most official at-bats by an individual (11, by Dave Schneck)
- Most plate appearances by an individual (12 by Felix Millan and John Milner)

| St. Louis | AB | R | H | I |
|---|---|---|---|---|
| Brock L, lf | 9 | 0 | 1 | 0 |
| Godby D, lf | 2 | 0 | 0 | 0 |
| Sizemore T, 2b | 10 | 1 | 1 | 0 |
| Smith R, rf | 8 | 0 | 1 | 0 |
| Torre J, 1b | 9 | 0 | 2 | 1 |
| Simmons T, c | 3 | 0 | 1 | 0 |
| Herndon L, pr | 0 | 1 | 0 | 0 |
| Hill M, c | 1 | 0 | 0 | 0 |
| Scheinblum R, ph | 1 | 0 | 0 | 0 |
| Billings D, c | 5 | 0 | 1 | 0 |
| McBride B, cf | 10 | 1 | 4 | 0 |
| Reitz K, 3b | 10 | 1 | 4 | 2 |
| Tyson M, ss | 2 | 0 | 0 | 0 |
| Hernandez K, ph | 1 | 0 | 0 | 0 |
| Folkers R, p | 0 | 0 | 0 | 0 |
| Cruz J, ph | 1 | 0 | 0 | 0 |
| Bare R, p | 0 | 0 | 0 | 0 |
| Osteen C, p | 4 | 0 | 0 | 0 |
| Siebert S, p | 1 | 0 | 0 | 0 |
| Forsch B, p | 1 | 0 | 0 | 0 |
| Melendez L, ph | 1 | 0 | 0 | 0 |
| Garman M, p | 0 | 0 | 0 | 0 |
| Hunt R, ph | 1 | 0 | 0 | 0 |
| Hrabosky A, p | 0 | 0 | 0 | 0 |
| Dwyer J, ph | 0 | 0 | 0 | 0 |
| Heidemann J, ss | 6 | 0 | 3 | 0 |
| | 86 | 4 | 18 | 3 |

| New York | AB | R | H | I |
|---|---|---|---|---|
| Harrelson B, ss | 7 | 0 | 0 | 0 |
| Boswell K, 3b | 4 | 0 | 0 | 0 |
| Millan F, 2b | 10 | 1 | 4 | 0 |
| Jones C, lf | 9 | 2 | 3 | 2 |
| Webb H, p | 0 | 0 | 0 | 0 |
| Pemberton B, ph | 1 | 0 | 1 | 0 |
| Milner J, 1b | 10 | 0 | 2 | 1 |
| Garrett W, 3b-ss | 10 | 0 | 0 | 0 |
| Schneck D, cf-rf | 11 | 0 | 2 | 0 |
| Ayala B, rf | 2 | 0 | 1 | 0 |
| Hahn D, ph-cf | 6 | 0 | 0 | 0 |
| Gosger J, lf | 0 | 0 | 0 | 0 |
| Dyer D, c | 9 | 0 | 2 | 0 |
| Boisclair B, pr | 0 | 0 | 0 | 0 |
| Hodges R, c | 0 | 0 | 0 | 0 |
| Koosman J, p | 2 | 0 | 0 | 0 |
| Martinez T, ph | 1 | 0 | 0 | 0 |
| Parker H, p | 0 | 0 | 0 | 0 |
| Kranepool E, ph | 1 | 0 | 0 | 0 |
| Miller B, p | 0 | 0 | 0 | 0 |
| Theodore G, ph | 1 | 0 | 0 | 0 |
| Apodaca B, p | 1 | 0 | 0 | 0 |
| Cram J, p | 3 | 0 | 1 | 0 |
| Staub R, ph-rf | 1 | 0 | 0 | 0 |
| | 89 | 3 | 16 | 3 |

| St. Louis | IP | H | R | ER | BB | SO |
|---|---|---|---|---|---|---|
| Forsch | 6.0 | 5 | 3 | 2 | 4 | 3 |
| Garman | 2.0 | 0 | 0 | 0 | 0 | 2 |
| Hrabosky | 3.0 | 2 | 0 | 0 | 0 | 3 |
| Folkers | 2.0 | 3 | 0 | 0 | 1 | 2 |
| Bare | 0.1 | 0 | 0 | 0 | 1 | 0 |
| Osteen | 9.1 | 4 | 0 | 0 | 2 | 5 |
| Siebert (W) | 2.1 | 2 | 0 | 0 | 3 | 1 |
| | 25.0 | 16 | 3 | 2 | 11 | 16 |

| New York | IP | H | R | ER | BB | SO |
|---|---|---|---|---|---|---|
| Koosman | 9.0 | 5 | 3 | 3 | 4 | 5 |
| Parker | 3.0 | 2 | 0 | 0 | 0 | 0 |
| Miller | 1.0 | 1 | 0 | 0 | 1 | 1 |
| Apodaca | 3.0 | 2 | 0 | 0 | 1 | 1 |
| Cram | 8.0 | 7 | 0 | 0 | 2 | 4 |
| Webb (L) | 1.0 | 1 | 1 | 0 | 0 | 1 |
| | 25.0 | 18 | 4 | 3 | 8 | 12 |

| | | | | | | | | | | | |
|---|---|---|---|---|---|---|---|---|---|---|---|
| St. Louis | 100 | 000 | 002 | 000 | 000 | 000 | 000 | 000 | 1 — 4 |
| New York | 100 | 020 | 000 | 000 | 000 | 000 | 000 | 000 | 0 — 3 |

OB: St. Louis 20, New York 25; ER: Tyson, Schneck, Dyer, Osteen, Webb, Hodges; DP: St. Louis 1, New York 2; 2B: Milner, Schneck 2; HR: Jones; SB: McBride; CS: Brock; PK: R.Smith; CI: Torre reached on catcher's interference by Dyer in the 20th; SH: Koosman, Forsch, Millan, McBride, Jones; HP: by Koosman(Tyson), by Parker(Dwyer); WP: Forsch, Koosman, Cram; PB: Simmons; BK: Webb; TI: 7:04; AT: 13,460; UM: Sudol, Weyer, Engel, Pulli

• Longest errorless game by a second baseman (25 by Felix Millan and Ted Sizemore)

• Most runners left on base by two teams (45)

National League records:

• Most official at-bats by one team (89, by the Mets)
• Most plate appearances by one team (103, by the Mets)

This marathon may even have continued had not New York's Hank Webb, the 13th hurler in the game, made a wild throw enabling the speedy Bake McBride to score from first. McBride had led off the 25th with an infield single. With the hit-and-run sign on, McBride broke for second, only too early. Webb had him picked off but threw wildly past first baseman John Milner. (It was later learned that Webb had balked, and in such a case, McBride was on his own once he passed second base.) McBride sped around the diamond and didn't even see third base coach Vern Benson's stop sign. Because there were no outs, Benson didn't want to risk a play at the plate, but McBride sailed home and scored when Mets' catcher Ron Hodges fumbled Milner's throw. That lone tally was all the Cardinals needed as the Mets then failed to cross the plate for the 20th straight inning.

Prior to McBride's heroics there was little offense and a lot of clutch pitching. After each club scored single runs in the first, Cleon Jones' two-run home run in the fifth gave the Mets a 3–1 lead that they carried into the ninth. Jerry Koosman then struck out two of the first three Cardinals and was one out away from a nine-inning victory. But Ken Reitz signaled the start of the marathon with a two-run homer to tie it. No runs scored for the next 15 innings.

Each team did have multiple scoring opportunities in overtime. In both the 16th and 17th, the Cardinals had two on with only one out but failed to score. In the 20th they got their first two batters on, and in the 24th they left the bases loaded. The Mets meanwhile stranded two baserunners in the 10th, 12th, 14th, and 22nd. They also left the bases loaded in the 23rd and 24th.

Home plate umpire Ed Sudol, who called every pitch in this and two other Mets' marathons in 1964 and 1968, may have set a record himself. During the seven hours and four minutes he never sat down, prompting amazement on the part of players.

Relief pitchers on both teams performed superbly. St. Louis hurler Claude Osteen twirled 9 and ⅓ scoreless innings, prompting teammate Alan Foster to question whether Claude should get credit for a shutout.

The approximately 1,000 diehards who saw this contest to its ugly conclusion witnessed five sweepings of the infield and 15 dozen balls put into play. St. Louis first baseman Joe Torre contradicted most of the other participants when he later said that this was the fastest 25-inning game he ever played in.

# *Reds Take the Flag on a Wild Pitch* **53**

## PITTSBURGH (NL) at CINCINNATI (NL)
### Wednesday, October 11, 1972, Riverfront Stadium
### Reds 4, Pirates 3

The two contenders for the 1972 National League pennant each finished with double-digit leads over their closest rivals. Dominating the West were the Cincinnati Reds, who not only led the majors in stolen bases, but also dressed the major league hit leader (Pete Rose), runs leader (Joe Morgan), and the home run and RBI leader (Johnny Bench). In the East, returning with their third consecutive crown, were the defending World Champion Pittsburgh Pirates, who exhibited their own array of stars, including Roberto Clemente and Willie Stargell.

As the five-game series unfolded, the Big Red Machine always seemed to be playing catch-up. Favored Pittsburgh won Games One and Three while Cincinnati retaliated in the even numbered contests. Game Five was a reflection of the first four as the Reds fell behind early and never drew even until the chaotic ninth.

In a pitching rematch of Game One, Cincinnati's Don Gullett squared off against Steve Blass. Neither starter made it through the eighth, despite effective pitching, and neither was involved in the decision.

After nearly an hour and a half rain delay, the Pirates jumped out to what amounted to a commanding lead with two runs in the second inning. Manny Sanguillen's single, Richie Hebner's double, and Dave Cash's single did the damage.

A single, a sacrifice, and a double by Rose put the Reds on the board in the bottom of the third, but Pete was left stranded at third.

Pittsburgh's two-run lead was restored in the fourth. Again it was consecutive singles by Sanguillen, Hebner, and Cash that gave Pittsburgh a 3–1 edge. Cincinnati relievers then retired the next 11 Pirates.

Fighting a 1-for-17 playoff slump, the Reds' Caesar Geronimo led off the bottom of the fifth with a home run. That brought Geronimo's club to within one, but Blass quieted Cincinnati bats by retiring eight of the next nine.

Both teams gave their fans something to cheer about in the eighth. The Pirates threatened when they put runners at first and second with only one out, but reliever Tom Hall struck out Stargell and got Sanguillen on a ground-out. A walk, sacrifice, and a ground-out, put a Cincinnati runner at third, but Pirate reliever Ramon Hernandez fanned Bobby Tolan.

| Pittsburgh | AB | R | H | I |
|---|---|---|---|---|
| Stennett R, lf | 4 | 0 | 1 | 0 |
| Oliver A, cf | 3 | 0 | 0 | 0 |
| Clemente R, rf | 3 | 0 | 1 | 0 |
| Stargell W, 1b | 4 | 0 | 0 | 0 |
| Robertson B, 1b | 0 | 0 | 0 | 0 |
| Sanguillen M, c | 4 | 2 | 2 | 0 |
| Hebner R, 3b | 4 | 1 | 2 | 0 |
| Cash D, 2b | 4 | 0 | 2 | 2 |
| Alley G, ss | 4 | 0 | 0 | 0 |
| Blass S, p | 3 | 0 | 0 | 0 |
| Hernandez R, p | 0 | 0 | 0 | 0 |
| Giusti D, p | 0 | 0 | 0 | 0 |
| Moose B, p | 0 | 0 | 0 | 0 |
|  | 33 | 3 | 8 | 2 |

| Cincinnati | AB | R | H | I |
|---|---|---|---|---|
| Rose P, lf | 3 | 0 | 1 | 1 |
| Morgan J, 2b | 4 | 0 | 0 | 0 |
| Tolan B, cf | 4 | 0 | 0 | 0 |
| Bench J, c | 4 | 1 | 2 | 1 |
| Perez T, 1b | 4 | 0 | 1 | 0 |
| Foster G, pr | 0 | 1 | 0 | 0 |
| Menke D, 3b | 3 | 0 | 1 | 0 |
| Geronimo C, rf | 4 | 1 | 1 | 1 |
| Chaney D, ss | 4 | 1 | 1 | 0 |
| Gullett D, p | 0 | 0 | 0 | 0 |
| Borbon P, p | 0 | 0 | 0 | 0 |
| Uhlaender T, ph | 1 | 0 | 0 | 0 |
| Hall T, p | 0 | 0 | 0 | 0 |
| Hague J, ph | 0 | 0 | 0 | 0 |
| Concepcion D, pr | 0 | 0 | 0 | 0 |
| Carroll C, p | 0 | 0 | 0 | 0 |
| McRae H, ph | 0 | 0 | 0 | 0 |
|  | 31 | 4 | 7 | 3 |

| Pittsburgh | IP | H | R | ER | BB | SO |
|---|---|---|---|---|---|---|
| Blass | 7.1 | 4 | 2 | 2 | 2 | 4 |
| Hernandez | 0.2 | 0 | 0 | 0 | 0 | 1 |
| Giusti (L) | 0.0 | 3 | 2 | 2 | 0 | 0 |
| Moose | 0.2 | 0 | 0 | 0 | 0 | 0 |
|  | 8.2 | 7 | 4 | 4 | 2 | 5 |

| Cincinnati | IP | H | R | ER | BB | SO |
|---|---|---|---|---|---|---|
| Gullett | 3.0 | 6 | 3 | 3 | 0 | 2 |
| Borbon | 2.0 | 1 | 0 | 0 | 0 | 1 |
| Hall | 3.0 | 1 | 0 | 0 | 1 | 4 |
| Carroll (W) | 1.0 | 0 | 0 | 0 | 0 | 0 |
|  | 9.0 | 8 | 3 | 3 | 1 | 7 |

```
Pittsburgh   020   100   000 — 3
Cincinnati   001   010   002 — 4
```

OB: Pittsburgh 5, Cincinnati 5; ER: Chaney; DP: Cincinnati 1; 2B: Hebner, Rose; HR: Geronimo, Bench; SH: Gullett, Oliver, Rose; WP: Gullett, Moose; TI: 2:19; AT: 41,887;UM: HP Donatelli, 1B Kibler, 2B Wendelstedt, 3B Burkhart, LF Harvey, RF Williams

Then came the turbulent ninth. Pittsburgh went down in order and subsequently entrusted their 3–2 lead, and ticket to the World Series, to their longtime relief ace, Dave Giusti. It was a calculated risk because left-hander Hernandez had pitched well and had an even lower ERA than Giusti. But with three right-handers due up for Cincinnati, the dye was cast. The Reds had just four hits all day, but Bench ignited the hometown fans by leading off with home run over the right-field fence. That drew Cincinnati even for the first time in the game. When Tony Perez and Denis Menke followed with singles, Bob Moose replaced Giusti. George Foster, pinch-running for Perez, moved to third on Geronimo's 370-foot fly-out to right. That put the World Series ticket within Cincinnati's reach, just 90 feet from home. Moose then disposed of Darrel Chaney on a pop-up to shortstop, leaving the contest one out away from extra innings. Amid deafening howls, pinch-hitter Hal McRae stepped to the plate. With the count 1-1, Moose bounced a waste pitch wide and into the dirt. It took a crazy hop over Sanguillen's head, and as it rolled toward the box seats, Foster raced home with that ticket to the World Series.

# *Mays and Rhodes Shock the Indians* 54

CLEVELAND (AL) at NEW YORK (NL)
Wednesday, September 29, 1954, Polo Grounds
Giants 5, Indians 2

After setting a torrid pace in winning an American League record 111 games, the Cleveland Indians were eight-to-five favorites to win the World Series. Pitching was the beacon that guided this Tribe, which sported the lowest ERA in the major leagues. Their opponents, the New York Giants, were no slouches on the mound either. In addition, they displayed considerable home-run power.

The first game was scheduled in New York's Polo Grounds, the ancient playing field with unique dimensions. Horseshoe shaped, the shallow fence in right (258 feet from home plate) and left (280 feet) quickly jutted out to a vast center field, 475 feet straight away to the clubhouses. Those parameters eventually became instrumental in the game's outcome on this brilliant, warm day with its stiff wind blowing in from left field.

Toeing the rubber for Cleveland was Bob Lemon, 23–7 on the regular season, while Sal Maglie, at 14–6, occupied the box for New York. Experts predicted a pitcher's duel, and that's exactly what they got, for despite an abundance of baserunners, each pitcher managed to exact crucial outs.

Cleveland took advantage of wildness by Maglie in the opening frame. Al Smith was hit by a pitch, and Bobby Avila was almost clipped before he singled. Maglie got the next two batters to pop out, but Vic Wertz drove both mates home with a triple. Wertz then became the first in a parade of runners from both teams stranded at third base — episodes that created a bounty of nail-biting drama.

In the bottom of the first, the Giants put men at the corners with only one out. Lemon was equal to the task, however, as he retired Willie Mays and Hank Thompson without sustaining damage.

The Giants tied it in the third and had an opportunity to take the lead. A walk and three singles tallied two, but New York stranded runners at the corners after just one out.

A potential Giants run again died at third base in the fourth inning. The same fate was met by the Indians in the fifth and sixth, giving the fans plenty to cheer about.

**View of the Polo Grounds from just above the point of Mays's catch (National Baseball Hall of Fame Library, Cooperstown, New York).**

It took one of the most dramatic plays in World Series history to keep the scoreboard clean in the eighth. Larry Doby led off for Cleveland with a walk, and Al Rosen singled, knocking Maglie out of the game. Wertz, with a perfect day at the plate, next faced southpaw Don Liddle. After trying unsuccessfully to bunt, Wertz drove a two-strike pitch deep into cavernous center field. He later said he had never hit a ball harder in his career. Mays raced with his back to the plate and made a spectacular over-the-shoulder catch, saving at least one, if not two runs. After effusive praise, radio announcer Jimmy Dudley called it the greatest catch he'd ever seen. Marv Grissom then took the mound for New York and walked the next batter, loading the bases. With stomachs churning, Grissom struck out pinch-hitter Dave Pope. The inning's suspense contained one more element as Jim Hegan crushed a ball to deep left-center field. Most thought it a sure grand slam, but the incoming wind pushed it into Monte Irvin's glove at the warning track about 400 feet from home.

The Giants got another runner to third in the bottom half of the eighth, but Lemon retired Wes Westrum on a line drive to center.

The ninth inning saw the Indians blow still another scoring chance. With two outs and runners at first and second, Grissom got Rosen on a fly ball to left. New York had no baserunners in the bottom half, but Alvin Dark electrified the fans when he sent Smith back to the wall in left to pull down his towering drive.

| Cleveland | AB | R | H | I |
|---|---|---|---|---|
| Smith A, lf | 4 | 1 | 1 | 0 |
| Avila B, 2b | 5 | 1 | 1 | 0 |
| Doby L, cf | 3 | 0 | 1 | 0 |
| Rosen A, 3b | 5 | 0 | 1 | 0 |
| Wertz V, 1b | 5 | 0 | 4 | 2 |
| Regalado R, pr | 0 | 0 | 0 | 0 |
| Grasso M, c | 0 | 0 | 0 | 0 |
| Philley D, rf | 3 | 0 | 0 | 0 |
| Majeski H, ph | 0 | 0 | 0 | 0 |
| Mitchell D, ph | 0 | 0 | 0 | 0 |
| Dente S, ss | 0 | 0 | 0 | 0 |
| Strickland G, ss | 3 | 0 | 0 | 0 |
| Pope D, ph-rf | 1 | 0 | 0 | 0 |
| Hegan J, c | 4 | 0 | 0 | 0 |
| Glynn B, ph-1b | 1 | 0 | 0 | 0 |
| Lemon B, p | 4 | 0 | 0 | 0 |
|  | 38 | 2 | 8 | 2 |

| New York | AB | R | H | I |
|---|---|---|---|---|
| Lockman W, 1b | 5 | 1 | 1 | 0 |
| Dark A, ss | 4 | 0 | 2 | 0 |
| Mueller D, rf | 5 | 1 | 2 | 1 |
| Mays W, cf | 3 | 1 | 0 | 0 |
| Thompson H, 3b | 3 | 1 | 1 | 1 |
| Irvin M, lf | 3 | 0 | 0 | 0 |
| Rhodes D, ph | 1 | 1 | 1 | 3 |
| Williams D, 2b | 4 | 0 | 0 | 0 |
| Westrum W, c | 4 | 0 | 2 | 0 |
| Maglie S, p | 3 | 0 | 0 | 0 |
| Liddle D, p | 0 | 0 | 0 | 0 |
| Grissom M, p | 1 | 0 | 0 | 0 |
|  | 36 | 5 | 9 | 5 |

| Cleveland | IP | H | R | ER | BB | SO |
|---|---|---|---|---|---|---|
| Lemon (L) | 9.1 | 9 | 5 | 5 | 5 | 6 |

| New York | IP | H | R | ER | BB | SO |
|---|---|---|---|---|---|---|
| Maglie | 7.0 | 7 | 2 | 2 | 2 | 2 |
| Liddle | 0.1 | 0 | 0 | 0 | 0 | 0 |
| Grissom (W) | 2.2 | 1 | 0 | 0 | 3 | 2 |
|  | 10.0 | 8 | 2 | 2 | 5 | 4 |

| Cleveland | 200 | 000 | 000 | 0 — 2 |
|---|---|---|---|---|
| New York | 002 | 000 | 000 | 3 — 5 |

OB: Cleveland 13, New York 9; ER: Mueller 2, Irvin; 2B: Wertz; 3B: Wertz; HR: Rhodes; SB: Mays; SH: Irvin, Dente; HP: by Maglie (Smith); WP: Lemon; TI: 3:11; AT: 52,751; UM: HP Barlick, 1B Berry, 2B Conlan, 3B Stevens, LF Warneke, RF Napp

More of the same fate befell Cleveland in the tenth. Wertz' double, the first extra-base hit since the opening inning, started a rally that was followed by a sacrifice and a base on balls. Once again Grissom quelled the uprising, this time by striking out pinch-hitter Bill Glynn. Then, with the crowd still buzzing, Lemon lined sharply to Whitey Lockman at first, marking the fifth inning in which the Tribe had stranded a runner just 90 feet from the plate.

The Giants started their half of the 10th inauspiciously as Don Mueller struck out. Mays walked and promptly stole second. Hank Thompson then was walked intentionally to set up a double play possibility, and Dusty Rhodes was summoned to pinch hit for Monte Irvin. Rhodes, with two pinch-hit homers during the regular season, lifted a lazy pop fly down the right-field line. Cleveland second baseman Avila raced out toward right field and, for seconds, neither announcer Al Helfer nor the crowd sounded very excited. But soon everyone erupted as the ball carried into the front row of spectators, about seven feet fair. The same wind that had stalled Hegan's blast in the eighth and Dark's in the ninth now played a part in Rhodes's heroics. Lemon threw his glove into the air and trudged off the field in disgust after watching a 270-foot fly ball — and perhaps the shortest home run in World Series history — win the nerve-tingling struggle.

# 55 *Browns Overcome 11-Run Deficit*

### PHILADELPHIA (AL) at ST. LOUIS (AL)
### Wednesday, June 17, 1936, Sportsmans Park
### Browns 14, Athletics 13

On this date the Philadelphia Athletics and St. Louis Browns were battling for little more than evasion of the basement. The game drew little attention from contemporary sportswriters, even in the home town of the visiting club, Philadelphia. After all, the two teams, who had finished seventh and eighth a year earlier, showed little more potential this season. This single game, however, proved to be something special, as the Browns pulled out a dramatic 14–13 victory in the bottom of the ninth after trailing by as many as 11 runs earlier in the game. Only two clubs during the century overcame a greater deficit to emerge victorious.

Through five and one-half innings, the Athletics used 17 hits to forge a 13–2 advantage. Then the Browns began their relentless comeback. In the final four innings they sent four Philadelphia pitchers to the showers, scoring one

| Philadelphia | AB | R | H | I |
|---|---|---|---|---|
| Finney L, 1b | 5 | 4 | 4 | 0 |
| Warstler R, 2b | 4 | 1 | 2 | 2 |
| Moses W, cf | 5 | 3 | 3 | 4 |
| Puccinelli G, rf | 5 | 2 | 3 | 3 |
| Higgins, P, 3b | 4 | 1 | 1 | 2 |
| Johnson B, lf | 5 | 0 | 2 | 1 |
| Peters R, ss | 5 | 0 | 0 | 0 |
| Hayes F, c | 4 | 0 | 0 | 0 |
| Flythe S, p | 1 | 1 | 1 | 0 |
| Ross B, p | 3 | 1 | 1 | 0 |
| Dietrich B, p | 0 | 0 | 0 | 0 |
| Kelley H, p | 1 | 0 | 0 | 0 |
| | 42 | 13 | 17 | 12 |

| St. Louis | AB | R | H | I |
|---|---|---|---|---|
| Lary L, ss | 5 | 2 | 4 | 4 |
| Clift H, 3b | 5 | 1 | 1 | 0 |
| Solters M, lf | 5 | 1 | 1 | 1 |
| Bottomley J, 1b | 3 | 2 | 2 | 4 |
| Bell B, rf | 5 | 1 | 1 | 1 |
| West S, cf | 3 | 2 | 1 | 1 |
| Carey T, 2b | 5 | 1 | 1 | 1 |
| Giuliani T, c | 3 | 2 | 1 | 1 |
| Caldwell E, p | 0 | 0 | 0 | 0 |
| Van Atta R, p | 1 | 0 | 0 | 1 |
| Bejma O, ph | 1 | 1 | 1 | 0 |
| Mahaffey R, p | 0 | 0 | 0 | 0 |
| Pepper R, ph | 1 | 0 | 0 | 0 |
| Andrews I, p | 0 | 0 | 0 | 0 |
| Coleman E, ph | 0 | 1 | 0 | 0 |
| Knott J, p | 0 | 0 | 0 | 0 |
| | 37 | 14 | 13 | 14 |

| Philadelphia | IP | H | R | ER | BB | SO |
|---|---|---|---|---|---|---|
| Flythe | 1.1 | 0 | 1 | – | 3 | 0 |
| Ross | 5.2 | 7 | 7 | – | 2 | 2 |
| Dietrich | 0.0 | 3 | 4 | – | 1 | 0 |
| Kelley (L) | 1.1 | 3 | 2 | – | 1 | 1 |
| | 8.1 | 13 | 14 | – | 7 | 3 |

| St. Louis | IP | H | R | ER | BB | SO |
|---|---|---|---|---|---|---|
| Caldwell | 1.2 | 7 | 6 | – | 1 | 1 |
| Van Atta | 3.1 | 5 | 3 | – | 0 | 2 |
| Mahaffey | 2.0 | 5 | 4 | – | 0 | 1 |
| Andrews | 1.0 | 0 | 0 | – | 0 | 0 |
| Knott (W) | 1.0 | 0 | 0 | – | 1 | 1 |
| | 9.0 | 17 | 13 | – | 2 | 5 |

```
Philadelphia   330   124   000 — 13
St. Louis      010   011   371 — 14
```

OB: Philadelphia 5, St. Louis 7; ER: Finney, Lary; DP: St. Louis 2; 2B: Finney 2, Ross, Solters, Bottomley; 3B: Moses, Bejma; HR: Moses, Higgins, Bottomley; SH: Warstler, Knott; HP: by Flythe (Bottomley); WP: Flythe, Mahaffey; PB: Hayes; TI: 2:25; UM: Hubbard, Dinneen, Geisel

run in the sixth, three in the seventh, and seven in the eighth to tie it. Meanwhile, the Athletics' bats went hitless.

The bottom of the historic ninth opened with Tony Giuliani being issued a free pass and then sacrificed to second. Lyn Larry next smacked a sharp grounder toward second that bad-hopped over the head of Rabbit Warstler for the game-ending RBI.

The win meant little for St. Louis in the final standings, though they did finish barely ahead of the eighth-place Athletics by season's end.

# Cardinals Overcome an 11-Run Deficit 56

### ST. LOUIS (NL) at NEW YORK (NL)
### Sunday, June 15, 1952, Polo Grounds
### Cardinals 14, Giants 12

Under blistering heat and humidity, the New York Giants flexed their muscles early in the first game of a doubleheader. Batting around for five runs in the second inning and six more in the third, they forged a commanding 11–0 lead that carried through the fourth inning. In addition, they had on the mound their pitching ace, Sal "The Barber" Maglie, bidding for his league-leading 10th victory. Manager Leo Durocher, confident in his lead and considerate of the heat, rested two of his veterans, Bob Elliott and Wes Westrum. Cardinal manager Eddie Stanky also thought about giving some of his veteran regulars a rest but, on a hunch, decided against it.

With the huge lead Maglie relaxed, and St. Louis took advantage by erupting for seven runs in the fifth and sending the Barber to the shop. Tommy Glaviano led off with a circuit smash. Then came four singles and a walk. It was still only 11–4, however, and with two outs, Maglie needed only one more to be eligible for his 10th victory. But Enos Slaughter ruined his day with a three-run homer, and Hoyt Wilhelm was beckoned to extinguish the Cardinals' merrymaking.

## First Game

| St. Louis | AB | R | H | I |
|---|---|---|---|---|
| Hemus S, ss | 5 | 3 | 2 | 3 |
| Schoendienst R, 2b | 6 | 1 | 2 | 0 |
| Musial S, cf-lf | 6 | 2 | 2 | 2 |
| Sisler D, 1b | 5 | 2 | 2 | 1 |
| Lowrey P, lf-cf | 4 | 1 | 1 | 0 |
| Slaughter E, rf | 5 | 2 | 3 | 5 |
| Glaviano T, 3b | 5 | 1 | 2 | 2 |
| Rice D, c | 5 | 1 | 3 | 0 |
| Presko J, p | 0 | 0 | 0 | 0 |
| Crimian J, p | 1 | 0 | 0 | 0 |
| Werle B, p | 2 | 1 | 1 | 0 |
| Rice H, ph | 1 | 0 | 0 | 1 |
| Yuhas E, p | 0 | 0 | 0 | 0 |
| Schmidt W, p | 0 | 0 | 0 | 0 |
| | 45 | 14 | 18 | 14 |

| New York | AB | R | H | I |
|---|---|---|---|---|
| Williams D, 2b | 6 | 0 | 3 | 1 |
| Lockman W, 1b | 5 | 0 | 3 | 3 |
| Thomson B, 3b | 5 | 0 | 0 | 0 |
| Thompson H, cf | 4 | 2 | 1 | 1 |
| Elliott B, lf | 2 | 1 | 0 | 0 |
| Diering C, lf | 1 | 0 | 0 | 0 |
| Howerton B, ph | 1 | 0 | 0 | 0 |
| Mueller D, rf | 4 | 3 | 2 | 1 |
| Dark A, ss | 4 | 2 | 2 | 2 |
| Westrum W, c | 2 | 2 | 2 | 3 |
| Noble R, c | 2 | 0 | 0 | 0 |
| Rigney B, ph | 1 | 0 | 0 | 0 |
| Maglie S, p | 1 | 2 | 1 | 0 |
| Wilhelm H, p | 1 | 0 | 0 | 0 |
| Spencer G, p | 0 | 0 | 0 | 0 |
| Lanier M, p | 0 | 0 | 0 | 0 |
| Wilson G, ph | 1 | 0 | 0 | 0 |
| Kennedy M, p | 0 | 0 | 0 | 0 |
| Yvars S, ph | 1 | 0 | 0 | 0 |
| | 41 | 12 | 14 | 11 |

| St. Louis | IP | H | R | ER | BB | SO |
|---|---|---|---|---|---|---|
| Presko | 1.2 | 6 | 5 | 4 | 1 | 0 |
| Crimian | 0.1 | 7 | 6 | 6 | 1 | 0 |
| Werle | 4.0 | 0 | 0 | 0 | 0 | 3 |
| Yuhas (W) | 2.2 | 1 | 1 | 0 | 2 | 0 |
| Schmidt | 0.1 | 0 | 0 | 0 | 0 | 0 |
| | 9.0 | 14 | 12 | 10 | 4 | 3 |

| New York | IP | H | R | ER | BB | SO |
|---|---|---|---|---|---|---|
| Maglie | 4.2 | 9 | 7 | 7 | 1 | 1 |
| Wilhelm | 1.2 | 4 | 3 | 1 | 0 | 1 |
| Spencer | 0.2 | 1 | 1 | 1 | 0 | 0 |
| Lanier (L) | 1.0 | 2 | 1 | 1 | 1 | 0 |
| Kennedy | 1.0 | 2 | 2 | 2 | 0 | 0 |
| | 9.0 | 18 | 14 | 12 | 2 | 2 |

St. Louis    000    070    322 — 14
New York    056    000    001 — 12

OB: St. Louis 7, New York 7; ER: Hemus, Glaviano 2, Williams, Lockman, Maglie; DP: St. Louis 2, New York 1; 2B: Slaughter; 3B: D. Rice; HR: Slaughter, Thompson, Westrum, Glaviano, Hemus 2; SH: Maglie, Yuhas; TI: 3:22; AT: 41,899; UM: Gorman, Donatelli, Ballanfant, Barlick

Three other Giants hurlers followed Wilhelm, and each was reached for additional hits and runs. With three in the seventh, St. Louis closed to within one run. In the eighth, the Redbirds finally forged ahead on a pair of runs including a solo homer by shortstop Solly Hemus. Just for insurance, Hemus blasted another circuit clout in the ninth, this one a two-run shot into the right-field upper deck. By the time New York batted in the bottom of the ninth, they were demoralized, embarrassed, and trailing 14–11. But the Cardinals, despite six innings of one-hit relief pitching, left the door open.

After the first two Giants were retired in the bottom of the ninth, both Don Mueller and Alvin Dark walked. Another pinch-hitter, Bill Rigney, grounded toward third but was safe on Glaviano's error, loading the bases. Another grounder by pinch-hitter Sal Yvars also was bobbled, this time by Hemus, enabling New York's 12th run to cross the plate. Now with the bases loaded the huge crowd was on its feet and screaming for one more hit. The suspense and

he game ended when the next batter, Davey Williams, fouled out to catcher
Del Rice.

# League Rules Halt 24-Inning Deadlock 57

DETROIT (AL) at PHILADELPHIA (AL)
Saturday, July 21, 1945, Shibe Park
Tigers 1, Athletics 1

Yes, Shibe Park did have lights in 1945, but a league rule prohibited their
use for continuation of a day game. Of course, when the first pitch for this contest was thrown at three-o'clock, no one ever expected the rule to become a
factor. But as the innings wore on, and neither the Detroit Tigers nor the
Philadelphia Athletics could deliver that one extra hit needed to score, the
lengthening shadows took on significance. Finally, after the last out of the 24th
inning, at 7:48 p.m., home plate umpire Bill Summers was forced to call off the
action. His decision came despite pleading by many of players who realized
they were on the brink of establishing a new major league record.

Both lineups were flavored with wartime replacement players, many of
whom would be relegated to reserve roles the following year. Despite that fact,
the visitors breathed first-place air while their hosts already had a stronghold
on their season-ending basement assignment. This day, however, the two clubs
were evenly matched.

Each club used two pitchers during the marathon. Russ Christopher and
Joe Berry split the duties for Philadelphia, while Detroit's Les Mueller tossed
nearly 20 innings before being relieved. For rookie Mueller, this would be his
last season in the majors.

All the scoring could have been avoided with some better play. The Athletics took a 1–0 lead in the fourth after one out when Dick Siebert reached first
on an error and went to third on a double by Bobby Estalella. Buddy Rosar then
singled to drive in the unearned run off Mueller. A walk loaded the sacks before
George Kell hit into an inning-ending double play.

The Tigers tied it in the seventh. With one out Roy Cullenbine walked and
went to third on a single by Rudy York. Roger Cramer then hit a hot grounder
directly at Dick Siebert. The first baseman scooped it cleanly but hesitated while
deciding whether to cut down Cullenbine, heading for the plate, or to try for

| Detroit | AB | R | H | I |
|---|---|---|---|---|
| Webb S, ss | 10 | 0 | 2 | 0 |
| Mayo E, 2b | 9 | 0 | 0 | 0 |
| Cullenbine R, rf | 7 | 1 | 2 | 0 |
| York R, 1b | 9 | 0 | 3 | 0 |
| Cramer D, cf | 10 | 0 | 1 | 1 |
| Outlaw J, lf | 8 | 0 | 1 | 0 |
| Greenberg H, ph | 0 | 0 | 0 | 0 |
| Hostetler C, lf | 0 | 0 | 0 | 0 |
| Maier B, 3b | 10 | 0 | 1 | 0 |
| Swift B, c | 9 | 0 | 0 | 0 |
| Mueller L, p | 7 | 0 | 1 | 0 |
| Trout, D, p | 2 | 0 | 0 | 0 |
| | 81 | 1 | 11 | 1 |

| Philadelphia | AB | R | H | I |
|---|---|---|---|---|
| Hall I, 2b | 11 | 0 | 2 | 0 |
| Peck H, rf | 8 | 0 | 2 | 0 |
| Siebert D, 1b | 9 | 1 | 1 | 0 |
| Estalella B, cf | 10 | 0 | 5 | 0 |
| Rosar, B, c | 9 | 0 | 2 | 1 |
| McGhee B, lf | 8 | 0 | 2 | 0 |
| Kell G, 3b | 10 | 0 | 0 | 0 |
| Busch E, ss | 10 | 0 | 1 | 0 |
| Christopher R, p | 5 | 0 | 0 | 0 |
| Berry J, p | 3 | 0 | 0 | 0 |
| Burns J, ph | 0 | 0 | 0 | 0 |
| Metro C, ph | 1 | 0 | 1 | 0 |
| | 84 | 1 | 16 | 1 |

| Detroit | IP | H | R | ER | BB | SO |
|---|---|---|---|---|---|---|
| Mueller | 19.2 | 13 | 1 | 0 | 5 | 6 |
| Trout | 4.1 | 3 | 0 | 0 | 0 | 2 |
| | 24.0 | 16 | 1 | 0 | 5 | 8 |

| Philadelphia | IP | H | R | ER | BB | SO |
|---|---|---|---|---|---|---|
| Christopher | 13.0 | 5 | 1 | 1 | 2 | 7 |
| Berry | 11.0 | 6 | 0 | 0 | 5 | 2 |
| | 24.0 | 11 | 1 | 1 | 7 | 9 |

| | | | | | | | | | |
|---|---|---|---|---|---|---|---|---|---|
| Detroit | 000 | 000 | 100 | 000 | 000 | 000 | 000 | 000 — 1 |
| Philadelphia | 000 | 100 | 000 | 000 | 000 | 000 | 000 | 000 — 1 |

OB: Detroit 15, Philadelphia 18; ER: Webb, Mayo, York, Busch; DP: Detroit 3, Philadelphia 1; 2B: Cullenbine, Estalella; SH: Siebert, Rosar; TI: 4:48; AT: 4,325; UM: HP Summers, Rue, Boyer

a 3–6–3 double play. Observers reported he could have done either had he had acted quickly. But his hesitation resulted in just one out at first and gave the Tigers their run. There was no further scoring during the following 17 innings.

Each club did have other scoring opportunities, however. The Athletics put runners at the corners with only one out in the sixth. But Mueller fanned Rosar and retired McGhee on a pop-up. In the 10th Philadelphia had men on first and second with two outs when Rosar singled sharply to left. With the winning run rounding third, Jimmy Outlaw unleashed a perfect peg to the plate for a hair-raising third out.

The Tigers made three exciting bids for victory. They loaded the bases with two outs in the 11th before York blistered a long drive toward the center-field bleachers. Estalella raced back and jumped to make the catch just in front of the wall, bringing down the house with cheers of elation. It wasn't until the 22nd that Detroit next seriously threatened. Again they loaded the bases with two outs, but 41-year-old Joe Berry retired Bob Maier on a fly-out to left. In the final frame, the Tigers executed their third and greatest bases-loaded threat. This time there was only one out, but Maier hit sharply into a 6–4–3 double play.

In the home half of the 24th both clubs had trouble seeing the ball, which forced Summers to halt the action. At the time, only one game in major league history had exceeded this one in length.

# *Williams's Homer Decides the All-Star Game* 58

## NATIONAL LEAGUE at AMERICAN LEAGUE
Tuesday, July 8, 1941, Briggs Stadium
AL All-Stars 7, NL All-Stars 5

Unlike All-Star Games of the latter part of the century, early confrontations were more hotly contested. Players had a tendency to remain with one club, or in one league, for most of their careers. As a result there was continuity and camaraderie within the each league, and a natural rivalry between the two. The American League had taken five of the first eight meetings, but this year the National League was hoping to win its second in a row. Highlighting the American League starting lineup were six future Hall of Famers, while the Senior Circuit had but two.

Twenty-two-year-old Bob Feller, from the Cleveland Indians, blazed through the first three innings with his fastball, facing only nine batters and fanning four. The Dodgers' Whit Wyatt, crafting his only 20-win season, also faced the minimum, although he was lifted for a pinch-hitter in the top of the third.

In the bottom of the fourth, Cincinnati's Paul Derringer, coming off three consecutive 20-win campaigns, was on the hill when the first run of the game scored. With one out, Washington's Cecil Travis doubled to left. Joe DiMaggio then flied out, but another youngster, 22-year-old Ted Williams, doubled home Travis.

The scoring pace accelerated in the sixth frame. First, the Senior Circuit tied it in the top half. A leadoff double by pitcher Bucky Walters, a sacrifice bunt, and a sacrifice fly by Terry Moore did the work. In the home half, Walters allowed two walks, then an RBI single by Lou Boudreau, as the American League regained the lead at 2–1.

Facing Washington's Sid Hudson, the National League forged ahead in the seventh. After Enos Slaughter led off with a single, Arky Vaughan homered to right making it 3–2. There was a chance for more when Billy Herman doubled, but Hudson closed the door.

The White Sox Eddie Smith was on the mound in the eighth when the National League struck again. Johnny Mize doubled, and Arky Vaughan hit his second two-run circuit blast, giving his team a 5–2 margin. But the American League got one back in the bottom half thanks to the DiMaggio brothers. Joe doubled, and, with two outs, Dom knocked him home with a single. Boudreau then also singled, but the Cubs' Claude Passeau struck out Jimmie Foxx to hold it at 5–3.

| National League | AB | R | H | I |
|---|---|---|---|---|
| Hack S, 3b | 2 | 0 | 1 | 0 |
| Lavagetto C, ph-3b | 1 | 0 | 0 | 0 |
| Moore T, lf | 5 | 0 | 0 | 1 |
| Reiser P, cf | 4 | 0 | 0 | 0 |
| Mize J, 1b | 4 | 1 | 1 | 0 |
| McCormick F, 1b | 0 | 0 | 0 | 0 |
| Nicholson B, rf | 1 | 0 | 0 | 0 |
| Elliott B, rf | 1 | 0 | 0 | 0 |
| Slaughter E, rf | 2 | 1 | 1 | 0 |
| Vaughan A, ss | 4 | 2 | 3 | 4 |
| Miller E, ss | 0 | 0 | 0 | 0 |
| Frey L, 2b | 1 | 0 | 1 | 0 |
| Herman B, ph-2b | 3 | 0 | 2 | 0 |
| Owen M, c | 1 | 0 | 0 | 0 |
| Lopez A, c | 1 | 0 | 0 | 0 |
| Danning H, c | 1 | 0 | 0 | 0 |
| Wyatt W, p | 0 | 0 | 0 | 0 |
| Ott M, ph | 1 | 0 | 0 | 0 |
| Derringer P, p | 0 | 0 | 0 | 0 |
| Walters B, p | 1 | 1 | 1 | 0 |
| Medwick J, ph | 1 | 0 | 0 | 0 |
| Passeau C, p | 1 | 0 | 0 | 0 |
| | 35 | 5 | 10 | 5 |

| American League | AB | R | H |
|---|---|---|---|
| Doerr B, 2b | 3 | 0 | 0 |
| Gordon J, 2b | 2 | 1 | 1 |
| Travis C, 3b | 4 | 1 | 1 |
| DiMaggio J, cf | 4 | 3 | 1 |
| Williams T, lf | 4 | 1 | 2 |
| Heath J, rf | 2 | 0 | 0 |
| DiMaggio D, rf | 1 | 0 | 1 |
| Cronin J, ss | 2 | 0 | 0 |
| Boudreau L, ss | 2 | 0 | 2 |
| York R, 1b | 3 | 0 | 1 |
| Foxx J, 1b | 1 | 0 | 0 |
| Dickey B, c | 3 | 0 | 1 |
| Hayes F, c | 1 | 0 | 0 |
| Feller B, p | 0 | 0 | 0 |
| Cullenbine R, ph | 1 | 0 | 0 |
| Lee T, p | 1 | 0 | 0 |
| Hudson S, p | 0 | 0 | 0 |
| Keller C, ph | 1 | 0 | 0 |
| Smith E, p | 0 | 0 | 0 |
| Keltner K, ph | 1 | 1 | 1 |
| | 36 | 7 | 11 |

| National League | IP | H | R | ER | BB | SO |
|---|---|---|---|---|---|---|
| Wyatt | 2.0 | 0 | 0 | 0 | 1 | 0 |
| Derringer | 2.0 | 2 | 1 | 1 | 0 | 1 |
| Walters | 2.0 | 3 | 1 | 1 | 2 | 2 |
| Passeau (L) | 2.2 | 6 | 5 | 5 | 1 | 3 |
| | 8.2 | 11 | 7 | 7 | 4 | 6 |

| American League | IP | H | R | ER | BB | SC |
|---|---|---|---|---|---|---|
| Feller | 3.0 | 1 | 0 | 0 | 0 | |
| Lee | 3.0 | 4 | 1 | 1 | 0 | |
| Hudson | 1.0 | 3 | 2 | 2 | 1 | |
| Smith (W) | 2.0 | 2 | 2 | 2 | 0 | |
| | 9.0 | 10 | 5 | 5 | 1 | |

| National League | 000 | 001 | 220 — 5 |
|---|---|---|---|
| American League | 000 | 101 | 014 — 7 |

OB: National League 6, American League 7; ER: Heath, Reiser 2, Williams, Smith; DP National League 1, American League 1; 2B: Travis, Williams, Walters, Herman, Mize DiMaggio J; HR: Vaughan 2, Williams; CS: Frey; SH: Hack, Lopez; TI: 2:23; AT: 54,674 UM: HP Summers, 1B Jorda, 2B Grieve, 3B Pinelli

Smith retired the side in order in the top of the ninth, leaving Passeau and the National League needing just three outs for the victory.

The right-hander retired the first American Leaguer on an infield pop-up but two singles and a walk loaded the sacks. That brought to the plate the grea Joe DiMaggio, who was in the midst of his much celebrated 56-game hitting streak and an MVP season. Joe drilled a sharp grounder to shortstop that should have ended the game, but Herman's wide relay to first spoiled a double play. I also enabled the fourth run to score, and put runners at the corners with two outs. Next up was Williams, leading the league with a .405 average and posses sor of an earlier RBI double. The spindly left-handed batter lashed a tremendou line drive off the right field roof amid a thunderous roar from the partisan crowd The American League had turned near defeat into a rousing 7–5 celebration.

# Frank Becomes "Home Run" Baker 59

PHILADELPHIA (AL) at NEW YORK (NL)
Tuesday, October 17, 1911, Polo Grounds
Athletics 3, Giants 2

In a rematch of the 1905 World Series, John McGraw and Connie Mack once again matched powerhouse clubs in 1911. This year, the New York Giants combined the National League's top batting average, lowest ERA, and the century's most stolen bases in a season — 357 — to easily outdistance their nearest rivals. Anchoring the pitching corps was the imposing right-hander left-hander duo of Christy Mathewson and Rube Marquard, winners of 26 and 24 games, respectively.

The Philadelphia Athletics dominated even more so in the American League. In addition to the best fielding average, they topped the league in runs, batting, on-base percentage and slugging average. Contributing to all categories in its first season was the $100,000 infield of Stuffy McInnis (1B), Eddie Collins (2B), Jack Barry (SS), and Frank Baker (3B). No slouches on the mound, starters Jack Coombs, Eddie Plank, and Chief Bender amassed a staggering 67–25 combined record.

Mathewson continued his dominance of 1905 — when he shut out the Athletics three times — by winning Game One. Game Two saw Philadelphia stalwart Eddie Plank stymie the Giants while a third-year player named Baker began molding a nickname for himself. In the sixth inning, with Marquard and Plank in command of a 1–1 duel, Baker broke it open with a two-run home run over the right-field fence. In 1905 home runs were still eye-opening. Baker's blow was only the eighth to clear a fence in the 42 World Series games. After the third baseman's heroics, Mathewson wrote in his syndicated newspaper column a criticism of Marquard's pitching to Baker. It would come back to haunt him in Game Three.

For the third game, Mathewson returned to the mound to face 28–12 Jack Coombs. What followed were a tremendous pitching confrontation, sparkling defensive plays, controversy, and another dramatic home run.

The Athletics reached Mathewson for only five hits through the first eight innings but had several scoring opportunities. Each was thwarted by an outstanding defensive play.

Leading off the third, Barry singled and stole second. Jack Lapp then launched a low liner that looked like it would find its way into the outfield. Barry started for home, but New York second baseman Larry Doyle made a fine catch and flipped to the bag for a double play.

Snodgrass, standing on third, also spiked Baker in Game One (National Baseball Hall of Fame Library, Cooperstown, New York).

An error, single, and a sacrifice put Athletics at second and third with one out in the fifth. Lapp then chopped a high bounder back through the middle. Mathewson made a leaping snare and trapped the Philadelphia runner attempting to score. The last batter popped out.

Philadelphia had two more runners thrown out at the plate in the eighth. Barry's leadoff double and Lapp's infield single put A's at the corners with no outs. Coombs sent a sizzling grounder to Doyle at second, who fired home to get Barry on a very close play. Bris Lord also grounded to Doyle. The second baseman wanted a force-out at second or possibly a double play, but shortstop Art Fletcher dropped the ball. Observing this, Lapp rounded third and took off for home but was also tagged out. Mathewson then fanned Rube Oldring to maintain his shutout.

Up to this point, Coombs had out pitched Mathewson, allowing only two hits through eight innings. However, the hits, helped by a misplay, produced a New York run in the third. With one out, Meyers and Mathewson singled putting Giants at the corners. The next batter sent a hard grounder to Barry. The shortstop had plenty of time to nip Meyers, who started for the plate, but Barry took his eye off the ball and fumbled it. He recovered in time to get a force-out at second, but Meyers crossed the plate with the game's first run.

Play entered the ninth with the lone run looming large. Mathewson retired the first batter, but with a 2–1 count on Baker, his criticism of Marquard was about to echo throughout the Polo Grounds. Baker then lashed a line drive high

| Philadelphia | AB | R | H | I |
|---|---|---|---|---|
| Lord B, lf | 5 | 0 | 0 | 0 |
| Oldring R, cf | 5 | 0 | 0 | 0 |
| Collins E, 2b | 5 | 1 | 2 | 0 |
| Baker F, 3b | 5 | 2 | 2 | 1 |
| Murphy D, rf | 5 | 0 | 0 | 1 |
| Davis H, 1b | 5 | 0 | 2 | 1 |
| Barry J, ss | 3 | 0 | 2 | 0 |
| Lapp J, c | 4 | 0 | 1 | 0 |
| Coombs J, p | 4 | 0 | 0 | 0 |
| | 41 | 3 | 9 | 3 |

| New York | AB | R | H | I |
|---|---|---|---|---|
| Devore J, lf | 4 | 0 | 0 | 1 |
| Doyle L, 2b | 4 | 0 | 0 | 0 |
| Snodgrass F, cf | 3 | 0 | 0 | 0 |
| Murray R, rf | 2 | 0 | 0 | 0 |
| Merkle F, 1b | 3 | 0 | 0 | 0 |
| Herzog B, 3b | 3 | 1 | 1 | 0 |
| Fletcher A, ss | 4 | 0 | 0 | 0 |
| Meyers C, c | 4 | 1 | 1 | 0 |
| Mathewson C, p | 3 | 0 | 1 | 0 |
| Becker B, ph | 1 | 0 | 0 | 0 |
| | 31 | 2 | 3 | 1 |

| Philadelphia | IP | H | R | ER | BB | SO |
|---|---|---|---|---|---|---|
| Coombs (W) | 11.0 | 3 | 2 | 1 | 4 | 7 |

| New York | IP | H | R | ER | BB | SO |
|---|---|---|---|---|---|---|
| Mathewson (L) | 11.0 | 9 | 3 | 1 | 0 | 3 |

| Philadelphia | 000 | 000 | 001 | 02 — 3 |
|---|---|---|---|---|
| New York | 001 | 000 | 000 | 01 — 2 |

OB: Philadelphia 6, New York 1; ER: Herzog 3, Fletcher 2, Collins; DP: New York 1; 2B: Barry, Herzog; HR: Baker; SB: Barry, Collins; CS: Devore, Herzog, Merkle, Davis, Becker; SH: Barry, Murray; TI: 2:25; AT: 37,216; UM: HP Brennan, 1B Connolly, 2B Klem, 3B Dinneen

into the right-field seats, even farther than the one a day earlier. That tied the game at 1–1, and the few fans that traveled from Philadelphia finally had a chance to raise their voices. Danny Murphy next reached second on an error, but two more ground-outs closed the frame.

Coombs continued his mastery over the Giants in the bottom of the ninth by retiring the side in order. Since New York scored their run in the third, Coombs faced just 19 batters over six innings.

The Giants threatened in the tenth, but the strong arm of Philadelphia catcher Jack Lapp saved the Athletics. Fred Snodgrass led off with a walk and was sacrificed to second. Coombs' second pitch to Fred Merkle dribbled a few feet behind Lapp. Snodgrass darted for third but Lapp recovered quickly and fired to Baker. When the ball arrived early, Snodgrass tried to kick it out of Baker's glove. In doing so he cut Baker and nearly tore off the third sacker's trousers. Worse, he continued kicking at Baker even after being called out. Philadelphia newspapers the next day blasted Snodgrass and the Giants for their dirty tactics. When the commotion died down, Merkle walked. But again Lapp helped his battery mate when he gunned down the Giant trying to steal second.

In the top of the 11th, with one out, Collins and Baker both singled and moved to second and third on an infield throwing error. Danny Murphy was safe when Fletcher bobbled his grounder, enabling Collins to score and giving Philadelphia its first lead of the game. Harry Davis also singled, knocking in Baker, but Murphy was thrown out at third. Davis was then caught stealing.

With a 3–1 lead, it looked easy for Coombs, but Buck Herzog led off the home half of the 11th with a double. Coombs got the next two outs as Herzog moved to third. Beals Becker, pinch-hitting for Mathewson, grounded toward second in what should have ended the game, but Collins mishandled it. Herzog scored on the play, making it 3–2. Trying to get himself into scoring position,

Becker then tried to steal second. But again Lapp's arm shined as he tossed out his fifth Giant on the basepaths, ending the thriller.

# 60 Déjà vu for the Giants and Dodgers

SAN FRANCISCO (NL) at LOS ANGELES (NL)
Wednesday, October 3, 1962, Dodger Stadium
Giants 6, Dodgers 4

Eleven years to the day after the "Shot Heard 'Round the World," a strikingly similar event occurred about 3,000 miles away. The scene again staged the Dodgers and Giants meeting for the third of a three-game playoff. The Dodgers had blown a sure pennant and allowed their arch rival to capture a share of the crown during the waning hours of the season. And now, just as on that fateful day in the Polo Grounds 11 years earlier, the Dodgers took a commanding lead into the ninth, only to lose a gut-wrenching decision.

The Dodgers demise was not as shocking as it had been in 1951. After all, they lost their best pitcher, Sandy Koufax, in July to circulatory problems in his pitching arm and fingers. But that aside, they still had a seemingly insurmountable lead of four games with just seven to play. While Los Angeles was dropping its final three in St. Louis, Willie Mays homered on the last day to lock the Giants into a tie for first.

San Francisco won the first playoff game in convincing style, 8–0, and took a commanding 5–0 lead in Game Two. But Los Angeles vengefully rallied twice to tie the series. Thus the 1962 National League pennant came down to a single contest.

In the decisive game, the Dodgers sent bygone hero Johnny Podres to face the Giants' Juan Marichal. Once again San Francisco scored first with a pair in the third inning and nearly broke it open in the sixth when they loaded the bases with no outs. Ed Roebuck quelled the uprising on just four pitches, however, and the Dodgers squirmed free of the hook — for now.

As they had in Game Two, Los Angeles rallied again to regain the lead, 3–2, in the bottom of the sixth. Another run by the Dodgers in the seventh gave them a 4–2 lead that they carried into the ninth. The lead was nearly greater, but the Giants' Don Larsen, in relief of Marichal, escaped potential disaster in

| San Francisco | AB | R | H | I |
|---|---|---|---|---|
| Kuenn H, lf | 5 | 1 | 2 | 1 |
| Hiller C, 2b | 3 | 0 | 1 | 0 |
| McCovey W, ph | 0 | 0 | 0 | 0 |
| Bowman E, pr-2b | 0 | 1 | 0 | 0 |
| Alou F, rf | 4 | 1 | 1 | 0 |
| Mays W, cf | 3 | 1 | 1 | 1 |
| Cepeda O, 1b | 4 | 0 | 1 | 1 |
| Bailey E, c | 4 | 0 | 2 | 0 |
| Davenport J, 3b | 4 | 0 | 1 | 1 |
| Pagan J, ss | 5 | 1 | 2 | 0 |
| Marichal J, p | 2 | 1 | 1 | 0 |
| Larsen D, p | 0 | 0 | 0 | 0 |
| Alou M, ph | 1 | 0 | 1 | 0 |
| Nieman B, ph | 1 | 0 | 0 | 0 |
| Pierce B, p | 0 | 0 | 0 | 0 |
|  | 36 | 6 | 13 | 4 |

| Los Angeles | AB | R | H | I |
|---|---|---|---|---|
| Wills M, ss | 5 | 1 | 4 | 0 |
| Gilliam J, 2b-3b | 5 | 0 | 0 | 0 |
| Snider D, lf | 3 | 2 | 2 | 0 |
| Burright L, 2b | 1 | 0 | 0 | 0 |
| Walls L, ph | 1 | 0 | 0 | 0 |
| Davis T, 3b-lf | 3 | 1 | 2 | 2 |
| Moon W, 1b | 3 | 0 | 0 | 0 |
| Fairly R, 1b-rf | 0 | 0 | 0 | 0 |
| Howard F, rf | 4 | 0 | 1 | 1 |
| Harkness T, 1b | 0 | 0 | 0 | 0 |
| Roseboro J, c | 3 | 0 | 0 | 0 |
| Davis W, cf | 3 | 0 | 0 | 0 |
| Podres J, p | 2 | 0 | 0 | 0 |
| Roebuck E, p | 2 | 0 | 0 | 0 |
| Williams S, p | 0 | 0 | 0 | 0 |
| Perranoski R, p | 0 | 0 | 0 | 0 |
|  | 35 | 4 | 9 | 3 |

| San Francisco | IP | H | R | ER | BB | SO |
|---|---|---|---|---|---|---|
| Marichal | 7.0 | 9 | 4 | 3 | 1 | 2 |
| Larsen (W) | 1.0 | 0 | 0 | 0 | 2 | 1 |
| Pierce | 1.0 | 0 | 0 | 0 | 0 | 0 |
|  | 9.0 | 9 | 4 | 3 | 3 | 3 |

| Los Angeles | IP | H | R | ER | BB | SO |
|---|---|---|---|---|---|---|
| Podres | 5.0 | 9 | 2 | 1 | 1 | 0 |
| Roebuck (L) | 3.1 | 4 | 4 | 3 | 3 | 0 |
| Williams | 0.1 | 0 | 0 | 0 | 2 | 0 |
| Perranoski | 0.1 | 0 | 0 | 0 | 0 | 1 |
|  | 9.0 | 13 | 6 | 4 | 6 | 1 |

```
San Francisco   002   000   004 — 6
Los Angeles     000   102   100 — 4
```

OB: San Francisco 12, Los Angeles 8; ER: Marichal, Podres, Roseboro, Gilliam, Bailey, Burright; DP: Los Angeles 3; 2B: Snider, Hiller; HR: Davis; SB: Wills 3, Davis; SH: Hiller, Marichal, Fairly; SF: Cepeda; WP: Williams; TI: 3:00; AT: 45,693; UM: HP Boggess, 1B Donatelli, 2B Conlan, 3B Barlick

the eighth by retiring Roebuck with the bases loaded. The Dodgers would later regret the decision not to lift the pitcher for a pinch-hitter.

In the ninth, the Giants touched Roebuck for two singles and a pair of walks, making it 4–3, before Stan Williams came in to relieve. Williams was also wild, walking two more and giving San Francisco a 5–4 lead. Ron Perranoski also entered the fray, but an infield error cost the Dodgers another run. By the time the dust settled, the Giants led 6–4.

San Francisco manager Alvin Dark, recalling how his club squandered their 5–0 lead a day earlier, decided to forsake his bullpen for the last of the ninth. Instead, he went to his reliable starter, Billy Pierce. The left-hander, who had blanked Los Angeles on three hits in the opening playoff game, sat down the stunned Dodgers in order to send the Giants on a familiar road to Yankee Stadium.

# 61 *The Century's Only 21-Strikeout Pitcher*

WASHINGTON (AL) at BALTIMORE (AL)
Wednesday, September 12, 1962, Memorial Stadium
Senators 2, Orioles 1

How many baseball fans would remember the likes of Zip Zabel, Phil Weintraub, Cesar Gutierrez, Mark Whiten, or Andy Hawkins were it not for their one phenomenal day on the diamond. Included in this list certainly must be Tom Cheney, winner of only 19 games during his eight major-league seasons. But on one September night, Cheney set the baseball world on its heels by fanning 21 batters in a single game, establishing a benchmark that still stands.

Prior to Cheney's heroics, no hurler struck out more than 18 in any one game during the 20th century, regardless of the number of innings pitched. During the 19th century Charlie Sweeney and Hugh Daily each fanned 19, and since Cheney's spectacle, 20 strikeouts has been reached three times.

The 27-year-old, who passed through St. Louis and Pittsburgh before settling in the nation's capital, demonstrated infrequent and erratic mound mastery. For example, through August of the 1962 campaign, he had completed only three games in 20 starts, but each was a shutout. Nor was the six-footer known as a strikeout artist, for on this night he struck out more batters than he had in all of 1961.

The game began inauspiciously for Cheney as he fanned no Orioles in the opening frame and only one in the second. The pace quickened, though, as he then fanned 16 over the next nine innings, and the modern strikeout mark of

| Washington | AB | R | H | I | | Baltimore | AB | R | H | I |
|---|---|---|---|---|---|---|---|---|---|---|
| Kennedy J, ss | 6 | 0 | 1 | 0 | | Adair J, ss | 6 | 0 | 2 | 0 |
| Stillwell R, 2b | 3 | 1 | 1 | 0 | | Snyder R, rf | 7 | 0 | 2 | 0 |
| King J, ph | 1 | 0 | 1 | 0 | | Robinson B, 3b | 5 | 0 | 1 | 0 |
| Cottier C, 2b | 2 | 0 | 0 | 0 | | Gentile J, 1b | 7 | 0 | 1 | 0 |
| Hinton C, rf | 7 | 0 | 1 | 0 | | Powell B, lf | 6 | 0 | 1 | 0 |
| Zipfel B, 1b | 7 | 1 | 3 | 2 | | Nicholson D, cf | 7 | 0 | 1 | 0 |
| Retzer K, c | 7 | 0 | 0 | 0 | | Landrith H, c | 6 | 0 | 0 | 0 |
| Osteen C, pr | 0 | 0 | 0 | 0 | | Brandt J, ph | 1 | 0 | 0 | 0 |
| Schmidt B, c | 0 | 0 | 0 | 0 | | Breeding M, 2b | 6 | 1 | 1 | 0 |
| Hicks J, cf | 5 | 0 | 1 | 0 | | Williams D, ph | 1 | 0 | 0 | 0 |
| Schaive J, ph | 1 | 0 | 0 | 0 | | Pappas M, p | 2 | 0 | 0 | 0 |
| Piersall J, cf | 0 | 0 | 0 | 0 | | Lau C, ph | 1 | 0 | 1 | 1 |
| Lock D, lf | 7 | 0 | 1 | 0 | | Hall D, p | 3 | 0 | 0 | 0 |
| Brinkman E, 3b | 5 | 0 | 1 | 0 | | Hoeft B, p | 0 | 0 | 0 | 0 |
| Cheney T, p | 6 | 0 | 0 | 0 | | Stock W, p | 0 | 0 | 0 | 0 |
| | 57 | 2 | 10 | 2 | | | 58 | 1 | 10 | 1 |

| Washington | IP | H | R | ER | BB | SO |
|---|---|---|---|---|---|---|
| Cheney (W) | 16.0 | 10 | 1 | 1 | 4 | 21 |

| Baltimore | IP | H | R | ER | BB | SO |
|---|---|---|---|---|---|---|
| Pappas | 7.0 | 4 | 1 | 1 | 3 | 4 |
| Hall (L) | 8.1 | 5 | 1 | 1 | 1 | 4 |
| Hoeft | 0.1 | 1 | 0 | 0 | 0 | 0 |
| Stock | 0.1 | 0 | 0 | 0 | 1 | 0 |
| | 16.0 | 10 | 2 | 2 | 5 | 8 |

| Washington | 100 | 000 | 000 | 000 | 000 | 1 — 2 |
|---|---|---|---|---|---|---|
| Baltimore | 000 | 000 | 100 | 000 | 000 | 0 — 1 |

OB: Washington 13, Baltimore 13; ER: Adair, Breeding; 2B: Hinton, Snyder, Adair, Gentile, Hicks, Breeding; HR: Zipfel; SB: Adair; CS: Kennedy; SH: Cheney; WP: Cheney; BK: Pappas; TI: 3:59; AT: 4,098; UM: McKinley, Chylak, Umont, Stewart

18 fell in the 14th frame. A new all-time standard of 20 was set in the 15th inning, and with two outs in the 16th, pinch-hitter Dick Williams watched a third strike go by to end the game and give Cheney his 21st marker. Every Baltimore starter fanned except Boog Powell; while Russ Snyder, Jim Gentile, Dave Nicholson, Marv Breeding and Dick Hall were each victimized three times.

But Cheney did more than simply strike out batters. His 228 pitches were reached for just 10 safeties, and he held the Orioles hitless from the eighth until the 16th. He used a variety of pitches including a fastball, slider, and knuckler, but it was his curveball that most baffled Baltimore hitters. Marv Breeding said after the game that Cheney had the best stuff he had seen all year. Brooks Robinson agreed.

In July of 1963, with an 8–9 record and a 2.71 ERA, Cheney suffered a severe elbow injury that cut short his major-league career. Comeback attempts in 1964 and again in 1966 proved unsuccessful.

# *Good Pitching* 62
# *Subdues Good Hitting*

CLEVELAND (AL) at ATLANTA (NL)
Saturday, October 28, 1995, Fulton County Stadium
Braves 1, Indians 0

The 1995 World Series promised a fresh world champion, for neither participant had worn that crown in nearly 40 years. This is not to suggest, however, that both teams were strangers to the post season. The Atlanta Braves had fielded quality teams since 1991, finishing first in their division four of the last

| Cleveland | AB | R | H | I |
|---|---|---|---|---|
| Lofton K, cf | 4 | 0 | 0 | 0 |
| Vizquel O, ss | 3 | 0 | 0 | 0 |
| Sorrento P, ph | 1 | 0 | 0 | 0 |
| Baerga C, 2b | 4 | 0 | 0 | 0 |
| Belle A, lf | 1 | 0 | 0 | 0 |
| Murray E, 1b | 2 | 0 | 0 | 0 |
| Ramirez M, rf | 3 | 0 | 0 | 0 |
| Embree A, p | 0 | 0 | 0 | 0 |
| Tavarez J, p | 0 | 0 | 0 | 0 |
| Assenmacher P, p | 0 | 0 | 0 | 0 |
| Thome J, 3b | 3 | 0 | 0 | 0 |
| Peña T, c | 3 | 0 | 1 | 0 |
| Martinez D, p | 1 | 0 | 0 | 0 |
| Poole J, p | 1 | 0 | 0 | 0 |
| Hill K, p | 0 | 0 | 0 | 0 |
| Amaro R, rf | 1 | 0 | 0 | 0 |
| | 27 | 0 | 1 | 0 |

| Atlanta | AB | R | H | I |
|---|---|---|---|---|
| Grissom M, cf | 4 | 0 | 1 | 0 |
| Lemke M, 2b | 2 | 0 | 1 | 0 |
| Jones C, 3b | 3 | 0 | 2 | 0 |
| McGriff F, 1b | 4 | 0 | 0 | 0 |
| Justice D, rf | 2 | 1 | 2 | 1 |
| Klesko R, lf | 1 | 0 | 0 | 0 |
| Devereaux M, lf | 1 | 0 | 0 | 0 |
| Lopez J, c | 3 | 0 | 0 | 0 |
| Belliard R, ss | 4 | 0 | 0 | 0 |
| Glavine T, p | 3 | 0 | 0 | 0 |
| Polonia L, ph | 1 | 0 | 0 | 0 |
| Wohlers M, p | 0 | 0 | 0 | 0 |
| | 28 | 1 | 6 | 1 |

| Cleveland | IP | H | R | ER | BB | SO |
|---|---|---|---|---|---|---|
| Martinez | 4.2 | 4 | 0 | 0 | 5 | 2 |
| Poole (L) | 1.1 | 1 | 1 | 1 | 0 | 1 |
| Hill | 0.0 | 1 | 0 | 0 | 0 | 0 |
| Embree | 1.0 | 0 | 0 | 0 | 2 | 0 |
| Tavarez | 0.2 | 0 | 0 | 0 | 0 | 0 |
| Assenmacher | 0.1 | 0 | 0 | 0 | 0 | 1 |
| | 8.0 | 6 | 1 | 1 | 7 | 4 |

| Atlanta | IP | H | R | ER | BB | SO |
|---|---|---|---|---|---|---|
| Glavine (W) | 8.0 | 1 | 0 | 0 | 3 | 8 |
| Wohlers (S) | 1.0 | 0 | 0 | 0 | 0 | 0 |
| | 9.0 | 1 | 0 | 0 | 3 | 8 |

| Cleveland | 000 | 000 | 000 — 0 |
|---|---|---|---|
| Atlanta | 000 | 001 | 00x — 1 |

OB: Cleveland 3, Atlanta 11; ER: Thome; DP: Cleveland; 2B: Justice; HR: Justice; SB: Lofton, Grissom; CS: Lemke, Belle; SH: Lemke; TI: 3:01; AT: 51,875; UM: HP Brinkman, 1B Wendelstedt, 2B McKean, 3B Froemming, LF Hirschbeck, RF Pulli

five years. Led by a pitching staff perennially among the best, they were making their third World Series appearance in four years. Still, not since 1957 had the franchise been able to proclaim itself world champion.

Standing in the Braves' path were the powerful Cleveland Indians, who reached the final dance in different fashion. They ascended quickly from mediocrity, finishing atop their division and league for the first time since 1954. They had not arrived, like the Braves, on the strength of pitching, but rather riding the bats of emerging offensive stars. The match-up provided the classic confrontation — good pitching against good hitting.

As the teams traveled back to Atlanta, the Braves held a three-games-to-two advantage. The scheduled pitching matchup was a repeat of Game Two, with Cleveland's Dennis Martinez pitted against Atlanta's Tom Glavine. The Braves' left-hander had won the first confrontation and later intimated that his change-in-speed delivery style was perfectly suited to the aggressive Indians' bats.

Unfortunately for Cleveland, Glavine was even better in Game Six. Through five innings, only Albert Belle reached base — twice, on walks, and once was thrown out attempting to steal. In the sixth, Cleveland managed their first hit, a leadoff single by veteran catcher Tony Peña. After one out, Kenny Lofton grounded into a fielder's choice and stole second, where he was stranded.

Atlanta's David Justice, who a day earlier had roused Braves fans by commenting on their lack of spirit, led off the home sixth with a long home run to right field. The villain-to-hero blow came at the expense of Jim Poole, who was pitching in relief of stiff-elbowed Martinez.

Glavine, tiring, came out after the eighth, but Mark Wohlers continued the Cleveland whitewash by retiring the side in order in the ninth. For the game, just four Indians reached base, and only one got as far as second. Atlanta had won their first world championship in 38 years and, at least in this Series, good pitching did overcome good hitting.

# Hack's Hit in the 12th Beats the Tigers 63

DETROIT (AL) at CHICAGO (NL)
Monday, October 8, 1945, Wrigley Field
Cubs 8, Tigers 7

Ten years earlier these same two clubs met in the Fall Classic with the Detroit Tigers prevailing in six games. This year the Chicago Cubs won two of the three in Detroit but dropped the first two games in Chicago, again leaving themselves on the brink of ending their season as runners-up.

For Game Six, Chicago patrons were greeted with a cloudy day and a wintry nip in the air that forced many to wrap themselves in blankets. Bats were anything but cold, however, as both teams clubbed the ball at a pace that delivered no fewer than nine pitchers into the fray.

Claude Passeau, who had tossed a one-hitter in Game Three, started for the Cubs against Virgil Trucks, the winner of Game Two. Neither hurler approached the success of their earlier outing.

After a leadoff out in the second, the Tigers filled the bases before Passeau walked in the first run. Further damage was averted when neither Trucks nor Skeeter Webb could get the ball out of the infield. Passeau killed another bases-loaded rally in the fourth by retiring Webb on a fly ball to center.

It was the Cubs' turn to load the bases in the fifth. They did it without making an out, giving fans the first opportunity to get their blood circulating. Stan Hack, one of the most popular players ever to wear a Chicago uniform,

| Detroit | AB | R | H | I |
|---|---|---|---|---|
| Webb S, ss | 3 | 0 | 0 | 0 |
| Hostetler C, ph | 1 | 0 | 0 | 0 |
| Hoover J, ss | 3 | 1 | 1 | 1 |
| Mayo E, 2b | 6 | 0 | 1 | 1 |
| Cramer D, cf | 6 | 1 | 2 | 1 |
| Greenberg H, lf | 5 | 2 | 1 | 1 |
| Cullenbine R, rf | 5 | 1 | 2 | 1 |
| York R, 1b | 6 | 0 | 2 | 1 |
| Outlaw J, 3b | 5 | 0 | 1 | 0 |
| Richards P, c | 0 | 0 | 0 | 1 |
| Maier B, ph | 1 | 0 | 1 | 0 |
| Swift B, c | 2 | 1 | 1 | 0 |
| Trucks V, p | 1 | 0 | 0 | 0 |
| Caster G, p | 0 | 0 | 0 | 0 |
| McHale J, ph | 1 | 0 | 0 | 0 |
| Bridges T, p | 0 | 0 | 0 | 0 |
| Benton A, p | 0 | 0 | 0 | 0 |
| Walker H, ph | 1 | 1 | 1 | 0 |
| Trout D, p | 2 | 0 | 0 | 0 |
| | 48 | 7 | 13 | 7 |

| Chicago | AB | R | H | I |
|---|---|---|---|---|
| Hack S, 3b | 5 | 1 | 4 | 3 |
| Johnson D, 2b | 4 | 0 | 0 | 0 |
| Lowrey P, lf | 5 | 1 | 1 | 0 |
| Cavarretta P, 1b | 5 | 1 | 2 | 2 |
| Pafko A, cf | 6 | 0 | 2 | 0 |
| Nicholson B, rf | 5 | 0 | 0 | 0 |
| Livingston M, c | 3 | 2 | 2 | 1 |
| Gillespie P, ph | 1 | 0 | 0 | 0 |
| Williams D, c | 1 | 0 | 0 | 0 |
| Hughes R, ss | 4 | 1 | 3 | 2 |
| Becker H, ph | 0 | 0 | 0 | 0 |
| Block C, pr | 0 | 0 | 0 | 0 |
| Merullo L, ss | 0 | 0 | 0 | 0 |
| Secory F, ph | 1 | 0 | 1 | 0 |
| Schuster B, pr | 0 | 1 | 0 | 0 |
| Passeau C, p | 3 | 1 | 0 | 0 |
| Wyse H, p | 1 | 0 | 0 | 0 |
| Prim R, p | 0 | 0 | 0 | 0 |
| Borowy H, p | 2 | 0 | 0 | 0 |
| | 46 | 8 | 15 | 8 |

| Detroit | IP | H | R | ER | BB | SO |
|---|---|---|---|---|---|---|
| Trucks | 4.1 | 7 | 4 | 4 | 2 | 3 |
| Caster | 0.2 | 0 | 0 | 0 | 0 | 1 |
| Bridges | 1.2 | 3 | 3 | 3 | 3 | 1 |
| Benton | 0.1 | 1 | 0 | 0 | 0 | 1 |
| Trout (L) | 4.2 | 4 | 1 | 1 | 2 | 3 |
| | 11.2 | 15 | 8 | 8 | 7 | 9 |

| Chicago | IP | H | R | ER | BB | SO |
|---|---|---|---|---|---|---|
| Passeau | 6.2 | 5 | 3 | 3 | 6 | 2 |
| Wyse | 0.2 | 3 | 3 | 2 | 1 | 0 |
| Prim | 0.2 | 1 | 1 | 0 | 0 | 0 |
| Borowy (W) | 4.0 | 4 | 0 | 0 | 0 | 0 |
| | 12.0 | 13 | 7 | 5 | 7 | 2 |

```
Detroit   010  000  240  000 — 7
Chicago   000  041  200  001 — 8
```

OB: Detroit 12, Chicago 12; ER: Johnson, Richards, Hack 2; DP: Detroit 2, Chicago 1; 2B: York, Livingston, Hughes, Walker, Pafko, Hack; HR: Greenberg; SB: Cullenbine; CS: Hoover; SH: Johnson 2; TI: 3:28; AT: 41,708; UM: HP Jorda, 1B Passarella, 2B Conlan, 3B Summers

delivered a two-run single. After a walk, Phil Cavarretta did the same, giving the home team a 4–1 advantage and starting a parade of Tiger relievers.

Tommy Bridges was the next Tiger reliever, and he fell victim to a pair of doubles in the sixth that extended the Cubs lead to 5–1.

In the seventh, Detroit answered with two runs but should have had more. A walk, three singles and a Chicago error let in a pair, but a third runner was tagged out at the plate when he tripped rounding third. The Cubs countered with two runs of their own in the home half. Three walks sandwiched between a pair of singles did the damage, and the Cubs regained their comfortable four-run lead at 7–3.

The Tigers allowed Chicago fans little time to savor their contentment. An eighth-inning rally pushed across four Detroit runs, concluded by a Hank Greenberg solo homer. They squandered another run when, preceding Greenberg's blast, Eddie Mayo got himself tossed out trying to stretch a single into a double.

Detroit nearly tallied the lead run in the ninth after two singles put runners at the corners with only one out. But Dizzy Trout's hot grounder to short resulted in a rundown put-out between third and home. The rally suffocated when the next batter popped out.

In the home half of the ninth, excitement surged when Andy Pafko led off with a double, but Trout quieted the crowd and wriggled out of the threat.

Hank Borowy, who had taken the mound for Chicago in the ninth, faced a total of just nine Tigers during the 10th, 11th, and 12th. Trout, too, was successful until he retired the first batter in the 12th. Then Frank Secory singled and gave way to pinch-runner Bill Shuster. Borowy struck out for the second out, bringing up Hack, who had already reached base five times. Stan laced a sharp drive into left that had all appearances of a harmless single. But the sphere took an unexpected hop over the head of Greenberg. Amid pandemonium, it rolled to the wall while Shuster cruised home with the winning tally and sent the Series to a seventh game.

# *Pilgrims Take the Flag on a Wild Pitch* 64

### BOSTON (AL) at NEW YORK (AL)
### Monday, October 10, 1904, Hilltop Park
### Pilgrims 3, Highlanders 2

On the final day of the season, the American League championship was yet undetermined, and the two contenders, the Boston Pilgrims and New York Highlanders, were scheduled to meet in New York. Only three days earlier New York right-hander Jack Chesbro had notched his astonishing 41st victory at the expense of the Pilgrims, giving his club a half-game lead. But Boston swept a doubleheader the following day vaulting them ahead by 1 and one-half games. After an off day, the two met for another doubleheader, with New York needing to win both for the pennant. Any other combination would crown the Pilgrims champions.

On the mound in the first game for New York was Chesbro, Boston countered with 23-game winner Big Bill Dinneen. More than 28,000 fans turned out for the showdown, including Boston's Royal Rooters. Seats were quickly filled, and the overflow lined the outfield, clustering along the foul lines and wedging into the aisles. Between the Royal Rooter band and the fans with their megaphones and tin horns, a constant din prevailed throughout the contest.

| Boston | AB | R | H | I |
|---|---|---|---|---|
| Selbach K, lf | 5 | 0 | 0 | 0 |
| Parent F, ss | 5 | 0 | 1 | 0 |
| Stahl C, cf | 5 | 0 | 1 | 0 |
| Collins J, 3b | 4 | 0 | 0 | 0 |
| Freeman B, rf | 4 | 0 | 2 | 0 |
| LaChance C, 1b | 4 | 1 | 2 | 0 |
| Ferris H, 2b | 4 | 1 | 1 | 0 |
| Criger L, c | 2 | 1 | 1 | 0 |
| Dinneen B, p | 3 | 0 | 0 | 0 |
| | 36 | 3 | 8 | 0 |

| New York | AB | R | H | I |
|---|---|---|---|---|
| Dougherty P, lf | 4 | 0 | 1 | 1 |
| Keeler W, rf | 2 | 0 | 0 | 0 |
| Elberfeld K, ss | 3 | 0 | 0 | 1 |
| Williams J, 2b | 4 | 0 | 0 | 0 |
| Anderson J, cf | 4 | 0 | 1 | 0 |
| Ganzel J, 1b | 4 | 0 | 0 | 0 |
| Conroy W, 3b | 3 | 0 | 0 | 0 |
| Kleinow J, c | 4 | 1 | 2 | 0 |
| Chesbro J, p | 3 | 1 | 2 | 0 |
| McGuire J, ph | 0 | 0 | 0 | 0 |
| Fultz D, pr | 0 | 0 | 0 | 0 |
| | 31 | 2 | 6 | 2 |

| Boston | IP | H | R | ER | BB | SO |
|---|---|---|---|---|---|---|
| Dinneen(W) | 9.0 | 6 | 2 | 2 | 5 | 7 |

| New York | IP | H | R | ER | BB | SO |
|---|---|---|---|---|---|---|
| Chesbro (L) | 9.0 | 8 | 3 | 1 | 1 | 5 |

| Boston | 000 | 000 | 201 — 3 |
|---|---|---|---|
| New York | 000 | 020 | 000 — 2 |

OB: Boston 9, New York 8; ER: Elberfield, Williams 2, Chesbro; 2B: LaChance; 3B: Chesbro; SB: Parent; SH: Criger, Dinneen, Keeler; WP: Chesbro 2; TI: 2:05; AT: 28,540; UM: Connolly, Sheridan

New York mounted the first threat in the third frame. With one out Chesbro tripled to right, but Dinneen rose to the challenge and fanned the next two batters.

In the fifth the Highlanders finally did break into the scoring column. After the first two batters were retired, three singles and two walks forced a pair of runs across the plate. New York left the bases loaded, however. They would later regret the squandered opportunity.

Boston had little success with Chesbro until the seventh, when some shoddy New York fielding provided a scoring opportunity. After an infield single, Highlander second baseman Jimmy Williams muffed an easy grounder, putting two Pilgrims aboard. (Some sources labeled this a hit rather than an error.) Both runners advanced on a sacrifice before Dinneen sent another routine bounder toward Williams. Seeing the runner on third trying to score, Williams threw home — wildly. Two runs crossed the plate.

The Pilgrims also collected three singles in the eighth but failed to score because of a scintillating play at the plate.

In the ninth, Boston took their first lead of the game. Lou Criger singled, was sacrificed to second, and moved to third on a ground-out. With two strikes on the next batter, Chesbro uncorked a wild pitch that allowed the go-ahead run to score.

With two outs and a man with a free pass already onboard, Dinneen walked his second Highlander in the bottom of the ninth, rekindling excitement in the home crowd. But Big Bill ended the game and gave Boston the flag when he fanned Patsy Dougherty.

For many years after, fans attributed the New York loss to Chesbro's wild pitch. But the Highlanders never would have been in position to contend without his 41 victories. In addition, wild pitch or not, Jack would have won this game with some better fielding or clutch hitting behind him.

# *Camp Provides Early Fireworks* 65

NEW YORK (NL) at ATLANTA (NL)
Thursday, July 4, 1985, Fulton County Stadium
Mets 16, Braves 13

In one of the most bizarre games of the century, the visiting New York Mets and their hosts, the Atlanta Braves, virtually emptied their benches through 19 innings of strategy, blown rallies, heroics, and rain delays. Soggy fans were treated to four ties and multiple lead changes, several of which occurred in the extra frames. Those who stayed would see ejections, a protest, a player hit for the cycle, and a lifetime .060 hitter tie the game in the bottom of the 18th with a home run. The rain not only delayed the first pitch for 84 minutes but also created conditions forcing players to slosh through puddles and retrieve balls that stopped dead in standing water.

Despite poor weather predictions, Fireworks Night in Atlanta attracted an Independence Day sellout crowd of nearly 45,000 enthusiasts. The initial rain delay may have taken the edge off both starters, because each team not only scored in the opening inning but also left the bases loaded. The Mets got one run home, but Ray Knight struck out to end the visitors' half. Atlanta tied it on Claudell Washington's triple and a ground-out. Three of the next four batters then walked before Rick Cerone grounded out.

Both teams generated some offense in the third, but only the Braves scored. After two were out in the top half, the Mets loaded the bases on three consecutive walks before Knight lined out. The home half was interrupted by a 41-minute rain delay, forcing the first of what would become a dozen pitching changes. During this frame Ken Oberkfell doubled home two mates, giving the Braves a 3–1 lead.

New York retaliated with four runs in the fourth. Their rally was marked by Wally Backman's single that stopped dead in a deep puddle and a triple by Keith Hernandez made possible in part by Washington's slipping and falling in the waterlogged outfield.

The Mets expanded their advantage to 6–4 in the top of the sixth and had

| New York | AB | R | H | I |
|---|---|---|---|---|
| Dykstra L, cf | 9 | 1 | 3 | 2 |
| Backman W, 2b | 10 | 2 | 4 | 2 |
| Hernandez K, 1b | 10 | 3 | 4 | 3 |
| Carter G, c | 9 | 1 | 5 | 2 |
| Strawberry D, rf | 7 | 0 | 3 | 1 |
| Christensen J, rf | 0 | 0 | 0 | 0 |
| Foster G, lf | 2 | 0 | 0 | 0 |
| Orosco J, p | 0 | 0 | 0 | 0 |
| Sisk D, p | 1 | 0 | 0 | 0 |
| Chapman K, ph | 1 | 0 | 0 | 0 |
| Gorman T, p | 2 | 0 | 0 | 0 |
| Staub R, ph | 0 | 1 | 0 | 0 |
| Darling R, p | 0 | 0 | 0 | 0 |
| Knight R, 3b | 10 | 2 | 3 | 1 |
| Santana R, ss | 4 | 1 | 1 | 0 |
| Johnson H, ph-ss | 5 | 4 | 3 | 2 |
| Gooden D, p | 1 | 0 | 0 | 0 |
| McDowell R, p | 0 | 0 | 0 | 0 |
| Hurdle C, ph | 1 | 0 | 0 | 0 |
| Leach T, p | 2 | 0 | 0 | 0 |
| Heep D, lf | 6 | 1 | 2 | 2 |
| | 80 | 16 | 28 | 15 |

| Atlanta | AB | R | H | I |
|---|---|---|---|---|
| Washington C, rf | 8 | 3 | 3 | 0 |
| Ramirez R, ss | 9 | 2 | 3 | 2 |
| Murphy D, cf | 8 | 1 | 1 | 3 |
| Horner B, 1b | 4 | 1 | 1 | 0 |
| Perry G, 1b | 4 | 0 | 0 | 0 |
| Harper T, lf | 10 | 3 | 5 | 4 |
| Oberkfell K, 3b | 6 | 1 | 3 | 2 |
| Camp R, p | 2 | 1 | 1 | 1 |
| Cerone R, c | 4 | 1 | 1 | 0 |
| Hall A, pr | 0 | 0 | 0 | 0 |
| Benedict B, c | 2 | 0 | 0 | 0 |
| Hubbard G, 2b | 3 | 0 | 0 | 0 |
| Shields S, p | 0 | 0 | 0 | 0 |
| Komminsk B, ph | 1 | 0 | 0 | 0 |
| Sutter B, p | 0 | 0 | 0 | 0 |
| Chambliss C, ph | 1 | 0 | 0 | 0 |
| Forster T, p | 1 | 0 | 0 | 0 |
| Garber G, p | 1 | 0 | 0 | 0 |
| Runge P, ph-3b | 2 | 0 | 0 | 0 |
| Mahler R, p | 1 | 0 | 0 | 0 |
| Dedmon J, p | 1 | 0 | 0 | 0 |
| Zuvella P, 2b | 7 | 0 | 0 | 0 |
| | 75 | 13 | 18 | 13 |

| New York | IP | H | R | ER | BB | SO |
|---|---|---|---|---|---|---|
| Gooden | 2.1 | 2 | 2 | 2 | 4 | 3 |
| McDowell | 0.2 | 2 | 1 | 1 | 0 | 1 |
| Leach | 4.0 | 4 | 1 | 1 | 0 | 3 |
| Orosco | 0.2 | 1 | 4 | 4 | 3 | 1 |
| Sisk | 4.1 | 3 | 0 | 0 | 1 | 0 |
| Gorman (W) | 6.0 | 5 | 3 | 3 | 2 | 2 |
| Darling | 1.0 | 1 | 2 | 0 | 2 | 1 |
| | 19.0 | 18 | 13 | 11 | 12 | 11 |

| Atlanta | IP | H | R | ER | BB | SO |
|---|---|---|---|---|---|---|
| Mahler | 3.1 | 6 | 3 | 3 | 4 | 2 |
| Dedmon | 2.0 | 5 | 3 | 3 | 0 | 1 |
| Shields | 2.2 | 4 | 1 | 1 | 1 | 1 |
| Sutter | 1.0 | 3 | 1 | 1 | 0 | 1 |
| Forster | 4.0 | 3 | 2 | 2 | 1 | 3 |
| Garber | 3.0 | 1 | 0 | 0 | 2 | 2 |
| Camp (L) | 3.0 | 6 | 6 | 5 | 2 | 2 |
| | 19.0 | 28 | 16 | 15 | 10 | 12 |

| New York | 100 | 401 | 011 | 000 | 200 | 001 | 5 — 16 |
|---|---|---|---|---|---|---|---|
| Atlanta | 102 | 010 | 040 | 000 | 200 | 001 | 2 — 13 |

OB: New York 20, Atlanta 17; ER: Ramirez, Johnson, Camp, Washington, Hernandez; DP: New York 1, Atlanta 3; 2B: Hernandez, Oberkfell, Murphy, Harper, Knight; 3B: Washington, Hernandez; HR: Hernandez, Johnson, Harper, Camp; SB: Backman, Strawberry; CS: Washington; SH: Backman, Christensen; SF: Dykstra; PB: Carter; TI: 6:10; AT: 44,947; UM: Unknown

further opportunity. For the third time they loaded the bases, but for the third time Knight left them stranded. This inning he hit into an inning-ending double play.

Hernandez expanded the visitors' margin to 7–4 with a leadoff homer in the eighth, but Atlanta came back with a vengeance. The Braves abused two pitchers for three walks, a single, and a three-run double by Dale Murphy that catapulted the home club to an 8–7 lead.

Facing a loss and the Braves' top reliever, Bruce Sutter, the Mets gathered three singles to tie the game and send it into extra innings.

In the 12th, Hernandez collected a single to complete his cycle, but there were few baserunners and no serious threats until the 13th. Then, the Mets took what looked like a game-winning lead. After Knight singled, Howard

Johnson homered to center, giving the visitors a 10–8 advantage. In the home half, Tom Gorman, the sixth New York pitcher, allowed a single but struck out the next two Braves. He then worked a 0–2 count on Terry Harper. One strike from defeat, Harper thrilled the dwindling crowd by sending a drive to the foul screen in left to tie it.

Through the 14th, 15th, and 16th, there was little threat of runs being scored. In the 17th, after Darryl Strawberry was called out on strikes, both he and Mets manager Davey Johnson were ejected for arguing. For the skipper, it added insult to injury, as he had earlier protested the game because of a disallowed batting-order change.

Leading off the 18th, Howard Johnson singled and reached third on an error by Atlanta's seventh hurler, Rick Camp. A sacrifice fly then sent Johnson home with the Mets' fourth lead of the game. In the home half of the inning, the first two Braves grounded out. Camp, a lifetime .060 hitter and the potential goat of the game, was scheduled to bat. By this time Atlanta manager Eddie Haas had used all his position players and had no pinch-hitters available. So Camp batted. Mets pitcher Gorman, who had already blown a two-run lead in the 13th, got ahead of Camp with two quick strikes. Then, to everyone's astonishment, Camp drove the third pitch over the left-field wall for his first major league home run. The contest was now tied at 11.

Camp's heroics were short-lived. In the 19th, he fell apart as the Mets assembled two walks, three singles, and a redemptive double by Knight to tally five times and take a 16–11 lead.

In such an outlandish game, nothing could further surprise the approximately 8,000 remaining fans. Ron Darling hadn't relieved since his college days but was called upon to hold the five-run margin. He would have escaped unscathed were it not for an error, but after the miscue and a few walks, Harper singled home a pair. The Braves then brought the tying run to the plate in the person of Camp. From goat-to-hero-to-goat, the right-hander now had a chance for another miracle. He struck out, however, ending the game at 3:55 a.m., 8 hours and 55 minutes after the scheduled opening pitch.

The two clubs had used 43 players of a possible 50, and the only position player who didn't see action was Ronn Reynolds, the Mets' third-string catcher. At 4:01 a.m., the remaining faithful finally got to see the official fireworks.

# 66 *The Mother of All Doubleheaders*

## SAN FRANCISCO (NL) at NEW YORK (NL)
### Sunday, May 31, 1964, Shea Stadium
### Giants 8, Mets 6

When the huge throng sat down for the 1:05 P.M. start of a doubleheader, little did they realize that many would not return home until the next day. Those who stayed until the bitter end saw endurance, performance, and attendance records tumble through nine innings of a first game and 23 frames of a nightcap. The 32 innings, as well as the 9 hours and 52 minutes of play, established the century's major league benchmarks for a doubleheader. But it was the second game, which alone ate up 7 hours and 23 minutes for a new National League standard, that remains one of the century's greatest games.

Although 57,037 paid their way into the park, less than 10,000 remained at 11:25 P.M. for the final out. The nightcap featured terrific relief pitching and 33 runners left on base. Del Crandall finally drove home the game's winning tally with his two-out, pinch-hit double in the top of the 23rd giving San Francisco a sweep.

In addition to endurance records, the largest crowd to date this season also saw a triple play in the 14th inning. After Jesus Alou singled, Willie Mays walked. Orlando Cepeda lined to Mets shortstop Roy McMillan, who stepped on second to retire Alou, then threw to first baseman Ed Kranepool to get Mays.

The crowd also saw Mays play shortstop for three innings before returning to center field, Cepeda steal home, and 12 pitchers share in the century's NL strikeout record, 36. Two pitchers, Galen Cisco of the Mets and Gaylord Perry of the Giants, each pitched nine or more innings in relief; and both catchers, Tom Haller of the Giants and Chris Cannizzaro of the Mets, survived the entire game behind the plate.

The Giants scored early and often, putting two on the board before making their first out of the game. They added four in the third inning on six singles. Meanwhile the Mets could generate only one unearned run in the second.

Several innings later the Mets fought back. In the sixth they surrounded a triple with a pair of singles to narrow the gap to 6–3. The home seventh began innocently with two routine outs, but then two singles and a home run by one of the National League's leading batters at the time, Joe Christopher, knotted the score at six.

Home plate then remained untouched for 15 innings, with only one player even reaching third base. In both the 10th and 15th, San Francisco's Tom Haller

## Second Game

| San Francisco | AB | R | H | I |
|---|---|---|---|---|
| Kuenn H, lf | 5 | 1 | 0 | 0 |
| Perry G, p | 3 | 0 | 0 | 0 |
| Crandall D, ph | 1 | 0 | 1 | 1 |
| Hendley B, p | 0 | 0 | 0 | 0 |
| Alou J, rf | 10 | 1 | 4 | 2 |
| Mays W, cf-ss-cf | 10 | 1 | 1 | 1 |
| Cepeda O, 1b | 9 | 1 | 3 | 0 |
| Haller T, c | 10 | 1 | 4 | 1 |
| Hiller C, 2b | 8 | 1 | 1 | 1 |
| Hart J, 3b | 4 | 0 | 1 | 1 |
| Alou M, ph-cf-lf | 6 | 0 | 0 | 0 |
| Garrido G, ss | 3 | 0 | 0 | 0 |
| McCovey W, ph | 1 | 0 | 0 | 0 |
| Davenport J, ss-3b-ss | 4 | 1 | 1 | 1 |
| Bolin B, p | 2 | 0 | 1 | 0 |
| MacKenzie K, p | 0 | 0 | 0 | 0 |
| Shaw B, p | 0 | 0 | 0 | 0 |
| Snider D, ph | 1 | 0 | 0 | 0 |
| Herbel R, p | 0 | 0 | 0 | 0 |
| Peterson C, ph-3b | 4 | 1 | 0 | 0 |
|  | 81 | 8 | 17 | 8 |

| New York | AB | R | H | I |
|---|---|---|---|---|
| Kanehl R, 2b | 1 | 0 | 0 | 0 |
| Gonder J, ph | 1 | 0 | 0 | 0 |
| Samuel A, 2b | 7 | 0 | 2 | 0 |
| McMillan R, ss | 10 | 1 | 2 | 0 |
| Thomas F, lf | 10 | 1 | 2 | 0 |
| Christopher J, rf | 10 | 2 | 4 | 3 |
| Kranepool E, 1b | 10 | 1 | 3 | 1 |
| Hickman J, cf | 10 | 1 | 2 | 0 |
| Smith C, 3b | 9 | 0 | 4 | 1 |
| Cannizzaro C, c | 9 | 0 | 1 | 1 |
| Wakefield B, p | 0 | 0 | 0 | 0 |
| Altman G, ph | 0 | 0 | 0 | 0 |
| Jackson A, pr | 0 | 0 | 0 | 0 |
| Anderson C, p | 0 | 0 | 0 | 0 |
| Sturdivant T, p | 0 | 0 | 0 | 0 |
| Smith D, ph | 1 | 0 | 0 | 0 |
| Lary F, p | 0 | 0 | 0 | 0 |
| Taylor H, ph | 1 | 0 | 0 | 0 |
| Bearnarth L, p | 3 | 0 | 0 | 0 |
| Cisco G, p | 2 | 0 | 0 | 0 |
| Stephenson J, ph | 1 | 0 | 0 | 0 |
|  | 85 | 6 | 20 | 6 |

| San Francisco | IP | H | R | ER | BB | SO |
|---|---|---|---|---|---|---|
| Bolin | 6.2 | 8 | 6 | 5 | 2 | 7 |
| MacKenzie | 0.0 | 1 | 0 | 0 | 0 | 0 |
| Shaw | 1.1 | 1 | 0 | 0 | 0 | 1 |
| Herbel | 4.0 | 3 | 0 | 0 | 0 | 3 |
| Perry (W) | 10.0 | 7 | 0 | 0 | 1 | 9 |
| Hendley | 1.0 | 0 | 0 | 0 | 0 | 2 |
|  | 23.0 | 20 | 6 | 5 | 3 | 22 |

| New York | IP | H | R | ER | BB | SO |
|---|---|---|---|---|---|---|
| Wakefield | 2.0 | 2 | 2 | 2 | 2 | 1 |
| Anderson | 0.1 | 4 | 4 | 4 | 0 | 0 |
| Sturdivant | 2.2 | 3 | 0 | 0 | 1 | 2 |
| Lary | 2.0 | 0 | 0 | 0 | 0 | 2 |
| Bearnarth | 7.0 | 3 | 0 | 0 | 4 | 4 |
| Cisco (L) | 9.0 | 5 | 2 | 2 | 2 | 5 |
|  | 23.0 | 17 | 8 | 8 | 9 | 14 |

| San Francisco | 204 | 000 | 000 | 000 | 000 | 000 | 000 | 02 — 8 |
|---|---|---|---|---|---|---|---|---|
| New York | 010 | 002 | 300 | 000 | 000 | 000 | 000 | 00 — 6 |

OB: San Francisco 16, New York 16; ER: Garrido, Haller, Cepeda, Cisco; DP: San Francisco 2, New York 1; TP: New York 1; 2B: J. Alou, Kranepool, Cepeda, Crandall; 3B: Kranepool, Haller, Davenport; HR: Christopher; CS: J. Alou, C. Smith; SH: Herbel, Hiller, C. Smith, Cisco; HP: by Shaw (Samuel); by Cisco (Cepeda); PB: Cannizzaro; TI: 7:23; AT: 57,037; UM: Sudol, Pryor, Secory, Burkhart

got around to third, both times with two outs. On each occasion he was left stranded. So stringent was the relief pitching that during those same 15 frames only eight other runners — four from each club — even reached second base.

Finally, in the top of the 23rd, San Francisco broke through. Cisco, who had been told by Mets manager Casey Stengel that he'd only have to work two innings in relief, began his ninth stanza by getting the first two batters out. But after Jim Davenport tripled, Peterson was walked intentionally. Crandall, pinch-hitting for Perry, doubled home Davenport, giving the Giants their first run in 20 innings. Next, Alou beat out an infield hit while Peterson crossed the plate, making it 8–6.

The Mets offered no resistance in the bottom of the 23rd as Bob Hendley retired the side in order, thereby ending the longest continuous game, in terms of time, played in the century. Twenty years later another marathon game exceeded eight hours, but that contest had to be stopped earlier and resumed the following day.

# 67 *Leyritz and the Cat and Mouse Game*

NEW YORK (AL) at ATLANTA (NL)
Wednesday, October 23, 1996, Fulton County Stadium
Yankees 8, Braves 6

On October 23, 1996, the New York Yankees mounted the second-greatest comeback in World Series history. And never, even in the storied history of the Yankees, had a more resounding post-season resurgence unfolded as what Atlanta began as a blowout, New York ended in the 10th with a game of cat and mouse.

The Braves arrived in the 1996 World Series to defend the title they had captured a year earlier. On the other hand, the Yankees had become strangers to the Fall Classic, having endured a 14-year hiatus. Now, entering Game Four, Atlanta held a two-games-to-one advantage.

Atlanta jumped on a shaky Kenny Rodgers for four runs in the second inning. After Fred McGriff's leadoff rocket over the center-field fence, two walks, a single and a double pushed across the fourth Braves' run. Left-hander Rodgers started the third inning, but the home team picked up where they left off the inning before. Two singles sent Rodgers packing, and Javy Lopez managed to drive home Atlanta's fifth marker with a sacrifice fly.

In the fifth, Andruw Jones doubled home another run, giving the Braves a daunting 6–0 lead. Meanwhile Denny Neagle froze New York bats, allowing only two hits through the first five innings.

The complexion of the game began to change in the sixth as the visitors not only solved Neagle but disposed of him, as well. Two walks along with three singles notched three runs on the New York scoresheet and left runners at first and second with no outs. Atlanta manager Bobby Cox then called on journeyman Mike Bielecki, who fanned the next three hitters, two of them pinch-hitters. The game of moves and counter-moves had begun.

Bielecki pitched another good inning and left after the seventh with his

| New York | AB | R | H | I |
|---|---|---|---|---|
| Raines T, lf | 5 | 1 | 0 | 0 |
| Jeter D, ss | 4 | 2 | 2 | 0 |
| Williams B, cf | 4 | 1 | 0 | 0 |
| Fielder C, 1b | 4 | 1 | 2 | 1 |
| Fox A, pr-3b | 0 | 0 | 0 | 0 |
| Boggs W, ph-3b | 0 | 0 | 0 | 1 |
| Hayes C, 3b-1b | 5 | 1 | 3 | 1 |
| Strawberry D, rf | 5 | 0 | 2 | 0 |
| Duncan M, 2b | 5 | 1 | 0 | 0 |
| Girardi J, c | 2 | 0 | 0 | 0 |
| O'Neill P, ph | 1 | 0 | 0 | 0 |
| Leyritz J, c | 2 | 1 | 1 | 3 |
| Rogers K, p | 1 | 0 | 1 | 0 |
| Boehringer B, p | 0 | 0 | 0 | 0 |
| Sojo L, ph | 1 | 0 | 1 | 0 |
| Weathers D, p | 0 | 0 | 0 | 0 |
| Martinez T, ph | 1 | 0 | 0 | 0 |
| Nelson J, p | 0 | 0 | 0 | 0 |
| Aldrete M, ph | 1 | 0 | 0 | 0 |
| Rivera M, p | 0 | 0 | 0 | 0 |
| Lloyd G, p | 1 | 0 | 0 | 0 |
| Wetteland J, p | 0 | 0 | 0 | 0 |
| | 42 | 8 | 12 | 6 |

| Atlanta | AB | R | H | I |
|---|---|---|---|---|
| Grissom M, cf | 5 | 0 | 1 | 2 |
| Lemke M, 2b | 5 | 0 | 1 | 0 |
| Jones C, 3b-ss | 3 | 2 | 1 | 0 |
| McGriff F, 1b | 3 | 1 | 2 | 1 |
| Clontz B, p | 0 | 0 | 0 | 0 |
| Lopez J, c | 2 | 1 | 0 | 1 |
| Wohlers M, p | 0 | 0 | 0 | 0 |
| Avery S, p | 0 | 0 | 0 | 0 |
| Klesko R, 1b | 1 | 0 | 0 | 0 |
| Jones A, lf | 4 | 1 | 3 | 1 |
| Dye J, rf | 4 | 0 | 0 | 0 |
| Blauser J, ss | 3 | 1 | 1 | 1 |
| Belliard R, ss | 0 | 0 | 0 | 0 |
| Polonia L, ph | 1 | 0 | 0 | 0 |
| Pendleton T, 3b | 1 | 0 | 0 | 0 |
| Neagle D, p | 1 | 0 | 0 | 0 |
| Wade T, p | 0 | 0 | 0 | 0 |
| Bielecki M, p | 1 | 0 | 0 | 0 |
| Perez E, c | 1 | 0 | 0 | 0 |
| | 35 | 6 | 9 | 6 |

| New York | IP | H | R | ER | BB | SO |
|---|---|---|---|---|---|---|
| Rogers | 2.0 | 5 | 5 | 5 | 2 | 0 |
| Boehringer | 2.0 | 0 | 0 | 0 | 0 | 3 |
| Weathers | 1.0 | 1 | 1 | 1 | 2 | 2 |
| Nelson | 2.0 | 0 | 0 | 0 | 1 | 2 |
| Rivera | 1.1 | 2 | 0 | 0 | 1 | 1 |
| Lloyd (W) | 1.0 | 0 | 0 | 0 | 0 | 1 |
| Wetteland (S) | 0.2 | 1 | 0 | 0 | 0 | 0 |
| | 10.0 | 9 | 6 | 6 | 6 | 9 |

| Atlanta | IP | H | R | ER | BB | SO |
|---|---|---|---|---|---|---|
| Neagle | 5.0 | 5 | 3 | 2 | 4 | 3 |
| Wade | 0.0 | 0 | 0 | 0 | 1 | 0 |
| Bielecki | 2.0 | 0 | 0 | 0 | 1 | 4 |
| Wohlers | 2.0 | 6 | 3 | 3 | 0 | 1 |
| Avery (L) | 0.2 | 1 | 2 | 1 | 3 | 0 |
| Clontz | 0.1 | 0 | 0 | 0 | 0 | 1 |
| | 10.0 | 12 | 8 | 6 | 9 | 9 |

| | | | |
|---|---|---|---|
| New York | 000 | 003 | 030 | 2 — 8 |
| Atlanta | 041 | 010 | 000 | 0 — 6 |

OB: New York 13, Atlanta 8; ER: Dye, Klesko; DP: New York 1, Atlanta 1; 2B: Grissom, Jones; HR: McGriff, Leyritz; SH: Neagle, Dye; SF: Lopez; BK: Weathers; TI: 4:17; AT: 51,881; UM: HP Rippley, 1B Young, 2B Davis, 3B Evans, LF Tata, RF Welke

club ahead 6–3. The National League's most intimidating closer, Mark Wohlers, then entered the fray as part of a double switch but was greeted by a pair of singles. With Yankees at first and second, a critical play followed. Mariano Duncan hit sharply to shortstop Rafael Belliard. It was a tailor-made double play ball, but Belliard bobbled it and could get only a forceout. That brought to the plate Jim Leyritz, who had entered the game as part of a double switch by New York manager Joe Torre in the sixth. On a 2–2 count, Leyritz drove a long home run to left, silencing the tomahawk choppers. It was a tie game, and skipper Torre seemed to be enjoying his team's visit to the National League city.

Yankee momentum carried into the ninth when, after a pair of outs, three straight singles loaded the bases. Wohlers finally stopped the assault by retiring Duncan.

Braves fans renewed their cheering in the bottom of the ninth. With one out, a single and a walk threatened to end it. But left-hander Graeme Lloyd relieved a struggling Mariano Rivera and got McGriff to ground into an inning-ending double play.

Lefty Steve Avery replaced Wohlers for the Braves in the 10th and quickly disposed of the first two Yankees. But Tim Raines walked and Derek Jeter got an infield hit, putting runners at first and second. Then came a curious and daring strategy. With red-hot, switch-hitting Bernie Williams the next batter, Cox elected to walk him intentionally to face a rookie, Andy Fox. With the bases then loaded Torre countered with his last pinch-hitter — left-handed Wade Boggs. Avery got ahead of Boggs with a one-ball, two-strike count before walking him to force in the lead run. It was New York's first lead all night. That brought about another double switch by Cox. On his line-up card, he penciled in pitcher Brad Clontz for McGriff and first baseman Ryan Klesko for Avery. But Cox's strategy again backfired when Clontz' first pitch was popped up toward first. Klesko got under it but lost it in the lights, allowing the eighth Yankee run to score.

Trailing 8–6 the Braves made one last gasp in the bottom of the 10th. After Lloyd retired Klesko, John Wetteland took the mound for the Yankees. Andruw Jones kept Atlanta hopes alive with a single, and Jermaine Dye took their breath away with a long fly to left that was caught by Tim Raines. That left it up to Terry Pendleton, who also sent a long drive to left. On the warning track, Raines circled under it and tumbled to the ground just as he caught it. The umpires had to wait for the left fielder to raise his glove, showing the ball in it, before the out signal was given.

Torre had used seven pitchers, five pinch-hitters and a pinch-runner, as well as his reserve catcher. He was completely out of reserve players and later said he and his coaches had been deciding which pitcher could bunt if they needed it. The selection turned out to be unnecessary, as the Yankees prevailed in the battle of wits and switches.

# 68 Coolidge's Cheers Can't Stop the Giants

NEW YORK (NL) at WASHINGTON (AL)
Saturday, October 4, 1924, Griffith Stadium
Giants 4, Senators 3

President Calvin Coolidge lobbed out the first pitch, but the last toss by the New York Giants' George Kelly represented the game winner. Between those two throws, a thrilling 12-inning struggle unfolded in Griffith Stadium, marking the first ever World Series game in the nation's capital.

Amid balmy weather, splendor surrounded the opening game revelry. A multitude of dignitaries, including many cabinet members, were afforded recognition by occupying the president's box just behind the Washington dugout. Meanwhile, senators, representatives, Supreme Court justices, as well as army and navy chieftains could be seen sprinkled throughout the stands. Walter "The Big Train" Johnson, idol of Washington fans, was presented a green Lincoln limousine and a silver plate inscribed with words proclaiming him baseball's greatest pitcher. Veteran backstop Roger Peckinpaugh received a tan Peerless touring car from his hometown admirers of Cleveland, Ohio, and outfielder Sam Rice was presented a medal by the secretary of the Navy commending him for heroism under fire at Vera Cruz, Mexico. Several other players received gold watches. Even a few non-participating ballplayers — Babe Ruth, Ty Cobb, and George Sisler — were afforded rousing ovations as they met the president. Once all awards were distributed, the pre-game ceremony concluded with a 100-piece band parading around the field followed by a platoon of marines.

Coolidge became the first chief executive to throw out the World Series ceremonial first pitch — a wild one to umpire Tom Connolly that required a leaping catch. Then, reminding all why they were assembled, a deafening roar discharged as the Big Train took the mound to start the game.

Johnson, normally steel-nerved and resolute, was understandably nervous. Having toiled for 18 seasons with a second-division club, the 37-year-old had finally reached the World Series and wanted desperately to succeed. But he appeared overly deliberate, uncertain, and wild. In just the second inning the Giants' Kelly led off with a home run into the temporary left-field bleachers. In the fourth Bill Terry did the same, staking New York to a 2–0 lead.

Meanwhile, diminutive Giants' hurler Art Nehf out-pitched Johnson. The left-hander didn't allow a hit until the fourth or a run until the sixth. Then, Washington center fielder Earl McNeely led off with a double and scored on two ground-outs, making it 2–1.

The Senators nearly tied it in the seventh. With two outs and runners at first and second, Johnson sent a sharp liner toward right. But New York captain Frankie Frisch leaped high in the air to snare it and save a run.

In the top of the ninth, the Giants narrowly missed scoring an insurance run. With Hack Wilson on second and two outs, Nehf singled to right; but Sam Rice made a strong throw home to nip Wilson at the plate.

The Washington crowd was silent as the Senators sank to their final three outs. Joe Judge was called out on strikes, but Ossie Bluege singled. When Peckinpaugh then doubled home the tying run, there erupted such pandemonium that the game had to be stopped. Cushions, programs, hats and coats sprayed onto the field, and someone even fired off a pistol. In addition, police were rushed into right field to herd the crowd back into their seats. When play resumed, Washington catcher Muddy Ruel grounded out, sending Peckinpaugh to third.

| New York | AB | R | H | I |
|---|---|---|---|---|
| Lindstrom F, 3b | 5 | 0 | 0 | 0 |
| Bentley J, ph | 0 | 0 | 0 | 0 |
| Southworth B, pr-cf | 0 | 1 | 0 | 0 |
| Frisch F, 2b-3b | 5 | 0 | 2 | 0 |
| Youngs R, rf | 6 | 0 | 2 | 1 |
| Kelly G, cf-2b | 5 | 1 | 1 | 2 |
| Terry B, 1b | 5 | 1 | 3 | 1 |
| Wilson H, lf | 6 | 0 | 2 | 0 |
| Jackson T, ss | 3 | 0 | 0 | 0 |
| Gowdy H, c | 3 | 0 | 1 | 0 |
| Nehf A, p | 5 | 1 | 3 | 0 |
| | 43 | 4 | 14 | 4 |

| Washington | AB | R | H | I |
|---|---|---|---|---|
| McNeely E, cf | 5 | 1 | 1 | 0 |
| Harris B, 2b | 6 | 0 | 2 | 1 |
| Rice S, rf | 5 | 0 | 2 | 1 |
| Goslin G, lf | 6 | 0 | 1 | 0 |
| Judge J, 1b | 4 | 0 | 1 | 0 |
| Bluege O, 3b | 5 | 1 | 1 | 0 |
| Peckinpaugh R, ss | 5 | 0 | 2 | 1 |
| Ruel M, c | 3 | 0 | 0 | 0 |
| Johnson W, p | 4 | 0 | 0 | 0 |
| Shirley M, ph | 1 | 1 | 0 | 0 |
| | 44 | 3 | 10 | 3 |

| New York | IP | H | R | ER | BB | SO |
|---|---|---|---|---|---|---|
| Nehf (W) | 12.0 | 10 | 3 | 2 | 5 | 3 |

| Washington | IP | H | R | ER | BB | SO |
|---|---|---|---|---|---|---|
| Johnson (L) | 12.0 | 14 | 4 | 3 | 6 | 12 |

| New York | 010 | 100 | 000 | 002 — 4 |
|---|---|---|---|---|
| Washington | 000 | 001 | 001 | 001 — 3 |

OB: New York 11, Washington 10; ER: McNeely, Jackson; DP: New York 1, Washington 2; 2B: Frisch, McNeely, Youngs, Peckinpaugh; HR: Kelly, Terry; SB: Peckinpaugh, Rice, Frisch; CS: Goslin, Youngs; SH: Jackson; SF: Kelly; WP: Johnson; TI: 3:07; AT: 35,760; UM: HP Connolly, 1B Klem, 2B Dinneen, 3B Quigley

With the game on the line, Nehf retired Johnson on a fly ball to center, sending the game into extra innings.

Each team got a runner to second base in the 10th, but both pitchers escaped. In the 11th, both sides were retired in order.

The 12th inning was not for the faint of heart. Johnson crumbled, allowing a walk, single, and another walk to load the bases for the Giants. With the infield in, Frisch grounded to Bucky Harris at second, who threw home for a forceout. Despite imploring by the home crowd for a miraculous escape, Ross Youngs next singled to drive in the go-ahead run, and Kelly hit a sacrifice fly to make it 4–2. The crowd was silent as Terry then singled to re-load the sacks before Wilson flied out.

Having used a pinch-hitter and a pinch-runner in the top of the 12th, the Giants then reconfigured their defense. Frisch moved from second to third and Kelly from center field to second base. Kelly was a natural first baseman but, to get Terry's bat into the lineup, he played center field this game. Now he was put in another unnatural position.

Pinch-hitting for Johnson, Mule Shirley led off for Washington and popped up. Giants shortstop Travis Jackson had plenty of time but dropped it for a two-base error. After a fly-out, Harris singled home Shirley, closing it to 4–3. Next, Sam Rice also singled, sending the tying run to third with only one out. But Rice made a fatal baserunning blunder by trying to stretch his hit into a double. On a close play, Kelly applied the tag, and there were two down. Nehf got two strikes on the next batter, Goose Goslin, before he dribbled a slow roller to the right side of the infield. Nehf couldn't quite reach it, and Terry covered first as the tying run approached the plate. Out of nowhere raced the long-legged first baseman–turned–second baseman Kelly, who scooped the ball barehanded and threw a bullet to Terry. Goslin was racing at top speed, but the ball beat him by a fraction of a step for the third out.

While greatly disappointed this day, Washington and Johnson emerged victorious six days later in this same park, by the same score and also in 12 innings, for their first world's championship.

# *Chambliss's Home Run* **69**
# *Wins the Pennant*

### KANSAS CITY (AL) at NEW YORK (AL)
### Thursday, October 14, 1976, Yankee Stadium
### Yankees 7, Royals 6

After a dozen years' absence, the New York Yankees revisited their successful post-season past. They arrived at the American League Championship Series by easily outdistancing second-place Baltimore in the East. For their opponents, the Kansas City Royals, who endured a much more difficult road to the five-game series, this was a novel experience. They had staggered to their first Western Division title despite losing nine of their last 11.

The two clubs traded victories through the first four games, setting the stage for the dramatic deciding contest. In a rematch of Game Two, each team tossed its top hurler into the fray — Ed Figueroa for New York against Dennis Leonard for Kansas City.

Both teams scored in the opening frame. After the first two Royals were retired, George Brett doubled before John Mayberry homered over the right field wall. Mickey Rivers led off the home half with a triple and scored on Roy White's single. When the third batter, Thurman Munson, also singled, Paul Splittorff replaced Leonard after only nine pitches. Chris Chambliss greeted the reliever with a sacrifice fly, making it 2–2.

Kansas City regained the lead in the following frame when Cookie Rojas singled, stole second, and scampered home on Buck Martinez's single.

The see-saw battle tipped back to the Yankees favor in the third when a walk, two singles, and a ground-out tallied a pair, giving New York a 4–3 advantage.

After the first two batters were retired in the home fourth, the Yankees loaded the bases and forced Splittorff from the game. But Marty Pattin came in to retire Munson and suppress the uprising.

In the fifth, the Yankees again loaded the bases with two outs. This time

| Kansas City | AB | R | H | I |
|---|---|---|---|---|
| Cowens A, cf | 4 | 1 | 1 | 0 |
| Poquette T, lf | 3 | 0 | 0 | 0 |
| Wohlford J, ph-lf | 2 | 1 | 1 | 0 |
| Brett G, 3b | 4 | 2 | 2 | 3 |
| Mayberry J, 1b | 4 | 1 | 2 | 2 |
| McRae H, rf | 4 | 0 | 0 | 0 |
| Quirk J, dh | 4 | 0 | 0 | 0 |
| Rojas C, 2b | 4 | 1 | 1 | 0 |
| Patek F, ss | 4 | 0 | 1 | 0 |
| Martinez B, c | 4 | 0 | 3 | 1 |
|  | 37 | 6 | 11 | 6 |

| New York | AB | R | H | I |
|---|---|---|---|---|
| Rivers M, cf | 5 | 3 | 4 | 0 |
| White R, lf | 2 | 2 | 1 | 1. |
| Munson T, c | 5 | 0 | 3 | 2 |
| Chambliss C, 1b | 4 | 2 | 3 | 3 |
| May C, dh | 4 | 0 | 0 | 0 |
| Alomar S, pr | 0 | 0 | 0 | 0 |
| Nettles G, 3b | 3 | 0 | 0 | 0 |
| Gamble O, rf | 2 | 0 | 0 | 0 |
| Randolph W, 2b | 3 | 0 | 0 | 0 |
| Stanley F, ss | 3 | 0 | 0 | 0 |
|  | 31 | 7 | 11 | 6 |

| Kansas City | IP | H | R | ER | BB | SO |
|---|---|---|---|---|---|---|
| Leonard | 0.0 | 3 | 2 | 2 | 0 | 0 |
| Splittorff | 3.2 | 3 | 2 | 2 | 3 | 1 |
| Pattin | 0.1 | 0 | 0 | 0 | 0 | 0 |
| Hassler | 2.1 | 4 | 2 | 1 | 3 | 1 |
| Littell (L) | 1.2 | 1 | 1 | 1 | 0 | 1 |
|  | 8.0 | 11 | 7 | 6 | 6 | 3 |

| New York | IP | H | R | ER | BB | SO |
|---|---|---|---|---|---|---|
| Figueroa | 7.0 | 8 | 4 | 4 | 0 | 3 |
| Jackson | 1.0 | 2 | 2 | 2 | 0 | 1 |
| Tidrow (W) | 1.0 | 1 | 0 | 0 | 1 | 0 |
|  | 9.0 | 11 | 6 | 6 | 1 | 4 |

```
Kansas City   210   000   030 — 6
New York      202   002   001 — 7
```

OB: Kansas City 5, New York 9; ER: Gamble, Brett; DP: New York 1; 2B: Brett, Chambliss; 3B: Rivers; HR: Mayberry, Brett, Chambliss; SB: White, Rojas, Chambliss; CS: Alomar; SH: White, Gamble; SF: Chambliss; TI: 3:13; AT: 56,821; UM: HP Frantz, 1B McCoy, 2B Brinkman, 3B Barnett, LF Maloney, RF Haller

it was against Andy Hassler, but the left-hander escaped when Fred Stanley lined out to second.

Having left six runners on base during the last two frames, New York finally tallied again in the sixth. Three singles and a costly error by George Brett ushered in two runs, making it 6–3. The Yankees stranded another runner on third base in the seventh but comfortably carried their lead into the eighth.

An Al Cowens's single leading off the Kansas City eighth resulted in Figueroa being relieved by Grant Jackson. Jim Wolford greeted the new moundsman with a single before Brett atoned for his earlier error with a three-run blast to right.

With the game deadlocked at six, the Royals put two on in the ninth but failed to score. The first batter for New York in the home half was Chambliss. The big first baseman, who had already driven in a pair of runs, stunned the crowd as he picked on the first offering from reliever Mark Littell and sent it far into the night. Yankee Stadium security was not prepared for what followed. In one of the wildest demonstrations of the century, fans poured onto the field. Chambliss rounded first but, by the time he reached the vicinity of second, an overzealous fan had already removed the base. Chambliss touched it with his hand as he ran past the fan. Between second and third he was knocked off his feet by the overwhelming horde. Rounding third Chambliss was forced to push people out of his way, twisting and spinning like a halfback. When he approached the vicinity of home plate he found such a tightly knit mass of humanity that he merely entered the area, uncertain whether he had touched the plate. It took every effort by the police to get him and several teammates off the field. Later

**Chambliss became an instant hero (National Baseball Hall of Fame Library, Cooperstown, New York).**

in the clubhouse Chambliss became concerned that he may not have touched the plate, thereby negating his heroic blast. So to the field he returned and found that home plate, along with every other base and much of the turf, had fallen victim to souvenir hunters. It mattered not. The Yankees had officially won and advanced to the World Series.

# 70 *Alexander and Lazzeri*

### ST. LOUIS (NL) at NEW YORK (AL)
### Sunday, October 10, 1926, Yankee Stadium
### Cardinals 3, Yankees 2

Make no mistake about it: Grover Alexander's dramatic relief appearance in the 1926 World Series was critical to the St. Louis Cardinals' victory. But there were several other crucial plays, probably even more instrumental in the outcome of the gripping seventh game.

The deciding contest was played on an overcast day in Yankee Stadium. It had rained most of the morning and past the noon hour, keeping the crowd far under capacity.

The championship was placed in the hands of two veteran right-handers — New York's Waite Hoyt, winner of Game Four, and the Cardinals' Jesse Haines, victor in Game Three. Haines was the first to crack; in the third, Babe Ruth sent a 1–1 pitch deep into the right-center field bleachers. It was Ruth's fourth home run of the Series, a record at the time. In retrospect, had it not been for some later poor fielding, this is how the 1926 Series may have ended with Ruth and Hoyt the heroes. But Fate had other ideas.

The visitors' fourth would become the turning point of the game. With one out, Jim Bottomley singled. Les Bell then grounded sharply to short. Young Mark Koenig, in his haste for an inning-ending double play, fumbled the ball, and all hands were safe. Chick Hafey loaded the bases when his lazy fly into left fell just beyond the reach of both Koenig and left fielder Bob Meusel. Next, Bob O'Farrell lifted a fly ball to left center. Meusel, with a stronger arm than his counterpart in center, signaled to make the catch. But concentrating on a play at the plate, he dropped the ball. Bottomley scored, and the surprised Cardinals each advanced one base. Tommy Thevenow, who batted .417 during the Series, then delivered a clutch single driving home two more Cardinals. By the time Haines grounded out, St. Louis led, 3–1, on the cluster of unearned runs.

The Yankees threatened in each of the next three innings. In the fifth Haines left two stranded by retiring Meusel on a ground-out. In the sixth, the New Yorkers did score their second run when Joe Dugan singled and Hank Severeid doubled him home.

Entering the seventh with a 3–2 lead, Haines gave up a single and a sacrifice before intentionally walking Ruth. Meusel hit into a forceout, but Gehrig walked, loading the bases. St. Louis player-manager Rogers Hornsby then called a conference at the mound with his catcher and entire infield. This would be

| St. Louis | AB | R | H | I |
|---|---|---|---|---|
| Holm W, cf | 5 | 0 | 0 | 0 |
| Southworth B, rf | 4 | 0 | 0 | 0 |
| Hornsby R, 2b | 4 | 0 | 2 | 0 |
| Bottomley J, 1b | 3 | 1 | 1 | 0 |
| Bell L, 3b | 4 | 1 | 0 | 0 |
| Hafey C, lf | 4 | 1 | 2 | 0 |
| O'Farrell B, c | 3 | 0 | 0 | 1 |
| Thevenow T, ss | 4 | 0 | 2 | 2 |
| Haines J, p | 2 | 0 | 1 | 0 |
| Alexander G, p | 1 | 0 | 0 | 0 |
| | 34 | 3 | 8 | 3 |

| New York | AB | R | H | I |
|---|---|---|---|---|
| Combs E, cf | 5 | 0 | 2 | 0 |
| Koenig M, ss | 4 | 0 | 0 | 0 |
| Ruth B, rf | 1 | 1 | 1 | 1 |
| Meusel B, lf | 4 | 0 | 1 | 0 |
| Gehrig L, 1b | 2 | 0 | 0 | 0 |
| Lazzeri T, 2b | 4 | 0 | 0 | 0 |
| Dugan J, 3b | 4 | 1 | 2 | 0 |
| Severeid H, c | 3 | 0 | 2 | 1 |
| Adams S, pr | 0 | 0 | 0 | 0 |
| Collins P, c | 1 | 0 | 0 | 0 |
| Hoyt W, p | 2 | 0 | 0 | 0 |
| Paschal B, ph | 1 | 0 | 0 | 0 |
| Pennock H, p | 1 | 0 | 0 | 0 |
| | 32 | 2 | 8 | 2 |

| St. Louis | IP | H | R | ER | BB | SO |
|---|---|---|---|---|---|---|
| Haines (W) | 6.2 | 8 | 2 | 2 | 5 | 2 |
| Alexander (S) | 2.1 | 0 | 0 | 0 | 1 | 1 |
| | 9.0 | 8 | 2 | 2 | 6 | 3 |

| New York | IP | H | R | ER | BB | SO |
|---|---|---|---|---|---|---|
| Hoyt (L) | 6.0 | 5 | 3 | 0 | 0 | 2 |
| Pennock | 3.0 | 3 | 0 | 0 | 0 | 0 |
| | 9.0 | 8 | 3 | 0 | 0 | 2 |

```
St. Louis   000  300  000 — 3
New York    001  001  000 — 2
```

OB: St. Louis 7, New York 10; ER: Koenig, Meusel, Dugan; 2B: Severeid; HR: Ruth; CS: Dugan, Hafey, Ruth; SH: Haines, Koenig, Bottomley; SF: O'Farrell; TI: 2:15; AT: 38,093; UM: HP Hildebrand, 1B Klem, 2B Dinneen, 3B O'Day

the turning point of the game and the championship, they decided, and Hornsby motioned for a relief pitcher. As nearly 40,000 pairs of eyes peered through the gray mist toward the bullpen in deep left field, in strode a tall, familiar figure wrapped in a Cardinals sweater. It was Grover Cleveland Alexander, or "Pete," as he had been called for most of his career. With cap askew, Pete shuffled like a man going nowhere and in no particular hurry. The crowd buckled under the tension of the moment, but with drooping shoulders, the outwardly unconcerned Alexander seemed without a frazzled nerve in his body. The 39-year-old right-hander had pitched a complete game a day earlier, but he was ready. Later stories about Alexander's having been hung over in celebration of his sixth game victory simply were not true.

Waiting at the plate was a 22-year-old rookie named Tony Lazzeri whom Alexander had collared the day before. Lazzeri, who led the league in strikeouts, would go on to a Hall of Fame career. But this day he belonged to the wily veteran. The half-mad crowd sounded and squirmed with every pitch — first a ball, then a called strike. Lazzeri ignited the frenzy as he sent the third pitch deep into the seats in left, but foul. When he swatted vainly at the fourth pitch, Alexander had strangled the rally. Unfathomable as it may seem to the modern fan, the nearly 40,000 Yankee fans gave Pete a roaring ovation as he walked expressionless to the dugout amid pounding and patting by teammates along the way.

The balance of the clash was anti-climactic. Alexander retired the Yankees in order in the eighth and, with two outs in the ninth, walked Ruth on a full count. Meusel then swung and missed at the first pitch while Ruth broke for second. Reporters differed on whether this was an attempted steal or a botched hit-and-run play. Regardless, catcher O'Farrell's throw beat the Babe to the bag, and the Cardinals were world champions.

# 71 *Tigers Out-Claw the Cubs in 11 Innings*

DETROIT (AL) at CHICAGO (NL)
Friday, October 4, 1935, Wrigley Field
Tigers 6, Cubs 5

Making their second straight appearance in the Fall Classic, the Detroit Tigers had ridden the back of American League Most Valuable Player Hank Greenberg. Now they were forced to play without the big first baseman, who broke his wrist during Game Two. Earlier in the Series, Greenberg had been the target of religious slurs. Umpire George Moriarty, among others, had been disgusted by the abuse and unruliness, and his rancor surfaced before this game ended.

The Chicago Cubs and National League MVP Gabby Hartnett were happy to get home after splitting in Detroit. The North siders had captured the National League flag with a dramatic 21-game winning streak in September and were hoping that familiar surroundings would facilitate their first world's championship in 27 years.

An autumn chill accompanied the sunshine for Game Three as Detroit's Eldon "Submarine" Auker squared off against Chicago's Big Bill Lee.

There were early roars from the home crowd as the Cubs touched Auker for two hits in the opening frame, but a smart double play quieted the faithful.

Al Demaree led off the Chicago second with a home run into the right-field bleachers. Stan Hack then singled, stole second and scored on two infield outs, giving the Cubs a 2–0 cushion.

The Tigers had runners at first and second with two outs in the third inning when a spectacular play saved Lee. Goose Goslin smashed a long drive to left-center, but Augie Galan made a running one-handed catch 364 feet from home.

In the fifth, Chicago added another run on a walk, sacrifice, and Galan's single. With a 3–0 lead, Windy City fans grew extremely confident. In the home half, two more magnificent catches in the outfield rescued Lee.

| Detroit | AB | R | H | I |
|---|---|---|---|---|
| White J, cf | 5 | 1 | 2 | 1 |
| Cochrane M, c | 5 | 0 | 0 | 0 |
| Gehringer C, 2b | 5 | 1 | 2 | 0 |
| Goslin G, lf | 5 | 2 | 3 | 2 |
| Fox P, rf | 5 | 1 | 2 | 1 |
| Rogell B, ss | 5 | 0 | 3 | 1 |
| Owen M, 1b | 5 | 1 | 0 | 0 |
| Clifton F, 3b | 4 | 0 | 0 | 0 |
| Auker E, p | 2 | 0 | 0 | 0 |
| Walker G, ph | 1 | 0 | 0 | 0 |
| Hogsett C, p | 0 | 0 | 0 | 0 |
| Rowe S, p | 2 | 0 | 0 | 0 |
| | 44 | 6 | 12 | 5 |

| Chicago | AB | R | H | I |
|---|---|---|---|---|
| Galan A, lf | 4 | 0 | 2 | 2 |
| Herman B, 2b | 5 | 0 | 1 | 0 |
| Lindstrom F, cf-3b | 5 | 0 | 2 | 0 |
| Hartnett G, c | 4 | 0 | 0 | 0 |
| Demaree F, rf-cf | 4 | 1 | 1 | 1 |
| Cavarretta P, 1b | 5 | 0 | 0 | 0 |
| Hack S, 3b-ss | 5 | 2 | 2 | 0 |
| Jurges B, ss | 1 | 1 | 0 | 0 |
| Klein C, ph-rf | 2 | 1 | 1 | 0 |
| Lee B, p | 1 | 0 | 0 | 1 |
| Warneke L, p | 0 | 0 | 0 | 0 |
| O'Dea K, ph | 1 | 0 | 1 | 1 |
| French L, p | 0 | 0 | 0 | 0 |
| Stephenson W, ph | 1 | 0 | 0 | 0 |
| | 38 | 5 | 10 | 5 |

| Detroit | IP | H | R | ER | BB | SO |
|---|---|---|---|---|---|---|
| Auker | 6.0 | 6 | 3 | 2 | 2 | 1 |
| Hogsett | 1.0 | 0 | 0 | 0 | 1 | 0 |
| Rowe (W) | 4.0 | 4 | 2 | 2 | 0 | 3 |
| | 11.0 | 10 | 5 | 4 | 3 | 4 |

| Chicago | IP | H | R | ER | BB | SO |
|---|---|---|---|---|---|---|
| Lee | 7.1 | 7 | 4 | 4 | 3 | 3 |
| Warneke | 1.2 | 2 | 1 | 1 | 0 | 2 |
| French (L) | 2.0 | 3 | 1 | 0 | 0 | 1 |
| | 11.0 | 12 | 6 | 5 | 3 | 6 |

```
Detroit    000  001  040  01 — 6
Chicago    020  010  002  00 — 5
```

OB: Detroit 8, Chicago 7; ER: Herman, Cavarretta, Clifton, Cochrane, Lindstrom; DP: Detroit 2, Chicago 1; 2B: Gehringer, Goslin, Lindstrom; 3B: Fox; HR: Demaree; SB: Hack; CS: Cavarretta, Rogell; SH: Lee 2, Hartnett; HP: by Hogsett (Jurges); TI: 2:27; AT: 45,532; UM: HP McGowan, 1B Stark, 2B Moriarty, 3B Quigley

The game took on an extra dimension in the sixth. With one out and one on, Detroit's Pete Fox tripled down the right field line to make it 3–1. The Tigers were in position to pull within one run, but Hartnett's snap throw picked off Fox at third on a very close play. Such a heated argument ensued that umpire Quigley ejected third base coach Del Baker, much to the glee of Chicago fans. In the home half, Phil Cavarretta attempted to steal second with two outs but was also called out. This time umpire George Moriarty was the center of wrath. Led by manager Charlie Grimm, a horde of Cubs ran onto the field and surrounded the umpire. Before the argument ended, Grimm was ordered to the locker room.

The harassment of Moriarty continued from the Chicago bench for another inning before he could stand it no longer. Before the eighth inning began, the arbiter walked from his position at second and engaged in a lengthy, heated discussion with the Cubs players before ejecting Woody English and Tuck Stainback. The two were substitutes that could have helped the Chicago cause later in the game.

The eighth inning fireworks were not confined to the sidelines. A Detroit walk, a double and Goslin's single off the first base bag tied the game at 3–3 and knocked Lee out of the game. Even Chicago's shutout hero of game one, Lon Warneke, couldn't stop the siege as singles by Fox and Billy Rogell tallied Detroit's fourth run and put runners at the corners. On the fourth pitch to the next batter, the Tigers launched a double steal. Rogell darted from first and drew a throw from Hartnett while Fox waited for an opportunity to score. It came as Rogell engaged the Cubs in a rundown long enough for Fox to sneak home with Detroit's fifth run.

With their first lead of the game, the Tigers summoned starter Schoolboy Rowe to carry them to victory. Rowe dispatched the Cubs in order in the eighth, but ran into trouble in the bottom of the ninth. After a routine out, Hack singled to start the crowd in a terrific uproar. Pinch-hitters Chuck Klein and Ken O'Dea also singled to make it 5–4. Amid ear-splitting racket, Galan then hit a fly ball to center that scored Klein and tied the game.

Each team threatened in the 10th. In the top half, Goslin doubled with two outs for Detroit, but Cavarretta made a sparkling catch to close it. The Cubs' threat was much more serious, as Fred Lindstrom led off with a double and was sacrificed to third. Here Rowe greatly disappointed the home crowd by inducing two ground balls to preserve Detroit's chances.

In the fateful 11th, Rogell singled, and Marv Owen tried to sacrifice. But Lindstrom made a fine play and forced Rogell at second. On the next play Lindstrom fumbled Flea Clifton's slow roller, putting Tigers at first and second with one out. After Rowe struck out, Chicago envisioned an escape. But hopes were dashed when Jo-Jo White singled home Owen with the lead run.

Chicago's last chance was anti-climactic. Rowe retired the Cubs in order, striking out the final two batters. The Tigers went on to win this Series in six games, walking away with Detroit's first world's championship.

# 72 Controversy Breeds a Dodgers Miracle

## LOS ANGELES (NL) at PHILADELPHIA (NL)
### Friday, October 7, 1977, Veterans Stadium
### Dodgers 6, Phillies 5

In a game replete with controversy, the Los Angeles Dodgers pulled off a shocking two-out, ninth-inning comeback over the Philadelphia Phillies to move within one game of the 1977 National League Championship.

The best-of-five series saw the clubs split the first two games in Los Angeles and travel to the East Coast for Game Three. Philadelphia fans turned out in droves, the second largest crowd in Veterans Stadium history, to urge their heroes on to the World Series for the first time in 27 years. Frustrated a year earlier, the Phillies finished first in the East but dropped three straight to Cincinnati in the playoffs.

A pair of right-handers assumed Game Three pitching duties — Larry Christenson for the home team and Burt Hooton for the visitors. Neither, however, lasted very long, and each was followed by a parade of relievers.

Both the scoring and the controversy began in the second inning. With one out, the Dodgers' Steve Garvey singled. On Dusty Baker's double, Garvey tried to score and apparently beat the throw by an eyelash. Phillies catcher Bob Boone, however, adroitly blocked the plate and tagged Garvey. But home plate umpire Harry Wendelstedt ruled Garvey safe, igniting both the Phillies and the fans. Had Wendelstedt had the luxury of viewing the instant replay, he would have seen that Garvey never touched the plate. Nevertheless, Los Angeles led 1–0. Rick Monday then flied out for what would have been the third out. Steve Yeager capitalized on the extra out by singling home Baker, increasing the visitors' lead to 2–0. Hooton also hit safely, doubling to left, but Yeager was thrown out at home. This time it was the Dodgers turn to argue the decision at the plate. Yeager had to be restrained by teammates.

Philadelphia bounced back in the home half with two singles sandwiching a pair of outs. Then Hooton walked Ted Sizemore to load the bases. The crowd was on its feet, hooting and howling as the next batter, pitcher Larry Christenson, took a called third strike — or so the Dodgers thought. Wendelstedt called it a ball. That so incensed and rattled Hooton that he walked not only Christenson but the next two batters as well. All the while Hooton questioned one call after another, waving his arms as if to ask, "Where was that one?" The umpire could hear nothing, however, as the passionate crowd screamed their delight. Finally, manager Tommy Lasorda had enough and the Dodger righthander was sent to the showers with the Phillies leading, 3–2. With the bases loaded Rick Rhoden was summoned, and the right-hander quelled the uprising by inducing slugger Mike Schmidt to pop out.

The Dodgers mounted another rally in the fourth. After a leadoff double by Ron Cey and a ground-out, Baker singled to tie it at 3–3. Another single and an intentional walk loaded the bases for pitcher Rhoden, who sent a fly ball to right field. Philadelphia's Bake McBride caught it for out number two and fired to the plate. Boone took the throw and the full impact of the onrushing Baker for an inning-ending double play. It marked the game's third close play at the plate.

The tie game extended through the seventh with neither team getting another runner as far as third base.

In the bottom of the eighth, facing Elias Sosa, the Phillies staged another fruitful attack. After Richie Hebner opened with a double, Gary Maddox singled him home and went to third on a throwing error. Another error allowed Maddox to cross the plate and gave Philadelphia a 5–3 advantage.

Needing just three outs for the victory, manager Danny Ozark called on his ace reliever, Gene Garber. The right-hander satisfied the shrieking fans by getting two quick outs. Down to their final out, the Dodgers sent pinch-hitter

| Los Angeles | AB | R | H | I |
|---|---|---|---|---|
| Lopes D, 2b | 5 | 1 | 1 | 1 |
| Russell B, ss | 5 | 0 | 2 | 1 |
| Smith R, rf | 5 | 0 | 0 | 0 |
| Cey R, 3b | 4 | 1 | 1 | 0 |
| Garvey S, 1b | 4 | 1 | 1 | 0 |
| Baker D, lf | 4 | 1 | 2 | 2 |
| Monday R, cf | 3 | 0 | 1 | 0 |
| Burke G, cf | 0 | 0 | 0 | 0 |
| Yeager S, c | 2 | 0 | 1 | 1 |
| Davalillo V, ph | 1 | 1 | 1 | 0 |
| Grote J, c | 0 | 0 | 0 | 0 |
| Hooton B, p | 1 | 0 | 1 | 0 |
| Rhoden R, p | 1 | 0 | 0 | 0 |
| Goodson E, ph | 1 | 0 | 0 | 0 |
| Rau D, p | 0 | 0 | 0 | 0 |
| Sosa E, p | 0 | 0 | 0 | 0 |
| Rautzhan L, p | 0 | 0 | 0 | 0 |
| Mota M, ph | 1 | 1 | 1 | 0 |
| Garman M, p | 0 | 0 | 0 | 0 |
| | 37 | 6 | 12 | 5 |

| Philadelphia | AB | R | H | |
|---|---|---|---|---|
| McBride B, rf | 4 | 0 | 0 | |
| Bowa L, ss | 4 | 0 | 0 | |
| Schmidt M, 3b | 4 | 0 | 1 | |
| Luzinski G, lf | 3 | 0 | 1 | |
| Hebner R, 1b | 5 | 2 | 1 | |
| Maddox G, cf | 4 | 1 | 1 | |
| Boone B, c | 4 | 1 | 2 | |
| Sizemore T, 2b | 3 | 1 | 1 | |
| Christenson L, p | 0 | 0 | 0 | |
| Brusstar W, p | 0 | 0 | 0 | |
| Hutton T, ph | 1 | 0 | 0 | |
| Reed R, p | 0 | 0 | 0 | |
| McCarver T, ph | 1 | 0 | 0 | |
| Garber G, p | 0 | 0 | 0 | |
| | 33 | 5 | 6 | |

| Los Angeles | IP | H | R | ER | BB | SO |
|---|---|---|---|---|---|---|
| Hooton | 1.2 | 2 | 3 | 3 | 4 | 1 |
| Rhoden | 4.1 | 2 | 0 | 0 | 2 | 0 |
| Rau | 1.0 | 0 | 0 | 0 | 0 | 1 |
| Sosa | 0.2 | 2 | 2 | 1 | 0 | 0 |
| Rautzhan (W) | 0.1 | 0 | 0 | 0 | 0 | 0 |
| Garman (S) | 1.0 | 0 | 0 | 0 | 0 | 0 |
| | 9.0 | 7 | 5 | 4 | 6 | 2 |

| Philadelphia | IP | H | R | ER | BB | SO |
|---|---|---|---|---|---|---|
| Christenson | 3.1 | 7 | 3 | 3 | 0 | |
| Brusstar | 0.2 | 0 | 0 | 0 | 1 | |
| Reed | 2.0 | 1 | 0 | 0 | 1 | |
| Garber (L) | 3.0 | 4 | 3 | 2 | 0 | |
| | 9.0 | 12 | 6 | 5 | 2 | |

| Los Angeles | 020 | 100 | 003 — 6 |
|---|---|---|---|
| Philadelphia | 030 | 000 | 020 — 5 |

OB: Los Angeles 6, Philadelphia 9; ER: Smith, Cey, Sizemore, Garber; DP: Philadelphia 1; 2B: Baker, Hooton, Cey, Russell, Hebner, Mota; SH: Garber; HP: by Garman (Luzinski); PB: Boone; TI: 2:59; AT: 63,719; UM: HP Wendelstedt, 1B Froemming, 2B Rennert, 3B Runge, LF Pryor, RF Engel

Vic Davalillo to the plate. The veteran dropped a perfect drag bunt toward second and beat it out for a hit. Lasorda then commissioned another pinch-hitter Manny Mota. Mota, who concluded his career with more pinch-hits than anyone in history, quickly got behind in an 0–2 count. Then he drove Garber's third pitch deep into left. Left fielder Greg Luzinski initially took one step in before realizing the ball would sail over his head. Racing back to the wall, Luzinski got his glove on it before it bounded against the Plexiglas, where he trapped it. His throw to second was late, but worse, it short-hopped past Sizemore enabling Davalillo to score and Mota to reach third. The Dodgers had the tying run 90 feet from the plate, and the batter was Davey Lopes.

Garber's first pitch to Lopes was driven hard toward Schmidt, playing shallow at third. The ball bounced off his glove but directly toward short where Larry Bowa made a bare handed pickup and fired a bullet to first. It was a very close play and, belying the replays, Lopes was called safe while Mota scored the tying run.

Garber immediately tried to pick off Lopes, but the ball glanced off Hebner's glove, allowing the runner to reach second. Then, with a 2–2 count, Bill Russell drove a ball through Garber's legs and into center field, sending Lopes home with the lead run.

Mike Garman was given the task of preserving the Dodger lead, and he performed admirably. Only Luzinski reached base, being hit by a pitch. The 63,719 stunned fans left the park realizing the Phillies needed to win two in a row to bring home the championship that seemed imminent only minutes earlier.

# *Dodger Comeback Wins Second Playoff Game* 73

SAN FRANCISCO (NL) at LOS ANGELES (NL)
Tuesday, October 2, 1962, Dodger Stadium
Dodgers 8, Giants 7

With two weeks left in the season, the Los Angeles Dodgers held a slim lead over their long-time rivals, the San Francisco Giants. But the loss of pitching ace Sandy Koufax to arm problems back in July, and the subsequent strain it put on the beleaguered pitching staff, finally exacted its toll. The Dodgers lost 10 of their final 13 games and barely stopped the bleeding in time. The charging Giants finally tied them on the last day of the season, forcing a three-game playoff to decide the National League champion.

The Giants won the first game in convincing fashion, 8–0, behind the three-hit pitching of Billy Pierce. On the brink of extinction, the Dodgers sent Don Drysdale to the mound for Game Two. With the loss of Koufax, the big right-hander had already tossed more than 300 innings and was making his fourth start in nine days. The Giants countered with their ace, Jack Sanford, who was also working on two days' rest and battling a bad cold.

San Francisco started the scoring in the second inning on an RBI double by Felipe Alou. In the sixth they erupted for four more and sent Drysdale to the showers.

The situation looked bleak for the home club but the organist bravely played a few rounds of "You Gotta Have Heart." Not only were the Dodgers trailing, 5–0, but they hadn't scored in their last 35 innings of play. So when Sanford opened the bottom of the sixth with a walk, there was little concern

| San Francisco | AB | R | H | I |
|---|---|---|---|---|
| Hiller C, 2b | 3 | 1 | 1 | 1 |
| Nieman B, ph | 1 | 0 | 0 | 0 |
| Bowman E, 2b | 1 | 0 | 0 | 0 |
| Davenport J, 3b | 6 | 1 | 2 | 1 |
| Mays W, cf | 5 | 0 | 1 | 0 |
| McCovey W, lf | 2 | 0 | 1 | 1 |
| Miller S, p | 0 | 0 | 0 | 0 |
| O'Dell B, p | 0 | 0 | 0 | 0 |
| Larsen D, p | 0 | 0 | 0 | 0 |
| Bailey E, ph | 1 | 0 | 1 | 1 |
| Boles C, pr | 0 | 1 | 0 | 0 |
| Bolin B, p | 0 | 0 | 0 | 0 |
| LeMay D, p | 0 | 0 | 0 | 0 |
| Perry G, p | 0 | 0 | 0 | 0 |
| McCormick M, p | 0 | 0 | 0 | 0 |
| Cepeda O, 1b | 5 | 1 | 1 | 0 |
| Alou F, rf | 4 | 0 | 2 | 1 |
| Haller T, c | 1 | 1 | 0 | 0 |
| Orsino J, c | 1 | 0 | 1 | 1 |
| Pagan J, ss | 5 | 1 | 3 | 0 |
| Sanford J, p | 3 | 1 | 0 | 0 |
| Alou M, lf | 0 | 0 | 0 | 0 |
| Kuenn H, ph-lf | 2 | 0 | 0 | 0 |
| | 40 | 7 | 13 | 6 |

| Los Angeles | AB | R | H | I |
|---|---|---|---|---|
| Wills M, ss | 4 | 1 | 0 | 0 |
| Gilliam J, 2b-3b | 3 | 1 | 0 | 0 |
| Snider D, lf | 3 | 1 | 1 | 0 |
| Spencer D, ph | 0 | 0 | 0 | 0 |
| Davis T, 3b-cf | 3 | 0 | 1 | 1 |
| Moon W, 1b | 2 | 1 | 1 | 0 |
| Fairly R, 1b | 1 | 0 | 1 | 1 |
| Howard F, rf | 3 | 1 | 1 | 1 |
| Roseboro J, c | 2 | 0 | 0 | 0 |
| Camilli D, ph-c | 2 | 1 | 1 | 0 |
| Davis W, cf | 2 | 0 | 0 | 0 |
| Carey A, ph | 0 | 0 | 0 | 1 |
| Burright L, pr-2b | 0 | 1 | 0 | 0 |
| Drysdale D, p | 2 | 0 | 0 | 0 |
| Roebuck E, p | 0 | 0 | 0 | 0 |
| Walls L, ph | 1 | 1 | 1 | 3 |
| Perranoski R, p | 0 | 0 | 0 | 0 |
| Smith J, p | 0 | 0 | 0 | 0 |
| Williams S, p | 1 | 0 | 0 | 0 |
| | 29 | 8 | 7 | 7 |

| San Francisco | IP | H | R | ER | BB | SO |
|---|---|---|---|---|---|---|
| Sanford | 5.0 | 2 | 1 | 1 | 3 | 4 |
| Miller | 0.1 | 2 | 3 | 3 | 1 | 0 |
| O'Dell | 0.0 | 2 | 3 | 2 | 0 | 0 |
| Larsen | 1.2 | 1 | 0 | 0 | 0 | 1 |
| Bolin (L) | 1.0 | 0 | 1 | 1 | 2 | 2 |
| LeMay | 0.0 | 0 | 0 | 0 | 1 | 0 |
| Perry | 0.1 | 0 | 0 | 0 | 0 | 0 |
| McCormick | 0.1 | 0 | 0 | 0 | 1 | 0 |
| | 8.2 | 7 | 8 | 7 | 8 | 7 |

| Los Angeles | IP | H | R | ER | BB | SO |
|---|---|---|---|---|---|---|
| Drysdale | 5.1 | 7 | 5 | 3 | 4 | 4 |
| Roebuck | 0.2 | 1 | 0 | 0 | 0 | 0 |
| Perranoski | 1.0 | 4 | 1 | 1 | 0 | 0 |
| Smith | 0.1 | 1 | 1 | 0 | 0 | 0 |
| Williams (W) | 1.2 | 0 | 0 | 0 | 1 | 2 |
| | 9.0 | 13 | 7 | 4 | 5 | 6 |

```
San Francisco   010   004   020 — 7
Los Angeles     000   007   001 — 8
```

OB: San Francisco 13, Los Angeles 7; ER: Drysdale, Haller, Howard; 2B: Alou, Pagan, Snider, Walls; SB: Wills; CS: Burright; SH: Spencer; SF: T. Davis, Orsino, Fairly; HP: by Drysdale (Hiller), by O'Dell (Carey); TI: 4:18; AT: 25,321; UM: HP Barlick, 1B Boggess, 2B Donatelli, 3B Conlan

among Giants fans. Manager Alvin Dark was concerned that Sanford's cold and lack of rest had drained him, however, and decided to bring in a reliever. It was a move he soon regretted.

Los Angeles released their pent-up offensive frustrations and erupted at the expense of three relievers. An error and a hit batsman accompanied two walks, two singles, and two doubles. By the time order was restored, the Dodgers had vaulted into a 7–5 advantage. With the season on the line, the sixth inning also marked the beginning of wholesale substitutions by both Dark and Dodgers manager Walter Alston.

In the seventh, the Giants put two men on with only one out, but relief specialist Ron Perranoski retired two pinch-hitters to keep the score stable.

San Francisco led off the eighth with two singles, forcing Perranoski's retreat. Another single and an error made it 7–6 and brought on the third Dodger hurler of the inning, Stan Williams. The right-hander issued another pass, and then a sacrifice fly tied the game. Williams did escape, however, leaving a pair of Giants aboard.

No further threats materialized until the bottom of the ninth when the first two Dodgers walked. Rookie pitcher Gaylord Perry then fielded a sacrifice and had plenty of time to throw out the lead runner at third. But failing to look to third, Perry instead threw to first. That led to an intentional walk, loading the bases. Ron Fairly next hit a line drive to shallow center field. The strong-armed Willie Mays made the catch, but the mercurial Maury Wills tagged and headed for home. It wasn't very close. Wills scored the winning run, and the Dodgers thrilling comeback enabled them to play another day.

# Defensive Replacement Turns Around the ALCS 74

## BOSTON (AL) at CALIFORNIA (AL)
### Sunday, October 12, 1986, Anaheim Stadium
### Red Sox 7, Angels 6

In 1985 the League Championship Series was expanded from a best-of-five-games format to a best-of-seven. And for the second year in a row a team that would have been eliminated in five games went on to take the pennant in seven.

This year it was the California Angels who took a commanding three-games-to-one lead over the Boston Red Sox for American League honors. California had won Game Four in dramatic style, tying it with three in the bottom of the ninth before winning it in the eleventh. They then needed to win just one of three remaining games in order to make the first World Series appearance in the franchise's 26-year history.

A third consecutive sellout crowd jammed Anaheim Stadium hoping to see their heroes win it at home. They were disappointed in the second inning when Boston's Rich Gedman smashed a two-run homer off their best pitcher, Mike Witt. But the Red Sox had led in both Games Three and Four before the Angels had come back to win both.

Bob Boone put California on the board with a solo home run leading off

| Boston | AB | R | H | I |
|---|---|---|---|---|
| Boggs W, 3b | 5 | 0 | 1 | 0 |
| Barrett M, 2b | 5 | 0 | 0 | 0 |
| Buckner B, 1b | 4 | 0 | 1 | 0 |
| Stapleton D, pr-1b | 1 | 1 | 1 | 0 |
| Rice J, lf | 5 | 1 | 1 | 0 |
| Baylor D, dh | 4 | 2 | 1 | 2 |
| Evans D, rf | 5 | 0 | 1 | 0 |
| Gedman R, c | 4 | 2 | 4 | 2 |
| Armas T, cf | 2 | 0 | 0 | 0 |
| Henderson D, cf | 2 | 1 | 1 | 3 |
| Owen S, ss | 2 | 0 | 0 | 0 |
| Greenwell M, ph | 1 | 0 | 1 | 0 |
| Romero E, pr-ss | 2 | 0 | 0 | 0 |
| | 42 | 7 | 12 | 7 |

| California | AB | R | H | I |
|---|---|---|---|---|
| Burleson R, 2b | 2 | 0 | 0 | 0 |
| Wilfong R, ph-2b | 3 | 0 | 2 | 2 |
| Schofield D, ss | 5 | 0 | 1 | 0 |
| Downing B, lf | 3 | 0 | 0 | 1 |
| DeCinces D, 3b | 5 | 1 | 2 | 0 |
| Grich B, 1b | 5 | 1 | 1 | 2 |
| Jackson R, dh | 5 | 0 | 1 | 0 |
| Hendrick G, rf | 3 | 0 | 1 | 0 |
| White D, pr-rf | 2 | 1 | 1 | 0 |
| Boone B, c | 3 | 1 | 3 | 1 |
| Jones R, pr | 0 | 1 | 0 | 0 |
| Narron J, c | 0 | 0 | 0 | 0 |
| Pettis G, cf | 3 | 1 | 1 | ? |
| | 39 | 6 | 13 | 6 |

| Boston | IP | H | R | ER | BB | SO |
|---|---|---|---|---|---|---|
| Hurst | 6.0 | 7 | 3 | 3 | 1 | 4 |
| Stanley | 2.1 | 4 | 3 | 3 | 2 | 1 |
| Sambito | 0.0 | 1 | 0 | 0 | 0 | 0 |
| Crawford (W) | 1.2 | 1 | 0 | 0 | 2 | 1 |
| Schiraldi | 1.0 | 0 | 0 | 0 | 0 | 2 |
| | 11.0 | 13 | 6 | 6 | 5 | 8 |

| California | IP | H | R | ER | BB | SO |
|---|---|---|---|---|---|---|
| Witt | 8.2 | 8 | 4 | 4 | 0 | 5 |
| Lucas | 0.0 | 0 | 1 | 1 | 0 | 0 |
| Moore (L) | 2.0 | 4 | 2 | 2 | 1 | 0 |
| Finley | 0.1 | 0 | 0 | 0 | 0 | 0 |
| | 11.0 | 12 | 7 | 7 | 1 | 5 |

Boston      020   000   004   01 — 7
California   001   002   201   00 — 6

OB: Boston 6, California 9; DP: California 2; 2B: DeCinces 2, Gedman, Wilfong; HR: Gedman, Boone, Grich, Baylor, Henderson; CS: Downing, White; SH: Burleson, Boone, Pettis; SF: Downing, Henderson; HP: by Lucas (Gedman), by Moore (Baylor); TI: 3:54; AT: 64,223; UM: HP Roe, 1B Garcia, 2B Barnett, 3B McCoy, LF Cooney, RF Bremigan

the third, but that was all the Angels could muster off Bruce Hurst through five innings.

In the home sixth, there were two outs when Doug DeCinces doubled. Bobby Grich then drove a ball deep toward the "386-foot" sign in center. Dave Henderson, who had replaced Tony Armas in the fifth inning after the latter sprained his ankle, raced back to the padded fence and leaped for the ball. He got his glove on it, but his momentum helped to bounce the ball over the wall for a gift home run. Anaheim Stadium erupted in ecstasy as the Angels seized a 3–2 lead.

California padded their lead in the seventh. Rob Wilfong's double and Brian Downing's sacrifice fly each drove in a run, making it 5–2.

Witt continued his mastery over the Sox until the dramatic ninth, for which 64,000 attendees stood transfixed. Bill Buckner led off with a single. After Jim Rice struck out, Don Baylor crushed a 3–2 pitch, sending it far over the left-field fence to make it 5–4. But Witt retired the next batter, leaving the Angels one out away from the World Series. Rich Gedman, a left-handed batter, was the next scheduled hitter. California manager Gene Mauch, who always played the percentages, decided to bring in a left-handed reliever, Gary Lucas, to get the last out. Lucas tossed one pitch, hitting Gedman. That brought up Henderson with a chance to redeem himself for having gifted the Angels two runs in the sixth. Mauch countered with right-hander Donnie Moore. When the count rose to 2–2, California was only one pitch away from that elusive Fall

Classic. Then Angel hopes were brutally dashed as Henderson sent a long drive over the left-field fence, giving the Red Sox the lead, 6–5. The shocked stadium crowd, deafening only minutes before, was silenced.

Gallantly, the Angels rallied in the bottom of the ninth. A single, a sacrifice, and Rob Wilfong's RBI single tied it at six. Another single and an intentional walk then loaded the bases, and a sacrifice fly would have won it. But Steve Crawford, Boston's third pitcher of the stanza, retired DeCinces and Grich to send it into extra innings.

In the 10th the Red Sox put runners at the corners with only one out, but Moore induced Rice to ground into an inning-ending double play.

Boston again threatened in the 11th when they loaded the bases with no outs. This time they dented the plate on a sacrifice fly by Henderson, giving them a 7–6 advantage. Calvin Schiraldi pitched the bottom of the frame and retired California in order, sealing the Sox' victory.

The loss took the heart out of the Angels. They were crushed in the following two games, 10–4 and 8–1, having come as close to the World Series as they would for the rest of the century.

# *Dent's Home Run Helps Eliminate the Red Sox* 75

### NEW YORK (AL) at BOSTON (AL)
### Monday, October 2, 1978, Fenway Park
### Yankees 5, Red Sox 4

In mid–July the Yankees trailed the Boston Red Sox in the American League East by 14 games. But after manager Billy Martin was replaced by Bob Lemon, New York surged toward the finish and occupied first place with just two weeks remaining in the season. Boston, meanwhile, staggered in September, at one point losing 14 of 17 before winning their last eight to catch the Yankees on the final day of the season. With identical records, the two clubs then were forced into a one-game playoff.

A pitcher's duel developed over the first six innings. Boston's Mike Torrez, a former Yankee, was working on a two-hit shutout while New York's Ron Guidry, 24–3 entering this game, had been touched for two runs. Boston scored single runs in the second, on Carl Yastrzemski's home run, and in the sixth, on an RBI single by Jim Rice. They nearly added more in the sixth, but right

**Dent put the Yankees ahead (National Baseball Hall of Fame Library, Cooperstown, New York).**

fielder Lou Piniella made a great lunging catch with two runners aboard for the third out.

The pennant picture began to fade for Torrez and the Red Sox in the seventh. With one out, Chris Chambliss and Roy White each singled. Another out brought Bucky Dent to the plate. Far from an obvious threat, Dent was a .242 hitter with four home runs during the season. Normally, the Yankees would have pinch hit for the shortstop, but they were out of infield replacements. So Dent batted and lifted a 1–1 pitch high in the air toward the Green Monster, the 37-foot wall in left field. To the surprise of most in attendance, including

| New York | AB | R | H | I |
|----------|----|----|----|----|
| Rivers M, cf | 2 | 1 | 1 | 0 |
| Blair P, ph-cf | 1 | 0 | 1 | 0 |
| Munson T, c | 5 | 0 | 1 | 1 |
| Piniella L, rf | 4 | 0 | 1 | 0 |
| Jackson R, dh | 4 | 1 | 1 | 1 |
| Nettles G, 3b | 4 | 0 | 0 | 0 |
| Chambliss C, 1b | 4 | 1 | 1 | 0 |
| White R, lf | 3 | 1 | 1 | 0 |
| Thomasson G, lf | 0 | 0 | 0 | 0 |
| Doyle B, 2b | 2 | 0 | 0 | 0 |
| Spencer J, ph | 1 | 0 | 0 | 0 |
| Stanley F, 2b | 1 | 0 | 0 | 0 |
| Dent B, ss | 4 | 1 | 1 | 3 |
| | 35 | 5 | 8 | 5 |

| Boston | AB | R | H | I |
|--------|----|----|----|----|
| Burleson R, ss | 4 | 1 | 1 | 0 |
| Remy J, 2b | 4 | 1 | 2 | 0 |
| Rice J, rf | 5 | 0 | 1 | 1 |
| Yastrzemski C, lf | 5 | 2 | 2 | 2 |
| Fisk C, c | 3 | 0 | 1 | 0 |
| Lynn F, cf | 4 | 0 | 1 | 1 |
| Hobson B, dh | 4 | 0 | 1 | 0 |
| Scott G, 1b | 4 | 0 | 2 | 0 |
| Brohamer J, 3b | 1 | 0 | 0 | 0 |
| Bailey B, ph | 1 | 0 | 0 | 0 |
| Duffy F, 3b | 0 | 0 | 0 | 0 |
| Evans D, ph | 1 | 0 | 0 | 0 |
| | 36 | 4 | 11 | 4 |

| New York | IP | H | R | ER | BB | SO |
|----------|----|----|----|----|----|----|
| Guidry (W) | 6.1 | 6 | 2 | 2 | 1 | 5 |
| Gossage (S) | 2.2 | 5 | 2 | 2 | 1 | 2 |
| | 9.0 | 11 | 4 | 4 | 2 | 7 |

| Boston | IP | H | R | ER | BB | SO |
|--------|----|----|----|----|----|----|
| Torrez (L) | 6.2 | 5 | 4 | 4 | 3 | 4 |
| Stanley | 0.1 | 2 | 1 | 1 | 0 | 0 |
| Hassler | 1.2 | 1 | 0 | 0 | 0 | 2 |
| Drago | 0.1 | 0 | 0 | 0 | 0 | 0 |
| | 9.0 | 8 | 5 | 5 | 3 | 6 |

| New York | 000 | 000 | 410 — 5 |
|----------|-----|-----|---------|
| Boston | 010 | 001 | 020 — 4 |

OB: New York 6, Boston 9; 2B: Rivers, Scott, Burleson, Munson, Remy; HR: Yastrzemski, Dent, Jackson; SB: Rivers 2; SH: Brohamer, Remy; PB: Munson; TI: 2:52; AT: 32,925; UM: HP Denkinger, 1B Evans, 2B Clark, 3B Palermo

Torrez and Dent himself, the ball carried over the wall and into the netting for a three-run homer, giving the Yankees their first lead at 3–2. Torrez then walked Mickey Rivers, and Bob Stanley relieved the shaken starter. Rivers promptly stole second and scored the Yankees fourth run on Thurman Munson's double.

Leading off the New York eighth, Reggie Jackson added a fifth run on a solo homer to center.

Boston responded with a rally in the home half of the eighth. A double by Jerry Remy along with successive singles by Yastrzemski, Carlton Fisk, and Fred Lynn made it 5–4. Then with Sox at first and second and only one out, Goose Gossage, having relieved Guidry in the seventh, slammed the door on any further mischief.

In the bottom of the ninth, the Red Sox mounted one last threat. After Gossage retired the first batter, Rick Burleson walked, and Remy rifled a line drive to right. Piniella took one step in, then signaled that he'd lost the ball in the sun. When it bounced in front of him and to the left, he quickly speared it, holding Remy to a single and Burleson to second. Piniella's recovery averted the tying run, for Burleson certainly would have scored had the ball gotten past the right fielder. Nevertheless, Boston had the tying and winning runs on base with their two best hitters, Rice and Yastrzemski, coming to bat. Jam packed Fenway rocked with excitement and anticipation of a happy ending to the season's storybook finish.

Gossage later told reporters that as far as pressure is concerned, nothing exceeded this one-game playoff situation, not even World Series games. The flame-throwing right-hander first retired Jim Rice on a fly ball to right deep enough for Burleson to tag and move to third. Then Yastrzemski, one of the game's great clutch players, lifted a high pop just foul behind third, dramatically ending the closest division race in history.

# 76 Teams Combine for 12 Home Runs in Nine-Inning Game

CHICAGO (AL) at DETROIT (AL)
Sunday, May 28, 1995, Tiger Stadium
White Sox 14, Tigers 12

The National Weather Service claimed there were wind gusts of up to 12 miles-per-hour in Detroit this day, but everyone involved in the home run derby at Tiger Stadium felt that estimate was grossly understated. Taking advantage of Mother Nature, a cozy ballpark and some generous pitching, an offensive assault unseen in baseball history was unleashed on the record books.

• Eight different players on the two clubs combined for a new major league standard of 12 home runs.
• Ten bases-empty circuit blasts shattered the previous major league record of seven.
• Four different players each struck two or more round-trippers, tying the ML benchmark
• Three teammates (Tigers) each clouted two or more homers to tie the ML record for one team.
• In addition, the two teams combined to set an American League mark with 21 extra-base hits.

Although the Tigers out-homered their guests seven to five and scored in each of the first six innings, they still lost the 385-pitch marathon. They also became the 41st team in major league history to club seven or more homers in one game, but the first of those to taste defeat.

| Chicago | AB | R | H | I |
|---|---|---|---|---|
| Martin N, rf | 3 | 1 | 0 | 0 |
| Newson W, ph-rf | 1 | 0 | 0 | 0 |
| Raines T, lf | 5 | 2 | 2 | 0 |
| Thomas F, 1b | 5 | 2 | 2 | 2 |
| Kruk J, dh | 4 | 2 | 1 | 1 |
| Ventura R, 3b | 4 | 0 | 1 | 1 |
| Devereaux M, cf | 5 | 3 | 1 | 2 |
| Durham R, 2b | 5 | 1 | 4 | 3 |
| Karkovice R, c | 3 | 2 | 2 | 4 |
| Grebeck C, ss | 3 | 1 | 1 | 1 |
| Guillen O, ph-ss | 1 | 0 | 0 | 0 |
|  | 39 | 14 | 14 | 14 |

| Detroit | AB | R | H | I |
|---|---|---|---|---|
| Curtis C, cf | 5 | 3 | 3 | 2 |
| Whitaker L, 2b | 4 | 3 | 3 | 2 |
| Trammell A, ss | 6 | 1 | 2 | 1 |
| Fielder C, 1b | 5 | 2 | 2 | 5 |
| Fletcher S, pr-1b | 0 | 0 | 0 | 0 |
| Gibson K, dh | 6 | 2 | 4 | 2 |
| Fryman T, 3b | 4 | 0 | 1 | 0 |
| Higginson B, lf | 2 | 0 | 0 | 0 |
| Samuel J, ph | 0 | 0 | 0 | 0 |
| Steverson T, lf | 0 | 0 | 0 | 0 |
| Stubbs F, ph | 1 | 0 | 0 | 0 |
| Bautista D, rf | 6 | 0 | 1 | 0 |
| Flaherty J, c | 5 | 1 | 1 | 0 |
|  | 44 | 12 | 17 | 12 |

| Chicago | IP | H | R | ER | BB | SO |
|---|---|---|---|---|---|---|
| Baldwin | 1.1 | 7 | 7 | 7 | 2 | 3 |
| McCaskill | 3.0 | 5 | 3 | 3 | 2 | 3 |
| Dibble | 1.1 | 2 | 1 | 1 | 2 | 2 |
| Radinsky (W) | 2.0 | 2 | 1 | 1 | 2 | 1 |
| Hernandez (S) | 1.1 | 1 | 0 | 0 | 0 | 2 |
|  | 9.0 | 17 | 12 | 12 | 8 | 11 |

| Detroit | IP | H | R | ER | BB | SO |
|---|---|---|---|---|---|---|
| Wells | 3.0 | 7 | 7 | 5 | 1 | 2 |
| Doherty | 3.2 | 5 | 4 | 4 | 2 | 1 |
| Groom (L) | .2 | 1 | 3 | 3 | 2 | 1 |
| Henneman | 1.2 | 1 | 0 | 0 | 1 | 0 |
|  | 9.0 | 14 | 14 | 12 | 6 | 4 |

```
Chicago   013  321  130 — 14
Detroit   431  111  010 — 12
```

OB: Chicago 7, Detroit 15; ER: Grebeck 2, Wells; DP: Chicago 2; 2B: Raines, Thomas, Kruk, Devereaux, Durham 2, Curtis, Gibson, Flaherty; HR: Curtis 2, Fielder 2, Durham, Karkovice 2, Grebeck, Gibson 2, Thomas, Whitaker; SB: Durham, Whitaker, Gibson 2, Higginson, Fryman; CS: Fryman; SF: Karkovice 2, Ventura; HP: by Dibble (Curtis), by Hernandez (Fielder); TI: 3:46; AT: 10,813; UM: Cederstrom, Phillips, Roe, McClelland

Along the way, several unlikely candidates contributed to the fusillade. The White Sox' Craig Grebeck, who hadn't hit a home run in more than a year, hit his lone home run of the season. Chicago's rookie second baseman, Ray Durham, had never hit a major league home run until this day when he smashed the first of the three successive Sox homers in the fourth.

Four players each provided two home runs. Chicago catcher Ron Karkovice sent a pair into the seats, as did three Detroit sluggers. Chad Curtis served notice of the day's events by homering to lead off both the first and second innings, and Kirk Gibson celebrated his 38th birthday with a pair. Cecil Fielder launched the longest homers of the day, with a 450-foot blast into the center-field bleachers in the first and a 420-foot shot in the second. His two blasts were the only ones in the contest with runners on base.

Chicago rookie right-hander James Baldwin was appearing in his sixth major league game, having been bombarded for 25 hits and 15 runs in 13.1 innings prior to this debacle. The first batter he faced, Curtis, homered. Then he walked Lou Whitaker, and Alan Trammell singled. That set the table for Fielder's first ponderous home run, and after four batters it was 4–0.

Chicago got on the board in the second on Karkovice's sacrifice fly, making it 4–1. In the home half, Curtis again led off with a homer. Whitaker singled before Fielder stroked another tape measure blast giving the home club a

7–1 advantage. That was all for Baldwin, who had given up as many homers as he had gotten outs.

Detroit entrusted their six-run lead to starter David Wells, who was not ready for the challenge. Chicago manufactured three runs in the top of the third and the Tigers one in the bottom half, all without a circuit clout. After three frames it was 8–4 in favor of Detroit.

Wells finally succumbed to the long ball in the fourth as Durham, Karkovice, and Grebeck connected successively for solo shots. Gibson answered with a solo blast for the Tigers in the home half, and after four innings Detroit precariously clung to a 9–7 lead.

The Sox scored a pair in the fifth (without a home run) to tie it, but the Tigers singled home one of their own. The sixth frame saw the teams exchange runs on solo homers by Frank Thomas and Gibson, preserving the Tiger's slim margin at 11–10.

Karkovice tied the score at 11 with his second home run in the top of the seventh. In the bottom half, batterymate Scott Radinsky held the Tigers scoreless for the first time in the game.

With the momentum having swung their way, Chicago pushed across three more runs in the eighth without a homer and led, 14–11. The hosts had just about run out of gas but mustered one more round-tripper, a solo blast by Whitaker, in the bottom of the eighth. Whitaker's clout was the record breaking 12th of the game and signified the extent of the scoring.

It was a particularly frustrating day for the home team. In addition to losing after blowing a 7–1 lead, they wasted multiple scoring opportunities, having left 15 runners on base. Despite 17 hits and eight walks, five of their seven homers came without a mate aboard.

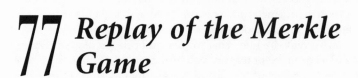

# 77 *Replay of the Merkle Game*

## CHICAGO (NL) at NEW YORK (NL)
### Thursday, October 8, 1908, Polo Grounds
### Cubs 4, Giants 2

On September 23, with both clubs in the heat of the pennant race, the Cubs and Giants met in the Polo Grounds. With two outs in the bottom of the ninth of a 1–1 game, the Giants had runners at the corners when Al Bridwell singled to center, scoring the apparent game winner. Fred Merkle, the baserunner at first, seeing his teammate cross the plate, assumed the game was over and headed for the clubhouse without touching second base. This was not an uncommon practice during the era, as the obligatory touching of second was rarely enforced. While a mass of celebrating humanity flooded the field, an alert Johnny Evers, Chicago second baseman, observed the situation. He realized the possibility of a delayed forceout — if only he could retrieve the ball. For each year that has passed since that day, there is another version of what next transpired. Suffice to say the reconciliation of the outcome reached the president of the National League, Harry Pulliam, who declared the game a tie. Pulliam further decreed that should the two combatants finish the regular season deadlocked, they would be required to replay the game in its entirety. Finish in a tie they did.

On October 8, with the pennant on the line, the teams met for a one-game tiebreaker. The *New York Times* reported that never had there been a sporting event in that city that so stirred its inhabitants. Despite a scheduled 3:00 P.M. start, by 10:30 A.M. more than 5,000 patrons covered the surrounding streets. The police, even those mounted on horseback, were helpless amid the throng. By 12:45 P.M., with every available seat filled, thousands broke onto the field to stake out dangerous standing positions along the foul lines. Meanwhile, hundreds overcame the double-barbed wire atop 15-foot walls to gain entrance. The steep grandstand rooftop was also reached by hundreds of the more agile, while thousands more covered the elevated railroad tracks that afforded an inexpensive view of the grounds. Even the fall and death of one hopeful observer did not deter the horde. Finally, Coogan's Bluff itself, affording long distance — although relatively safe — vantage points, was covered by spectators. Estimates of the crowd were 40,000 inside and from 40,000 to 60,000 outside the grounds.

Opposing moundsmen were identical to the September 23 match — Jack Pfeister for the visitors against the idol of New York, Christy Mathewson.

A deafening roar, both from within the grounds as well as outside, greeted Mathewson when he fanned the first two Cubs with his patented fadeaway pitch. The din was ear-splitting as he returned to the bench, horns and megaphones punctuating the wild cries of exultant fans.

Pfeister lasted only two-thirds of an inning before New York crossed the plate with their first run. Giants fans could already imagine their pennant flying, and they let the intruders know it while Chicago manager–first baseman Frank Chance replaced his starter with the great Mordecai "Three-Finger" Brown. The future Hall of Famer had fashioned a 28–9 slate along with five saves before today's contest. It was a stroke of genius, for Brown silenced the faithful with machine-like precision.

Mathewson fanned two more Cubs in the second frame but sustained major damage in the third. A triple, double, walk, and two singles pushed across four runs for the visitors.

It remained 4–1 until the seventh, when Brown weakened and brought the crowd back into the game. The first two New York batters singled and the third walked, loading the bases with no outs. Mathewson was lifted for a pinch-hitter,

| Chicago | AB | R | H | I |
|---|---|---|---|---|
| Sheckard J, lf | 4 | 0 | 0 | 0 |
| Evers J, 2b | 3 | 1 | 1 | 0 |
| Schulte W, rf | 4 | 1 | 1 | 1 |
| Chance F, 1b | 4 | 0 | 3 | 2 |
| Steinfeldt H, 3b | 4 | 0 | 1 | 0 |
| Hofman S, cf | 0 | 0 | 0 | 0 |
| Howard D, cf | 4 | 0 | 0 | 0 |
| Tinker J, ss | 4 | 1 | 1 | 0 |
| Kling J, c | 3 | 1 | 1 | 1 |
| Pfeister J, p | 0 | 0 | 0 | 0 |
| Brown, M, p | 2 | 0 | 0 | 0 |
| | 32 | 4 | 8 | 4 |

| New York | AB | R | H | I |
|---|---|---|---|---|
| Tenney F, 1b | 2 | 1 | 1 | 1 |
| Herzog B, 2b | 3 | 0 | 0 | 0 |
| Bresnahan R, c | 4 | 0 | 1 | 0 |
| Donlin M, rf | 4 | 0 | 1 | 1 |
| Seymour C, cf | 3 | 0 | 0 | 0 |
| Devlin A, 3b | 4 | 1 | 1 | 0 |
| McCormick M, lf | 4 | 0 | 1 | 0 |
| Bridwell A, ss | 3 | 0 | 0 | 0 |
| Mathewson C, p | 2 | 0 | 0 | 0 |
| Doyle L, ph | 1 | 0 | 0 | 0 |
| Wiltse H, p | 0 | 0 | 0 | 0 |
| | 30 | 2 | 5 | 2 |

| Chicago | IP | H | R | ER | BB | SO |
|---|---|---|---|---|---|---|
| Pfeister | 0.2 | 1 | 1 | 1 | 2 | 1 |
| Brown (W) | 8.1 | 4 | 1 | 1 | 1 | 1 |
| | 9.0 | 5 | 2 | 2 | 3 | 2 |

| New York | IP | H | R | ER | BB | SO |
|---|---|---|---|---|---|---|
| Mathewson (L) | 7.0 | 7 | 4 | 4 | 1 | 7 |
| Wiltse | 2.0 | 1 | 0 | 0 | 0 | 2 |
| | 9.0 | 8 | 4 | 4 | 1 | 9 |

| | | | | |
|---|---|---|---|---|
| Chicago | 004 | 000 | 000 — 4 |
| New York | 100 | 000 | 100 — 2 |

OB: Chicago 3, New York 6; ER: Tenney; DP: Chicago 1, New York 1; 2B: Donlin, Schulte, Chance, Evers; 3B: Tinker; CS: Chance; PK: Chance; SH: Brown; SF: Tenney; HP: by Pfeister (Tenney); TI: 1:40; AT: 40,000; UM: Johnstone, Klem

Larry Doyle, who popped up to catcher Johnny Kling. So frustrated was the crowd that, as Kling made the easy catch, they showered him with bottles, cushions, and newspapers. A long sacrifice fly then scored the second Giants run, but Buck Herzog grounded out to end the threat. The Giants had squandered their best opportunity of the day, and Brown didn't give them another chance. He faced only six batters in the eighth and ninth to send the Cubs into the World Series.

# 78 Cubs Score Seven After Two Outs in the Ninth

CHICAGO (NL) at CINCINNATI (NL)
Sunday, June 29, 1952, Crosley Field
Cubs 9, Reds 8

The Chicago Cubs established a National League record on this date when, in the ninth inning with two outs and no baserunners, they scored seven runs to pull out a 9–8 victory over the Cincinnati Reds.

Crosley Field, scene of the Cubs' miracle (National Baseball Hall of Fame Library, Cooperstown, New York).

Playing in 100-degree heat and oppressive humidity, the two clubs squared off for a Sunday doubleheader in Cincinnati. In the historic first game, the Reds' Bubba Church was coasting along in the ninth with an 8–2 lead, having allowed just eight hits and no walks. Cub chances for victory were about as soggy as the fans' shirt collars, especially when Church routinely retired the first two batters. With just one out remaining the miraculous rally unfolded.

• Bill Serena doubled.
• Roy Smalley walked.
• Pinch-hitting for Joe Hatten, Gene Hermanski singled, driving home Serena and sending Smalley to third. The score then stood at 8–3.
• Eddie Miksis then bunted toward third. Cincinnati's Ed Kazak hurriedly tried for a play at the plate but threw wildly allowing Smalley to score, making it 8–4.
• That was all for the drenched Church, who was relieved by Frank Smith. The ace reliever hit Hal Jeffcoat with his first pitch, loading the bases.
• Dee Fondy's third hit of the game was a single, driving home Hermanski and Miksis with the Cubs' fifth and sixth runs. Fondy was then lifted for a pinch-runner, Randy Jackson.
• Hank Sauer lashed a screaming line drive off the left-field wall for a

| Chicago | AB | R | H | I |
|---|---|---|---|---|
| Miksis E, 2b | 5 | 1 | 1 | 0 |
| Jeffcoat H, cf | 4 | 1 | 0 | 0 |
| Fondy D, 1b | 5 | 2 | 3 | 3 |
| Jackson R, pr | 0 | 1 | 0 | 0 |
| Cavarretta P, 1b | 0 | 0 | 0 | 0 |
| Sauer H, lf | 5 | 1 | 1 | 1 |
| Atwell T, c | 4 | 0 | 2 | 1 |
| Edwards B, ph-c | 0 | 0 | 0 | 0 |
| Addis B, rf | 4 | 0 | 1 | 0 |
| Pramesa J, ph | 1 | 0 | 1 | 2 |
| Leonard D, p | 0 | 0 | 0 | 0 |
| Serena B, 3b | 5 | 1 | 2 | 0 |
| Smalley R, ss | 3 | 1 | 1 | 0 |
| Klippstein J, p | 2 | 0 | 0 | 0 |
| Ramsdell W, p | 0 | 0 | 0 | 0 |
| Brown T, ph | 1 | 0 | 0 | 0 |
| Schultz B, p | 0 | 0 | 0 | 0 |
| Hatten J, p | 0 | 0 | 0 | 0 |
| Hermanski G, ph-rf | 1 | 1 | 1 | 1 |
| | 40 | 9 | 13 | 8 |

| Cincinnati | AB | R | H | I |
|---|---|---|---|---|
| Abrams C, cf | 1 | 1 | 1 | 0 |
| Borkowski B, cf-lf | 3 | 1 | 1 | 0 |
| Adams B, 3b | 3 | 3 | 3 | 1 |
| Kazak E, 3b | 1 | 0 | 0 | 0 |
| Hatton G, 2b | 4 | 1 | 1 | 0 |
| Kluszewski T, 1b | 3 | 1 | 1 | 1 |
| Westlake W, cf | 1 | 0 | 0 | 0 |
| Marshall W, rf | 4 | 0 | 2 | 2 |
| Adcock J, lf-1b | 5 | 0 | 2 | 2 |
| Seminick A, c | 5 | 1 | 1 | 0 |
| McMillan R, ss | 4 | 0 | 2 | 0 |
| Church B, p | 4 | 0 | 1 | 1 |
| Smith F, p | 0 | 0 | 0 | 0 |
| Raffensberger K, p | 0 | 0 | 0 | 0 |
| | 38 | 8 | 15 | 7 |

| Chicago | IP | H | R | ER | BB | SO |
|---|---|---|---|---|---|---|
| Klippstein | 4.1 | 9 | 6 | 6 | 1 | 0 |
| Ramsdell | 1.2 | 2 | 0 | 0 | 0 | 0 |
| Schultz | 1.0 | 4 | 2 | 2 | 1 | 1 |
| Hatten (W) | 1.0 | 0 | 0 | 0 | 0 | 0 |
| Leonard | 1.0 | 0 | 0 | 0 | 1 | 0 |
| | 9.0 | 15 | 8 | 8 | 3 | 1 |

| Cincinnati | IP | H | R | ER | BB | SO |
|---|---|---|---|---|---|---|
| Church | 8.2 | 10 | 6 | 3 | 1 | 4 |
| Smith (L) | 0.0 | 2 | 3 | 0 | 0 | 0 |
| Raffensberger | 0.1 | 1 | 0 | 0 | 1 | 0 |
| | 9.0 | 13 | 9 | 3 | 2 | 4 |

| | | | |
|---|---|---|---|
| Chicago | 100 | 100 | 007 — 9 |
| Cincinnati | 210 | 030 | 110 — 8 |

OB: Chicago 7, Cincinnati 8; ER: Smalley, Kazak; DP: Cincinnati 1, Chicago 1; 2B: Serena 2, Fondy, Adams, Sauer; HR: Fondy; SH: Hatten, Marshall; HP: by Smith (Jeffcoat); TI: 2:22; AT: 13,622; UM: Gorman, Donatelli, Ballanfant, Barlick

double, scoring Jeffcoat and pushing Chicago to within one run. Jackson held at third, but the tying and winning runs were in scoring position.

• With left-handed Toby Atwell due to bat, a frantic Luke Sewell, the Cincinnati manager, summoned the ace of his staff, lefty Ken Raffensberger. Cub manager Phil Cavarretta countered with a right-handed pinch-hitter, Bruce Edwards. The chess game continued with Edwards' being intentionally walked to fill the bases while the Reds were still looking for that elusive third out.

• Left-handed Bob Addis was the next scheduled hitter, so Cavarretta sent to the plate the right-handed former Red, Johnny Pramesa. Pramesa crowned the magnificent comeback when he singled to right, driving in Jackson and Sauer. At 9–8, the Cubs had their first lead since the first half-inning.

• Serena, who had begun the rally with a double, now ended it with a weak pop out.

Chicago's Dutch Leonard then ably retired the demoralized Reds in the bottom of the ninth to sew up the victory.

# A Giant, Two-Out Rally in the Ninth 79

PITTSBURGH (NL) at SAN FRANCISCO (NL)
Tuesday, May 1, 1973, Candlestick Park
Giants 8, Pirates 7

Trailing 7–1 with two outs in the ninth and a runner on first, only an innocent would have given the Giants any chance to win this game. Pittsburgh right-hander Bob Moose had allowed only five hits, no walks, and was one out away from victory when San Francisco mounted one of the most remarkable two-out comebacks in baseball history.

- Moose issued his first walk of the game to the previously hitless Bobby Bonds.
- Tito Fuentes forced Bonds at second for the first out.
- Chris Speier also grounded into a fielder's choice, Fuentes being retired at second for out number two.
- Willie McCovey walked.
- Ed Goodson, also hitless on the day, collected the Giants' third walk of the inning, loading the bases.
- Pittsburgh manager Bill Virdon sent Moose to the showers and brought in Ramon Hernandez to get the final out.
- Pinch-hitter Chris Arnold had other ideas, however, and clouted a grand slam home run. That made it 7–5, and the elusive third out still beckoned.
- Gary Matthews doubled to left.
- Dave Rader, like Bonds and Goodson before him, was hitless but took the fourth walk of the frame.
- Another pinch-hitter, Jim Howarth, also walked, re-loading the bases. This infuriated Virdon, who ran on the field to argue the call and was ejected.
- Dave Guisti was then summoned to relieve Hernandez and extinguish the rally.
- Bobby Bonds, batting for the second time in the inning, now doubled to left field, sending the three runners, including the game winner, plateward.

This game retains a share of the National League record for most runs scored in the ninth inning after two outs, tying the Chicago Cubs' effort of June 29, 1952. Three American League teams have also scored nine runs in the ninth after two outs.

| Pittsburgh | AB | R | H | I |
|---|---|---|---|---|
| Cash D, 2b | 5 | 0 | 1 | 1 |
| Alley G, ss | 0 | 0 | 0 | 0 |
| Oliver A, cf | 5 | 1 | 0 | 0 |
| Sanguillen M, rf | 4 | 2 | 1 | 0 |
| Stargell W, lf | 5 | 1 | 3 | 3 |
| Robertson B, 1b | 3 | 2 | 1 | 0 |
| Hebner R, 3b | 4 | 1 | 2 | 1 |
| Stennett R, ss-2b | 5 | 0 | 1 | 1 |
| May M, c | 5 | 0 | 2 | 0 |
| Moose B, p | 4 | 0 | 1 | 0 |
| Hernandez R, p | 0 | 0 | 0 | 0 |
| Giusti D, p | 0 | 0 | 0 | 0 |
| | 40 | 7 | 12 | 6 |

| San Francisco | AB | R | H | I |
|---|---|---|---|---|
| Bonds B, rf | 4 | 0 | 1 | 3 |
| Fuentes T, 2b | 4 | 0 | 0 | 0 |
| Speier C, ss | 4 | 1 | 1 | 0 |
| McCovey W, 1b | 3 | 0 | 2 | 0 |
| Blanco D, pr | 0 | 1 | 0 | 0 |
| Goodson E, 3b | 3 | 1 | 0 | 0 |
| Thomasson G, cf | 3 | 1 | 1 | 1 |
| Arnold C, ph | 1 | 1 | 1 | 4 |
| Matthews G, lf | 4 | 1 | 2 | 0 |
| Rader D, c | 3 | 1 | 0 | 0 |
| Bryant R, p | 1 | 0 | 0 | 0 |
| Phillips M, ph | 1 | 0 | 0 | 0 |
| McDowell S, p | 0 | 0 | 0 | 0 |
| Kingman D, ph | 1 | 0 | 0 | 0 |
| Sosa E, p | 0 | 0 | 0 | 0 |
| Howarth J, ph | 0 | 1 | 0 | 0 |
| | 32 | 8 | 8 | 8 |

| Pittsburgh | IP | H | R | ER | BB | SO |
|---|---|---|---|---|---|---|
| Moose | 8.2 | 5 | 4 | 4 | 3 | 4 |
| Hernandez (L) | 0.0 | 2 | 4 | 4 | 2 | 0 |
| Giusti | 0.0 | 1 | 0 | 0 | 0 | 0 |
| | 8.2 | 8 | 8 | 8 | 5 | 4 |

| San Francisco | IP | H | R | ER | BB | SO |
|---|---|---|---|---|---|---|
| Bryant | 6.0 | 6 | 4 | 2 | 2 | 4 |
| McDowell | 2.0 | 4 | 2 | 2 | 2 | 3 |
| Sosa (W) | 1.0 | 2 | 1 | 1 | 1 | 0 |
| | 9.0 | 12 | 7 | 5 | 5 | 7 |

```
Pittsburgh      301   000   111 — 7
San Francisco   000   010   007 — 8
```

OB: Pittsburgh 11, San Francisco 3; ER: Speier, Thomasson; DP: Pittsburgh 1; 2B: Stargell 2, Matthews, Bonds; HR: Thomasson, Arnold; TI: 2:45; AT: 7,972; UM: HP Harvey, 1B Olson, 2B A.Williams, 3B Crawford

# 80 Mets on the Brink of Their Miracle

BALTIMORE (AL) at NEW YORK (NL)
Wednesday, October 15, 1969, Shea Stadium
Mets 2, Orioles 1

In 1969, another tier of excitement was layered into the baseball season with the addition of divisional playoffs in each league. It was also the year the upstart New York Mets, who had never finished higher than ninth during their seven-year history, combined a talented young pitching staff, outstanding defense, and a 38–11 stretch run to prevail in the National League East. They then swept the Atlanta Braves in the League Championship Series to vault into the franchise's first World Series. Their opponents, the favored Baltimore Orioles, were appearing in the first of three consecutive World Series. The Orioles had crushed their nearest eastern rival by 19 games and then swept Minnesota for the American League Championship.

Outstanding pitching and sparkling defensive plays punctuated the first three games. The New York staff was particularly parsimonious, allowing only five runs and 12 hits in 36 innings. The heart of the Orioles' batting order—Paul Blair, Frank Robinson, Boog Powell, and Brooks Robinson—was a combined 5 for 44, and the Series leaders in RBI, with two each, were the Mets' Al Weis, a .215 regular season hitter, and Gary Gentry, a pitcher.

Game Four opened in Shea Stadium amid crystal clear skies and a brisk 57 degrees. It was a pitching rematch of Game One Cy Young Award candidates—New York's Tom Seaver, a 25-game winner, and Mike Cuellar, with 23 regular season wins.

The Mets jumped out to a 1–0 lead on Donn Clendenon's home run leading off the bottom of the second. In the top of the third, Baltimore showed the frustration of 13 consecutive scoreless innings when manager Earl Weaver was ejected for arguing balls and strikes.

With the help of some fine fielding plays, most notably a diving catch by Cleon Jones in short left field during the fifth, Seaver continued to mow down the Orioles. A lone walk in the sixth was the only baserunner Baltimore could muster between the fourth and eighth innings. By the time the eighth frame ended the aforementioned heart of the Orioles was a combined 7 for 52 in the Series, and Seaver drew a standing ovation when he batted.

The ninth inning opened in front of a boisterous New York crowd that muffled the radio announcers' calls and drew listeners ever closer to the suspense. Over the course of the entire season the Orioles had been shut out only eight times. Now, for the first time, they were in danger of being whitewashed twice in a row. A New York victory also would put the Series underdogs on the doorstep of a world championship, but Baltimore was not yet finished.

After Blair routinely flied out, Frank Robinson and Powell each singled putting runners at the corners. Brooks Robinson then sent a drive into right-center that was ticketed for extra bases, but Ron Swoboda made a diving one-handed catch. Frank Robinson tagged and scored, tying the game. Ellie Hendricks then nearly put Baltimore ahead when he slammed a ball into the right-field seats. Hesitating for what seemed like an eternity, the announcers finally reported the drive as foul. Hendricks followed with a line drive into right on which Swoboda made another fine catch.

New York had an opportunity to end it in the bottom of the ninth. Jones and Swoboda singled around a pair of outs placing runners at the corners, and Art Shamsky was called upon to pinch hit for third baseman Ed Charles. When Baltimore reliever Eddie Watt induced a routine ground out, it signaled the first extra-inning World Series game in five years.

Wayne Garrett assumed the hot corner for New York in the 10th and fumbled

| Baltimore | AB | R | H | I |
|---|---|---|---|---|
| Buford D, lf | 5 | 0 | 0 | 0 |
| Blair P, cf | 4 | 0 | 1 | 0 |
| Robinson F, rf | 4 | 1 | 1 | 0 |
| Powell B, 1b | 4 | 0 | 1 | 0 |
| Robinson B, 3b | 3 | 0 | 0 | 1 |
| Hendricks E, c | 3 | 0 | 0 | 0 |
| Johnson D, 2b | 4 | 0 | 0 | 0 |
| Belanger M, ss | 4 | 0 | 1 | 0 |
| Cuellar M, p | 2 | 0 | 1 | 0 |
| May D, ph | 1 | 0 | 0 | 0 |
| Watt E, p | 0 | 0 | 0 | 0 |
| Dalrymple C, ph | 1 | 0 | 1 | 0 |
| Hall D, p | 0 | 0 | 0 | 0 |
| Richert P, p | 0 | 0 | 0 | 0 |
|  | 35 | 1 | 6 | 1 |

| New York | AB | R | H | I |
|---|---|---|---|---|
| Agee T, cf | 4 | 0 | 1 | 0 |
| Harrelson B, ss | 4 | 0 | 1 | 0 |
| Jones C, lf | 4 | 0 | 1 | 0 |
| Clendenon D, 1b | 4 | 1 | 1 | 1 |
| Swoboda R, rf | 4 | 0 | 3 | 0 |
| Charles E, 3b | 3 | 0 | 0 | 0 |
| Shamsky A, ph | 1 | 0 | 0 | 0 |
| Garrett W, 3b | 0 | 0 | 0 | 0 |
| Grote J, c | 4 | 0 | 1 | 0 |
| Gaspar R, pr | 0 | 1 | 0 | 0 |
| Weis A, 2b | 3 | 0 | 2 | 0 |
| Seaver T, p | 3 | 0 | 0 | 0 |
| Martin J, ph | 0 | 0 | 0 | 0 |
|  | 34 | 2 | 10 | 1 |

| Baltimore | IP | H | R | ER | BB | SO |
|---|---|---|---|---|---|---|
| Cuellar | 7.0 | 7 | 1 | 1 | 0 | 5 |
| Watt | 2.0 | 2 | 0 | 0 | 0 | 2 |
| Hall (L) | 0.0 | 1 | 1 | 0 | 1 | 0 |
| Richert | 0.0 | 0 | 0 | 0 | 0 | 0 |
|  | 9.0 | 10 | 2 | 1 | 1 | 7 |

| New York | IP | H | R | ER | BB | SO |
|---|---|---|---|---|---|---|
| Seaver (W) | 10.0 | 6 | 1 | 1 | 2 | 6 |

| Baltimore | 000 | 000 | 001 | 0 — 1 |
|---|---|---|---|---|
| New York | 010 | 000 | 000 | 1 — 2 |

OB: Baltimore 7, New York 7; ER: Garrett, Richert; DP: Baltimore 3; 2B: Grote; HR: Clendenon; CS: Johnson, Swoboda; SH: Martin; SF: B. Robinson; TI: 2:33; AT: 57,367; UM: HP Crawford, 1B DiMuro, 2B Weyer, 3B Soar, LF Secory, RF Napp

the first ball sent his way by Dave Johnson. After a foul out by Mark Belanger, Clay Dalrymple pinch-hit for Watt and singled, sending Johnson to second. Don Buford sent a chill through the crowd with a fly to right that was deep enough to allow Johnson to advance to third. But Seaver bore down and fanned Blair to end the threat.

Right-hander Dick Hall took the hill for the Orioles in the bottom of the 10th and was greeted with a looping double into short left field by Jerry Grote. Ron Gaspar was sent in to run for Grote, and a series of strategic moves followed. To set up a possible double play or force at any base, Weis was walked. The Mets smelled blood and sent J.C. Martin to hit for Seaver. Baltimore countered with lefty Pete Richert.

When Martin bunted, Richert fielded it cleanly, but his throw to first hit Martin on the wrist and bounded into the outfield. Gasper never stopped as he rounded third and crossed home, sending the Mets to the brink of completing a fairy tale season. The story ended the following day when the Mets clinched the championship with a 5–3 victory.

# *Schoendienst Ends a* 81
# *Thriller in the 14th*

## NATIONAL LEAGUE at AMERICAN LEAGUE
## Tuesday, July 11, 1950, Comiskey Park I
## NL All-Stars 4, AL All-Stars 3

As the 1950 mid-summer classic approached, the American League had dominated All-Star competition, winning 12 of the 16 played. This year they were favored to win their fifth straight on the grounds of the exhibition's origin, Comiskey Park.

Pre-game controversy stirred in the National League camp when manager Burt Shotton tested the rules of player selection. The fans had voted into their starting lineup three outfielders, none of whom was a legitimate center fielder. When Shotton asked Commissioner Happy Chandler if he could replace the Cubs' Hank Sauer in the starting lineup with a true center fielder, he was rebuffed. Unfortunately the story leaked, and with the game being played in Chicago, fans unleashed a tide of vitriol upon the gentlemanly pilot during the opening ceremonies. But the black mark could not detract from what many consider the most exciting All-Star game of the century.

Limiting the star-studded lineups to precious few runs, a parade of hurlers distinguished themselves. Only two of the 11 moundsmen allowed more hits than innings pitched in this, the first extra-inning affair. But there was also spectacular defense and explosive offense by the most unlikely characters, particularly the majestic home run that finally won the game.

The excitement began in the very first inning with a thrilling catch of a drive off the bat of the National League's long-ball leader, Ralph Kiner. Left fielder Ted Williams, not known for his fielding, raced back and made a one-handed catch before crashing into the wall. Newspapers reported that Williams was slightly shaken but rubbed his elbow vigorously and continued playing. The following day X-rays revealed a fracture, and seven bone fragments were surgically removed.

In the second inning Jackie Robinson led off with a single to right. Enos Slaughter, Shotton's designated center fielder, then tripled to left center, driving home the game's first run. Hank Sauer followed with a long fly ball, giving the National League a 2–0 advantage. In the home half Slaughter also shined on defense. The American League first baseman, Walt Dropo, rocketed a ball to the deepest part of the park, but Slaughter raced to the 415-foot mark in center and made a remarkable running one-handed catch.

Kiner delivered another line drive to left in the third. This one was sinking

| National League | AB | R | H | I |
|---|---|---|---|---|
| Jones W, 3b | 7 | 0 | 1 | 0 |
| Kiner R, lf | 6 | 1 | 2 | 1 |
| Musial S, 1b | 5 | 0 | 0 | 0 |
| Robinson J, 2b | 4 | 1 | 1 | 0 |
| Wyrostek J, ph-rf | 2 | 0 | 0 | 0 |
| Slaughter E, cf-rf | 4 | 1 | 2 | 1 |
| Schoendienst R, 2b | 1 | 1 | 1 | 1 |
| Sauer H, rf | 2 | 0 | 0 | 1 |
| Pafko A, cf | 4 | 0 | 2 | 0 |
| Campanella R, c | 6 | 0 | 0 | 0 |
| Marion M, ss | 2 | 0 | 0 | 0 |
| Konstanty J, p | 0 | 0 | 0 | 0 |
| Jansen L, p | 2 | 0 | 0 | 0 |
| Snider D, ph | 1 | 0 | 0 | 0 |
| Blackwell E, p | 1 | 0 | 0 | 0 |
| Roberts R, p | 1 | 0 | 0 | 0 |
| Newcombe D, p | 0 | 0 | 0 | 0 |
| Sisler D, ph | 1 | 0 | 1 | 0 |
| Reese P, pr-ss | 3 | 0 | 0 | 0 |
|  | 52 | 4 | 10 | 4 |

| American League | AB | R | H | I |
|---|---|---|---|---|
| Rizzuto P, ss | 6 | 0 | 2 | 0 |
| Doby L, cf | 6 | 1 | 2 | 0 |
| Kell G, 3b | 6 | 0 | 0 | 2 |
| Williams T, lf | 4 | 0 | 1 | 1 |
| DiMaggio D, lf | 2 | 0 | 0 | 0 |
| Dropo W, 1b | 3 | 0 | 1 | 0 |
| Fain F, ph-1b | 3 | 0 | 1 | 0 |
| Evers H, rf | 2 | 0 | 0 | 0 |
| DiMaggio J, rf | 3 | 0 | 0 | 0 |
| Berra Y, c | 2 | 0 | 0 | 0 |
| Hegan J, pr-c | 3 | 0 | 0 | 0 |
| Doerr B, 2b | 3 | 0 | 0 | 0 |
| Coleman J, 2b | 2 | 0 | 0 | 0 |
| Raschi V, p | 0 | 0 | 0 | 0 |
| Michaels C, ph | 1 | 1 | 1 | 0 |
| Lemon B, p | 0 | 1 | 0 | 0 |
| Houtteman A, p | 1 | 0 | 0 | 0 |
| Reynolds A, p | 1 | 0 | 0 | 0 |
| Henrich T, ph | 1 | 0 | 0 | 0 |
| Gray T, p | 0 | 0 | 0 | 0 |
| Feller B, p | 0 | 0 | 0 | 0 |
|  | 49 | 3 | 8 | 3 |

| NL | IP | H | R | ER | BB | SO |
|---|---|---|---|---|---|---|
| Roberts | 3.0 | 3 | 1 | 1 | 1 | 1 |
| Newcombe | 2.0 | 3 | 2 | 2 | 1 | 1 |
| Konstanty | 1.0 | 0 | 0 | 0 | 0 | 2 |
| Jansen | 5.0 | 1 | 0 | 0 | 0 | 6 |
| Blackwell (W) | 3.0 | 1 | 0 | 0 | 0 | 2 |
|  | 14.0 | 8 | 3 | 3 | 2 | 12 |

| AL | IP | H | R | ER | BB | SO |
|---|---|---|---|---|---|---|
| Raschi | 3.0 | 2 | 2 | 2 | 0 | 1 |
| Lemon | 3.0 | 1 | 0 | 0 | 0 | 2 |
| Houtteman | 3.0 | 3 | 1 | 1 | 1 | 0 |
| Reynolds | 3.0 | 1 | 0 | 0 | 1 | 2 |
| Gray (L) | 1.1 | 3 | 1 | 1 | 0 | 1 |
| Feller | 0.2 | 0 | 0 | 0 | 1 | 1 |
|  | 14.0 | 10 | 4 | 4 | 3 | 7 |

| National | 020 | 000 | 001 | 000 | 01 — 4 |
|---|---|---|---|---|---|
| American | 001 | 020 | 000 | 000 | 00 — 3 |

OB: NL 9, AL 6; ER: Coleman; DP: NL 1, AL 1; 2B: Michaels, Doby, Kiner; 3B: Slaughter, Dropo; HR: Kiner, Schoendienst; WP: Roberts; PB: Hegan; TI: 3:14; AT: 46,127; UM: HP McGowan, 1B Pinelli, 2B Rommel, 3B Conlan, LF Robb, RF Stevens

fast, but Williams, despite his throbbing elbow, made another spectacular catch, netting the ball just off his shoe tops. The Junior Circuit got on the board in the home half. Cass Michaels pinch-hit for starter Vic Raschi and bounced a drive into the center-field bullpen area for a ground-rule double. Phil Rizzuto bunt-singled him to third before George Kell delivered a long sacrifice fly to make it 2–1.

With Don Newcombe taking the hill for the National League, the fourth inning began auspiciously for the home team. Dropo opened by sizzling a triple that caromed crazily off the center-field wall. After a ground-out, Yogi Berra drilled one back to the box. Foolishly, Dropo had ventured off third and was caught during a rundown, essentially ending the threat.

The American League vaulted into the lead in the fifth. Pitcher Bob Lemon walked, and after Rizzuto fanned, Larry Doby lashed a ground ball through the box. Robinson made a terrific play to get his glove on the ball, but it trickled into center field, enabling the runners to advance to second and third. Kell again flied deep to center, allowing Lemon to score the tying run. That brought to the plate Williams, whose elbow by now must have been delivering considerable pain. Nevertheless, he singled soundly to right, giving the AL their first lead at 3–2.

It was at this point that the pitchers took command of the action, as neither team could mount a serious threat in the sixth, seventh, or eighth. The National League's Larry Jansen was particularly effective, allowing only one hit in five innings of work.

The ninth opened with the American League on the verge of their fifth consecutive All-Star victory. But Kiner led off and lofted a shot that dropped into the lower left-field seats, tying the game at three.

No further scoring opportunities developed until the visitors' 11th. With one away, Kiner doubled and Stan Musial was passed intentionally. Despite the fact that he was the league's leading hitter, Robinson was lifted for pinch-hitter Johnny Wyrostek. The substitute swinger flied out, but the maneuver had important implications, as Red Schoendienst came on to play second base. The next National League batter was Slaughter, who reached first on an error, loading the bases. But Allie Reynolds, with a reputation as a clutch performer, retired Andy Pafko to avert any alteration to the scoreboard.

Through the 12th and 13th, the moundsmen on both sides muffled any offense. Then switch-hitter Schoendienst led off the 14th batting right-handed against Detroit southpaw Ted Gray. Possessing little power, the redhead averaged but one home run every 263 times at bat during his first five big-league campaigns. But now, on a 2–2 pitch, he swung and delivered a minor miracle into the upper deck of the left-field stands. It was a blow worthy of many of the great sluggers who graced the field that day. The National Leaguers proceeded to load the bases later in the inning, but further scoring was unnecessary; Ewell Blackwell faced only three batters in the home half to complete the upset.

# *Zabel Shines in Relief* 82

## BROOKLYN (NL) at CHICAGO (NL)
### Thursday, June 17, 1915, West Side Park
### Cubs 4, Robins 3

Relief pitchers in the early years of the century were not in great demand. Most moundsmen finished what they started, and "relievers" were usually the young or aged pitchers who could no longer carry their own weight. And

| Brooklyn | AB | R | H | I |
|---|---|---|---|---|
| O'Mara O, ss | 8 | 1 | 1 | 0 |
| Myers H, cf | 8 | 0 | 2 | 1 |
| Daubert J, 1b | 8 | 1 | 1 | 0 |
| Cutshaw G, 2b | 8 | 1 | 3 | 0 |
| Wheat Z, lf | 7 | 0 | 2 | 1 |
| Stengel C, rf | 6 | 0 | 1 | 0 |
| McCarty L, c | 4 | 0 | 1 | 0 |
| Miller O, c | 3 | 0 | 1 | 1 |
| Getz G, 3b | 6 | 0 | 0 | 0 |
| Pfeffer J, p | 7 | 0 | 0 | 0 |
|  | 65 | 3 | 12 | 3 |

| Chicago | AB | R | H | I |
|---|---|---|---|---|
| Good W, rf | 9 | 1 | 1 | 0 |
| Fisher B, ss | 8 | 1 | 3 | 0 |
| Schulte W, lf | 8 | 1 | 2 | 1 |
| McLarry P, 2b | 7 | 0 | 0 | 0 |
| Saier V, 1b | 6 | 1 | 1 | 1 |
| Williams C, cf | 9 | 0 | 2 | 1 |
| Bresnahan R, c | 8 | 0 | 1 | 0 |
| Phelan A, 3b | 5 | 0 | 2 | 0 |
| Humphries B, p | 0 | 0 | 0 | 0 |
| Zabel Z, p | 7 | 0 | 1 | 0 |
|  | 67 | 4 | 13 | 3 |

| Brooklyn | IP | H | R | ER | BB | SO |
|---|---|---|---|---|---|---|
| Pfeffer (L) | 18.2 | 13 | 4 | 2 | 8 | 6 |

| Chicago | IP | H | R | ER | BB | SO |
|---|---|---|---|---|---|---|
| Humphries | 0.2 | 2 | 1 | 1 | 0 | 0 |
| Zabel (W) | 18.1 | 10 | 2 | 0 | 1 | 6 |
|  | 19.0 | 12 | 3 | 1 | 1 | 6 |

| Brooklyn | 100 | 000 | 010 | 000 | 001 | 000 | 0 — 3 |
|---|---|---|---|---|---|---|---|
| Chicago | 200 | 000 | 000 | 000 | 001 | 000 | 1 — 4 |

OB: Brooklyn 8, Chicago 18; ER: Myers, Cutshaw, Stengel 2, McCarty, Fisher, McLarry, Phelan; DP: Brooklyn 1; 2B: Phelan, Bresnahan, Schulte, Myers, O'Mara; HR: Saier; SB: Williams, Getz; CS: Cutshaw 2; SH: Fisher, Zabel, Schulte, Getz, Wheat; TI: 3:30; AT: Unknown; UM: Rigler, Hart

although "saves" would not be charted for many decades, retrofitting statisticians found scant few during this time period. From 1901–1914: only two teams amassed more than 20 saves; 167 team seasons had less than 10; and 7 team seasons had zero.

George Washington "Zip" Zabel was one of those youngsters trying to find his way into a rotation. He hadn't had much luck during his first two big league seasons, starting just 8 of the 30 games in which he appeared. And he would have no further opportunities after this season, his last in the major leagues. But on this day the 24-year-old right-hander gained immortality by tossing 18⅓ innings in relief, the longest in major league history, while leading the Chicago Cubs to victory over the Brooklyn Robins.

A torn fingernail by starter Bert Humphries opened the door for Zabel as he took the mound in the first with two outs and two on. Without warming up he quickly extinguished the rally by helping thwart a double-steal attempt by the Robins.

From that point Zabel was masterful, employing a sweeping curve and active fastball to allow only nine hits and one intentional walk over the next 18 innings. Only twice, in the fifth and 15th, were the Robins able to manage two hits in the same frame. And from the eighth through the 14th, no Robin hit safely. Some porous fielding enabled Brooklyn to dent the plate twice against Zabel, but both runs were unearned. The Cubs, however, did provide some solid fielding support, particularly in the 16th. Then, with Hy Myers on first and one away, George Cutshaw drove a liner to deep center field. Chicago's Cy Williams raced with his back to the infield, lunged, and made a sensational one-handed catch, turning a somersault in the process.

In the 15th, each team scored. Brooklyn benefited from an error by third baseman Art Phelan, but Chicago tied it in the home half on a home run by Vic Saier.

The game was finally decided on an error in the bottom of the 19th. Bobby Fisher led off with a single. Wildfire Schulte then drove a deep fly to right that forced Casey Stengel back to the fence. Fisher tagged and went to second. Polly McLarry walked, but Saier flied out to center for the second out. Cy Williams then sent a screaming grounder toward right on which Cutshaw made a nice pick-up. The inning seemed over, but the second baseman slipped and threw high over first. Before the ball could be retrieved, Fisher raced home with the game winner.

# *Gowdy's Bat Punctuates a Miracle Season* 83

### PHILADELPHIA (AL) at BOSTON (NL)
### Monday, October 12, 1914, Fenway Park
### Braves 5, Athletics 4

The 1914 World Series was a tale of David and Goliath. For the heavily favored Philadelphia Athletics, this was their fourth appearance in five years. The Boston Braves, meanwhile, not only had never participated in the Fall Classic but as late as July 18 occupied the basement of the National League. But the Miracle Braves caught fire, advanced to second place on August 12 and first reached the summit on September 2. This band of cast-offs not only won 34 of their final 44 games, but also finished 10 and one-half games in front.

On the strength of great pitching, the Braves sustained their momentum in Philadelphia by taking the first two games of the Series. Connie Mack's juggernaut, which had led the major leagues in batting and runs scored, could generate only seven hits and one run in the two games. Still, as the scene of conflict switched to Boston, the public as well as the oddsmakers anticipated the awakening of the slumbering giant.

The Braves had played their home games in a decaying 19th-century arena known as South End Grounds, but for the World Series they utilized the nearby, newly constructed Fenway Park. Monday, Columbus Day — or "Discovery Day," as it was termed — was a holiday enticing more than 35,000 fans to the park. That figure nearly equaled the two-game total in Philadelphia, and temporary stands were erected in left field to seat the lively crowd. In pre-game ceremonies the avid band of Boston's Royal Rooters presented manager George Stallings with a golden baseball, and sparkplug second baseman Johnny Evers received a new automobile for being the "most valuable and best all-around player in the league." Evers immediately gave a few of his teammates a ride around the ballpark.

Starters for the third game were 21-year-old Leslie "Bullet Joe" Bush for Philadelphia and George "Lefty" Tyler for the home club.

The first batter in the game, Eddie Murphy, doubled and was sacrificed to third and then home, giving the visitors a quick 1–0 lead.

The Braves tied it in the second when, after the first two batters were retired, Rabbit Maranville walked and stole second. Catcher Hank Gowdy, batting star of Game One, then hit a fly ball into the temporary seats in left field for a ground rule RBI double.

In the fourth, Philadelphia's first two batters made outs before Stuffy McInnis also lifted one into the left field bleachers for a double. Left fielder Joe Connolly disappeared into the seats trying to make the catch, but to no avail. Jimmy Walsh then singled home McInnis to give the Athletics a 2–1 margin.

The feisty Braves struck back in the home half of the inning as Butch Schmidt singled, moved up on a ground-out, and scored on Maranville's single. Maranville then stole second, moved to third on an error, but was caught stealing home.

With the score tied at two, both pitchers strengthened. Bush allowed just two hits from the fifth through the ninth, while Tyler was touched for three. Several spectacular fielding plays also helped to preserve the tie through regulation. In the eighth, Schmidt ignited the home crowd when he made an acrobatic stop of Bush's hard drive down the first-base line and tossed to Tyler for the out. The drive would have gone for at least two bases and perhaps three. In the bottom of the ninth, McInnis saved Frank Baker's wide-bouncing throw to first with a beautiful outstretched catch.

Philadelphia crafted their third lead of the game in the 10th. With runners at first and second and one away, Rube Oldring sent a sharp drive toward second that was ticketed for a hit. But Tyler lunged for the smash and deflected it to Evers, who nipped Oldring by an eyelash. Eddie Collins was passed intentionally, loading the bases for Frank Baker. The third baseman was one-for-four with two strikeouts and had grounded into a double play. This time he grounded between first and second. Evers raced back to the outfield grass and knocked it down, but then inexplicably held it while two runs scored. Now, leading 4–2, it appeared the Athletics were back in the Series.

Hank Gowdy led off for Boston in the bottom of the 10th with a first-pitch home run to right-center field. The clout rekindled hope and ovation from his teammates and the Royal Rooters. After a strikeout, Herbie Moran walked and Evers singled him to third. Joe Connolly then flied out to center, but deep enough to score Moran with the tying run. For the third time the Braves had come back to tie, and the fans slipped into a frenzy.

| Philadelphia | AB | R | H | I |
|---|---|---|---|---|
| Murphy E, rf | 5 | 2 | 2 | 0 |
| Oldring R, lf | 5 | 0 | 0 | 0 |
| Collins E, 2b | 4 | 0 | 1 | 1 |
| Baker F, 3b | 5 | 0 | 2 | 2 |
| McInnis S, 1b | 5 | 1 | 1 | 0 |
| Walsh J, cf | 4 | 0 | 1 | 1 |
| Barry J, ss | 5 | 0 | 0 | 0 |
| Schang W, c | 4 | 1 | 1 | 0 |
| Bush J, p | 5 | 0 | 0 | 0 |
| | 42 | 4 | 8 | 4 |

| Boston | AB | R | H | I |
|---|---|---|---|---|
| Moran H, rf | 4 | 1 | 0 | 0 |
| Evers J, 2b | 5 | 0 | 3 | 0 |
| Connolly J, lf | 4 | 0 | 0 | 1 |
| Whitted P, cf | 5 | 0 | 0 | 0 |
| Schmidt B, 1b | 5 | 1 | 1 | 0 |
| Deal C, 3b | 5 | 0 | 1 | 0 |
| Maranville R, ss | 4 | 1 | 1 | 1 |
| Gowdy H, c | 4 | 1 | 3 | 2 |
| Mann L, pr | 0 | 1 | 0 | 0 |
| Tyler L, p | 3 | 0 | 0 | 0 |
| Devore J, ph | 1 | 0 | 0 | 0 |
| James B, p | 0 | 0 | 0 | 0 |
| Gilbert L, ph | 0 | 0 | 0 | 0 |
| | 40 | 5 | 9 | 4 |

| Philadelphia | IP | H | R | ER | BB | SO |
|---|---|---|---|---|---|---|
| Bush (L) | 11.0 | 9 | 5 | 4 | 4 | 4 |

| Boston | IP | H | R | ER | BB | SO |
|---|---|---|---|---|---|---|
| Tyler | 10.0 | 8 | 4 | 4 | 3 | 4 |
| James (W) | 2.0 | 0 | 0 | 0 | 3 | 1 |
| | 12.0 | 10 | 4 | 4 | 6 | 5 |

| | | | | |
|---|---|---|---|---|
| Philadelphia | 100 | 100 | 000 | 200 — 4 |
| Boston | 010 | 100 | 000 | 201 — 5 |

OB: Philadelphia 10, Boston 8; ER: Connolly, Schang, Bush; DP: Boston 1; 2B: Murphy 2, Gowdy 2, McInnis, Deal, Baker; HR: Gowdy; SB: Collins, Evers, Maranville 2; CS: Maranville; PK: Collins; SH: Oldring, Moran; SF: Collins, Connolly; TI: 3:06; AT: 35,520; UM: HP Klem, 1B Dinneen, 2B Byron, 3B Hildebrand

Bill James replaced Tyler, who was lifted for a pinch-hitter during the dramatic 10th. The big right-hander, 26–7 on the regular season, shut out the Athletics just two days earlier while winning Game Two. Now, despite three walks, he tossed a hitless 11th and 12th.

Between the top and bottom halves of the 12th, umpires Bill Klem and Bill Dinneen discussed the wisdom of continuing the game amid the growing darkness. It was then past 5:00 P.M., so it was likely this game would be called a tie after the Braves batted.

Bush threw 172 pitches through the first 11 frames but returned to the mound for the 12th. Gowdy led off with another fly ball into the temporary seats in left for his second double. Realizing play would not continue into another inning, Stallings commissioned Les Mann to run for his catcher and Larry Gilbert to pinch-hit for James. After Mack ordered Gilbert intentionally passed, Moran bunted toward third to advance the runners. Bush thought he could get the lead runner at third but threw wildly past Baker, enabling the winning run to score.

The loss broke the spirit of the Athletics. They lost again the following day, becoming the first team in the century to be swept in World Series play. Goliath had fallen decisively.

# 84 *Seaver Fans 10 Straight*

## SAN DIEGO (NL) at NEW YORK (NL)
### Wednesday, April 22, 1970, Shea Stadium
### Mets 2, Padres 1

Just before this game, the New York Mets' Tom Seaver accepted the Cy Young Award as the outstanding pitcher of the National League for 1969. With a 25–7 record and a 2.21 ERA, he won his last 10 decisions and had added two more already in 1970. The 25-year-old right-hander continued his streak this day while striking out 19 San Diego Padres, including the last 10 consecutively. His 19 strikeouts tied the major league mark set a season earlier by Steve Carlton; but the 10 straight put Seaver in a class by himself.

The masterpiece consisted of 136 pitches: 81 fastballs, 34 sliders, 19 curves, and two change-ups. All the San Diego baserunners came in the first four frames, although the tight score kept the outcome undecided until the final out. Al Ferrara touched Seaver for a solo home run, and the only run, in the second. Bob Barton walked in the third, while Ferrara walked and Dave Campbell

| San Diego | AB | R | H | I |
|---|---|---|---|---|
| Arcia J, ss | 3 | 0 | 0 | 0 |
| Murrell I, ph | 1 | 0 | 0 | 0 |
| Roberts D, p | 0 | 0 | 0 | 0 |
| Kelly V, 3b | 4 | 0 | 0 | 0 |
| Gaston C, cf | 4 | 0 | 0 | 0 |
| Ferrara A, lf | 3 | 1 | 1 | 1 |
| Colbert N, 1b | 3 | 0 | 0 | 0 |
| Campbell D, 2b | 3 | 0 | 1 | 0 |
| Morales J, rf | 3 | 0 | 0 | 0 |
| Barton B, c | 2 | 0 | 0 | 0 |
| Corkins M, p | 2 | 0 | 0 | 0 |
| Webster R, ph | 1 | 0 | 0 | 0 |
| Slocum R, ss | 0 | 0 | 0 | 0 |
|  | 29 | 1 | 2 | 1 |

| New York | AB | R | H | I |
|---|---|---|---|---|
| Agee T, cf | 3 | 1 | 1 | 0 |
| Harrelson B, ss | 3 | 1 | 2 | 1 |
| Boswell K, 2b | 4 | 0 | 1 | 1 |
| Jones C, lf | 4 | 0 | 0 | 0 |
| Shamsky A, rf | 2 | 0 | 0 | 0 |
| Swoboda R, ph-rf | 1 | 0 | 0 | 0 |
| Foy J, 3b | 2 | 0 | 0 | 0 |
| Kranepool E, 1b | 2 | 0 | 0 | 0 |
| Grote J, c | 3 | 0 | 0 | 0 |
| Seaver T, p | 3 | 0 | 0 | 0 |
|  | 27 | 2 | 4 | 2 |

| San Diego | IP | H | R | ER | BB | SO |
|---|---|---|---|---|---|---|
| Corkins (L) | 7.0 | 4 | 2 | 2 | 5 | 5 |
| Roberts | 1.0 | 0 | 0 | 0 | 0 | 2 |
|  | 8.0 | 4 | 2 | 2 | 5 | 7 |

| New York | IP | H | R | ER | BB | SO |
|---|---|---|---|---|---|---|
| Seaver (W) | 9.0 | 2 | 1 | 1 | 2 | 19 |

```
San Diego   010   000   000 — 1
New York    101   000   00x — 2
```

OB: San Diego 3, New York 6; 2B: Boswell; 3B: Harrelson; HR: Ferrara; SB: Agee; CS: Harrelson; TI: 2:14; AT: 14,197; UM: Wendelstedt, Venzon, Secory, Engel

ingled in the fourth. But Seaver strengthened as the game progressed, the cool weather helping in that regard.

The Cy Young Award–winner struck out each Padres batter at least once, except Jose Arcia, who ironically was lifted for a pinch-hitter in the eighth. Both San Diego pinch-hitters were among the eight who went down swinging, along with 11 others who were caught looking.

Despite Seaver's dominance, his teammates' paltry offensive support kept the contest suspenseful. The Mets tallied in the opening round when shortstop Arcia made a leaping stab of Bud Harrelson's liner, but it dropped safely for a ingle. Ken Boswell then doubled home Harrelson. In the third, Tommie Agee bounced a single off pitcher Mike Corkins' hand before Harrelson tripled him home.

Mindful of Carlton's 19-strikeout losing performance and holding just a one-run lead, Seaver never felt at ease. He worried about making a mistake right up to the last batter, Ferrara, who had homered earlier. But when he got two strikes on the outfielder in the ninth, Seaver let loose with his overpowering fastball, collecting his record strikeout along with the victory.

# *Home Run Barrage Keeps Outcome in Suspense* 85

PITTSBURGH (NL) at CINCINNATI (NL)
Friday, August 12, 1966, Crosely Field
Pirates 14, Reds 11

Forget the fact that witnesses saw one of the greatest long-ball demonstrations of the century — a then–record-tying 11 home runs. What the final score didn't show was that the visiting Pittsburgh Pirates and their hosts, the Cincinnati Reds, engaged in one of the most bewildering seesaw battles ever staged on a major league diamond. In addition to four ties, the Pirates led six different times, while the Reds led three times. After the game was tied for the second time in the ninth inning, each team scored once more in the 10th and twice in the 11th to push fans to the brink of emotional exhaustion.

Art Shamsky, who didn't step to the plate for the first time until the eighth, led the home run barrage with blasts off of three different Pirate hurlers. His first round-tripper gave the Reds their second lead in that eighth inning. His second homer tied the game in the tenth, and his third tied it again in the 11th.

| Pittsburgh | AB | R | H | I |
|---|---|---|---|---|
| Alou M, cf | 5 | 4 | 3 | 0 |
| Bailey B, 3b | 7 | 3 | 3 | 5 |
| Clemente R, rf | 5 | 2 | 1 | 1 |
| Stargell W, lf | 4 | 1 | 1 | 1 |
| Mota M, lf | 2 | 0 | 1 | 2 |
| Pagan J, ss | 7 | 0 | 0 | 0 |
| Clendenon D, 1b | 5 | 0 | 0 | 0 |
| Mazeroski B, 2b | 5 | 1 | 2 | 0 |
| Gonder J, c | 2 | 1 | 1 | 2 |
| May J, c | 1 | 0 | 0 | 0 |
| Lynch J, ph | 1 | 1 | 1 | 1 |
| Face E, p | 1 | 0 | 0 | 0 |
| O'Dell B, p | 0 | 0 | 0 | 0 |
| Mikkelsen P, p | 0 | 0 | 0 | 0 |
| Michael G, ph | 1 | 0 | 0 | 0 |
| Sisk T, p | 1 | 0 | 0 | 0 |
| Veale B, p | 2 | 0 | 0 | 0 |
| Rodgers A, ph | 1 | 0 | 0 | 0 |
| McBean A, p | 0 | 0 | 0 | 0 |
| Pagliaroni J, c | 1 | 1 | 0 | 0 |
| | 51 | 14 | 13 | 12 |

| Cincinnati | AB | R | H | I |
|---|---|---|---|---|
| Harper T, rf | 6 | 1 | 2 | 1 |
| Pinson V, cf | 7 | 0 | 3 | 0 |
| Rose P, 2b | 4 | 2 | 2 | 2 |
| Johnson D, lf | 7 | 1 | 1 | 2 |
| Perez T, 1b | 3 | 0 | 0 | 0 |
| Coleman G, 1b | 1 | 0 | 0 | 0 |
| Nottebart D, p | 1 | 0 | 0 | 0 |
| Queen M, ph | 1 | 0 | 0 | 0 |
| McCool B, p | 0 | 0 | 0 | 0 |
| Baldshun J, p | 0 | 0 | 0 | 0 |
| Ruiz C, ph | 1 | 0 | 1 | 0 |
| Helms T, 3b | 7 | 1 | 1 | 0 |
| Cardenas L, ss | 6 | 1 | 2 | 0 |
| Coker J, c | 2 | 0 | 1 | 0 |
| Simpson D, pr | 0 | 1 | 0 | 0 |
| Edwards J, c | 1 | 1 | 0 | 0 |
| Ellis S, p | 2 | 0 | 0 | 0 |
| Pavletich D, c | 0 | 0 | 0 | 1 |
| Nuxhall J, p | 0 | 0 | 0 | 0 |
| Shamsky A, lf | 3 | 3 | 3 | 5 |
| | 52 | 11 | 16 | 11 |

| Pittsburgh | IP | H | R | ER | BB | SO |
|---|---|---|---|---|---|---|
| Veale | 6.0 | 8 | 6 | 6 | 3 | 4 |
| McBean | 2.0 | 4 | 2 | 2 | 1 | 1 |
| Face | 2.2 | 2 | 2 | 2 | 3 | 5 |
| O'Dell | 0.0 | 1 | 1 | 1 | 0 | 0 |
| Mikkelsen | 0.1 | 0 | 0 | 0 | 0 | 1 |
| Sisk (W) | 2.0 | 1 | 0 | 0 | 0 | 1 |
| | 13.0 | 16 | 11 | 11 | 7 | 12 |

| Cincinnati | IP | H | R | ER | BB | SO |
|---|---|---|---|---|---|---|
| Ellis | 6.0 | 5 | 5 | 5 | 2 | 7 |
| Nuxhall | 1.1 | 1 | 2 | 2 | 0 | 0 |
| Nottebart | 2.2 | 3 | 2 | 2 | 1 | 1 |
| McCool (L) | 2.0 | 4 | 5 | 4 | 6 | 2 |
| Baldshun | 1.0 | 0 | 0 | 0 | 1 | 1 |
| | 13.0 | 13 | 14 | 13 | 10 | 11 |

```
Pittsburgh   004   001   201   120   3 — 14
Cincinnati   200   022   020   120   0 — 11
```

OB: Pittsburgh 9, Cincinnati 11; ER: Coker, Alou, Helms; DP: Pittsburgh 1, Cincinnati 2;
2B: Pinson, Bailey; HR: Johnson, Gonder, Clemente, Rose, Bailey 2, Shamsky 3, Lynch,
Stargell; SB: Alou ; SH: Coker ; SF: Pavletitch; HP: by Nuxhall (Alou); WP: Baldshun; PB:
Gonder; TI: 4:22; AT: 25,477; UM: Unknown

Other temporary heroes included Pittsburgh's Jerry Lynch, who hit his
18th career pinch-hit homer to tie it in the ninth, and Willie Stargell, who gave
the visitors one of their leads with a homer in the tenth.

Pittsburgh finally tallied three unanswered runs in the 13th, ironically
without an extra-base hit. Two singles, a walk, an error, and a wild pitch sent
25,477 fans home to rest for the weekend.

# Erskine, Snider, and Defense Win in 11   86

BROOKLYN (NL) at NEW YORK (AL)
Sunday, October 5, 1952, Yankee Stadium
Dodgers 6, Yankees 5

In three recent World Series confrontations, 1941, 1947, and 1949, the Yankees dominated the Dodgers. Although Brooklyn took New York to a seventh game in 1947, only to lose, they won just one game in each of the other encounters. This year, with the Series tied at two games each, the Dodgers forged their most compelling opportunity for a championship. It came with a thrilling, come-from-behind victory in the 11th inning of Game Five.

A warm and cloudless day encouraged many Yankee Stadium bleacherites to watch the game in shirtsleeves. They came to see New York's side-winding Ewell Blackwell, a recent National League cast-off, take the mound against perhaps Brooklyn's best starter, Carl Erskine. Arm miseries put Blackwell at the end of his career, having accumulated a horrific 3–12 mark for Cincinnati before the Yankees got him in a late August trade. Now, manager Casey Stengel was hoping for some of the magic that carried Ewell to 22 wins in 1947.

In the bottom of the first, the crowd witnessed the first of many sensational defensive plays. Phil Rizzuto sent a liner to left that looked to be a triple. But George Shuba, not known for his defensive prowess, made a wonderful running catch.

Opening the visitors' second inning, Jackie Robinson walked before Shuba knocked a sharp grounder toward second. It looked like a sure double play ball but took a sudden high bounce into right field for a single. Next, with the Yankees rushing in for an expected sacrifice bunt, Robinson stole third. After Roy Campanella fanned, Andy Pafko singled home Robinson. Gil Hodges then walked to load the bases, but Blackwell got a force-out at home and another at second to escape further damage.

Again there was larceny in the air in the bottom of the second. With a Yankee on first, Gene Woodling lifted a fly ball that was ticketed for the right-field bleacher fans, but Pafko leaped high above the short wall to steal two runs from the home team.

Brooklyn launched another attack on Blackwell in the fifth. A walk, an error, and a sacrifice put Dodgers at second and third before Pee Wee Reese's long fly made it 2–0. Brooklyn fans were well represented among the crowd, and they went wild when the next batter, Duke Snider, deposited a pitch into the right-field seats, giving the visitors a 4–0 margin.

| Brooklyn | AB | R | H | I |
|---|---|---|---|---|
| Cox B, 3b | 5 | 2 | 3 | 0 |
| Reese P, ss | 5 | 0 | 1 | 1 |
| Snider D, cf | 5 | 1 | 3 | 4 |
| Robinson J, 2b | 2 | 1 | 0 | 0 |
| Shuba G, lf | 2 | 0 | 1 | 0 |
| Furillo C, rf | 4 | 0 | 1 | 0 |
| Campanella R, c | 5 | 0 | 0 | 0 |
| Pafko A, rf-lf | 4 | 0 | 1 | 1 |
| Holmes T, lf | 1 | 0 | 0 | 0 |
| Hodges G, 1b | 3 | 1 | 0 | 0 |
| Erskine C, p | 4 | 1 | 0 | 0 |
| | 40 | 6 | 10 | 6 |

| New York | AB | R | H | |
|---|---|---|---|---|
| McDougald G, 3b | 4 | 1 | 0 | |
| Rizzuto P, ss | 5 | 1 | 1 | |
| Mantle M, cf | 5 | 0 | 1 | |
| Mize J, 1b | 5 | 1 | 1 | |
| Berra Y, c | 4 | 0 | 0 | |
| Woodling G, lf | 4 | 0 | 0 | |
| Bauer H, rf | 3 | 1 | 0 | |
| Martin B, 2b | 4 | 1 | 1 | |
| Blackwell E, p | 1 | 0 | 0 | |
| Noren I, ph | 1 | 0 | 1 | |
| Sain J, p | 2 | 0 | 0 | |
| | 38 | 5 | 5 | |

| Brooklyn | IP | H | R | ER | BB | SO |
|---|---|---|---|---|---|---|
| Erskine (W) | 11.0 | 5 | 5 | 5 | 3 | 6 |

| New York | IP | H | R | ER | BB | SC |
|---|---|---|---|---|---|---|
| Blackwell | 5.0 | 4 | 4 | 4 | 3 | |
| Sain (L) | 6.0 | 6 | 2 | 2 | 3 | |
| | 11.0 | 10 | 6 | 6 | 6 | |

```
Brooklyn   010  030  100  01 — 6
New York   000  050  000  00 — 5
```

OB: Brooklyn 11, New York 3; ER: Rizzuto; DP: New York 2; 2B: Furillo, Snider; HR: Snider Mize; SB: Robinson; SH: Erskine, Cox, Reese; HP: by Sain (Snider); TI: 3:00; AT: 70,536 UM: HP Pinelli, 1B Passarella, 2B Goetz, 3B McKinley, LF Boggess, RF Honochick

Erskine had allowed but one hit through the first four innings, but in the fifth the Yankees erupted. A walk, three singles and a majestic three-run home run by veteran Johnny Mize delighted the hometown fans. The blow marked the 39-year-old's third homer in three days. The Yankees had captured the lead 5–4, and it looked like the end of the line for Erskine. Dodger manager Chuck Dressen had other notions, however, and stuck with his right-hander.

In the seventh, with Johnny Sain on the hill for New York, Brooklyn tied it. An infield hit, a sacrifice, and a single by Snider made it 5–5.

Erskine and Sain then gained control of the contest, and there were few new scoring opportunities. The Dodgers got two men on with two out in the ninth, but Sain retired Carl Furillo on a ground-out.

The 10th inning was packed with fielding gems. In the top half, New York's Gene Woodling made a diving, rolling catch on a Gil Hodges fly ball. In the home half Robinson dashed behind second to gather Sain's grounder and nip him at first. It was such a close play that the Yankees argued vehemently, as coach Bil Dickey slammed his cap to the ground and jumped on it. Later, Billy Cox made a marvelous stop of Rizzuto's hot grounder for the third out.

Brooklyn broke the tie in the top of the 11th. After Cox and Reese singled Snider drove in his fourth run of the game with a double, sending Dodger fans into ecstasy once again.

The game was then in the hands of Erskine, who had not allowed New York a hit since their five-run fifth. True to form, he retired his 17th, 18th and 19th Yankees in order, although it took another great catch to do so. With one out Mize forced Furillo back to the barrier in right to make another leaping catch and stave off a game-tying home run. Erskine then fanned Berra, sending the Dodgers home needing to win just one of two games for the championship.

# Hartnett's Homer Beats the Darkness 87

## PITTSBURGH (NL) at CHICAGO (NL)
### Wednesday, September 28, 1938, Wrigley Field
### Cubs 6, Pirates 5

The visiting Pittsburgh Pirates had occupied first place in the National League since July 12 but, with the season coming to a close, were faltering. Entering a three-game series with the second-place Chicago Cubs, the Pittsburgh lead had been reduced to one and one-half games. Meanwhile, the Cubs had won seven straight, and 17 of 20. The first game of the set went to Chicago, giving them eight straight and narrowing the gap to a half-game. This second match-up, on a dark and dreary day, would be one of the most sensational ever played in Wrigley Field.

A hit and two errors got Chicago on the board in the second inning, and Cubs right-hander Clay Bryant had little trouble until the sixth. Then, a solo homer by Johnny Rizzo, followed by two walks and a pair of singles, gave the Pirates a 3–1 advantage.

The Cubs came roaring back to tie the score in the home half of the frame. A pair of doubles and a bunt single knotted it at 3–3.

In the eighth a walk and three singles pushed across two more for Pittsburgh, giving them a 5–3 lead. They nearly had another, but Heinie Manush was nailed at the plate on a ground-out.

Again the Cubs retaliated in the home half. A single, walk, and a double by pinch-hitter Tony Lazzeri netted the first run. When Stan Hack walked, it loaded the bases. Billy Herman then singled home the tying run, but the lead run was cut down at the plate on a great throw by Paul Waner. Further damage was averted when reliever Mace Brown induced a double play.

The umpires conferred regarding the encroaching darkness and whether to allow play to continue, deciding to go another round. For the Cubs it was a monumental decision. They needed to get this game in to avoid a doubleheader the next day, which would strain their already overtaxed pitching staff.

| Pittsburgh | AB | R | H | I |
|---|---|---|---|---|
| Waner L, cf | 4 | 0 | 2 | 0 |
| Waner P, rf | 5 | 0 | 2 | 0 |
| Rizzo J, lf | 4 | 1 | 1 | 1 |
| Vaughan A, ss | 2 | 2 | 1 | 0 |
| Suhr G, 1b | 3 | 2 | 1 | 0 |
| Young P, 2b | 2 | 0 | 0 | 0 |
| Manush H, ph | 1 | 0 | 1 | 1 |
| Thevenow T, 2b | 0 | 0 | 0 | 0 |
| Handley L, 3b | 4 | 0 | 2 | 3 |
| Todd A, c | 4 | 0 | 0 | 0 |
| Klinger B, p | 4 | 0 | 0 | 0 |
| Swift B, p | 0 | 0 | 0 | 0 |
| Brown M, p | 0 | 0 | 0 | 0 |
|  | 33 | 5 | 10 | 5 |

| Chicago | AB | R | H | I |
|---|---|---|---|---|
| Hack S, 3b | 3 | 0 | 0 | 1 |
| Herman B, 2b | 5 | 0 | 3 | 1 |
| Demaree F, lf | 5 | 0 | 0 | 0 |
| Cavarretta P, rf | 5 | 0 | 0 | 0 |
| Reynolds C, cf | 5 | 0 | 1 | 0 |
| Hartnett G, c | 4 | 2 | 2 | 1 |
| Collins R, 1b | 4 | 3 | 3 | 1 |
| Jurges B, ss | 3 | 1 | 1 | 0 |
| Bryant C, p | 2 | 0 | 1 | 0 |
| Russell J, p | 0 | 0 | 0 | 0 |
| O'Dea K, ph | 1 | 0 | 0 | 0 |
| Page V, p | 0 | 0 | 0 | 0 |
| French L, p | 0 | 0 | 0 | 0 |
| Lee B, p | 0 | 0 | 0 | 0 |
| Lazzeri T, ph | 1 | 0 | 1 | 1 |
| Marty J, pr | 0 | 0 | 0 | 0 |
| Root C, p | 0 | 0 | 0 | 0 |
|  | 38 | 6 | 12 | 5 |

| Pittsburgh | IP | H | R | ER | BB | SO |
|---|---|---|---|---|---|---|
| Klinger | 7.0 | 8 | 5 | 4 | 2 | 6 |
| Swift | 0.1 | 3 | 0 | 0 | 2 | 0 |
| Brown (L) | 1.1 | 1 | 1 | 1 | 0 | 0 |
|  | 8.2 | 12 | 6 | 5 | 4 | 6 |

| Chicago | IP | H | R | ER | BB | SO |
|---|---|---|---|---|---|---|
| Bryant | 5.2 | 4 | 3 | 3 | 5 | 1 |
| Russell | 0.1 | 0 | 0 | 0 | 0 | 0 |
| Page | 1.0 | 3 | 2 | 2 | 1 | 1 |
| French | 0.0 | 1 | 0 | 0 | 0 | 0 |
| Lee | 1.0 | 1 | 0 | 0 | 0 | 0 |
| Root (W) | 1.0 | 1 | 0 | 0 | 0 | 0 |
|  | 9.0 | 10 | 5 | 5 | 6 | 2 |

| Pittsburgh | 000 | 003 | 020 — 5 |
|---|---|---|---|
| Chicago | 010 | 002 | 021 — 6 |

OB: Pittsburgh 7, Chicago 10; ER: P. Waner, Vaughan, Handley, Todd; DP: Pittsburgh 1, Chicago 3; 2B: L. Waner, Hartnett, Collins, Lazzeri; HR: Rizzo, Hartnett; WP: Lee; PB: Todd; TI: 2:37; AT: 34,465; UM: Barr, Stark, Goetz, Campbell

In the top of the ninth the Pirates could muster a single but no scoring threat. The first two Cubs also went down easily before player-manager Gabby Hartnett appeared at the plate. Brown got ahead in the count 0–2 when Hartnett slashed the third pitch into the darkness of the left-field bleachers. Such pandemonium erupted that Hartnett had to fight his way through a swirling, hysterical mob that poured onto the field. Only with assistance from his players and the ushers was he able to find his way to the dugout. The Cubs had claimed first place and subsequently held on to advance to the World Series.

Gabby Hartnett (National Baseball Hall of Fame Library, Cooperstown, New York).

# 88 *Williams Frustrates Boudreau's Shift*

## CLEVELAND (AL) at BOSTON (AL)
### Sunday, July 14, 1946, Fenway Park
### Red Sox 11, Indians 10

In what proved to be one of the century's most memorable dramas, the Boston Red Sox hosted the Cleveland Indians for a Sunday doubleheader in Fenway Park. The occasion afforded two future Hall of Famers, Ted Williams and Lou Boudreau, center stage for displaying their talents before a near capacity crowd of 31,984.

Ted Williams was only five days removed from a prolific All-Star Game in which he led his team to a 12–0 thrashing of the National League. In the process he had collected a walk, two singles, and two home runs while scoring four times and driving home five of the American League runs.

The extraordinary became expected of Williams, and the first game of this doubleheader provided more of the same. When the dead-pull hitter stepped to the plate for the first time, he faced an expected unorthodox Cleveland defense. For some time, the Indians had been stationing their first baseman, second baseman, and shortstop all between first and second base whenever Williams batted. Despite the inviting open space on the left side of the infield, Ted had refused to hit or bunt in that direction. The strategy worked as Williams sent a line drive toward what would have been the hole between first and second. But with three infielders jammed between the sacks, second baseman Jack Conway had little trouble snaring the scorcher. Despite the shift, this would be the only time Williams was retired in this game.

By the time Ted batted again in the third, the Indians had forged a 5–0 lead, but the Sox had loaded the bases. Williams rendered the shift moot as he plastered Steve Gromek's second pitch over the Cleveland bullpen, bringing his team to within a run. His teammates added another run later in the frame to tie it at five.

In the fourth, Boston notched a go-ahead run and led 6–5, but the Tribe erupted for three in the top of the fifth to reclaim the lead at 8–6.

Ted led off the home fifth and deposited Don Black's first pitch beyond the Boston bullpen, again pulling his team to within one run.

Cleveland tallied single runs in the sixth and seventh, inflating their lead to 10–7. In the bottom of the seventh Williams singled and scored his third run, cutting the Indians' lead to 10–8.

That's how it stood when, in the eighth, Ted stepped to the plate with two

## FIRST GAME

| Cleveland | AB | R | H | I |
|---|---|---|---|---|
| Case G, lf | 6 | 1 | 2 | 1 |
| Conway J, 2b | 6 | 0 | 2 | 0 |
| Seerey P, cf | 3 | 2 | 2 | 0 |
| Edwards H, rf | 6 | 1 | 1 | 1 |
| Boudreau L, ss | 5 | 3 | 5 | 4 |
| Keltner K, 3b | 3 | 1 | 2 | 3 |
| Wasdell J, 1b | 5 | 0 | 1 | 0 |
| Hegan J, c | 5 | 2 | 2 | 0 |
| Gromek S, p | 2 | 0 | 0 | 0 |
| Black D, p | 2 | 0 | 1 | 1 |
| Berry J, p | 0 | 0 | 0 | 0 |
| Mackiewicz F, ph | 1 | 0 | 0 | 0 |
| | 44 | 10 | 18 | 10 |

| Boston | AB | R | H | I |
|---|---|---|---|---|
| Culberson L, rf | 5 | 2 | 3 | 0 |
| Pesky J, ss | 4 | 2 | 0 | 0 |
| DiMaggio D, cf | 5 | 0 | 1 | 0 |
| Williams T, lf | 5 | 4 | 4 | 8 |
| Doerr B, 2b | 5 | 1 | 4 | 0 |
| York R, 1b | 5 | 0 | 1 | 1 |
| Russell R, 3b | 4 | 0 | 0 | 0 |
| Partee R, c | 4 | 2 | 3 | 0 |
| Wagner H, c | 0 | 0 | 0 | 0 |
| Dobson J, p | 0 | 0 | 0 | 0 |
| Dreiserd C, p | 1 | 0 | 0 | 0 |
| Bagby J, p | 1 | 0 | 0 | 0 |
| Lazor J, ph | 1 | 0 | 0 | 0 |
| Hughson T, p | 0 | 0 | 0 | 0 |
| | 40 | 11 | 16 | 9 |

| Cleveland | IP | H | R | ER | BB | SO |
|---|---|---|---|---|---|---|
| Gromek | 2.2 | 6 | 5 | 5 | 1 | 3 |
| Black | 3.1 | 7 | 3 | 2 | 0 | 0 |
| Berry (L) | 2.0 | 3 | 3 | 0 | 0 | 1 |
| | 8.0 | 16 | 11 | 7 | 1 | 4 |

| Boston | IP | H | R | ER | BB | SO |
|---|---|---|---|---|---|---|
| Dobson | 0.2 | 4 | 4 | 4 | 1 | 0 |
| Dreiserd | 4.0 | 7 | 4 | 4 | 1 | 1 |
| Bagby (W) | 3.1 | 5 | 2 | 2 | 3 | 1 |
| Hughson | 1.0 | 2 | 0 | 0 | 0 | 1 |
| | 9.0 | 18 | 10 | 10 | 5 | 3 |

| Cleveland | 401 | 031 | 100 — 10 |
|---|---|---|---|
| Boston | 005 | 110 | 13x — 11 |

OB: Cleveland 12, Boston 7; ER: Boudreau, Wasdell 2; DP: Cleveland 2, Boston 1; 2B: Case, Boudreau 4, Hegan, Black, York, DiMaggio; 3B: Hegan, Conway; HR: Boudreau, Keltner, Williams 3; SB: Pesky; SH: Dreiserd; TI: 2:32; UM: Rommel, Boyer, Grieve

outs and two mates aboard. Joe Berry, the third Cleveland hurler, started Ted with two wide ones and then tried to sneak a curve ball over the plate. Williams pulled it mightily into the right-field seats just inside the foul marker for his third home run of the game. The blow gave Boston an 11–10 lead that endured the final frame.

Williams's three home runs and eight RBI overshadowed a remarkable offensive performance by Cleveland player-manager Lou Boudreau. The shortstop provided his own club with plenty of offense, beginning in the first inning when he clouted a three-run homer to left. In his next four plate appearances he doubled each time, amassing five extra-base hits, four RBI and three runs scored. The five extra-base hits set a modern major-league mark that since has been tied many times. It wasn't enough, however, to offset Williams.

Boudreau's exasperation over trying to stop the Boston superstar led to a revolutionary strategy in the nightcap. As Williams approached the plate in the third inning, there was commotion on the field as well as in the stands. The fans and the Boston players, including Williams, began laughing as Boudreau now moved his third baseman to the right of second base on the edge of the outfield grass. Shortstop Boudreau also played on the outfield fringe midway between first and second. The first baseman was positioned in the outfield grass about six feet from the right-field foul line and about 35 feet behind the bag. The second baseman became an extra right fielder, playing shallow and about 25 feet off the line. Right and center fielders stood on the lip of the right and right-center field warning track. That left only the left fielder to cover all the territory to the left of second base in both the infield and outfield. Williams went one-for-two with two walks in this second game as the Sox swept the doubleheader.

# 89 *Derringer Pitches Reds to the Summit*

### DETROIT (AL) at CINCINNATI (NL)
### Tuesday, October 8, 1940, Crosley Field
### Reds 2, Tigers 1

Only once since the inception of the modern World Series had the Cincinnati Reds been able to call themselves world champions — and tainted ones at that. In 1919 the Queen City club had taken their only Series from the notorious Chicago Black Sox in a victory later proven hollow. Twenty-one years later, despite several key injuries and the tragic death of their back-up catcher, they captured the Senior Circuit pennant by 12 games over Brooklyn. Now the doughty National Leaguers faced an offensive machine in the Detroit Tigers, who had broken the four-year Yankees' stranglehold on the American League flag. Fans, officials, and scribes agreed this would be a battle of Cincinnati pitching versus Detroit slugging.

The two clubs alternated victories through the first six games, reducing the season to one sunny, chilly day in Cincinnati. Into the skirmish strode a pair of veterans, repeat starters from the first game — Detroit's Buck "Bobo" Newsom and Cincinnati's Paul "Duke" Derringer. Newsom won the opener as well as Game Five via a shutout and would pitch this deciding contest on just a single day's rest. In addition, he mourned the sudden death of his father during the Series. Derringer, hammered in Game One, recovered to win the fourth game on October 5. The wily, tenacious right-handers now engaged in a pitcher's duel worthy of a championship.

Detroit mounted the game's first threat and scored an unearned run in the third. Billy Sullivan led off with an infield single and was sacrificed to second. A pop-up registered out number two before Barney McCosky walked. Charlie Gehringer then dribbled a slow roller toward third for another infield single that would have merely loaded the bases. But third baseman Bill Werber tried to make a heroic play by firing to first. His low throw glanced off the mitt of

| Detroit | AB | R | H | I |
|---|---|---|---|---|
| Bartell D, ss | 4 | 0 | 0 | 0 |
| McCosky B, cf | 3 | 0 | 0 | 0 |
| Gehringer C, 2b | 4 | 0 | 2 | 0 |
| Greenberg H, lf | 4 | 0 | 2 | 0 |
| York R, 1b | 4 | 0 | 0 | 0 |
| Campbell B, rf | 3 | 0 | 0 | 0 |
| Higgins M, 3b | 4 | 0 | 1 | 0 |
| Sullivan B, c | 3 | 1 | 1 | 0 |
| Newsom B, p | 2 | 0 | 1 | 0 |
| Averill E, ph | 1 | 0 | 0 | 0 |
| | 32 | 1 | 7 | 0 |

| Cincinnati | AB | R | H | I |
|---|---|---|---|---|
| Werber B, 3b | 4 | 0 | 0 | 0 |
| McCormick M, cf | 4 | 0 | 2 | 0 |
| Goodman I, rf | 4 | 0 | 0 | 0 |
| McCormick F, 1b | 4 | 1 | 1 | 0 |
| Ripple J, lf | 3 | 1 | 1 | 1 |
| Wilson J, c | 2 | 0 | 2 | 0 |
| Joost E, 2b | 2 | 0 | 0 | 0 |
| Lombardi E, ph | 0 | 0 | 0 | 0 |
| Frey L, pr-2b | 0 | 0 | 0 | 0 |
| Myers B, ss | 3 | 0 | 1 | 1 |
| Derringer P, p | 3 | 0 | 0 | 0 |
| | 29 | 2 | 7 | 2 |

| Detroit | IP | H | R | ER | BB | SO |
|---|---|---|---|---|---|---|
| Newsom (L) | 8.0 | 7 | 2 | 2 | 1 | 6 |

| Cincinnati | IP | H | R | ER | BB | SO |
|---|---|---|---|---|---|---|
| Derringer (W) | 9.0 | 7 | 1 | 0 | 3 | 1 |

```
Detroit      001  000  000 — 1
Cincinnati   000  000  20x — 2
```

OB: Detroit 8, Cincinnati 5; ER: Werber; DP: Detroit 1; 2B: Higgins, McCormick, McCormick, Ripple; SB: Wilson; SH: Newsom, Wilson; TI: 1:47; AT: 26,854; UM: HP Ballanfant, 1B Basil, 2B Klem, 3B Ormsby

first baseman Frank McCormick, and as McCormick chased the ball, Sullivan easily dashed home. Derringer then fanned Hank Greenberg to end the inning with Detroit ahead 1–0.

Ill fortune prohibited the Tigers from adding to their lead in the fourth. With two outs, Pinky Higgins doubled and Sullivan was passed intentionally. Newsom swung at the first offering and bounced toward short, where the ball hit baserunner Higgins for the third out.

The Tigers threatened again in the sixth as Greenberg led off with a single. After Rudy York popped out, Bruce Campbell walked. Next Higgins shot a drive through the box that was ticketed for center field and an RBI. But shortstop Billy Myers made a dazzling stop and raced to second for a force-out on Campbell. Still there were runners at the corners, but again Derringer quelled the uprising, retiring Sullivan on a ground-out.

In the seventh, hanging precariously to a 1–0 lead, Newsom appeared to tire. The first two Reds, McCormick and Jimmy Ripple, crashed solid doubles to tie the game. A sacrifice put the lead run on third, and the stands erupted in cheers as Ernie Lombardi, nursing an ankle injury, stepped to the plate as a pinch-hitter. Lombardi had already won the first of his two batting championships and was a Cincinnati favorite. But the cheers quickly turned to boos when Lombardi was passed intentionally. Myers then sent a long fly to center that forced McCosky to the fence and easily scored Ripple, making it 2–1.

Riding his first lead of the game, Derringer strengthened and blanked the Tigers over the final two frames on just 19 pitches. After the last out, teammates and fans mobbed the pitcher as he struggled to reach the dugout. Automobile horns, streetcar gongs, and factory whistles announced the news, and the city carried its championship celebration deep into the night.

# 90 *Red Barrett Wasted No Time*

BOSTON (NL) at CINCINNATI (NL)
Thursday, August 10, 1944, Crosley Field
Braves 2, Red 0

Through the end of the century, pitch counts were not among the official statistics charted by the major leagues. Recent years have incorporated such data in box scores, yet the unofficial nature renders such information susceptible to variation, and contention. During the early decades, few team statisticians, writers, or scorers noted pitch counts for regular season contests, but baseball researchers and historians have exhumed some exceptional low-pitch performances. None known, however, can compare with the pitching masterpiece that transpired on this date.

Charles "Red" Barrett of the Boston Braves was a right-handed hurler toiling in just his second full season. An eccentric personality of average pitching talent, the redhead excelled in building team morale with his constant clowning and joking. His former teammates, the Cincinnati Reds, little appreciated his humor this day, as Barrett delivered only 58 pitches over nine innings for a shutout victory. As the century closed this was believed to be the fewest number of pitches ever thrown in a nine-inning game. And, when the game was completed in only one hour and fifteen minutes, it also established the still-standing mark as the fastest night game in major league annals.

Facing his more publicized opponent, Bucky Walters, Barrett never fell behind in the count to a single batter, surrendered just two singles, and neither walked nor struck out anyone. The only two players to reach first safely were Gee Walker, who singled with two out in the first, and Eddie Miller, who singled leading off the sixth. Miller was the only Red who got as far as second. Barrett induced 13 ground-outs, five fly balls, three pop-ups in fair territory, four foul outs, and two line-drive outs.

The Braves' victory resulted from two tainted runs. Butch Nieman opened the second frame with a sharp grounder that scooted through Woody Williams's legs. Frank Grayson, official scorer this night, charitably accorded a single on the play. Two infield outs moved Butch to third, from whence he scored on a Damon Phillips single. Boston scored its second run when, with one out in the fifth, Phillips doubled over center fielder Gee Walker's head. Whitey Wietelmann then lifted a high fly to deep right field that dropped for a three-base error as Cincinnati's Tony Criscola tripped and fell while ascending the outfield terrace.

Barrett's teammate, Damon Phillips, later remembered him as the fastest-working pitcher he ever played behind. In a letter written to the author, Phillips

| Boston | AB | R | H | I |
|---|---|---|---|---|
| Macon M, lf | 4 | 0 | 0 | 0 |
| Holmes T, cf | 4 | 0 | 2 | 0 |
| Workman C, 3b | 3 | 0 | 0 | 0 |
| Nieman B, rf | 4 | 1 | 1 | 0 |
| Hofferth S, c | 4 | 0 | 0 | 0 |
| Etchison B, 1b | 3 | 0 | 0 | 0 |
| Phillips D, ss | 4 | 1 | 3 | 1 |
| Wietelmann W, 2b | 4 | 0 | 0 | 0 |
| Barrett R, p | 3 | 0 | 0 | 0 |
| | 33 | 2 | 6 | 1 |

| Cincinnati | AB | R | H | I |
|---|---|---|---|---|
| Williams W, 2b | 4 | 0 | 0 | 0 |
| Criscola T, rf | 4 | 0 | 0 | 0 |
| Walker G, cf | 3 | 0 | 1 | 0 |
| McCormick F, 1b | 3 | 0 | 0 | 0 |
| Mueller R, c | 3 | 0 | 0 | 0 |
| Tipton E, lf | 3 | 0 | 0 | 0 |
| Mesner S, 3b | 3 | 0 | 0 | 0 |
| Miller E, ss | 3 | 0 | 1 | 0 |
| Walters B, p | 2 | 0 | 0 | 0 |
| Crabtree E, ph | 1 | 0 | 0 | 0 |
| | 29 | 0 | 2 | 0 |

| Boston | IP | H | R | ER | BB | SO |
|---|---|---|---|---|---|---|
| Barrett (W) | 9.0 | 2 | 0 | 0 | 0 | 0 |

| Cincinnati | IP | H | R | ER | BB | SO |
|---|---|---|---|---|---|---|
| Walters (L) | 9.0 | 6 | 2 | 1 | 1 | 1 |

| Boston | 010 | 010 | 000 — 2 |
|---|---|---|---|
| Cincinnati | 000 | 000 | 000 — 0 |

OB: Boston 6, Cincinnati 2; ER: Criscola; 2B: Phillips, Holmes; SO: Barrett; BB: Etchison; SH: Workman; TI: 1:15; AT: 7,783; UM: Conlan, Barr, Sears

related that the less time Red spent between deliveries, the better he pitched: "The catcher knew that when he returned a pitch to Red that he [Barrett] wanted a sign for the next pitch as soon as the ball reached Red's glove. As an infielder it was great to play behind him because there was no wasted time and the fielders had to stay ready for action. He had pin-point control and could throw strikes with consistency."

The following season, Barrett was shipped to St. Louis, where for one partial season he enjoyed brilliant success, recording 21 wins against only 9 losses. Combining his efforts in both Boston and St. Louis, he led the league in wins (23), complete games (24), and innings pitched (285). After that, he returned to mediocrity and finished his career back in Boston with a 69–69 lifetime log.

# *Traynor's Blow Ends It in the 13th* 91

## PITTSBURGH (NL) at PHILADELPHIA (NL)
### Wednesday, July 23, 1930, Baker Bowl
### Pirates 16, Phillies 15

Though often omitted from discussions of history's great games, this turbulent and remarkable uphill battle nevertheless deserves its place among the greatest near-miss comebacks of the century. The line score reveals the host Philadelphia Phillies falling behind the Pittsburgh Pirates 7–0, finally tying the game in the eighth, again in the ninth, a third time in the 12th, and nearly again in the 13th. Of the 26 half-innings, 23 included hits, contributing to a game total of 50, including eight home runs. In addition, there were five outfield assists: one for an out at second, two at third, and two at home.

In part, the offensive barrage was made possible by that hitter's fantasy known as Baker Bowl. The ancient and now-decrepit park featured a 60-foot-high wall in right field just 280 feet from home plate. The pockmarked tin surface scarred by doubles and long singles, attested to its close proximity to home plate.

On this cloudy day, in the second game of a doubleheader, the Pirates scored early and often, taking a 7–0 advantage after three and one-half innings. Left-handed pitcher Erv Brame climaxed a three-run second-inning rally with a home run over the inviting right-field barrier. A walk and four singles added three more in the third, and Pie Traynor singled home the seventh marker in the fourth. Then the momentum swung to the home club.

The Phillies opened their scoring with four runs in the home half of the fourth. During the flurry, lefty Trip Sigman lofted his only home run of the season over the 60-foot partition.

In the fifth, Philadelphia first baseman Don Hurst, another lefty, led off with the game's third blast over the alluring wall, closing the gap to 7–5.

At the expense of the Phillies' fourth hurler, Pittsburgh increased its lead to 10–5 in the sixth. A single, double, two walks and an error provided the cushion, although the Phillies cut off an additional run at the plate.

In the bottom of the sixth, Lefty O'Doul doubled before Hurst repeated his long-ball effort of an inning earlier, keeping Philadelphia in the chase at 10–7.

The Pirates nearly scored in the seventh when Adam Comorosky doubled with a runner aboard, but a great relay play cut down Paul Waner at home.

It appeared there wasn't a competent pitcher in the house as the Phillies loaded the bases in their half of the seventh. Chuck Klein then singled home a pair, making it 10–9.

Barney Friberg, the Philadelphia second sacker, had only four homers all season, but in the eighth he hit one of them, tying the game for the first time since the opening stanza. The score was soon unknotted, however.

The Pirates quickly regained the lead when Paul Waner crashed a solo homer to right-center in the ninth. It was Paul's first circuit blast of the season.

Philadelphia, who had labored for seven innings and finally caught up, now faced another hurdle. When the first two batters grounded out, it appeared their heroics would go for naught, but O'Doul took another measure of the friendly right-field wall and tied it once again at 11.

The 10th inning was a landmark in that neither club got a hit or a baserunner. It was the first time six batters were retired consecutively.

Both teams lost golden opportunities in the 11th. Pittsburgh got its first

| Pittsburgh | AB | R | H | I |
|---|---|---|---|---|
| Waner L, cf | 6 | 0 | 3 | 0 |
| Flagstead I, ph-lf | 1 | 0 | 0 | 0 |
| Waner P, rf | 7 | 1 | 1 | 1 |
| Grantham G, 2b | 4 | 5 | 2 | 0 |
| Comorosky A, lf-cf | 7 | 3 | 3 | 0 |
| Traynor P, 3b | 7 | 4 | 5 | 4 |
| Bartell D, ss | 6 | 1 | 2 | 3 |
| Suhr G, 1b | 4 | 0 | 1 | 3 |
| Hemsley R, c | 7 | 1 | 4 | 1 |
| Brame E, p | 3 | 1 | 2 | 3 |
| Spencer G, p | 1 | 0 | 0 | 0 |
| Swetonic S, p | 2 | 0 | 0 | 0 |
| French L, p | 0 | 0 | 0 | 0 |
|  | 55 | 16 | 23 | 15 |

| Philadelphia | AB | R | H | I |
|---|---|---|---|---|
| Sigman T, cf | 8 | 2 | 3 | 1 |
| O'Doul L, lf | 4 | 3 | 3 | 1 |
| Klein C, rf | 8 | 2 | 3 | 3 |
| Hurst D, 1b | 8 | 3 | 4 | 4 |
| Whitney P, 3b | 8 | 1 | 3 | 1 |
| Friberg B, 2b | 6 | 2 | 4 | 1 |
| Thevenow T, ss | 7 | 0 | 3 | 1 |
| Davis S, c | 2 | 1 | 1 | 0 |
| McCurdy H, c | 4 | 1 | 1 | 0 |
| Benge R, p | 1 | 0 | 0 | 0 |
| Smythe H, p | 0 | 0 | 0 | 0 |
| Nichols C, p | 0 | 0 | 0 | 0 |
| Thompson F, ph | 1 | 0 | 1 | 3 |
| Elliott H, p | 1 | 0 | 0 | 0 |
| Sothern D, ph | 1 | 0 | 1 | 0 |
| Collard H, p | 0 | 0 | 0 | 0 |
| Sherlock M, ph | 1 | 0 | 0 | 0 |
| Sweetland L, p | 1 | 0 | 0 | 0 |
| Collins P, ph | 1 | 0 | 0 | 0 |
|  | 62 | 15 | 27 | 15 |

| Pittsburgh | IP | H | R | ER | BB | SO |
|---|---|---|---|---|---|---|
| Brame | 4.0 | 8 | 5 | 5 | 4 | 1 |
| Spencer | 2.0 | 8 | 4 | 4 | 0 | 1 |
| Swetonic | 5.2 | 8 | 4 | 4 | 1 | 2 |
| French (W) | 1.1 | 3 | 2 | 2 | 0 | 2 |
|  | 13.0 | 27 | 15 | 15 | 5 | 6 |

| Philadelphia | IP | H | R | ER | BB | SO |
|---|---|---|---|---|---|---|
| Benge | 2.0 | 6 | 6 | 6 | 2 | 0 |
| Smythe | 1.2 | 4 | 1 | 1 | 2 | 0 |
| Nichols | 0.1 | 0 | 0 | 0 | 0 | 0 |
| Elliott | 3.0 | 5 | 3 | 2 | 2 | 1 |
| Collard | 2.0 | 3 | 1 | 1 | 0 | 0 |
| Sweetland (L) | 4.0 | 5 | 5 | 3 | 5 | 1 |
|  | 13.0 | 23 | 16 | 13 | 11 | 2 |

| | | | | |
|---|---|---|---|---|
| Pittsburgh | 033 | 103 | 001 | 002 | 3 — 16 |
| Philadelphia | 000 | 412 | 211 | 002 | 2 — 15 |

OB: Pittsburgh 16, Philadelphia 14; ER: Thevenow, Whitney, McCurdy; DP: Pittsburgh 2, Philadelphia 2; 2B: Sigman, Traynor, Grantham, Whitney, Thompson, Bartell 2, O'Doul, Comorosky, Thevenow, Hurst; HR: Brame, Sigman, Hurst 2, Friberg, Waner, O'Doul, Traynor; SH: Waner, McCurdy, Comorosky; SF: Suhr 2, Bartell; WP: Sweetland; TI: 3:41; AT: unknown; UM: HP Pfirman, 1B Quigley, 2B (none), 3B Scott

two men on base, and a sacrifice moved them along before Paul Waner lined into a double play. Philadelphia also got a runner to third with only one out, but reliever Steve Swetonic escaped by getting a strikeout and a ground-out.

The Pirates capitalized on two Philadelphia errors in the 12th. In addition to the two miscues, two walks and a single enabled them to push over a pair of runs and take a 13–11 lead.

For the second time, the Phillies were down to their final three outs. O'Doul led off the bottom of the 12th and popped out. But Klein, Hurst, Pinky Whitney and Tommy Thevenow all singled to send it into yet another inning.

In the 13th, the first two Pirates were retired, but then a walk and a single brought Pie Traynor to the plate. Traynor had hit a fluke homer in the first game to win it in the ninth. It was a line drive that had bounced a few feet fair, hit a concrete wall in left field, and bounced into the bleachers. By the rules of the day, it was a home run. In this at-bat he used no such chicanery but blasted a pitch over the left-field fence for a three-run homer.

No lead was safe in this game, but in the bottom of the 13th the first two Phillies struck out. Then O'Doul singled and advanced to second, then third, because of defensive indifference. When Klein singled, O'Doul scored to make it 16–14. Klein followed O'Doul's example and also advanced his way to third when the Pirates paid him little attention. Hurst was the batter during this exhibition, and he doubled, making it 16–15. Now the Phillies had a chance to tie it with a single, but Whitney grounded back to the pitcher to end the suspense and one of most thrilling extra-inning games of the century.

# 92 Rigney and Hack Match Wits

## NEW YORK (NL) at CHICAGO (NL)
### Wednesday, May 2, 1956, Wrigley Field
### Giants 6, Cubs 5

Two clubs destined for second-division finishes played a game on this date as if their lives depended on it. Countering one strategic move with another, managers Bill Rigney of the New York Giants and Stan Hack of the Chicago Cubs bewildered observers with their maneuvers while orchestrating a game for the ages. A small Chicago crowd saw the clubs battle their way through four ties, multiple lead changes, 17 innings, 48 players, and five hours and 13 minutes before a winner was decided at Wrigley Field. Along the way a number of records were established or tied.

  • The Giants used 25 players, and the two clubs combined for 48, new major league standards at the time.
  • Chicago's Don Hoak earned the dubious distinction of striking out six times, establishing a National League benchmark and tying the major league mark set 43 years earlier.
  • New York tied the National League mark by using eight pitchers in the marathon, although that mark since has been exceeded.
  • In matching wits, the two managers each sent seven pinch-hitters to the plate. The two-team total of 14 was later tied but never exceeded.
  • Intentional bases on balls were not distinguished from the unintentional variety prior to 1955, but when the two clubs issued 11 intentional passes (four

| New York | AB | R | H | I |
|---|---|---|---|---|
| Lockman W, lf-1b-lf-1b | 8 | 0 | 2 | 0 |
| Dark A, ss | 8 | 1 | 3 | 1 |
| Mays W, cf | 6 | 1 | 0 | 0 |
| Lennon B, rf-lf | 5 | 0 | 0 | 0 |
| Hofman B, ph-1b | 2 | 0 | 0 | 0 |
| Rhodes D, ph-lf | 1 | 0 | 0 | 0 |
| Spencer D, 2b | 7 | 2 | 4 | 3 |
| Castleman F, 3b | 8 | 0 | 4 | 1 |
| Harris G, 1b | 4 | 0 | 1 | 0 |
| Mueller D, ph-rf | 2 | 0 | 0 | 0 |
| Katt R, c | 2 | 0 | 0 | 0 |
| Wilson G, ph | 1 | 0 | 0 | 0 |
| Westrum W, c | 1 | 0 | 0 | 0 |
| Thompson H, ph | 0 | 0 | 0 | 0 |
| Mangan J, c | 0 | 0 | 0 | 0 |
| Worthington A, p | 2 | 1 | 1 | 0 |
| Liddle D, p | 2 | 1 | 1 | 0 |
| Wilhelm H, p | 0 | 0 | 0 | 0 |
| Ridzik S, p | 1 | 0 | 0 | 0 |
| Terwilliger W, ph | 1 | 0 | 0 | 0 |
| Grissom M, p | 0 | 0 | 0 | 0 |
| McCall W, p | 1 | 0 | 0 | 0 |
| Antonelli J, ph | 1 | 0 | 0 | 0 |
| Margoneri J, p | 0 | 0 | 0 | 0 |
| Gomez R, p | 0 | 0 | 0 | 0 |
| | 63 | 6 | 16 | 5 |

| Chicago | AB | R | H | I |
|---|---|---|---|---|
| Hoak D, 3b | 7 | 0 | 1 | 0 |
| Drake S, cf | 8 | 1 | 2 | 1 |
| Fondy D, 1b | 7 | 1 | 3 | 0 |
| Banks E, ss | 5 | 1 | 2 | 2 |
| Moryn W, rf | 7 | 0 | 2 | 0 |
| King J, lf | 3 | 0 | 0 | 0 |
| Irvin M, ph-lf | 5 | 0 | 0 | 0 |
| Baker G, 2b | 8 | 2 | 4 | 1 |
| Landrith H, c | 2 | 0 | 0 | 0 |
| Miksis E, ph | 1 | 0 | 1 | 0 |
| Tappe E, c | 0 | 0 | 0 | 0 |
| Wade G, ph | 0 | 0 | 0 | 0 |
| Chiti H, c | 2 | 0 | 0 | 0 |
| Meyer R, p | 2 | 0 | 0 | 0 |
| Kellert F, ph | 1 | 0 | 0 | 0 |
| Lown T, p | 0 | 0 | 0 | 0 |
| Davis J, p | 1 | 0 | 0 | 0 |
| Whisenant P, ph | 0 | 0 | 0 | 0 |
| Valentinetti V, p | 0 | 0 | 0 | 0 |
| Friend O, ph | 1 | 0 | 0 | 0 |
| Brosnan J, p | 0 | 0 | 0 | 0 |
| McCullough C, ph | 1 | 0 | 1 | 0 |
| Myers R, pr | 0 | 0 | 0 | 0 |
| | 61 | 5 | 16 | 4 |

| New York | IP | H | R | ER | BB | SO |
|---|---|---|---|---|---|---|
| Worthington | 4.0 | 9 | 4 | 4 | 3 | 1 |
| Liddle | 3.0 | 3 | 1 | 0 | 1 | 4 |
| Wilhelm | 1.1 | 1 | 0 | 0 | 2 | 1 |
| Ridzik | 2.2 | 0 | 0 | 0 | 1 | 4 |
| Grissom | 1.2 | 0 | 0 | 0 | 1 | 1 |
| McCall | 2.1 | 2 | 0 | 0 | 0 | 3 |
| Margoneri (W) | 1.2 | 1 | 0 | 0 | 1 | 1 |
| Gomez | 0.1 | 0 | 0 | 0 | 0 | 1 |
| | 17.0 | 16 | 5 | 4 | 9 | 16 |

| Chicago | IP | H | R | ER | BB | SO |
|---|---|---|---|---|---|---|
| Meyer | 8.0 | 10 | 5 | 4 | 1 | 5 |
| Lown | 1.1 | 1 | 0 | 0 | 1 | 2 |
| Davis | 3.2 | 3 | 0 | 0 | 3 | 3 |
| Valentinetti | 2.0 | 0 | 0 | 0 | 1 | 0 |
| Brosnan (L) | 2.0 | 2 | 1 | 1 | 4 | 1 |
| | 17.0 | 16 | 6 | 5 | 10 | 11 |

```
New York   011  002  100  000  000  01 — 6
Chicago    100  120  010  000  000  00 — 5
```

OB: New York 21, Chicago 17; ER: Lockman, Castleman, Westrum, Margoneri, Fondy; DP: New York 1, Chicago 1; 2B: Baker, Dark 2, Castleman 2, McCullough; 3B: Spencer, Harris; HR: Drake, Baker, Banks, Spencer; SB: Moryn; CS: Lockman, Banks; SH: Lockman, Mueller, Hoak, Chiti, Fondy; SF: Castleman, Spencer; HP: by Meyer (Mays); WP: Wilhelm, Davis, Brosnan; PB: Chiti; TI: 5:13; AT: 2,389; UM: Gorman, Dixon, Pinelli, Boggess

by New York hurlers, seven by their counterpart Cubs), it established a record that survived the century. The Cubs set the single-game, single-team mark.

• Finally, the two clubs tied the major league mark by engaging six catchers.

The hero of the game was Giants rookie Daryl Spencer. The second baseman had two singles, a triple, a home run, and knocked in the game-winning tally with a sacrifice fly in the 17th inning. Another New York rookie, pitcher Joe Margoneri, notched his first major league victory in front of only 2,389 weary but die-hard Chicagoans.

Hoak's sixth strikeout carried ignominy. He was at the plate with the tying run at second and two outs in the bottom of the 17th — a perfect opportunity to redeem himself. Hoak worked a 3–2 count before watching a called third strike zip by. With the pitch, the game ended and his name was etched in baseball's austere registers: He had struck out six times — and against six different pitchers.

By the time of Hoak's final strikeout, the Giants had only two men left on their bench. Jim Hearn, who had pitched the day before, and Ray Monzant, who was nursing a sore shoulder. The Cubs, on the other hand, still had nine men, a veritable army, available.

The 11 intentional walks were the result of lavish managerial strategy. In the 17th, for example, Alvin Dark doubled with one away. Jim Brosnan then wild-pitched him to third, so Cubs manager Stan Hack ordered both Willie Mays and Dusty Rhodes walked to establish double-play possibilities. Hack may have taken the idea from Rigney, who in a similar situation in the ninth, directed walks to Walt Moryn and Ernie Banks. The New York media described Rigney's maneuvers as "out–Stengeling" his American League counterpart. For the record, Mays, Wes Westrum, and Banks were intentionally passed twice; Rhodes, Don Mueller, Hank Thompson, Moryn, and Hobie Landrith were each gifted once.

Jim Brosnan not only lost this game, but thanks to the excessive managerial manipulation, all four of his walks were ordered from the bench. In addition to Brosnan, Jim Davis and Hoyt Wilhelm were commanded to walk two, while Russ Meyer, Margoneri, and Al Worthington each issued one intentional pass. The maze of player orchestration was also responsible for Whitey Lockman's pilgrimage back and forth from first base to left field.

# 93 Blue Jays Overtake Phillies in Shameless Slugfest

TORONTO (AL) at PHILADELPHIA (NL)
Wednesday, October 20, 1993, Veterans Stadium
Blue Jays 15, Phillies 14

What a mess it was in Philadelphia this night. After having rained most of the day, a fine mist enveloped Veterans Stadium for the first pitch of the fourth World Series game. Throughout the contest, precipitation worsened, vacillating between drizzle and downpour and producing slick fielding conditions. The weather, however, was bright compared to the pitching. Seven of the game's 11 hurlers embarrassed themselves, either on the mound, the basepaths, or both. And when the offenses weren't pounding the ball, the moundsmen simply issued free passes. In the end, batters set a nine-inning, World Series record for at-bats and established Fall Classic benchmarks for hits, runs, extra-base hits, total bases, and RBI in a game of any length. It wasn't all ugliness, however; the game, despite sloppy, permissive defense, enthralled on-lookers with its excitement, dramatic momentum swings, and nail-biting pitcher-batter confrontations.

Philadelphia starter Tommy Greene was the first hurler to be torched by the Toronto Blue Jays. The right-hander got himself into a bases-loaded jam with two outs in the opening frame. He then walked Paul Molitor on four pitches before Tony Fernandez singled home a pair, giving the visitors a 3–0 advantage.

Experiencing an even more trying time, Blue Jays' right-hander Todd Stottlemyre walked four of the first five batters. It was a singular event, marking the first time in World Series history that a pitcher issued four free passes in the opening frame. Milt Thompson then cleared the bases with a triple, shifting the lead to the home team, 4–3.

Opening the second inning, Greene further demonstrated his own lack of control when he walked Stottlemyre. Accustomed to designated hitter play, this marked the first time all season that Stottlemyre had reached base. Two outs later, a single to center sent the baserunning novice foolishly racing for third. The relay beat Stottlemyre by a mile, but his zest sent him into a headfirst slide. After easily being tagged out, his momentum carried him across the bag, tearing a gash in his chin and delaying the game.

With blood still oozing from his wound, Stottlemyre opened the home second by giving up a single to opposing moundsman Greene. Lenny Dykstra then deposited an 0–1 pitch beyond the right-field wall, just left of the foul pole, increasing the Philadelphia advantage to 6–3.

Greene retired the first Toronto batter in the third before a walk and three consecutive singles narrowed the gap to 6–5 and forced manager Jim Fregosi to reach out for bullpen aid. The skipper was understandably hesitant; though the club won 97 regular season games, their erratic relievers sported inflated ERAs and led the league in blown saves. As reliever Roger Mason took his warm-up tosses, a pinch-hitter was announced for Stottlemyre, meaning both starters concluded their work before the 14th out of the game was recorded. Mason registered the second out of the frame before another walk and a two-run single by Tony Fernandez shifted the lead back to the visitors, 7–6. By now, frustrated fans had persevered in the fluctuating rain for one hour and 28 minutes, and the battle was only halfway through the third inning.

After tying it in the fourth, the Phillies erupted for five additional runs in the fifth. A pair of two-run homers, by Darren Daulton and Dykstra, highlighted the fireworks. Philadelphia, which once trailed by three, led by three and then

| Toronto | AB | R | H | I |
|---|---|---|---|---|
| Henderson R, lf | 5 | 2 | 2 | 2 |
| White D, cf | 5 | 2 | 3 | 4 |
| Alomar R, 2b | 6 | 1 | 2 | 1 |
| Carter J, rf | 6 | 2 | 3 | 0 |
| Olerud J, 1b | 4 | 2 | 1 | 0 |
| Molitor P, 3b | 4 | 2 | 2 | 2 |
| Griffin A, 3b | 0 | 0 | 0 | 0 |
| Fernandez T, ss | 6 | 2 | 3 | 5 |
| Borders P, c | 4 | 1 | 1 | 1 |
| Stottlemyre T, p | 0 | 0 | 0 | 0 |
| Butler R, ph | 1 | 1 | 0 | 0 |
| Leiter A, p | 1 | 0 | 1 | 0 |
| Castillo T, p | 1 | 0 | 0 | 0 |
| Sprague E, ph | 1 | 0 | 0 | 0 |
| Timlin M, p | 0 | 0 | 0 | 0 |
| Ward D, p | 0 | 0 | 0 | 0 |
|  | 44 | 15 | 18 | 15 |

| Philadelphia | AB | R | H | I |
|---|---|---|---|---|
| Dykstra L, cf | 5 | 4 | 3 | 4 |
| Duncan M, 2b | 6 | 1 | 3 | 1 |
| Kruk J, 1b | 5 | 0 | 0 | 0 |
| Hollins D, 3b | 4 | 3 | 2 | 0 |
| Daulton D, c | 3 | 2 | 1 | 3 |
| Eisenreich J, rf | 4 | 2 | 1 | 1 |
| Thompson M, lf | 5 | 1 | 3 | 5 |
| Stocker K, ss | 4 | 0 | 0 | 0 |
| Greene T, p | 1 | 1 | 1 | 0 |
| Mason R, p | 1 | 0 | 0 | 0 |
| Jordan R, ph | 1 | 0 | 0 | 0 |
| West D, p | 0 | 0 | 0 | 0 |
| Chamberlain W, ph | 1 | 0 | 0 | 0 |
| Andersen L, p | 0 | 0 | 0 | 0 |
| Williams M, p | 0 | 0 | 0 | 0 |
| Morandini M, ph | 1 | 0 | 0 | 0 |
| Thigpen B, p | 0 | 0 | 0 | 0 |
|  | 41 | 14 | 14 | 14 |

| Toronto | IP | H | R | ER | BB | SO |
|---|---|---|---|---|---|---|
| Stottlemyre | 2.0 | 3 | 6 | 6 | 4 | 1 |
| Leiter | 2.2 | 8 | 6 | 6 | 0 | 1 |
| Castillo (W) | 2.1 | 3 | 2 | 2 | 3 | 1 |
| Timlin | 0.2 | 0 | 0 | 0 | 0 | 2 |
| Ward (S) | 1.1 | 0 | 0 | 0 | 0 | 2 |
|  | 9.0 | 14 | 14 | 14 | 7 | 7 |

| Philadelphia | IP | H | R | ER | BB | SO |
|---|---|---|---|---|---|---|
| Greene | 2.1 | 7 | 7 | 7 | 4 | 1 |
| Mason | 2.2 | 2 | 0 | 0 | 1 | 2 |
| West | 1.0 | 3 | 2 | 2 | 0 | 0 |
| Andersen | 1.1 | 2 | 3 | 3 | 1 | 2 |
| Williams (L) | 0.2 | 3 | 3 | 3 | 1 | 1 |
| Thigpen | 1.0 | 1 | 0 | 0 | 0 | 0 |
|  | 9.0 | 18 | 15 | 15 | 7 | 6 |

Toronto        304  002  060 — 15
Philadelphia   420  151  100 — 14

OB: Toronto 10, Philadelphia 8; 2B: Henderson, Dykstra, Leiter, Thompson, White, Hollins, Molitor, Carter; 3B: Thompson, White; HR: Dykstra 2, Daulton; SB: Dykstra, White, Henderson, Duncan; HP: by West (Molitor), by Castillo (Daulton); TI: 4:14; AT: 62,731; UM: HP Williams, 1B McClelland, 2B DeMuth, 3B Phillips, LF Runge, RF Johnson

was tied, now commanded a five-run margin at 12–7. But Toronto was a powerful offensive club and had feasted on Philadelphia's hospitable bullpen.

David West was Fregosi's next hopeful, but announcers were quick to note that the portly left-hander had retired only one of the 10 previous World Series opponents he had faced. True to form, he allowed the first batter he faced to double, and the next singled the runner home. West then broke precedent and retired the third hitter, eliciting derisive cheers from the disgusted crowd. Another single and a hit batsman loaded the sacks before a ground-out tallied a second run. West got the third out, but Toronto had drawn to within three.

In the home half of the sixth, the Phillies recouped one run, making it 13–9. By this time each club had been retired in order just once. The two pitching staffs had already allowed 22 runs, 25 hits, 10 walks, four steals, and a hit batsman.

With a single, three more walks, and another hit batsman, the Phillies scored their 14th run, their second five-run lead. But with the bases loaded and only one out, Philadelphia could do no further damage, a fact they would long regret.

Toronto opened the eighth with an out, but then a single, walk, and a double pushed across their 10th run and brought reliever Mitch "The Wild Thing" Williams into the fray for Philadelphia. The left-hander had thrilled fans and caused heartaches for the three major league clubs that had employed him during his career. Despite 43 saves this campaign, it seemed he could not end an inning or a game until he put runners into scoring position. Now there already were runners at second and third, and Williams was at his worst. He allowed two singles, a walk, and a triple by Devon White that put the Blue Jays back into the lead, 15–14.

So devastated were the Phillies by the last half-inning that in the eighth they went down in order for only the second time in the game. In the ninth they proved equally fruitless, and closer Duane Ward quietly secured the Toronto victory.

# *Greenberg's Slam Clinches Pennant* 94

## DETROIT (AL) at ST. LOUIS (AL)
### Sunday, September 30, 1945, Sportsman's Park
### Tigers 6, Browns 3

The 1945 campaign witnessed a contentious pennant battle in the American League between the Detroit Tigers and the Washington Senators. The Tigers struggled through the first half of the season while their top slugger, Hank Greenberg, finished his four-year stint in the U.S. Army. After his return on July 1, the big outfielder made up for lost time, hitting .311 with 13 homers and 60 RBI over the last 78 games.

Although a week remained in the season for most teams, the Senators had concluded their schedule early to make Griffith Stadium available for pro football. Washington ended their season at 87–67. Detroit, meanwhile, had an 86–64 mark with four games remaining. A Wednesday doubleheader split left them at 87–65 and needing to win just one of their two remaining weekend games against the St. Louis Browns to take the flag. Two losses would have precipitated a playoff, but all Washington could do was wait.

Heavy rains in St. Louis postponed Saturday's scheduled game, forcing a doubleheader for the following day. But Sunday's weather wasn't much better, beginning overcast and foggy. A light rain delayed the first game for nearly an

| Detroit | AB | R | H | I |
|---|---|---|---|---|
| Webb S, ss | 3 | 1 | 1 | 0 |
| Mayo E, 2b | 4 | 0 | 1 | 1 |
| Cramer D, cf | 5 | 1 | 1 | 0 |
| Greenberg H, lf | 5 | 1 | 2 | 4 |
| Cullenbine R, rf | 4 | 1 | 1 | 0 |
| York R, 1b | 5 | 0 | 0 | 0 |
| Outlaw J, 3b | 2 | 0 | 1 | 0 |
| Richards P, c | 4 | 0 | 1 | 1 |
| Trucks V, p | 2 | 1 | 0 | 0 |
| Newhouser H, p | 0 | 0 | 0 | 0 |
| Walker H, ph | 1 | 0 | 1 | 0 |
| Borum R, pr | 0 | 1 | 0 | 0 |
| Benton A, p | 0 | 0 | 0 | 0 |
|  | 35 | 6 | 9 | 6 |

| St. Louis | AB | R | H | I |
|---|---|---|---|---|
| Gutteridge D, 2b | 3 | 1 | 1 | 0 |
| Finney L, lf | 2 | 0 | 2 | 1 |
| Byrnes M, cf | 2 | 0 | 0 | 0 |
| Christman M, ph | 1 | 0 | 0 | 0 |
| Gray P, cf | 1 | 1 | 0 | 0 |
| McQuinn G, 1b | 4 | 0 | 1 | 1 |
| Moore G, rf | 4 | 1 | 1 | 0 |
| Stephens V, ss | 4 | 0 | 2 | 1 |
| Mancuso F, c | 4 | 0 | 0 | 0 |
| Schulte L, 3b | 4 | 0 | 0 | 0 |
| Potter N, p | 3 | 0 | 1 | 0 |
|  | 32 | 3 | 8 | 3 |

| Detroit | IP | H | R | ER | BB | SO |
|---|---|---|---|---|---|---|
| Trucks | 5.1 | 3 | 2 | 2 | 2 | 3 |
| Newhouser (W) | 2.2 | 4 | 1 | 1 | 1 | 5 |
| Benton | 1.0 | 1 | 0 | 0 | 0 | 0 |
|  | 9.0 | 8 | 3 | 3 | 3 | 8 |

| St. Louis | IP | H | R | ER | BB | SO |
|---|---|---|---|---|---|---|
| Potter (L) | 9.0 | 9 | 6 | 6 | 5 | 4 |

```
Detroit     000  011  004 — 6
St. Louis   100  000  110 — 3
```

OB: Detroit 9, St. Louis 5; DP: Detroit 2; 2B: Gutteridge, Potter, McQuinn, Moore; HR: Greenberg; SH: Webb, Mayo; TI: 2:23; AT: 5,582; UM: Pipgras, Berry, Rue, Hubbard

hour, and the cumulative precipitation produced deplorable playing conditions.

Starting for Detroit was Virgil Trucks, recently discharged from service in the Navy. The big right-hander was not yet in pitching condition, but given the thin Tiger rotation, manager Steve O'Neill gave him his first start of the season. Nels Potter, veteran right-hander, took the ball for the Browns.

St. Louis jumped into the lead when their first two batters, Don Gutteridge and Lou Finney, greeted Trucks with a double and a single.

The Tigers fought back, scoring one in the fifth when Trucks walked in front of singles by Skeeter Webb and Eddie Mayo. They then pulled ahead in the sixth, 2–1, on a pair of walks and Paul Richards's single to left.

Lack of work caught up with Trucks in the home half of the sixth. After the tiring starter gave up a double to Potter and walked Gutteridge, skipper O'Neill called in his ace, Hal Newhouser. The tall left-hander, who already owned 24 wins, escaped the inning without damage.

In the seventh, the Browns tied it on Gene Moore's double and a single by Vern Stephens, the soon-to-be American League home run champ. They then regained the lead in the eighth, 3–2, on Finney's single and a two-bagger by George McQuinn.

Tiger hopes were as gloomy as the weather when the team batted in the ninth. But pinch-hitter Hub Walker started things with a single to center. Webb bunted, but a throw to second was late, putting two on with no outs. After Mayo sacrificed the runners to second and third, a conference was called at the mound. Browns' manager Luke Sewell decided to walk lefty Doc Cramer, hoping for a game-ending double play at the expense of the slow-footed Greenberg.

With light mist falling, Greenberg stepped in against Potter. Fewer than 6,000 St. Louis fans remained, but all eyes followed the Potter screwball that Greenberg drove far down the left-field line. It had plenty of distance but was so close to the line that not until third base umpire Cal Hubbard signaled a fair ball did the entire Detroit team leap from their dugout. They mobbed Greenberg at the plate and joyously escorted him to the dugout, leading, 6–3.

The Browns still had to bat in the bottom of the ninth, but Detroit right-hander Al Benton made the most of a slick double play to preserve the victory and give the Tigers the pennant.

# Overflow Crowd Fosters Doubles Record 95

## CHICAGO (NL) at ST. LOUIS (NL)
### Sunday, July 12, 1931, Sportsman's Park
### Cardinals 17, Cubs 13

Seventy years ago, the conduct of baseball fans was vastly different from the modern versions. Greedy owners, permitting dangerous numbers in their ballparks, and loosely enforced safety laws often allowed large, unruly crowds to affect game outcomes. Such was the case on this day, when two teams combined for 23 doubles in one game, a record that has yet to be approached.

Locked in a tight pennant race, the Chicago Cubs visited the St. Louis Cardinals for a twin bill. On a sweltering hot, cloudy day, the long-standing rivalry was heightened by an incident that occurred in Chicago only five days earlier. Bitter feelings resulted from Cub-inflicted Cardinal spike wounds, and this day's encounter held the potential for a turbulent grudge match. The *St. Louis Post-Dispatch* even referred to the visitors as "the hated Cubs."

With the main gates opened at 9:00 A.M., all reserved seats were occupied before noon. Others jammed the aisles. Ropes were then stretched around the outfield from foul line to foul line, 30 feet in from the walls, and the bleacher gates were opened. Invading hordes surged into the park, and seeing no police to contain them behind the ropes, they flooded the playing field like swarming bees. This happened about the same time the Cubs were taking fielding practice, and soon several enterprising patrons visited the infield and joined the visitors in their session. Before long there were hundreds of transgressors scrambling for batted balls that were immediately claimed as souvenirs. When the pseudo-infielders had consumed all of the Cubs' spare balls, they turned their attention to the dugouts, peering at the players and exchanging unpleasantries with the Cubs. The *St. Louis Globe-Democrat* estimated that at least 8,000 patrons walked the field, including children and infants being carried by their mothers.

With rain a distinct threat but refunds anathema to any owner, Cardinal president Sam Breadon roused the umpires, grounds crew, ushers, players, coaches, and all available policemen to clear the infield in preparation for the start of the first contest. Evacuating the infield went fairly smoothly, but the outfield was another story. There were so many fans without seats that they formed a sea of Redbird partisans covering most of the outfield. Attempts to move them back to the walls were fruitless. When pressure was applied in the middle, both ends surged forward; if pressure was applied to the ends, the center bulged forward. Finally, the crowd-control element decided it was hopeless and opted simply to begin the first game. The few hundred fearless patrons who had climbed to the pavilion roof had a birds-eye view of the throng milling about the field in fair territory. With the crowd of onlookers encroaching to within 70 feet behind first base, not more than 150 feet behind second, and about 100 feet behind third base, the field of play was shrunk to farcical proportions. In foul territory, furthermore, the throng bulged in front of both dugouts, blocking players' views and forcing box seat holders to stand to see any of the action. When all the receipts were tallied, a new St. Louis attendance record had been established, although more than 11,000 fans were without seats.

The games themselves were as ludicrous as the preliminary affairs. The overwhelming crowd necessitated a special ground rule calling for a double whenever a ball was hit into it. Ordinary fly balls, as well as some ground balls, miraculously transformed into two-base blows when fans fought among themselves and with the outfielders whenever a prospective souvenir approached. On a few occasions the Redbird sea was parted, allowing St. Louis outfielders to sneak through and make a catch. One *St. Louis Post-Dispatch* reporter felt that of the 32 "doubles" hit in the two games, all but five or six easily would have been caught.

Despite the hostile crowd, the Cubs won the opener, 7–5. The second game, which is one of the century's greatest, was even more outlandish than the first. The Cubs sent six hurlers into the maelstrom who allowed 21 hits and 17 runs. And while there had been only nine doubles awarded in the opener, the nightcap provided a two-team total of 23. By the time the second game began, fans had moved to just about wherever they pleased. There was as much room *behind* the right-field mob as in front of it, and the outfielders were forced to play just beyond the infield. Hundreds placed themselves in great danger to view the action, occupying the area in front of the backstop (scene of foul tips and wild pitches), as well as the first and third base foul lines. Fearless, these intrepid observers heartily flung themselves in front of balls traveling at blinding speeds in order to carry home souvenirs. Fortunately, no viewer was wounded through

### Second Game

| Chicago | AB | R | H | I |
|---|---|---|---|---|
| Blair F, 2b | 6 | 3 | 3 | 4 |
| English W, ss | 6 | 1 | 3 | 2 |
| Cuyler K, rf | 3 | 0 | 0 | 0 |
| Wilson H, lf | 6 | 0 | 1 | 0 |
| Hornsby R, 3b | 4 | 1 | 2 | 0 |
| Taylor D, cf | 4 | 1 | 0 | 0 |
| Grimm C, 1b | 5 | 2 | 1 | 0 |
| Hartnett G, c | 5 | 3 | 5 | 1 |
| Malone P, p | 0 | 1 | 0 | 0 |
| Bush G, p | 0 | 0 | 0 | 0 |
| Bell L, ph | 1 | 1 | 1 | 2 |
| Baecht E, p | 0 | 0 | 0 | 0 |
| Root C, p | 0 | 0 | 0 | 0 |
| Sweetland L, ph | 1 | 0 | 0 | 0 |
| Blake S, p | 0 | 0 | 0 | 0 |
| Warneke L, p | 0 | 0 | 0 | 0 |
| Stephenson R, ph | 1 | 0 | 0 | 0 |
| | 42 | 13 | 16 | 9 |

| St. Louis | AB | R | H | I |
|---|---|---|---|---|
| Adams S, ss | 4 | 3 | 1 | 0 |
| Watkins G, rf | 5 | 3 | 1 | 1 |
| Frisch F, 2b | 5 | 3 | 3 | 1 |
| Collins R, 1b | 6 | 2 | 4 | 4 |
| Hafey C, lf | 5 | 2 | 3 | 3 |
| Martin P, cf | 6 | 1 | 3 | 3 |
| High A, 3b | 4 | 1 | 1 | 1 |
| Mancuso G, c | 5 | 1 | 4 | 2 |
| Rhem F, p | 1 | 0 | 0 | 0 |
| Orsatti E, ph | 2 | 1 | 1 | 1 |
| Stout A, p | 0 | 0 | 0 | 0 |
| Derringer P, p | 3 | 0 | 0 | 0 |
| | 46 | 17 | 21 | 16 |

| Chicago | IP | H | R | ER | BB | SO |
|---|---|---|---|---|---|---|
| Malone | 3.1 | 10 | 7 | 4 | 0 | 3 |
| Bush | 0.2 | 3 | 3 | 3 | 1 | 0 |
| Baecht (L) | 0.0 | 0 | 2 | 2 | 2 | 0 |
| Root | 1.0 | 2 | 1 | 1 | 0 | 0 |
| Blake | 2.0 | 6 | 4 | 4 | 3 | 3 |
| Warneke | 1.0 | 0 | 0 | 0 | 1 | 0 |
| | 8.0 | 21 | 17 | 14 | 7 | 6 |

| St. Louis | IP | H | R | ER | BB | SO |
|---|---|---|---|---|---|---|
| Rhem | 4.0 | 7 | 6 | 3 | 3 | 5 |
| Stout | 0.0 | 2 | 4 | 3 | 1 | 0 |
| Derringer (W) | 5.0 | 7 | 3 | 3 | 1 | 6 |
| | 9.0 | 16 | 13 | 9 | 5 | 11 |

| | | | | |
|---|---|---|---|---|
| Chicago | 200 | 441 | 002 — 13 | |
| St. Louis | 300 | 732 | 02x — 17 | |

OB: Chicago 9, St. Louis 13; ER: Blair, English, Taylor, Adams 4, Rhem; DP: Chicago 1, St. Louis 2; 2B: Blair 2, English 3, Hornsby, Hartnett 3, Bell, Watkins, Frisch 2, Collins 3, Hafey 2, High, Mancuso 3, Orsatti; HR: Blair; SH: Cuyler, Malone; HP: by Root (High); WP: Blake, Stout, Derringer 2; TI: 2:44; AT: 45,715; UM: Pfirman, Rigler, Clarke

such action, although one patron was badly injured when pushed over the railing from his upper-deck grandstand seat.

Although the crowd and its influence were impossible to ignore, the game itself turned out to be quite exciting. Chicago forged three leads, 2–0, 6–3, and 11–10, but each one slipped away. And Pepper Martin made a great throw to retire Kiki Cuyler at the plate on a play so close that Chicago manager Charley Grimm was ejected after an ensuing argument. Rookie pitching sensation Paul Derringer tamed the Cubs in relief and won his 10th decision en route to an 18–8 season.

# 96 Blair's Single Wins It in the Twelfth

LOS ANGELES (NL) at NEW YORK (AL)
Tuesday, October 11, 1977, Yankee Stadium
Yankees 4, Dodgers 3

Old rivals opened the 74th World Series in New York when the Yankees and Dodgers met for the ninth time in the Fall Classic. Each team, too, had already traveled an exciting road through either the regular campaign or post-season. The Dodgers lost the first game of their playoff with Philadelphia but rebounded with three straight victories. For the Yankees, internecine wars and numerous injuries, more than the American League, had made the summer more trying than it otherwise might have been. Constant feuding between their volatile manager, Billy Martin, and the club's majority owner, George Steinbrenner, kept the Yankees in the headlines, win or lose. Martin feuded, too, with Steinbrenner's favorite player, Reggie Jackson, and the two nearly came to public blows in June.

Pitching this opener for New York was a 27-year-old who had beaten them in the first game of the World Series a year earlier. Don Gullet, former Cincinnati left-hander, had joined the Yankees as part of the first wave of free agents who offered their services on the open market. His mound opponent was Don Sutton, the Los Angeles wily veteran right-hander.

Gullet, who had been bombed in the first game of the American League Championship Series, looked as if he were in for more of the same in the opening frame. After walking Davey Lopes, Bill Russell tripled. Another walk and a sacrifice fly quickly made it 2–0.

New York countered in the home half on three consecutive two-out singles to make it 2–1. But over the next four innings the two hurlers dominated, and each team could generate just one single.

A critical play developed in the sixth. Steve Garvey singled and, with two outs, Glenn Burke did the same. Garvey had been running with the pitch, and the ball whizzed past him as he approached second. Nearing third, he received a signal to continue home. It was a scintillating play at the plate, but umpire Nestor Chylak called Garvey out.

In the home half of the sixth Willie Randolph led off with a home run to left, tying the game at two.

The Yankees scored the go-ahead run in the eighth when Randolph opened with a walk, and Munson doubled him home, making it 3–2. Two more walks loaded the bases, but Elias Sosa, third Dodger pitcher of the inning, closed matters.

| Los Angeles | AB | R | H | I | | New York | AB | R | H | I |
|---|---|---|---|---|---|---|---|---|---|---|
| Lopes D, 2b | 5 | 1 | 0 | 0 | | Rivers M, cf | 6 | 0 | 0 | 0 |
| Russell B, ss | 6 | 1 | 1 | 1 | | Randolph W, 2b | 5 | 3 | 2 | 1 |
| Smith R, rf | 4 | 0 | 1 | 0 | | Munson T, c | 4 | 1 | 2 | 1 |
| Cey R, 3b | 3 | 0 | 0 | 1 | | Jackson R, rf | 2 | 0 | 1 | 0 |
| Garvey S, 1b | 4 | 0 | 1 | 0 | | Blair P, rf | 2 | 0 | 1 | 1 |
| Baker D, lf | 4 | 1 | 1 | 0 | | Chambliss C, 1b | 5 | 0 | 1 | 1 |
| Burke G, cf | 3 | 0 | 1 | 0 | | Nettles G, 3b | 4 | 0 | 0 | 0 |
| Mota M, ph | 1 | 0 | 0 | 0 | | Piniella L, lf | 5 | 0 | 2 | 0 |
| Monday R, cf | 1 | 0 | 0 | 0 | | Dent B, ss | 5 | 0 | 2 | 0 |
| Yeager S, c | 3 | 0 | 0 | 0 | | Gullett D, p | 1 | 0 | 0 | 0 |
| Landestoy R, pr | 0 | 0 | 0 | 0 | | Lyle S, p | 2 | 0 | 0 | 0 |
| Grote J, c | 1 | 0 | 0 | 0 | | | 41 | 4 | 11 | 4 |
| Sutton D, p | 2 | 0 | 0 | 0 | | | | | | |
| Rautzhan L, p | 0 | 0 | 0 | 0 | | | | | | |
| Sosa E, p | 0 | 0 | 0 | 0 | | | | | | |
| Lacy L, ph | 1 | 0 | 1 | 1 | | | | | | |
| Garman M, p | 0 | 0 | 0 | 0 | | | | | | |
| Davalillo V, ph | 1 | 0 | 0 | 0 | | | | | | |
| Rhoden R, p | 0 | 0 | 0 | 0 | | | | | | |
| | 39 | 3 | 6 | 3 | | | | | | |

| Los Angeles | IP | H | R | ER | BB | SO | | New York | IP | H | R | ER | BB | SO |
|---|---|---|---|---|---|---|---|---|---|---|---|---|---|---|
| Sutton | 7.0 | 8 | 3 | 3 | 1 | 4 | | Gullett | 8.1 | 5 | 3 | 3 | 6 | 6 |
| Rautzhan | 0.1 | 0 | 0 | 0 | 2 | 0 | | Lyle (W) | 3.2 | 1 | 0 | 0 | 0 | 2 |
| Sosa | 0.2 | 0 | 0 | 0 | 0 | 1 | | | 12.0 | 6 | 3 | 3 | 6 | 8 |
| Garman | 3.0 | 1 | 0 | 0 | 1 | 3 | | | | | | | | |
| Rhoden (L) | 0.0 | 2 | 1 | 1 | 1 | 0 | | | | | | | | |
| | 11.0 | 11 | 4 | 4 | 5 | 8 | | | | | | | | |

| Los Angeles | 200 | 000 | 001 | 000 — 3 |
|---|---|---|---|---|
| New York | 100 | 001 | 010 | 001 — 4 |

OB: Los Angeles 8, New York 12; 2B: Munson, Randolph; 3B: Russell; HR: Randolph; CS: Smith; SH: Gullett 2; SF: Cey; HP: by Gullett (Baker), by Sutton (Jackson); TI: 3:24; AT: 56,668; UM: HP Chylak, 1B Sudol, 2B McCoy, 3B Dale, LF Evans, RF McSherry

While liberal with bases on balls, Gullet opened the ninth having allowed only three hits since the first inning. With the Dodgers needing one run to tie, Dusty Baker opened with a single to left. Gullet retired the next batter but walked Steve Yeager. Having logged 133 pitches, Gullet was relieved by Sparky Lyle. Pinch-hitter Lee Lacy greeted Lyle with a single that scored Baker and tied the game once more.

Only two of the next 20 batters reached base, and neither advanced as far as second. That set the stage for the New York 12th, when Rick Rhoden, a starter with a 16–10 regular-season mark, took the hill for Los Angeles. Randolph welcomed the right-hander with a double, encouraging an intentional pass to Thurman Munson. That brought to the plate Paul Blair, who had been commissioned as a defensive replacement for Jackson in the ninth. Blair was instructed to move the runners along with a bunt but failed as the count rose to 2–2. Normally an artful bunter, Blair was about to try again when third base coach Dick Howser yelled for time and motioned a second time to remove the bunt. On the next pitch, Blair poked at an outside pitch and sent it into right field for a single, scoring Randoph with the winning run and starting New York on their way to the championship.

# 97 *The Schoolboy Was Scholarly*

ST. LOUIS (NL) at DETROIT (AL)
Thursday, October 4, 1934, Navin Field
Tigers 3, Cardinals 2

After an absence of a quarter century, Detroit buzzed with excitement over the Tigers' appearance in the Fall Classic. Their new player-manager and American League Most Valuable Player, Mickey Cochrane, instilled a new spirit in the club. After a fifth-place finish a year earlier, Detroit this year mounted the league's top offense and defense to finish seven games ahead of the second-place Yankees.

Their opponents, the St. Louis Cardinals, did much the same in the Senior Circuit. Their hustling, colorful style earned them the nickname "The Gashouse Gang." Not only did they lead their league in hits, runs, and slugging, but they also boasted the dynamic pitching duo of the Dean brothers, Jerome and Paul. "Dizzy" and "Daffy," as they were better known, combined to win 49 games for the Cardinals this year. So intimidating was the 30–7 Dizzy that Detroit held back their ace, Lynwood "Schoolboy Rowe," from the first game of the Series — one that Dean won, 8–3.

The second game opened on a crisp, sunny afternoon before another sell-out crowd in Detroit. There was also a swirling wind, however, one that the gods of chance would use to smile upon the Tigers this day. Rowe, 24–8, was to face the Cardinals' Wild Bill Hallahan, so nicknamed because of his control struggles.

St. Louis broke into the scoring column in the second frame on a one-out single and Ernie Orsatti's triple. Rowe retired the next two batters to keep the damage to a minimum.

The Cardinals added another run in the third and nearly had more. With two outs, Joe Medwick singled, driving in Pepper Martin, and went to second on a play at home. When Ripper Collins also singled, Medwick sped toward the plate, sending Cochrane sprawling, but was called out.

Detroit got on the board in the fourth with two doubles. The gods blessed

Detroit player-manager Mickey Cochrane with owner Walter Briggs (National Baseball Hall of Fame Library, Cooperstown, New York).

the first, by Billy Rogell, when his routine fly ball to center was caught in a bewildering whirlwind and dropped safely. Pete Fox drove him home with another double over third base that was so close to the line that a long argument ensued.

Despite allowing Tiger runners in every inning but the eighth, Hallahan held the Tigers at bay and carried his 2–1 lead into the ninth. Then, Fox led off

| *St. Louis* | AB | R | H | I |
|---|---|---|---|---|
| Martin P, 3b | 5 | 1 | 2 | 0 |
| Rothrock J, rf | 4 | 0 | 0 | 0 |
| Frisch F, 2b | 5 | 0 | 1 | 0 |
| Medwick J, lf | 5 | 0 | 1 | 1 |
| Collins R, 1b | 5 | 0 | 1 | 0 |
| DeLancey B, c | 5 | 1 | 1 | 0 |
| Orsatti E, cf | 4 | 0 | 1 | 1 |
| Durocher L, ss | 4 | 0 | 0 | 0 |
| Hallahan B, p | 3 | 0 | 0 | 0 |
| Walker B, p | 1 | 0 | 0 | 0 |
| | 41 | 2 | 7 | 2 |

| *Detroit* | AB | R | H | I |
|---|---|---|---|---|
| White J, cf | 4 | 0 | 0 | 0 |
| Walker G, ph | 1 | 0 | 1 | 1 |
| Doljack F, cf | 1 | 0 | 0 | 0 |
| Cochrane M, c | 4 | 0 | 0 | 0 |
| Gehringer C, 2b | 4 | 1 | 1 | 0 |
| Greenberg H, 1b | 4 | 0 | 0 | 0 |
| Goslin G, lf | 6 | 0 | 2 | 1 |
| Rogell B, ss | 4 | 1 | 1 | 0 |
| Owen M, 3b | 5 | 0 | 0 | 0 |
| Fox P, rf | 5 | 1 | 2 | 1 |
| Rowe S, p | 4 | 0 | 0 | 0 |
| | 42 | 3 | 7 | 3 |

| *St. Louis* | IP | H | R | ER | BB | SO |
|---|---|---|---|---|---|---|
| Hallahan | 8.1 | 6 | 2 | 2 | 4 | 6 |
| Walker (L) | 3.0 | 1 | 1 | 1 | 3 | 2 |
| | 11.1 | 7 | 3 | 3 | 7 | 8 |

| *Detroit* | IP | H | R | ER | BB | SO |
|---|---|---|---|---|---|---|
| Rowe (W) | 12.0 | 7 | 2 | 2 | 0 | 7 |

```
St. Louis   011   000   000   000 — 2
Detroit     000   100   001   001 — 3
```

OB: St. Louis 4, Detroit 13; ER: Hallahan, Martin, Frisch; 2B: Rogell, Fox, Martin; 3B: Orsatti; SB: Gehringer; SH: Rothrock, Rowe; TI: 2:49; AT: 43,451; UM: HP Klem, 1B Geisel, 2B Reardon, 3B Owens

with a single, and Rowe sacrificed him to second. Again lady luck visited the Tigers when pinch-hitter Gee Walker lifted a high fly straight up in the air. St. Louis catcher Bill DeLancey stood firm after deciding it would fall near first. First baseman Collins hesitated but then came racing toward the plate as the ball fell several feet in front of home and bounced foul. Given another chance, Walker singled home the tying run and sent the game into extra innings.

Meanwhile, Rowe became unhittable. He retired the Cardinals in order again in the 10th, marking 21 straight outs.

The Tigers in the 10th and the Cardinals in the 11th got a runner to second, but neither could deliver a scoring blow.

Left-hander Bill Walker, who had replaced Hallahan in the ninth, faltered in the 12th. After getting Cochrane on a ground-out, he walked the next two batters on nine pitches, later claiming the swirling wind affected his control. Veteran Goose Goslin took one ball before singling sharply to center, sending the winning run across the plate and delirium throughout the park.

The Dean brothers eventually proved too much for Detroit, each winning two games in the Series. Daffy won Game Six, and Dizzy, pitching his third game in seven days, shut out the Tigers in Game Seven.

# Seerey Electrifies Shibe Park 98

CHICAGO (AL) at PHILADELPHIA (AL)
Sunday, July 18, 1948, Shibe Park
White Sox 12, Athletics 11

When Pat Seerey joined the Chicago White Sox via a trade on June 2, the Chicago press affectionately dubbed him "Fat Pat," "Mr. Five by Five," and once referred to him as "the portly member of the White Sox ensemble." The 25-year-old right-handed slugger had opened some eyes with an astonishing strikeout ratio while still with his first club, the Cleveland Indians. In 1944, his first full season, Pat led the league by fanning 99 times in only 342 official at-bats. Seerey followed with similar futility during his next two campaigns, again leading the league despite playing less than full time. But the 1948 White Sox were desperate for power. As a team, they had hit only 53 circuit blasts a year earlier and had bid farewell to their leading long-ball hitter, Rudy York, whose skills were dissipating. Thus Seerey moved into the Chicago lineup, usually in the clean-up position. This day, in the dramatic first game of a doubleheader, Pat electrified the Philadelphia crowd by smashing four titanic home runs, including a game-winning blast in extra innings.

Philadelphia opened the contest by pouncing on Chicago southpaw Frank Papish for a run in the first and four more in the second.

The Sox collected a run in the third, and each club tallied once in the fourth. Chicago's second run came off the bat of Seerey, who launched Carl Scheib's first delivery out of the park, clearing the roof atop the double-decked left-field stands.

In the fifth, after Chicago's Don Kolloway tripled, Seerey again blasted Scheib's first pitch toward the left-field roof. This one bounced on the tar paper before decorating the adjoining neighborhood. That made it 6–4, but the Athletics increased it to 7–4 in the home half.

By the time Seerey again stepped to the plate, it was the sixth inning, and Bob Savage had relieved Scheib. Two runs were already across, and there were two Sox aboard. On a 2–2 count, Seerey rocketed the next ball again onto the left-field roof. This blast, however, didn't have quite the distance of his first two blows and bounced back onto the playing field. But it did give the visitors their first lead at 9–7.

Chicago added two more to their advantage in the seventh, this time without the aid of Seerey, who fouled out. In the home half, Philadelphia exploded for four runs to tie it at 11. Three of those runs came on a home run by Eddie Joost.

## First Game

| Chicago | AB | R | H | I |
|---|---|---|---|---|
| Kolloway D, 2b | 7 | 2 | 5 | 3 |
| Lupien T, 1b | 7 | 1 | 1 | 0 |
| Appling L, 3b | 7 | 1 | 3 | 1 |
| Seerey P, lf | 6 | 4 | 4 | 7 |
| Robinson A, c | 6 | 0 | 3 | 0 |
| Wright T, rf | 6 | 0 | 2 | 0 |
| Philley D, cf | 6 | 1 | 2 | 0 |
| Michaels C, ss | 6 | 3 | 4 | 0 |
| Papish F, p | 0 | 0 | 0 | 0 |
| Moulder G, p | 1 | 0 | 0 | 0 |
| Hodgin R, ph | 1 | 0 | 0 | 0 |
| Caldwell E, p | 0 | 0 | 0 | 0 |
| Baker F, ph | 1 | 0 | 0 | 1 |
| Judson H, p | 3 | 0 | 0 | 0 |
| Pieretti M, p | 0 | 0 | 0 | 0 |
| | 57 | 12 | 24 | 12 |

| Philadelphia | AB | R | H | I |
|---|---|---|---|---|
| Joost E, ss | 7 | 4 | 4 | 5 |
| McCosky B, lf | 2 | 2 | 1 | 1 |
| White D, cf | 4 | 1 | 2 | 0 |
| Brissie L, p | 0 | 0 | 0 | 0 |
| Chapman S, ph | 0 | 0 | 0 | 0 |
| DeMars B, pr | 0 | 0 | 0 | 0 |
| Fain F, 1b | 5 | 0 | 0 | 2 |
| Majeski H, 3b | 5 | 0 | 1 | 1 |
| Valo E, rf | 3 | 0 | 1 | 0 |
| Rosar B, c | 3 | 0 | 0 | 0 |
| Guerra M, c | 3 | 0 | 0 | 0 |
| Suder P, 2b | 5 | 2 | 1 | 0 |
| Scheib C, p | 1 | 1 | 0 | 0 |
| Savage B, p | 1 | 0 | 0 | 0 |
| Harris C, p | 1 | 1 | 1 | 0 |
| Coleman J, p | 0 | 0 | 0 | 0 |
| Coleman R, ph-cf | 2 | 0 | 1 | 0 |
| | 42 | 11 | 12 | 9 |

| Chicago | IP | H | R | ER | BB | SO |
|---|---|---|---|---|---|---|
| Papish | 1.0 | 3 | 5 | 4 | 4 | 0 |
| Moulder | 2.0 | 0 | 0 | 0 | 0 | 1 |
| Caldwell | 2.0 | 4 | 2 | 2 | 1 | 1 |
| Judson (W) | 5.2 | 5 | 4 | 4 | 7 | 2 |
| Pieretti | 0.1 | 0 | 0 | 0 | 0 | 0 |
| | 11.0 | 12 | 11 | 10 | 12 | 4 |

| Philadelphia | IP | H | R | ER | BB | SO |
|---|---|---|---|---|---|---|
| Scheib | 4.2 | 9 | 4 | 4 | 1 | 2 |
| Savage | 1.0 | 5 | 5 | 5 | 1 | 0 |
| Harris | 1.2 | 4 | 2 | 1 | 0 | 0 |
| J.Coleman | 1.2 | 2 | 0 | 0 | 1 | 1 |
| Brissie (L) | 2.0 | 4 | 1 | 1 | 0 | 0 |
| | 11.0 | 24 | 12 | 11 | 3 | 4 |

```
Chicago        001  125  200  01 — 12
Philadelphia   140  110  400  00 — 11
```

OB: Chicago 15, Philadelphia 14; ER: Michaels, Harris; DP: Chicago 1, Philadelphia 1; 2B: Robinson, Wright, Kolloway, Philley, Joost 2, Majeski; 3B: Kolloway; HR: Seerey 4, Joost; SB: Appling; SH: McCosky, White 2; HP: by Papish (Valo); WP: Papish, Moulder, Savage; BK: Judson; TI: 3:44; AT: 17,296; UM: Hurley, Berry, Grieve

The White Sox loaded the sacks in the ninth (Seerey was onboard with a walk), but right-hander Joe Coleman escaped unscathed. Philadelphia mounted a threat of their own in the bottom of the frame when they put two runners aboard but failed to score, sending the battle into extra innings.

Chicago also got two men aboard in the tenth, but this time Lou Brissie, the fifth Philadelphia hurler, wriggled out of it.

While the score remained 11–11, left-hander Brissie retired the first two batters in the 11th. Seerey then stepped in and victimized his third Athletics pitcher, depositing Brissie's first pitch into the upper-deck seats in left. It was his shortest hit of the day, but it reclaimed the lead for the Sox.

Philadelphia wasn't finished, however. In the bottom of the 11th, they loaded the bases with two outs before Marino Pieretti choked the rally by retiring Ferris Fain on a foul-out to third.

When the final scoresheet was tallied, Seerey had driven in seven runs and become only the fifth man in major league history to hit four home runs in a game.

In the second game of the doubleheader, called after five because of a Pennsylvania curfew law, Seerey was 0 for 2. Six days later, Pat displayed the other side of his game when he became the first major leaguer to strike out seven times in a doubleheader.

# *Nationals Comeback Highlighted by Musial Home Run* 99

AMERICAN LEAGUE at NATIONAL LEAGUE
Tuesday, July 12, 1955, County Stadium
NL All-Stars 6, AL All-Stars 5

Poignancy accompanied the 22nd annual All-Star Game, for it was on this day that funeral services were held for Arch Ward, the *Chicago Tribune* sports editor who founded the mid-summer classic. Since the inception of Ward's brainchild, the American League had dominated by winning 14, and this year's contest began in similar fashion.

The Junior Circuit wasted no time in pummeling Robin Roberts. After the first two batters singled, the normally steady right-hander wild-pitched the first run home. He then walked Ted Williams in front of a long home run to center field by Mickey Mantle, and the American League led 4–0 before making their first out.

Roberts then settled down and joined his AL counterpart, Billy Pierce, in shutting down the offense.

In the fourth, Harvey Haddix and Early Wynn assumed the pitching duties for the hosts and visitors, respectively, and the two continued to register scoreboard goose eggs through the fifth.

With one out in the visitors' sixth, Yogi Berra singled and went to third on Al Kaline's double. Mickey Vernon then grounded out, pushing Berra's run across the plate and giving the AL a commanding 5–0 lead.

Whitey Ford took the hill for the AL in the seventh. Willie Mays, who had just robbed Williams of a two-run homer with an electrifying catch above the center-field fence, greeted Ford with a single. After two batters lined out, Henry Aaron walked. Johnny Logan then singled home Mays with the first run for the Senior Circuit. An error later allowed Aaron to score as well, making it 5–2.

| American League | AB | R | H | I |
|---|---|---|---|---|
| Kuenn H, ss | 3 | 1 | 1 | 0 |
| Carrasquel C, ss | 3 | 0 | 2 | 0 |
| Fox N, 2b | 3 | 1 | 1 | 0 |
| Avila B, 2b | 1 | 0 | 0 | 0 |
| Williams T, lf | 3 | 1 | 1 | 0 |
| Smith A, lf | 1 | 0 | 0 | 0 |
| Mantle M, cf | 6 | 1 | 2 | 3 |
| Berra Y, c | 6 | 1 | 1 | 0 |
| Kaline A, rf | 4 | 0 | 1 | 0 |
| Vernon M, 1b | 5 | 0 | 1 | 1 |
| Finigan J, 3b | 3 | 0 | 0 | 0 |
| Rosen A, 3b | 2 | 0 | 0 | 0 |
| Pierce B, p | 0 | 0 | 0 | 0 |
| Jensen J, ph | 1 | 0 | 0 | 0 |
| Wynn E, p | 0 | 0 | 0 | 0 |
| Power V, ph | 1 | 0 | 0 | 0 |
| Ford W, p | 1 | 0 | 0 | 0 |
| Sullivan F, p | 1 | 0 | 0 | 0 |
| | 44 | 5 | 10 | 4 |

| National League | AB | R | H | I |
|---|---|---|---|---|
| Schoendienst R, 2b | 6 | 0 | 2 | 0 |
| Ennis D, lf | 1 | 0 | 0 | 0 |
| Musial S, ph-lf | 4 | 1 | 1 | 1 |
| Snider D, cf | 2 | 0 | 0 | 0 |
| Mays W, cf | 3 | 2 | 2 | 0 |
| Kluszewski T, 1b | 5 | 1 | 2 | 0 |
| Mathews E, 3b | 2 | 0 | 0 | 0 |
| Jackson R, 3b | 3 | 1 | 1 | 1 |
| Mueller D, rf | 2 | 0 | 1 | 0 |
| Aaron H, pr-rf | 2 | 1 | 2 | 1 |
| Banks E, ss | 2 | 0 | 0 | 0 |
| Logan J, ss | 3 | 0 | 1 | 1 |
| Crandall D, c | 1 | 0 | 0 | 0 |
| Burgess S, ph-c | 1 | 0 | 0 | 0 |
| Lopata S, ph-c | 3 | 0 | 0 | 0 |
| Roberts R, p | 0 | 0 | 0 | 0 |
| Thomas F, ph | 1 | 0 | 0 | 0 |
| Haddix H, p | 0 | 0 | 0 | 0 |
| Hodges G, ph | 1 | 0 | 1 | 0 |
| Newcombe D, p | 0 | 0 | 0 | 0 |
| Baker G, ph | 1 | 0 | 0 | 0 |
| Jones S, p | 0 | 0 | 0 | 0 |
| Nuxhall J, p | 2 | 0 | 0 | 0 |
| Conley G, p | 0 | 0 | 0 | 0 |
| | 45 | 6 | 13 | 4 |

| AL | IP | H | R | ER | BB | SO |
|---|---|---|---|---|---|---|
| Pierce | 3.0 | 1 | 0 | 0 | 0 | 3 |
| Wynn | 3.0 | 3 | 0 | 0 | 0 | 1 |
| Ford | 1.2 | 5 | 5 | 4 | 1 | 0 |
| Sullivan (L) | 3.1 | 4 | 1 | 1 | 1 | 4 |
| | 11.0 | 13 | 6 | 5 | 2 | 8 |

| NL | IP | H | R | ER | BB | SO |
|---|---|---|---|---|---|---|
| Roberts | 3.0 | 4 | 4 | 4 | 1 | 0 |
| Haddix | 3.0 | 3 | 1 | 1 | 0 | 2 |
| Newcombe | 1.0 | 1 | 0 | 0 | 0 | 1 |
| Jones | 0.2 | 0 | 0 | 0 | 2 | 1 |
| Nuxhall | 3.1 | 2 | 0 | 0 | 3 | 5 |
| Conley (W) | 1.0 | 0 | 0 | 0 | 0 | 3 |
| | 12.0 | 10 | 5 | 5 | 6 | 12 |

| American | 400 | 001 | 000 | 000 — 5 |
|---|---|---|---|---|
| National | 000 | 000 | 230 | 001 — 6 |

ER: Mathews, Carrasquel, Rosen; DP: AL 1, NL 1; OB: AL 12, NL 8; 2B: Kluszewski, Kaline; HR: Mantle, Musial; SH: Pierce, Avila; HP: by Jones (Kaline); WP: Roberts; PB: Crandall; TI: 3:17; AT: 45,643; UM: HP Barlick, 1B Soar, 2B Boggess, 3B Summers, LF Secory, RF Runge

Sam Jones took the ball for the NL in the eighth and retired the first two batters. But when he hit Kaline with a pitch and issued free passes to both Vernon and Al Rosen, manager Leo Durocher summoned left-hander Joe Nuxhall. The Cincinnati stalwart struck out Ford to squirm out of difficulty.

American League manager Al Lopez was second-guessed for allowing Ford to bat, especially after Ford had more trouble in the home eighth. After retiring the first two batters, four consecutive singles and an error brought home three runs and tied the game at five.

Each team put two runners aboard in the ninth and one aboard in the 10th, but neither team could score. In the 11th, the American League again managed to get runners on first and second. But as he had in the ninth, Nuxhall retired Berra to escape harm. This time, however, it took a miraculous play by Red

Schoendienst, who fielded a ground ball over second and nipped Berra by an eyelash at first.

Gene Conley of the hometown Braves hurled the top of the 12th and struck out the side, much to the delight of the Milwaukee crowd. In the home half, Stan Musial led off against Frank Sullivan, ace right-hander of the Boston Red Sox, who had blanked the NL through three and one-third innings. The cheers for Conley had barely settled down when Sullivan's first pitch to Musial was launched into the right-field bleachers, suddenly ending the contest and marking the fifth National League victory in six years.

# Pirate Perseverance Pays Off in the Seventeenth 100

## SAN DIEGO (NL) at PITTSBURGH (NL)
### Thursday, July 15, 1971, Three Rivers Stadium
### Pirates 4, Padres 3

In a relatively unknown and little-celebrated game, the San Diego Padres and the Pittsburgh Pirates engaged in a remarkable struggle that featured excellent pitching and dramatic two-out offensive heroics. Through 17 innings the two clubs battled, with the Pirates tying it in the bottom of the ninth, the 13th, and the 16th, before finally winning it in the 17th.

The contest began as a pitcher's duel between southpaw Dave Roberts of the Padres and the Pirates' right-hander Steve Blass. San Diego mustered only two hits through the first six innings, the Pirates three. Only one runner reached third, that being Pittsburgh's Bill Mazeroski in the opening frame with one out. But Roberts then proceeded to strike out Willie Stargell and dispatch Manny Sanguillen on a ground-out.

With one away in the seventh, the Padres loaded the bases and scored the game's first run on a passed ball by Sanguillen. Blass then struck out Bob Barton before intentionally walking pinch-hitter Leron Lee. The threat ended as Roberts grounded out.

In the eighth, Pittsburgh assembled a two-out rally, but Roberts again fanned Stargell to quash the uprising.

Roberts carried his 1–0 advantage into the bottom of the ninth and retired the first batter. But Bob Robertson walked, and pinch-runner Vic Davalillo went to third on Jose Pagan's single. Gene Alley then sent a fly ball to center,

| San Diego | AB | R | H | I |
|---|---|---|---|---|
| Hernandez E, ss | 7 | 0 | 1 | 0 |
| Mason D, 3b-2b | 7 | 1 | 1 | 0 |
| Gaston C, cf | 6 | 1 | 1 | 0 |
| Severinsen A, p | 0 | 0 | 0 | 0 |
| Dean T, ph | 1 | 0 | 1 | 0 |
| Coombs D, p | 0 | 0 | 0 | 0 |
| Colbert N, 1b | 7 | 0 | 0 | 0 |
| Stahl L, lf | 7 | 0 | 1 | 0 |
| Brown O, rf | 6 | 0 | 2 | 0 |
| Barton B, c | 4 | 0 | 2 | 0 |
| Norman F, pr | 0 | 0 | 0 | 0 |
| Kendall F, c | 3 | 0 | 0 | 0 |
| Campbell D, 2b | 2 | 0 | 0 | 0 |
| Lee L, ph | 0 | 0 | 0 | 0 |
| Jestadt G, 3b | 1 | 0 | 0 | 0 |
| Spiezio E, ph-3b | 3 | 0 | 0 | 0 |
| Roberts D, p | 3 | 0 | 0 | 0 |
| Bravo A, ph | 1 | 0 | 0 | 0 |
| Miller B, p | 0 | 0 | 0 | 0 |
| Murrell I, ph-cf | 2 | 1 | 1 | 1 |
| | 60 | 3 | 10 | 1 |

| Pittsburgh | AB | R | H | I |
|---|---|---|---|---|
| Mazeroski B, 2b | 8 | 0 | 3 | 0 |
| Clines G, cf | 8 | 0 | 4 | 0 |
| Clemente R, rf | 8 | 1 | 1 | 1 |
| Stargell W, lf | 6 | 1 | 1 | 1 |
| Sanguillen M, c | 6 | 0 | 0 | 0 |
| Robertson B, 1b | 3 | 0 | 0 | 0 |
| Davalillo V, pr-1b | 3 | 1 | 1 | 0 |
| Pagan J, 3b | 4 | 0 | 1 | 0 |
| Hernandez J, pr-3b | 0 | 0 | 0 | 0 |
| Hebner R, ph-3b | 3 | 1 | 1 | 1 |
| Alley G, ss | 6 | 0 | 2 | 1 |
| Blass S, p | 2 | 0 | 0 | 0 |
| Stennett R, ph | 1 | 0 | 0 | 0 |
| Giusti D, p | 1 | 0 | 0 | 0 |
| Oliver A, ph | 1 | 0 | 0 | 0 |
| Grant J, p | 0 | 0 | 0 | 0 |
| Sands C, ph | 0 | 0 | 0 | 0 |
| Ellis D, pr | 0 | 0 | 0 | 0 |
| Veale B, p | 0 | 0 | 0 | 0 |
| Nelson J, p | 1 | 0 | 1 | 0 |
| | 61 | 4 | 15 | 4 |

| San Diego | IP | H | R | ER | BB | SO |
|---|---|---|---|---|---|---|
| Roberts | 9.0 | 7 | 1 | 1 | 1 | 9 |
| Miller | 3.0 | 2 | 0 | 0 | 0 | 1 |
| Severinsen | 3.0 | 3 | 1 | 2 | 2 | 2 |
| Coombs (L) | 1.1 | 3 | 2 | 2 | 0 | 1 |
| | 16.1 | 15 | 4 | 4 | 3 | 13 |

| Pittsburgh | IP | H | R | ER | BB | SO |
|---|---|---|---|---|---|---|
| Blass | 8.0 | 4 | 1 | 1 | 2 | 7 |
| Giusti | 4.0 | 1 | 0 | 0 | 0 | 4 |
| Grant | 2.0 | 2 | 1 | 1 | 0 | 3 |
| Veale | 1.1 | 2 | 1 | 1 | 0 | 0 |
| Nelson (W) | 1.2 | 1 | 0 | 0 | 0 | 0 |
| | 17.0 | 10 | 3 | 3 | 2 | 14 |

| | | | | | | |
|---|---|---|---|---|---|---|
| San Diego | 000 | 000 | 100 | 000 | 100 | 10 — 3 |
| Pittsburgh | 000 | 000 | 001 | 000 | 100 | 11 — 4 |

OB: San Diego 8, Pittsburgh 13; ER: Barton; DP: San Diego 1, Pittsburgh 1; 2B: Alley; HR: Murrell, Stargell, Hebner, Clemente; SB: Davalillo, Alley; CS: Sanguillen, Clines; SF: Alley; HP: by Roberts (Sanguillen); WP: Nelson; PB: Sanguillen; TI: 4:12; AT: 17,405; UM: HP Sudol, 1B Vargo, 2B Colosi, 3B Stello

deep enough for Davalillo to scamper home with the tying run and send the game into extra innings.

During the first three extra innings, each club collected just one hit. Then in the 13th, San Diego pinch-hitter Ivan Murrell hit a solo home run, giving the Padres their second lead of the contest.

Al Severinsen got the call to save the game and responded by striking out Gene Clines and Roberto Clemente before Stargell stepped to the plate. The big left fielder had been 0 for 5 with four strikeouts, but he promptly redeemed himself with a dramatic game-tying homer, delighting the hometown crowd. It was the second time the Pirates had tied the game while only one out from defeat.

The Padres struck again in the 16th when, after two singles, Pirate reliever Jim Nelson uncorked a wild pitch, giving San Diego their third lead.

Pittsburgh fans this night had grown accustomed to their team's valiant comebacks, and now it was Richie Hebner who homered to tie it at three.

Moving to the home half of the 17th, Danny Coombs fanned Clines, bringing Clemente to the plate. The future Hall of Famer had been hitless in seven plate appearances but rocked Coombs and the Padres with the Pirates' third extra-inning homer, this one the game winner.

# Bibliography

## Books, Articles, Interviews, and Audio Recordings

Alexander, Charles C. *Ty Cobb*. New York: Oxford University Press, 1984, 272 pp., indexed.

Allen, Mel. Recorded broadcast. NBC Radio. 8 October 1956.

Ashburn, Richie. Recorded broadcast. WCAU Radio. 17 May 1979.

*The Baseball Encyclopedia*. 10th ed. New York: Macmillan, 1996, 2857 pp.

The Baseball Workshop. (Gary Gillette, 619 Wadsworth Ave., Phila., Pa. 19119). Computer data bank of all games, pitch-by-pitch, 1984 to 1996.

Benson, Michael. *Ballparks of North America*. Jefferson, N.C.: McFarland, 1989, 475 pp., indexed.

Brennaman, Marty. Recorded broadcast. NBC Radio. 21 October 1975.

Buck, Jack. Recorded broadcast. CBS Radio. 12 October 1980.

Carmichael, John P. *My Greatest Day in Baseball*. New York: Grosset & Dunlap, 1951, 250 pp.

Carter, Craig, ed. *The Sporting News Complete Baseball Record Book*. St. Louis: The Sporting News, 1995, 500 pp.

Cavenaugh, Dick. Personal interview. 8 June 1999.

Charlton, James, ed. *The Baseball Chronology*. New York: Macmillan, 707 pp., indexed.

Cohen, Richard M., David Neft, and Roland Johnson. *The World Series*. New York: The Dial Press, 1976, 398 pp.

Coleman, Jerry. Recorded broadcast. CBS Radio. 12 October 1980.

Dewey, Donald, and Nicholas Acocella. *The Biographical History of Baseball*. New York: Carroll & Groff, 1995, 533 pp.

Dittmar, Joseph J. *Baseball Records Registry*. Jefferson, N.C.: McFarland, 1997, 674 pp., indexed.

Dudley, Jimmy. Recorded broadcast. Mutual Radio Network. 29 September 1954.

Farmer, Ted. "Joss vs. Walsh." In *The National Pastime*. Cleveland: Society for American Baseball Research, 1995, pp. 71–73.

Hoppel, Joe. *The Series*. St. Louis: The Sporting News, 1992, 391 pp.

Longert, Scott. *Addie Joss — King of the Pitchers*. Cleveland: Society for American Baseball Research, 1998, pp. 91–104.

Gershman, Michael. *The 1992 Baseball Engagement Book*. Boston: Houghton Mifflin, 1991.

Gowdy, Curt. Recorded broadcast. NBC Radio. 21 October 1975.

*Great Moments in Baseball*. Lincolnwood, Ill.: Beekman House, 192 pp., illustrated.

Helfer, Al. Recorded broadcast. Mutual Radio Network. 29 September 1954.

Kalas, Harry. Recorded broadcast. WCAU Radio. 17 May 1979.

Karst, Gene, and Martin J. Jones, Jr. *Who's Who in Professional Baseball.* New Rochelle N.Y.: Arlington House, 1973, 919 pp.

Lowry, Philip J. *Green Cathedrals.* Reading, Mass.: Addison-Wesley, 1992, 275 pp., in dexed.

Mann, Arthur. *Branch Rickey.* Boston: Houghton-Mifflin, 1957, 288 pp., indexed.

McLendon, Gordon. Recorded broadcast. Liberty Mutual Network. 3 October 1951.

Musser, Andy. Recorded broadcast. WCAU Radio. 17 May 1979.

Nadel, Eric, and Craig R. Wright. *The Man Who Stole First Base.* Dallas: Taylor, 1989 172 pp., indexed.

Neft, David S., Richard M. Cohen, and Michael L. Neft. *The Sports Encyclopedia: Base ball.* 18th ed. New York: St. Martin's, 1998, 727 pp.

O'Donnell, Bill. Recorded broadcast. NBC Radio. 15 October 1969.

Okkonen, Marc. *Baseball Memories 1900–1909.* New York: Sterling, 1992, 234 pp., in dexed.

Phillips, Damon. Letter to the author. 20 August 1993.

Quinlan, Jack. Recorded broadcast. Mutual Broadcasting System. 13 October 1960.

Reichler, Joseph, and Ben Olan. *Baseball's Unforgettable Games.* New York: Ronald Press 1960, 362 pp., indexed.

Reidenbaugh, Lowell. *The Sporting News Selects Baseball's 50 Greatest Games.* St. Louis The Sporting News, 1986, 288 pp.

Retrosheet. (David W. Smith, 20 Sunset Road, Newark, Del. 19711-5236). Computer dat bank of play-by-play for many games played between 1901 and 1983.

Schoor, Gene. *The History of the World Series.* New York. William Morrow, 1990, 431 pp indexed.

Scully, Vin. Recorded broadcast. NBC Radio. 8 October 1956.

_____. Recorded broadcast. CBS Radio Sports. 26 October 1997.

Shatzkin, Mike, ed. *The Ballplayers.* New York: William Morrow & Co., 1990, 1230 pp illustrated.

Simpson, Jim. Recorded broadcast. NBC Radio. 15 October 1969.

Siwoff, Seymour, ed. *The Book of Baseball Records.* New York: Seymour Siwoff, 1999, 39 pp.

Solomon, Burt. *The Baseball Timeline.* New York: Avon, 1997, 1082 pp., indexed

Stout, Steve. "The Greatest Game Ever Pitched." In *The National Pastime.* Cleveland Society for American Baseball Research, 1994, p.4.

Thompson, Chuck. Recorded broadcast. Mutual Broadcasting System. 13 October 1960

Thorn, John, Pete Palmer, Michael Gershman, David Petrusza, eds. *Total Baseball.* 5th ed. New York: Viking, 1997, 2458 pp.

Torborg, Jeff. Recorded broadcast. CBS Radio Sports. 26 October 1997.

Total Sports. Computer data bank of play-by-play for many games played between 199 and 1999.

Weigand, Jim. *The Greatest Game: Joss vs. Walsh, 1991.* Barberton, Ohio: n. pub., 4 pp.

## Newspapers

Akron Beacon Journal
Atlanta Constitution
Atlanta Journal
Boston Globe

Boston Herald
Boston Journal
Boston Post
Brooklyn Daily Eagle

Chicago American
Chicago Chronicle
Chicago Daily Journal
Chicago Daily News
Chicago Evening Post
Chicago Herald American
Chicago Herald Examiner
Chicago Record-Herald
Chicago Sun Times
Chicago Today
Chicago Tribune
Cincinnati Enquirer
Cincinnati Post
Cincinnati Times-Star
Cleveland Leader
Cleveland Plain Dealer
Cleveland Press
Commercial Tribune (Cincinnati)
Daily Mirror (New York)
Daily News (New York)
Daily Times (Chicago)
Dallas Morning News
Dallas Times Herald
Detroit Free Press
Detroit Journal
Detroit Times
Detroit Tribune
Evening Bulletin (Philadelphia)
Evening News (Detroit)
Evening Public Ledger (Philadelphia)
Evening Star (Washington)
Evening Telegraph (Philadelphia)
Evening Times (Philadelphia)
Evening Wisconsin (Milwaukee)
Fort Worth Star-Telegram
Gazette (Montreal)
Gazette Times (Pittsburgh)
Globe and Mail (Canada)
Houston Chronicle
Houston Post
Inter-Ocean (Chicago)
Kansas City Star
Kansas City Times
Kansas Star & Times
Los Angeles Herald-Examiner
Los Angeles Times
Milwaukee Daily News
Milwaukee Journal

Milwaukee Sentinel
Minneapolis Star
Minneapolis Star Tribune
New York American
New York Evening Post
New York Herald
New York Herald Tribune
New York Journal American
New York Press
The New York Times
New York Tribune
New York World Telegram
New York World Telegram and The Sun
North American (Philadelphia)
Oakland Tribune
Philadelphia Daily News
Philadelphia Evening Item
Philadelphia Inquirer
Philadelphia Record
Pittsburgh Dispatch
Pittsburgh Gazette
Pittsburgh Leader
Pittsburgh Post
Pittsburgh Post-Gazette
Pittsburgh Press
Pittsburgh Sun Telegraph
Press (Philadelphia)
Public Ledger (Philadelphia)
St. Louis Globe-Democrat
St. Louis Post-Dispatch
St. Louis Republic
St. Louis Star
St. Louis Times
San Diego Union
San Francisco Chronicle
San Francisco Examiner
Sporting Life
Sporting News
Standard Union (Brooklyn)
Sun (Baltimore)
Sun (New York)
Toronto Star
USA Today
USA Today Baseball Weekly
Washington Herald
Washington Post
Washington Times
World (New York)

# Index

248 Index